The Best
AMERICAN
ESSAYS
College Edition

The Best AMERICAN ESSAYS College Edition

Fourth Edition

Edited and with an Introduction
by ROBERT ATWAN

*Director, The Blue Hills Writing Institute
at Curry College*

Houghton Mifflin Company   Boston   New York

Executive Editor: Suzanne Phelps Weir
Senior Developmental Editor: Sarah Helyar Smith
Project Editor: Ylang Nguyen/Jane Lee
Production/Design Assistant: Bethany Schlegel
Senior Manufacturing Coordinator: Marie Barnes
Marketing Manager: Cindy Graff Cohen

Cover image: © Nina Wishnok

Printed in the U.S.A.

Library of Congress Control Number: 2002116630

ISBN: 0-618-33370-3

123456789-QUF-07 06 05 04 03

Credits

In Memory of

Stephen Jay Gould
(1941–2002)

Lucy Grealy
(1963–2002)

Vicki Hearne
(1946–2001)

Contents

1. THE PERSONAL VOICE: IDENTITY, DIVERSITY, SELF-DISCOVERY • 33

ANWAR F. ACCAWI, *The Telephone* • 34

"When I was growing up in Magdaluna, a small Lebanese village in the terraced, rocky mountains east of Sidon, time didn't mean much to anybody, except maybe to those who were dying, or those waiting to appear in court because they had tampered with the boundary markers on their land."

MARCIA ALDRICH, *Hair* • 43

"In maturity, I'm incapable of assuming a coherent or consistent philosophy. I have wayward hair: it's always becoming something else."

JUDITH ORTIZ COFER, *Silent Dancing* • 51

"The men drank Palo Viejo rum, and some of the younger ones got weepy. The first time I saw a grown man cry was at a New Year's Eve party: he had been reminded of his mother by the smells in the kitchen."

"Though there was graffiti on most of the walls of Westbury Court, and hills of trash piled up outside, and though the elevator wasn't always there when we opened the door to step inside and the heat and hot water weren't always on, I never dreamed of leaving Westbury Court until the year of the fire."

"Everybody I knew as a child wanted to have good hair. You could be as ugly as homemade sin dipped in misery and still be thought attractive if you had good hair."

"I once thought that truth was eternal, that when you understood something it was with you forever. I know now that this isn't so, that most truths are inherently unretainable, that we have to work hard all our lives to remember the most basic things."

"Did education mean moving from one class to the next? My grandmothers told me again and again that one could scale a mountain with a good education. But could I still talk to them, to my parents, my siblings? I would try to live in two worlds — at the very least. That was now my task."

"What terrified me that late summer day was the sudden greenness of the trees, the way their beauty insinuated itself into my vision — peripherally at first, vaguely, and without my consent. I blinked to stop what felt like tears, which I hadn't tasted for so long I'd forgotten that they were made of salt, that they were something my body was producing on its own, long after I thought I had shut down. O.K., I said to the steering wheel, the padded dashboard, the pines. If I can think of five reasons not to die, I won't."

"It has been alleged that when I was in college she heard that I had stayed up all night playing poker and wrote me a letter that used the word 'shame' forty-two times. I do not recall this."

"How could a young woman whom we had presumably cured, who had been so alive and healthy three days ago, be brain dead now?"

"The tools in my workbench are a double inheritance, for each hammer and level and saw is wrapped in a cloud of knowing."

"Language is the tool of my trade. And I use them all — all the Englishes I grew up with."

2. THE ATTENTIVE MIND: OBSERVATION, REFLECTION, INSIGHT • 155

"A week before his twenty-sixth birthday, the nimble Petit clandestinely strung a cable between the not-yet-completed Twin Towers, already dominating Manhattan's skyline, and for the better part of an hour walked back and forth over the void, demonstrating his astonishing obsession to one hundred thousand or so wide-eyed gawkers gathered so far below."

"Nothing on earth is more gladdening than knowing we must roll up our sleeves and move back the boundaries of the humanly possible once more."

"Last spring at this time I was coming out of a bout with pneumonia. I went to bed on January first and didn't get up until the end of February. Winter was a cocoon in which my gagging, basso cough shook the dark figures at the end of my bed."

"In October of 1998 I finally gave in and signed up for e-mail. I had resisted for a long time. My husband and I were proud of our retrograde
status. Not only did we lack a modem, but we didn't have a car, a microwave, a Cuisinart, an electric can opener, a cellular phone, a CD
player, or cable television."

" 'What are you *doing?*' The question pursues me still. When I go fishing
and catch no fish, the idea that it's fun simply to be out on the river consoles me for not one second. I must catch fish; and if I do, I must then
catch more and bigger fish."

"People with sunny natures do seem to live longer than people who are
nervous wrecks; yet mankind didn't evolve out of the animal kingdom by
being unduly sunny-minded."

"I've always wondered about dog food. Is a Gaines-burger really like a
hamburger?"

"I waited until I held his eye. I assured him I would not tell anyone else
how to get there. He looked at me with stoical despair, like a man who
had been robbed twice, whose belief in human beings was offered without conviction."

"As a woman and a writer, I have long wondered at the wellsprings of female masochism. Or what, in despair of a more subtle, less reductive
phrase, we can call the congeries of predilections toward self-hurt, self-
erasure, self-repudiation in women."

"Once my children leave the house, I will never again have to participate
in a mind-numbing discussion about where my children or my friends'

children or my neighbors' children are going to college, and why. On this subject, I am completely tapped out."

"The road to Fidel Castro's Palace of the Revolution leads through a memory lane of old American automobiles chugging along at about twenty-five miles an hour — springless, pre-embargo Ford coupes and Plymouth sedans, DeSotos and LaSalles, Nashes and Studebakers, and various vehicular collages created out of Cadillac grilles and Oldsmobile axles and Buick fenders patched with pieces of oil-drum metal and powered by engines interlinked with kitchen utensils and pre-Batista lawn mowers and other gadgets that have elevated the craft of tinkering in Cuba to the status of high art."

"Inhabiting a male body is much like having a bank account; as long as it's healthy, you don't think much about it. Compared to the female body, it is a low-maintenance proposition. . . ."

3. THE PUBLIC SPHERE: ADVOCACY, ARGUMENT, CONTROVERSY • 289

"People in movements too readily learn to deny to others the rights and privileges they demand for themselves. They too easily become unable to mean their own language, as when a 'peace movement' becomes violent."

"Education doesn't end until life ends, because you never know when you're going to understand something you hadn't understood before."

"Justice Oliver Wendell Holmes's classic example of unprotected speech — falsely shouting 'Fire!' in a crowded theater — has been invoked so often, by so many people, in such diverse contexts, that it has become part of our national folk language."

"We rarely wonder about or discuss the brother who shot him because we already know everything about him. When the call came, my first thought was the same one I'd had when I'd heard about Rosa Parks's beating: A brother did it."

"Of the many results of the end of the Cold War — the most amazing surge in the American economy, the rise of nationalism and tribalism in certain parts of the world — the most surprising and distressing was the trivialization of the American political agenda."

"Animal-rights publications are illustrated largely with photographs of two kinds of animals — 'Helpless Fluff' and 'Agonized Fluff,' the two conditions in which some people seem to prefer their animals, because any other version of an animal is too complicated for propaganda."

"When my teacher had pinned this map up on the blackboard, she said, 'This is England' — and she said it with authority, seriousness, and adoration, and we all sat up. It was as if she had said, 'This is Jerusalem, the place you will go to when you die but only if you have been good.'"

"The body of Emmett Till — 'his head . . . swollen and bashed in, his mouth twisted and broken' — became a new kind of icon. Emmett Till showed the world exactly what white supremacy looked like."

"In the world as it is now, I can see no escape from the conclusion that each one of us with wealth surplus to his or her essential needs should be giving most of it to help people suffering from poverty so dire as to be life-threatening. That's right: I'm saying that you shouldn't buy that new car, take that cruise, redecorate the house, or get that pricy new suit. After all, a thousand-dollar suit could save five children's lives."

"Black though I may be, it is impossible for me to sit in my single-family house with *two* cars in the driveway and a swing set in the back yard and *not* see the role class has played in my life."

"To kill is to put to death, extinguish, nullify, cancel, destroy. But from the hunter's point of view, it's just a tiny part of the experience."

"Having given up on most of the previous justifications for the death penalty, we cling to a mere vestige of the practice, relying most urgently on one of the least defensible defenses of it."

Preface

What Is *The Best American Essays* Series?

Back in the 1970s Edward Hoagland wondered why no one compiled an annual collection of the year's best essays, especially since comparable short story volumes had been around for decades. I agreed with Hoagland, and after a few false starts (I thought at first of calling the series "The E. B. White Awards" and later "The Emerson Awards"), I founded *The Best American Essays* as a companion volume to Houghton Mifflin's *The Best American Short Stories*. The first volume was published in 1986. Since then, the series has grown in popularity; each year more and more readers seem drawn to the vitality and versatility of the contemporary American essay.

For readers unfamiliar with the series, a brief introduction may be useful. As the series editor, I screen hundreds of essays from an enormous variety of general, specialized, and literary magazines. I then turn over a large number of candidates to a guest editor, a prominent American writer, who makes the final selection of approximately twenty essays. To qualify for selection, the essays must be works of high literary quality intended as fully developed, independent essays on subjects of general interest, originally written in English for first appearance in an American periodical during a calendar year. In general, selections for the book are included on the basis of literary achievement: they must be admirably written and demonstrate an awareness of craft as well as a forcefulness of thought. Since each guest editor, of course, possesses a different idea about what comprises a fine essay, each book also represents a unique literary sensibility. This variety of literary taste and opinion (which can be sampled in the prologue, "Essayists on the Essay") keeps the series healthy and diverse.

The College Edition

This version of *The Best American Essays* is designed for college students and classroom use. Essays have long been a staple of writing courses, so why not a collection of the "best" contemporary essays for today's students? I believe that many writing instructors wish to expose their students to high-quality, socially relevant, and intellectually challenging prose. With this end in mind, I selected particular essays from *The Best American Essays* series that I thought would work best for writing instructors and their students. Among the considerations for selection were length, topicality, diverse perspectives, and rhetorical and thematic variety.

Since the majority of essays we encounter today tend to fall into three general, though fairly distinct, categories — personal, informative, and argumentative — I arranged the selections accordingly. The book reflects the types of writing most often taught in introductory and even advanced composition courses. Instructors will find a generous number of selections to use if they want to teach excellent writing within the context of personal narratives, expository patterns, and persuasive strategies. In addition, I included within these three categories selections that also reflect many of the topics and issues that currently enliven discussion and debate: multiculturalism, race and gender, sexual and identity politics, popular culture, and media studies.

For instructors who prefer to teach essays along different lines, I've included three alternative arrangements: (a) a rhetorical table of contents that rearranges the essays into ten traditional modes or patterns; (b) a table of contents that focuses on salient literary and journalistic features; and (c) a thematic and topical organization that places the essays in a context of current issues. I've also drawn from the various "Forewords" I contribute to the annual volumes to develop an introduction to the literary and compositional features of the contemporary American essay. And, though space would not permit the inclusion of the seventeen guest-editor introductions, I orchestrated incisive excerpts into a prologue that should stimulate critical discussion of the genre and lead to writing assignments.

In addition, to help orient student readers, the volume contains an informative "lead-in" to each essay and a brief biographical note. "Reflections and Responses," a set of questions designed to assist class discussion or to instigate ideas for papers, follows each selection. The questions range from a consideration of compositional details to broader reflections on theme and issue. Instructors who wish to delve deeper into the literary and rhetorical features of the essays will appreciate the thorough and perceptive instructor's manual prepared by Elizabeth Huyck (Princeton University).

Given its arrangement, flexibility, and emphasis on recently published essays, the college edition of *The Best American Essays* is suitable for various writing courses. It can be used in mainstream freshman composition programs with a focus on personal, expository, and argumentative essays. Instructors who want to concentrate on the contemporary essay, creative nonfiction techniques, or the essay as a literary genre will also find the collection and its instructional apparatus extremely suitable.

For this fourth college edition, I revised a third of the book; of the thirty-six selections, twelve are new. All of these selections are drawn from the 2000, 2001, and 2002 volumes. My choices were partially guided by several useful reviews from writing instructors who shared with me some of their classroom experiences with particular selections.

Marcia Aldrich, *Michigan State University*

Ted Anton, *DePaul University*

Andrea De Fusco, *Boston College*

Brennan Enos, *Palm Beach Community College*

Andrea Herrmann, *University of Arkansas at Little Rock*

Elizabeth Hutton, *University of Michigan*

Tom Irish, *Western Illinois University*

Bonnie J. Marshall, *Grand Valley State University*

Christine Murray, *University of Texas at Arlington*

Lad Tobin, *Boston College*

No collection, of course, can entirely please everyone. I have listened carefully to reviewers and have relied on my own classroom experience in choosing contemporary essays that — in their variety of subject, style, and structure — would best serve as an introduction to the genre. I ought to add that I based my choices on the essays themselves, considering mainly their relevance to writing courses, not the reputations of their authors. You will certainly find many well-known essayists in the collection; but you will also discover several unfamiliar writers, some of whom have rarely been anthologized. A large part of my purpose in editing *The Best American Essays* series is to introduce to the reading public young and emerging writers.

I am always interested in comments and suggestions, especially regarding the book's classroom utility, and invite responses from teachers and students. Please address responses to: Robert Atwan/ Series Editor/The Best American Essays/P.O. Box 220/Readville, MA 02137.

Although anthologies such as this one may appear simple to construct, they actually involve the professional efforts of many people. I wish to extend my thanks, first of all, to the distinguished guest editors I've worked with and whose presence is felt throughout this edition: Elizabeth Hardwick, Gay Talese, Annie Dillard, Geoffrey Wolff, Justin Kaplan, Joyce Carol Oates, Susan Sontag, Joseph Epstein, Tracy Kidder, Jamaica Kincaid, Geoffrey C. Ward, Ian Frazier, Cynthia Ozick, Edward Hoagland, Alan Lightman, Kathleen Norris, and the late Stephen Jay Gould. Without them there would be no series.

I appreciate the enthusiasm for the project and the help I've received from the Houghton Mifflin college staff: I especially appreciate the advice and support I received from my editors, Suzanne Phelps Weir and Sarah Helyar Smith. I would also like to thank Project Editors Ylang Nguyen and Jane Lee, who handled production; permissions editors Craig D. Mertens and Katie Huha; and the copyeditor, Karen Keady. I'm especially grateful again to Elizabeth Huyck for producing a superb instructor's manual. As always, I'm indebted to my wife, Hélène, for her indispensable support and advice.

R. A.

The Best AMERICAN ESSAYS College Edition

Encountering the Essay

What Are Essays?

Like poems, plays, novels, and short stories, essays resist simple definition or classification. There are so many types of essays that any attempt to come up with a single, authoritative description of *the* essay is likely to be overly general or critically useless. A well-known handbook to literary terms, for example, doesn't even attempt to define the form: "A moderately brief prose discussion of a restricted topic," the entry begins. But it then goes on to say: "Because of the wide application of the term, no satisfactory definition can be arrived at; nor can a wholly acceptable 'classification' of essay types be made." So much writing today goes under the name of essay — celebrity profiles, interviews, political commentary, reviews, reportage, scientific papers, scholarly articles, snippets of humor, and newspaper columns — that it's virtually impossible for readers to obtain any clear and consistent impression of the form.

Though many illustrious examples of "brief prose discussion" can be found in classical Greek and Latin literature, the modern essay had its origins in the European Renaissance. At a time when writers and artists throughout Europe were exploring ways to express their personalities more freely in painting and literature, a French magistrate, Michel de Montaigne, retired to his Bordeaux estate in 1570 and began experimenting with a new kind of prose. Impatient with formal philosophy and academic disquisition, he soon found a way to create a more flexible and personal discourse. Realizing that his efforts fit no conventional category — they could not be termed letters, or memoirs, or treatises — he simply referred to them by the French word *essais,* meaning *attempts, trials,* or *experiments.* By adopting a casual, everyday word to describe his endeavors, Montaigne called attention to the informal character of this new literary genre. His essays were personal, tentative, highly digressive, and wholly unsystematic in their approach to a topic.

Montaigne's brand of essay became for many later writers *the* genuine essay. For William Hazlitt, Virginia Woolf, and E. B. White, this was the only type of essay that could be considered a literary form. It went under different names; sometimes it was called the periodical, informal, or familiar essay. This was to differentiate it from types of prose discourse composed in a more systematic and formal fashion, writing that conformed to objective rather than subjective standards. Some examples of the formal essay are philosophical and ethical arguments, historical and scientific papers, dissertations and critical articles. Today the informal essay is best represented by the personal essay, whereas the most popular type of formal essay is the magazine article. Although writers and editors may use the terms interchangeably, many periodicals routinely distinguish between essay and article in their tables of contents, a distinction that usually boils down to personal memoir or reflection as opposed to reportage, interviews, or feature stories.

Essays and Articles

If it's impossible to produce an airtight definition of an essay, it's equally impossible to define an article. Like "essay," this all-purpose literary label has a long, complex history. The word goes back to the Latin term for a joint *(artus)* connecting two parts of a body, and its literal use was eventually extended to include the components of writing and discourse. By the eighteenth century, "article" was used regularly for literary compositions that treated a specific topic. The first to use the term in its modern journalistic sense was one of English literature's foremost essayists, Joseph Addison.

Articles require not just a topic, but a timely topic. Unlike essays, articles are usually (a) about something specific and (b) about something of *current* interest. Essays, on the other hand, can take large liberties with subject, theme, organization, and point of view. Essayists tend to be personal, reflective, leisurely; article writers (they used to be called "articlers") usually stay close to the facts, rarely stray from "the point," and seldom interrupt the flow of information with personal opinion or reflection. The essayist will feel comfortable writing about various general topics — friendship, envy, manners, nature. The article writer is often looking for an angle, or "hook," that will directly relate the article to some current event or fashionable trend.

For example: assign the topic of "revenge" to two authors — one who prefers to write personal or familiar essays and one who specializes in journalistic articles or feature stories. Chances are the essayist will take a first-person, reflective look at the nature of revenge, blending together personal experience and literary references. The journalist will most likely conduct several interviews with psychologists and then skillfully choreograph these into an informative piece on how to deal constructively with vengeful emotions. These are, of course, extremes, but they suggest the divergent routes of the essay and article in today's literature. In general, the personal, reflective essay is often found in the literary quarterlies and periodicals; articles, like the example above, are the mainstay of popular magazines.

With a few exceptions, our major magazines print relatively few personal essays. Editors believe that their readers want news and information, not personal reminiscence or leisurely reflection. As a result, the weekly and monthly magazines depend on hard news stories, interviews, profiles, and "service articles" that offer readers practical advice on everything from child rearing to the latest diet. Few of these pieces could be called "literary"; most of them fall rapidly out of date and are not likely to be read even a few months after their appearance. If the personal essayist faces the challenge of making his or her experiences and reflections interesting and relevant, the article writer faces a different challenge: how to handle current issues and topics in such a way that people will still read the work with pleasure long after those issues and topics have vanished from public discussion.

Yet, as the selections in this volume show, most good prose is not easy to pigeonhole. At either end of the spectrum, it's fairly easy to distinguish a literary essay from a journalistic article. But as we move toward the center of the spectrum, the distinctions become less clear. We begin to find a compositional mix: personal essays that depend on research and reporting, topical articles that feature a personal voice and individual viewpoint. Such literary mixtures have become increasingly prevalent in today's magazines and literary periodicals. Note, for example, the selection by Gay Talese, the writer who was one of the founders of a literary movement known as "The New Journalism." This movement attracted many prominent authors (Joan Didion, Truman Capote, Norman Mailer, among others) who wanted to incorporate a variety of literary techniques — many borrowed from novels and essays — into the conventionally "objective" magazine article. In Talese's talented hands, the ordinary celebrity profile becomes infused with mood, atmosphere, and conflict as personalities develop within a narrative that bristles with dramatic tension. Many readers coming across "Ali in Havana" (see page 261) in *Esquire* magazine would naturally consider Talese's profile of the world's most famous athlete an article; yet a close reading will demonstrate not only Talese's meticulous skills as a journalist but his mastery of dramatic irony and literary form. Readers will want to note, too, how Annie Dillard (see page 167) elevates a "profile" of a famous stunt pilot into an essay of astonishing lyric power. In a number of the essays collected here, the writers move between the topical requirements of an article and the literary demands of an essay, adroitly balancing fact and observation with the nuances of voice and style, irony and wit.

Essays and Fiction

What ultimately makes a piece of prose an essay is usually found in the personal quality of its writing. Many of the essays in this book are not only written in the first-person singular but they are also *about* the first-person singular. As Montaigne proved long ago, the essay is the perfect literary vehicle for both self-disclosure and self-discovery: "The wisdom of my lesson," he wrote, "is wholly in truth, in freedom, in reality." Writers today use the essay to explore their personal relationships, their individual identities, and their ethnic or racial heritages. Personal essays like Judith Ortiz Cofer's "Silent Dancing" and Scott Russell Sanders's "The Inheritance of Tools" are intimate, candid, revealing, close to the pulse of everyday human experience.

Yet *personal* can be a tricky term. Its roots reach back to the Latin *persona,* the literal term for "mask." The word was traditionally used for a theatrical character, a *dramatis persona.* Thus, oddly enough, the word we use to convey intimacy and sincerity — we often approvingly speak of someone's *personal* touch — has hidden overtones of disguise and performance. Readers may overlook this double sense of the term, but personal essayists rarely do. They know that the first-person singular is not a simple equivalent of the self, a mere matter of slapping down the word "I" in front of every sentence. They know that the single letter "I" is one of the English language's most complex words.

Who is the "I" of the essay — a real person or a *dramatis persona?* Did Scott Russell Sanders really bang his thumb with a hammer just before learning of his father's death? Did Ann Hodgman actually sample Gaines-burgers to see if they tasted like human food? Or have these essayists contrived incidents and fabricated moods in the interests of creating a story or endorsing a position? Unless we personally know the writers, how can we verify their accounts?

When the essay is philosophical or argumentative, we can decide whether we accept an essayist's opinions or not on the basis of logic, evidence, proof, or internal consistency. For example, we would base our agreement or disagreement with Ashraf Rushdy's "Exquisite Corpse" entirely on information that has nothing to do with the author's personal life. But once essayists begin to tell stories — about sampling dog food or playing with their children — they move dangerously close to fiction, especially when they add characters, dialogue, episodes, and climaxes. When constructing personal narratives, the essayist confronts the toughest challenge of the craft: telling stories that are at once artful, true, and *believable.* One of the essayist's most frustrating moments is when he or she relates a true story with the utmost candor and discovers that nobody believes it.

The personal essayist, then, must balance craft and credibility, aesthetics and accuracy. The first-person singular is both person and *persona,* a real person and a literary construct. The "I" is both reporting a story and simultaneously *shaping* one. If essayists hope to be wholly believable, however, they need to worry about too much shaping. A true story doesn't usually come prepackaged in a compellingly dramatic shape — many elements just don't fit in. To be believable, the essayist may narrate a story that doesn't — like much of life itself — possess a satisfying narrative closure. Sometimes what one expects to happen doesn't happen. "The writer in me," writes Frank Conroy in "Think About It," "is tempted to create a scene here — to invent one for dramatic purposes — but of course I can't do that." His literary impulse as a novelist is to create a scene; his honesty as an essayist won't let him. An essay like "Think About It" places the reader directly inside the conflict between essay and story. In fact, the tension between personal essays and stories recurs throughout this collection and is especially apparent in such selections as Anwar F. Accawi's "The Telephone" and Edwidge Danticat's "Westbury Court."

Essays and Memoir

In college writing courses years ago, instructors referred to a syllogism that may help explain the enormous popularity of the personal memoir. It went something like this: "You write best when you write about what you know; what you know best is yourself; therefore, you write best when you write about yourself." As a syllogism, this seemed valid: the conclusion followed logically from its premises, no? So why didn't teachers always receive better essays when they assigned personal topics?

As anyone can see, the conclusion rests on dubious assumptions. The premises sound reasonable, but they raise some fundamental questions. Do people really write best about the subjects they know best? We see evidence all the time of experts being unable to communicate the basic concepts of their professions, which explains why so many technical books are authored by both an expert and a writer. Brilliant academics so committed to their vast research that they can't bear to part with any detail thus clog up their sentences with an excess of information. If a little knowledge is a dangerous thing, too much can sometimes be an impediment to clear and robust expression. Shakespeareans do not always write the best books on Shakespeare.

Can we also safely conclude that we know ourselves best of all? If so, then why do so many of us spend so much time in psychotherapy or counseling sessions? Surely, the pursuit of the self — especially the "hidden" self — has been a major twentieth-century industry. Self-knowledge, of course, confronts us with another logical problem: how can the self be at the same time the knower and the known? That's why biographies can be so much more revealing than autobiographies. As Dostoyevsky said in his *Notes from Underground:* "A true autobiography is almost an impossibility . . . man is bound to lie about himself."

Yet the illusion that we do know ourselves best must serve as both comfort and inspiration to the growing wave of memoirists who seem to write with one finger glued to the shift key and another to the letter *I,* which on the keyboard looks nothing like it does on the page, thus appropriately symbolizing the relationship between that single letter and the "self" it presumes to represent. Today's writer's market is flooded with autobiography — now more likely to be labeled "memoir" in the singular, as though the more fashionable literary label promises something grander. Memoirs (the term was almost always used in the plural) were customarily written by public figures who recorded their participation in historical events and their encounters with other prominent individuals. General Ulysses S. Grant's two-volume *Personal Memoirs* (1885–86) were bestsellers. The old memoirs were penned by well-established individuals in the twilight of their careers; the new memoir is frequently the work of an emerging writer aspiring to be well established.

The memoir is easily abused by those who believe the genre automatically confers upon the author some sort of importance. It's only natural, isn't it, to be the heroes or heroines of our own lives? And as the main protagonists, how can we resist the impulse to occupy center stage and not consider ourselves gifted with greater sensitivity, finer values, higher moral authority, and especially keener powers of recollection than any member of our supporting cast of characters? The most interesting autobiography ever conceived must be Mark Twain's. Partly written, partly dictated, never published in its entirety, and never according to his intentions — in many ways a colossal failure of a book — Twain's autobiography grappled with every psychological and compositional difficulty characteristic of the genre. Twain knew how easy it was to exhibit ourselves in "creditable attitudes exclusively" and tried to display himself as honestly as he could. It was a noble experiment, but it proved impossible: "I have been dictating this autobiography of mine," he wrote, "for three months; I have thought of fifteen hundred or two thousand incidents in my life which I am ashamed of but I have not gotten one of them to consent to go on paper yet."

To say that memoir, autobiography, and the personal essay are easily abused is not to disparage these vigorous genres. Democratizing the memoir has resulted in many wonderful books, not a few crafted by young or relatively young writers who have learned to ask themselves how to prevent their personal writing from deteriorating into narcissism and self-absorption. This is a question anyone setting out to write personally must face sooner or later. The solution requires a healthy regimen of self-skepticism and a respect for uncertainty. Though the first-person singular may abound, it should be a richly complex and mutable "I," never one that designates a reliably known, wholly static entity. In some of the best memoirs and personal essays, the writers are mysteries to themselves and the work evolves into an enactment of surprise and self-discovery. These elements keep "life writing" *live* writing, as a mysterious "I" converses with an equally mysterious "I."

The Five-Paragraph Essay

Many students who enter their first-year writing courses already know how to manufacture the "perfect paper." For some reason, they know it should begin with an introductory paragraph that contains a thesis statement and often cites an expert named Webster. It then pursues its expository path through three paragraphs that develop the main idea until it finally reaches a concluding paragraph that industriously summarizes all three previous paragraphs. The conclusion often begins, "Thus we see that. . . ." If the paper tells a personal story, it might conclude, "Suddenly I realized. . . ." Epiphanies abound.

What is especially maddening about the typical five-paragraph paper has less to do with its tedious, predictable structure than with its implicit message that writing should be the end product of thought and not the enactment of its process. Many students seem unaware that writing can be an act of discovery, an opportunity to say something they had never before thought of saying. The worst papers instructors receive are largely the products of premature conclusions, of unearned assurances, of minds irrevocably made up. As Robert Frost once put it, for many people thinking merely means voting. Why go through the trouble of writing papers on an issue when all that's required is an opinion poll? Do you agree? Disagree? It makes sense to call such productions "papers" (or "themes" or "assignments") since what is written has almost no connection with the true sense of "essaying" — trying out ideas and positions, writing while in a state of uncertainty, of not knowing.

The five-paragraph theme is also a charade. It not only parades in lock-step toward its conclusion; it begins with its conclusion. It is all about its conclusion. Its structure permits no change of direction, no reconsideration, no wrestling with ideas. It is — and has long been — the perfect vehicle for the sort of reader who solemnly likes to ask: "And your point is . . . ?"

The most talented essayists have aims other than merely getting a point across or a position announced or an identity established. It may help to imagine an essay as a sort of Cubist rendition of an idea: the essayist would rather you consider all sides and aspects of a thought or concept, much in the same multi-perspectival fashion that Picasso or Braque portrayed an ordinary table on canvas. Some essayists — Montaigne again was the first — seem literally to be turning ideas over in their minds. The intellectual essay is nothing if not ruminative; the autobiographical essay may continually lose its sense of direction. Both kinds of essays, like Samuel Johnson's eighteenth-century fable, *Rasselas,* will often reach a "conclusion in which nothing is concluded."

Can a Computer Evaluate an Essay?

This question has been on people's minds since Educational Testing Service recently unveiled e-rater®, their new computer program that will grade essay questions on the Graduate Management Admissions Test. As news of e-rater spread, newspaper reports appeared across the nation nervously wondering how essays can be machine-scored. Objective tests, with their multiple choices, are one thing; but aren't sentences, paragraphs, and organization quite another?

The answer is that a computer can very easily score the results of essay questions, assuming that all anyone wanted to know was whether the writing conformed to standard English usage and reflected a few other elements of style, like syntactic variety, that can be measured conveniently and objectively. Computers have been able to do this for quite some time, and most word-processing applications currently provide a few (though still rudimentary) tools to check grammar and style. But can a computer detect humor and irony (which skilled readers themselves sometimes fail to catch)? Can it evaluate the use of imagery and metaphor, or discern the nuances of a writer's tone of voice? E-rater's developer honestly admitted to the *New York Times* that it cannot: "It's not designed to score Montaigne," she said. "It's designed for a specific purpose: to score the kinds of essays we see on standardized tests." Admittedly, these would be "standard" essays.

Are these what we talk about when we talk about essays? Montaigne's term for his eccentric and digressive meditations is now employed so broadly and indiscriminately that its traditional literary meaning is all but forgotten. An essay, it seems, is anything we want it to be. Our dailies, weeklies, and monthlies are chock full of nonfiction prose, but little of it is either creative or literary. Most of it is informative, functional, or advisory, and that's as it should be. Produced with built-in obsolescence, such writing is made for the month (at best) and not for the years. E-rater may do fine evaluating standardized expression, but it is educationally unfortunate that its name and use will continue to confuse people about the true literary nature of essays.

The Essay and Risk

"Where there's a will there's a way," an excited William Hazlitt says to himself as he hurries down Chancery Lane "about half-past six o'clock, on Monday the 10th of December, to enquire at Jack Randall's where the fight the next day was to be." The year is 1821, the city is London, and Hazlitt is pursuing his way to an out-of-town boxing match, his first fight ever. He's eager to see big Bill Neate, the raging Bristol "Bull," take on the "Gas-Man," Tom Hickman, the bravest and cruelest fighter in all of England. "I was determined to see this fight, come what would, and see it I did, in great style."

You can consult all the handbooks on literary fiction for all the elements of style, structure, and composition, but you'll rarely find mention of what Hazlitt just noted — *determination*. Yet its literary value is inestimable.

This collection is filled with determination. You can see the fight

in great style. You can narrate it with equally great style. But as
Hazlitt reminds us, you first have to get there. No sitting in your
study with a boxing encyclopedia, no telephone interviews with experts, no electronic highway; and the travel involved takes you beyond your local library.

Such narratives can be a risky business. For one thing, the des-
tinations are often uncertain. When Jamaica Kincaid decides to
see England for the first time, or when Barry Lopez strays far
from the beaten track in search of an ancient stone horse, or even
when Ian Frazier journeys around his Ohio and Montana neigh-
borhoods, they have no idea what surprising emotions or events
they will encounter. But there's an additional risk. After writing
"The Fight," Hazlitt was surprised to find that people considered
his eyewitness report a "vulgar thing." This wasn't simply because
his story took readers into an unfamiliar subculture, but because it
took them into unfamiliar prose territory as well. In other words,
Hazlitt risked the unliterary; he was determined to find a way to
develop an essay out of "unsuitable" material. We can find a similar
determination throughout this volume: look at how such writers
as Marcia Aldrich, Rebecca McClanahan, Frank Conroy, or Debra
Dickerson creatively confront ordinary, unpromising, uncomfortable, or even intractable subjects. Where there's a will there's a way.

Risk and determination — at both a personal and creative level —
will often transform a piece of nonfiction prose into a memorable
literary work. Our finest essayists seek out challenges, go for the
toughest questions on the board. The challenges may spring from
the demands of the assignment or of the composition — or both.
These essayists resist the plodding memoir, the facile discovery of
identity, the predictable opinion, or the unearned assertion. What
many of the essays collected here have in common is their determination to take on the tough assignment, to raise the difficulty
level of the game.

The Contemporary American Essay:
A Diversity of Forms and Voices

The personal essay has long existed in a literary twilight zone. Because it presumes to tell a true story yet often employs fictional or
poetic techniques, it stands awkwardly with one foot in and one

foot out of "imaginative" literature. It was partially for this reason that one of America's foremost essayists, E. B. White, complained in 1977 that the essayist "unlike the novelist, the poet, and the playwright, must be content in his self-imposed role of second-class citizen." Writers who have their eyes on a Nobel Prize or "other earthly triumphs," White continued, "had best write a novel, a poem, or a play." White was responding not only to the critical reception of his own work but to a general decline in the literary quality of the American essay. Essays struck a lot of readers as "old-fashioned." When readers thought of essays, they thought of writing that was stiff, stuffy, textbookish — things teachers forced them to read and write in school.

A century ago, however, the essay occupied a prominent position in American literature. It fell into the class of writing that critics called "polite letters." The essayists, mostly men, addressed the literate world in an urbane, congenial, comfortable manner. These gentlemen, it seemed, always possessed three names — James Russell Lowell, Oliver Wendell Holmes, Thomas Wentworth Higginson — and more often than not lived in New England. In this era, when "coming out" referred only to a young woman's debut, the typical essay was proper, genteel, and Anglophilic. Although it atrophied during the 1930s, the polite essay retained for many years an insidious power over American students, who were often forced to imitate its polished civility in that shadow genre known as the "freshman theme." The goal of English teachers, Kurt Vonnegut recalls, was to get you "to write like cultivated Englishmen of a century or more ago."

Essays began to seem old-fashioned to the American reader mainly because they were too slow in coming to terms with twentieth-century modernism. While William Faulkner, T. S. Eliot, and Eugene O'Neill were radically transforming fiction, poetry, and drama, the essay retained much of its relaxed, genteel manner. Adventurous writers considered the essay a holdover from Victorian times. With few exceptions, the essay broke no new ground, violated no literary conventions. Instead of standing as modern works of literature in themselves, essays simply tried to explain those works. For the academic community as well as for many general readers, the essay gradually grew synonymous with literary criticism. Essays were written *about* literature, not *as* literature.

Since E. B. White issued his complaint, the literary status of the essay has been steadily improving. As Annie Dillard says, the essay "has joined the modern world." Essays are now written in the same imaginative spirit as fiction and poetry. Contemporary essays can rival the best fiction and poetry in artistic accomplishment. Far from being hesitant about literary aims and methods, today's essayists delight in the use of imagery, symbol, and metaphor, often interweaving them into such complex mosaic patterns as those we find in Gretel Ehrlich's "Spring" and Joyce Carol Oates's "They All Just Went Away." Boundary lines — between life and art, prose and poetry, truth and fiction, the world and self — are often blurred, as essayists take greater liberties with language and form. This is now true even of essays grounded in information and explanation.

Nor can the essay be characterized any longer by its homogeneity. In fact, its diversity may now be its most noticeable feature. In light of the essay's transformation, today's poetry and fiction appear stagnant: the essay may be our most exciting literary form. We see narrative essays that are indistinguishable from short stories, mosaic essays that read like prose poems. We find literary criticism with an autobiographical spin, journalism sensitively attuned to drama and metaphor, reflection with a heavy dose of information. Some essayists write polemic that sounds like poetry. Physicists, mathematicians, and philosophers are finding that complex ideas and a memorable prose style are not irreconcilable. Even law review articles have taken a literary turn. Today's essays are incredibly difficult to categorize and pin down.

This volume collects and celebrates the contemporary American essay. Never before — except perhaps in the days of Ralph Waldo Emerson and Henry David Thoreau — have so many fine young American writers begun to explore the essay's literary possibilities. They come to the form with a renewed enthusiasm for its astonishing flexibility and versatility — the essay can incorporate an enormously wide range of subjects and styles. The personal essay has grown increasingly candid, more intimate, less polite. Essayists seem willing to take greater emotional risks. Essayists today seem less relaxed and more eager to confront urgent social questions. Journalism has contributed to this sense of risk and urgency, encouraging essayists to fuse within a single style both personal experience and public issues, dual themes that Barry Lopez brilliantly combines in "The Stone Horse."

The Essay and Public Events

As Stephen Jay Gould was making selections for the 2002 volume of *The Best American Essays* he observed how everything seemed "shaped by 9/11," regardless of whether it was written before or after. Later, I realized how every few years some pivotal event dominates the national attention and dramatically narrows the literary scope of this series. In 1995 it seemed that half the essays published in magazines dealt either directly or tangentially with the O. J. Simpson trial. The nation couldn't stop talking about it, and many distinguished writers weighed in with insightful and sometimes brilliant commentary. In a similar occurrence toward the end of 2000, the American political process was put on hold during the most bizarre presidential election in our history. Yet coverage of these events — as influential and absorbing as they still are — did not necessarily find their way into the volumes featuring the best essays of those years.

But the terrorist attacks of 9/11 and their aftermath were altogether another story. The written response was overwhelming, and not merely because of the immediate and massive news coverage. One could expect the coverage, commentary, and reportage; unexpected was their astonishingly high quality. Anticipating that thoughtful essays would require months of reflection and deliberation, the "literature of 9/11" was surely several years away. But essays such as David Halberstam's "Who We Are" (page 319) were written within weeks of the incident.

In fact, we should have expected the abundance of fine 9/11 essays. The essay always seems to revitalize in times of war and conflict — and usually with the return of peace and prosperity, fiction and poetry regain their literary stature. The First World War resulted in an eruption of essays and introduced the work of some of our finest nonfiction writers, many of whom, like Randolph Bourne, took up the pacifist cause. But then the postwar years saw the flourishing of some of our most celebrated poets and novelists, those members of the "lost generation." This was true, too, in the Second World War (E. B. White published his greatest essay collection in 1942) and especially true during Vietnam. It seems to me no coincidence that the Vietnam years saw the emergence of the New Journalism, an exciting and innovative brand of nonfiction pioneered (as mentioned earlier) by Gay Talese, a writer included in this volume.

This theory about essays in time of war is not easily proven, but the idea also appears in Czeslaw Milosz's brilliant long poem, *A Treatise on Poetry,* which appeared shortly before the 9/11 carnage. Though he promotes the value of poetry in difficult times, Milosz, who won the Nobel Prize in 1980, prefaces *Treatise* with the recognition that in our time: "serious combat, where life is at stake, is fought in prose." Perhaps in times of conflict and crisis people want to be in the presence of less mediated voices; we need more debate and directives, we desire more public discourse. We instinctively turn to writing that displays a greater sense of immediacy and urgency. "These are the times that try men's souls," Tom Paine memorably wrote in 1776, in what would be the first essay of *The American Crisis.* At that moment in history, radicalism and nationalism could go hand in hand.

Whatever other consequences arise from 9/11, the attacks have had enormous cultural repercussions. One of these is the reemergence of the essay as a broadly relevant, even indispensable, genre — a vital source of voices, ideas, and personal histories that the public will turn to with perhaps greater attention than ever before.

The Essay in the Twenty-First Century

The year 1995 marked the 400th anniversary of the first complete edition of Montaigne's essays. As we progress into the twenty-first century, it will be natural to speculate on how the essay will change. Will essays be shaped in new, surprising ways by the digital revolution? Will cyberspace breed new essayists and new kinds of essays? Will original, literary prose works begin appearing in underground sites without benefit of agents, editors, publishers, and prestige periodicals? Will young, struggling writers find a quicker and less stressful way to break into print? As voice and video become increasingly common, will a new age of graphic/audio texts dramatically alter the reading habits of a future generation? In 2020, as one commentator wondered, will book publishers as a trade be as obsolete as blacksmiths?

Predictions of a bookless future have, of course, been

commonplace for decades, and there's good reason to be skeptical about the announced "end" of anything, whether it be books, literature, or history itself. When Bill Gates wanted to evangelize on America's electronic future, he didn't go online but produced an old-fashioned thirty-dollar hardcover book with a first printing of 800,000 copies. The first thing most young people probably did when they got the book, however, was run the inserted "companion interactive CD-ROM" that contained the complete text, multimedia hyperlinks, video demonstrations, and an audio interview with Gates. Unbelievers continually say that nobody wants to read a book on a screen, and for that reason alone they consider books to be irreplaceable. But for the next generation, books may routinely be read on screen, a cozy lightweight "papery" screen you can pop a CD into, carry anywhere, and comfortably curl up with and read in the dark. Why not? The practical advantages will be tremendous, and parents will finally be able to lift their kids' backpacks.

There's no reason to oppose technology; the digital revolution is here to stay, and one can amply enjoy its products and conveniences. A younger generation may be more comfortable reading electronic books, but if they are reading something worth reading, they will more than likely — to borrow the title of critic Ruben Brower's seminal essay — do their "reading in slow motion." Though retrieving and downloading *Walden* or *Portrait of a Lady* can be done in the blink of an eye, savoring the prose, word by word, sentence by sentence, will always take time. One danger, of course, is that as people become more accustomed to instantaneous acquisition of texts, they will simultaneously grow so impatient with the time-consuming process of reading them that reading itself may become as obsolete as Sunday family strolls down Main Street.

The issue really isn't the future of books but of reading, and since people were reading long before the paginated book was developed some five hundred years ago, chances are they'll be reading long after it has been radically transformed. It is hardly a coincidence that the essay was invented not long after the book, for we owe to the physical feature of books the personal essay's idiosyncratic and circuitous manner. Montaigne equipped his home office with one of the earliest book-lined studies, where he loved to spend his time *browsing*. His mind too mercurial to concentrate wholeheartedly on any one volume, he would "leaf through now one book now another, without order and without plan, by disconnected fragments." An idea took hold; he began to write just the way he read. His medium became his message, and the personal essay was born.

For those who enjoy leisurely reading, the essay remains the ideal form, as the selections in this volume amply demonstrate. A ruminative, unhurried style has long been part of the essay's tradition. Early in the twentieth century, literary critics were predicting that the slow-paced "old-fashioned essay" would soon disappear. It was, as William Dean Howells observed in 1902, being driven out by newsworthy articles with no interest in the "lounging gait," and the "wilding nature" that characterized what Howells called the "right" essay. His concerns about a readership so corrupted and depraved, so bereft of a lyrical sense that they preferred articles to essays, have been echoed through every decade of the twentieth century. Yet somehow "right" or true essays still manage to be written, published, and admired. This volume — with its many sinuous selections that wind through time and memory, that blur the distinctions between past and present, that take us intimately into the multilayered processes of thought — attests to that fact.

Robert Atwan

PROLOGUE

Essayists on the Essay

Each edition of The Best American Essays *features a guest editor who makes the final selections and writes an introduction to the volume. The guest editors themselves are distinguished American writers, many of whom have excelled in various literary forms. In their introductions, they almost always address the question of the essay: its history, definition, style, audience, composition. Their essays on the essay would in themselves make an interesting collection. What follows are some of their most incisive remarks.*

What Is an Essay?

What *is* an essay, and what, if anything, is it about? "Formal" and "informal," "personal," "familiar," "review-essay," "article-essay," "critical essay," essays literary, biographical, polemic, and historical — the standard lit-crit lexicon and similar attempts at genre definition and subclassification in the end simply tell you how like an eel this essay creature is. It wriggles between narcissism and detachment, opinion and fact, the private party and the public meeting, omphalos and brain, analysis and polemics, confession and reportage, persuasion and provocation. All you can safely say is that it's not poetry and it's not fiction.
— Justin Kaplan

Resisting Definitions

AN ESSAY! The fixed form or the fixed category of any kind, any definition at all, fills me with such despair that I feel compelled to do or be its opposite. And if I cannot do its opposite, if I can in fact complete the task that is the fixed form, or fill the fixed category, I then deny it, I then decline to participate at all. Is this a complex view? But I believe I have stated it simply: anything that I might do, anything that I might be, I cannot bear to be enclosed by, I cannot bear to have its meaning applied to me.

The Essay: and this is not a form of literary expression unfamiliar to me. I can remember being introduced to it. It was the opinions and observations of people I did not know, and their opinions and observations bore no relationship to my life as I lived it then. But even now, especially now, I do not find anything peculiar or wrong about this; after all, the opinions and observations of people you do not know are the most interesting, and even the most important, for your own opinions and observations can only, ultimately, fix you, categorize you — the very thing that leads me to dissent or denial.

— Jamaica Kincaid

The Ideal Essay

In reading an essay, I want to feel that I'm communing with a real person, and a person who cares about what he or she's writing about. The words sound sentimental and trite, but the qualities are rare. For me, the ideal essay is not an assignment, to be dispatched efficiently and intelligently, but an exploration, a questioning, an introspection. I want to see a piece of the essayist. I want to see a mind at work, imagining, spinning, struggling to understand. If the essayist has all the answers, then he isn't struggling to grasp, and I won't either. When you care about something, you continually grapple with it, because it is alive in you. It thrashes and moves, like all living things.

When I'm reading a good essay, I feel that I'm going on a journey. The essayist is searching for something and taking me along. That something could be a particular idea, an unraveling of identity, a meaning in the wallow of observations and facts. The facts are important but never enough. An essay, for me, must go past the facts, an essay must travel and move. Even the facts of the essayist's own history, the personal memoir, are insufficient alone.

The facts of personal history provide anchor, but the essayist then swings in a wide arc on his anchor line, testing and pulling hard.
      — Alan Lightman

The Essay As Object

If kids still write essays in school the way people my age used to, they meet the essay first as pure object. In school, it is (or was) a written paper of a certain length, on an assigned subject, with specified margins and neatness, due on the teacher's desk at a certain date. From about fourth grade on, I wrote many essays. "An essay a week" was a philosophy lots of grammar school teachers subscribed to back then. Recently I came across an essay of mine I'd saved from the fifth grade. It's called "If I Had Three Wishes." My first wish, as I described it, was for lots of fishing equipment, my second was for a canoe in which to go fishing, and my third was for a cabin in the woods somewhere near good fishing. I have more or less gotten those wishes, writing occasional essays about fishing all the while. Even in its present state as childhood artifact, "If I Had Three Wishes" retains its purposeful object-ness: the three-ring-binder paper with regular lines and space at the top for student's name, teacher's name, and date; the slow, newly-learned script, in blue ballpoint, almost without mistakes; and the circled good grade in the teacher's hand.
      — Ian Frazier

The Essay As Action

Beneath the object, the physical piece of writing with its unpredictable content, is the action that produced it. The action, it seems to me, is easier to predict. The difference is like that between a golf ball in the air and the swing of the golfer that propelled it; the flight of a struck ball varies, but the swing tends always to be the same. An essay is a golf swing, an angler's cast, a tennis serve. For example, say, an experience happens to you, one that seems to have literary potential. You wait for it to grow in your mind into a short story or even just an episode of "Friends," but somehow it doesn't. Then a further experience, or an odd chance, or something a friend says, or something in the newspaper chimes with the first experience, and suddenly you understand you can write about it, and you do. You quit longing for form and write what's there, with whatever serviceable prose comes to hand, for no better reason than the fun and release of saying. That sequence — that combination of patience with sudden impatience, that eventual yielding to the simple desire to tell — identifies the essay.

    — Ian Frazier

Essays and the Real World

The essay can do everything a poem can do, and everything a short story can do — everything but fake it. The elements in any nonfiction should be true not only artistically — the connections must hold at base and must be veracious, for that is the convention and the covenant between the nonfiction writer and his reader. Veracity isn't much of a drawback to the writer; there's a lot of truth out there to work with. And veracity isn't much of a drawback to the reader. The real world arguably exerts a greater fascination on people than any fictional one; many people, at least, spend their whole lives there, apparently by choice. The essayist does what we do with our lives; the essayist thinks about actual things. He can make sense of them analytically or artistically. In either case he renders the real world coherent and meaningful, even if only bits of it, and even if that coherence and meaning reside only inside small texts.

    — Annie Dillard

No Standard Essay

As there is no standard human type who writes essays, so is there no standard essay: no set style, length, or subject. But what does unite almost all successful essays, no matter how divergent the subject, is that a strong personal presence is felt behind them. This is so even if the essayist never comes out to tell you his view of the matter being discussed, never attempts directly to assert his personality, never even slips into the first-person singular. Without that strong personal presence, the essay doesn't quite exist; it becomes an article, a piece, or some other indefinable verbal construction. Even when the subject seems a distant and impersonal one, the self of the writer is in good part what the essay is about.

— Joseph Epstein

The Essay's Diversity

It is not only that the essay *could* be about anything. It usually was. The good health of essay writing depends on writers continuing to address eccentric subjects. In contrast to poetry and fiction, the nature of the essay is diversity — diversity of level, subject, tone, diction. Essays on being old and falling in love and the nature of poetry are still being written. And there are also essays on Rita Hayworth's zipper and Mickey Mouse's ears.

— Susan Sontag

The Memorable Essay

I am predisposed to the essay with knowledge to impart — but, unlike journalism, which exists primarily to present facts, the essays transcend their data, or transmute it into personal meaning. The memorable essay, unlike the article, is not place- or time-bound; it survives the occasion of its original composition. Indeed, in the most brilliant essays, language is not merely the medium of communication; it *is* communication.

— Joyce Carol Oates

The Author's Gumption

Given the confusion of genre minglings and overlaps, what finally distinguishes an essay from an article may just be the author's gumption, the extent to which personal voice, vision, and style are the prime movers and shapers, even though the authorial "I" may be only a remote energy, nowhere visible but everywhere present. ("We commonly do not remember," Thoreau wrote in the opening paragraphs of *Walden*, "that it is, after all, always the first person that is speaking.")

— Justin Kaplan

Essays and the Imagination

An essay is a thing of the imagination. If there is information in an essay, it is by-the-by, and if there is an opinion in it, you need not trust it for the long run. A genuine essay has no educational, polemical, or sociopolitical use; it is the movement of a free mind at play. Though it is written in prose, it is closer in kind to poetry than to any other form. Like a poem, a genuine essay is made out of language and character and mood and temperament and pluck and chance.

— Cynthia Ozick

Essays Versus Articles

And if I speak of a genuine essay, it is because fakes abound. Here the old-fashioned term poetaster may apply, if only obliquely. As the poetaster is to the poet — a lesser aspirant — so the article is to the essay: a look-alike knockoff guaranteed not to wear well. An article is gossip. An essay is reflection and insight. An article has the temporary advantage of social heat — what's hot out there right now. An essay's heat is interior. An article is timely, topical, engaged in the issues and personalities of the moment; it is likely to be stale within the month. In five years it will have acquired the quaint aura of a rotary phone. An article is Siamese-twinned to its date of birth. An essay defies its date of birth, and ours too.

— Cynthia Ozick

Essays Versus Stories

In some ways the essay can deal in both events and ideas better than the short story can, because the essayist — unlike the poet — may introduce the plain, unadorned thought without the contrived entrances of long-winded characters who mouth discourses. This sort of awful device killed "the novel of idea." (But eschewing it served to limit fiction's materials a little further, and likely contributed to our being left with the short story of scant idea.) The essayist may reason; he may treat of historical, cultural, or natural events, as well as personal events, for their interest and meaning alone, without resort to fabricated dramatic occasions. So the essay's materials are larger than the story's.

— Annie Dillard

Essays Versus Poems

The essay may deal in metaphor better than the poem can, in some ways, because prose may expand what the lyric poem must compress. Instead of confining a metaphor to half a line, the essayist can devote to it a narrative, descriptive, or reflective couple of pages, and bring forth vividly its meanings. Prose welcomes all sorts of figurative language, of course, as well as alliteration, and even rhyme. The range of rhythms in prose is larger and grander than that of poetry. And it can handle discursive idea, and plain fact, as well as character and story.

— Annie Dillard

Essays Are Not Scientific Documents

An essay is not a scientific document. It can be serendipitous or domestic, satire or testimony, tongue-in-cheek or a wail of grief. Mulched perhaps in its own contradictions, it promises no sure objectivity, just the condiment of opinion on a base of observation, and sometimes such leaps of illogic or superlogic that they may work a bit like magic realism in a novel: namely, to simulate the mind's own processes in a murky and incongruous world. More than being instructive, as a magazine article is, an essay has a slant, a seasoned personality behind it that ought to weather well. Even if we think the author is telling us the earth is flat, we might want to listen to him elaborate upon the fringes of his premise because the bristle of his narrative and what he's seen intrigues us. He has a cutting edge, yet balance too. A given body of information is going to be eclipsed, but what lives in art is spirit, not factuality, and we respond to Montaigne's human touch despite four centuries of technological and social change.

— Edward Hoagland

The Essayist's Defensiveness

No poet has a problem saying, I am a poet. No fiction writer hesitates to say, I am writing a story. "Poem" and "story" are still relatively stable, easily identified literary forms or genres. The essay is not, in that sense, a genre. Rather, "essay" is just one name, the most sonorous name, bestowed on a wide range of writings. Writers and editors usually call them "pieces." This is not just modesty or American casualness. A certain defensiveness now surrounds the notion of the essay. And many of the best essayists today are quick to declare that their best work lies elsewhere: in writing that is more "creative" (fiction, poetry) or more exacting (scholarship, theory, philosophy).

— Susan Sontag

On Being an Essayist

As someone who takes some pride in being known as "Joseph Epstein, an essayist" — or, even better, "the essayist Joseph Epstein" — who takes the term "essayist" as an honorific, I have both an interest and a stake in the form. I hate to see it put down, defamed, spat upon, even mildly slighted. The best luck that any writer can have is to find his or her form, and I feel fortunate in having found mine some twenty years ago in the familiar essay. It happened quite by luck: I was not then a frequent reader of Montaigne and Hazlitt; in those days I was even put off by Charles Lamb, who sometimes seemed to me a bit precious. For me the novel was the form of forms, and easily the one I most admired and should most have liked to master. Although I have published a dozen or so short stories, I have not yet written a novel — nor have I one in mind to write — and so I have to conclude that despite my enormous regard for that form, it just isn't mine. Perhaps it is quite useless for a writer to search for his perfect form; that form, it may well be, has to find him.

— Joseph Epstein

Essayists Must Tell the Truth

I work by Hemingway's precept that a writer's root charge is to distinguish what you really felt in the moment from the false sentiment of what you now believe you should have felt. The personal essay, autobiography, has been a red flag to professional classifiers and epistemologists; a critical industry has flourished for the refinement of generic protocols (many in French, with as much fine print as an installment purchase agreement), subcontracted principally to skeptics. In the judgment of Northrop Frye, for instance, a piece of work is shelved with autobiography or with fiction according to whether the librarian chooses to believe it.

Well. I've written one, and I've written the other, and I'm here to testify that the issue is at once weightier and simpler: a personal essayist means to tell the truth. The contract between a personal essayist and a reader is absolute, an agreement about intention. Because memory is fallible, and point of view by its nature biased, the personal essayist will tell a slant tale, willy-nilly. But not by design.

— Geoffrey Wolff

The Essayist's Voice

The influential essayist is someone with an acute sense of what has not been (properly) talked about, what should be talked about (but differently). But what makes essays last is less their argument than the display of a complex mind and a distinctive prose voice.

— Susan Sontag

The Demands of the First Person Singular

The thoroughgoing first person is a demanding mode. It asks for the literary equivalent of perfect pitch. Even good writers occa-

sionally lose control of their tone and let a self-congratulatory quality slip in. Eager to explain that their heart is in the right place, they
baldly state that they care deeply about matters with which they appear to be only marginally acquainted. Pretending to confess to
their bad behavior, they revel in their colorfulness. Insistently describing their own biases, they make it all too obvious that they wish
to appear uncommonly reliable. Obviously, the first person doesn't
guarantee honesty. Just because they are committing words to paper
does not mean that writers stop telling themselves the lies that
they've invented for getting through the night. Not everyone has
Montaigne's gift for candor. Certainly some people are less likely to
write honestly about themselves than about anyone else on earth.

— Tracy Kidder

The "Who Cares?" Factor

Not every voice a great soliloquy makes, a truth at odds with
the education of many an American writer, with the education of
this American writer. I remember (see how difficult, even now,
to break the habit of that pronoun, that solipsistic verb), at board-
ing school in England, writing about Cordelia in the moment when
she recognizes how mistaken is her father's measurement of affection. I spent the greater part of my allotted space telling about a
tangled misunderstanding between my dad and myself: "So I understand just how Cordelia felt." Of course my teacher wrote "who
cares?" Of course he was right to write that: to filter all data
through the mesh of personal relevance is the voice's tyrannical
sway over listener and speaker alike. Sometimes it should be okay to
take facts in, quietly manipulate them behind an opaque scrim,
and display them as though the arranger never arranged. It should
be all right to mediate, let another voice speak through your spirit
medium, pretend as a writer not to be front and center on stage.

— Geoffrey Wolff

What "Confessional Writing" Must Do

I knew that "confessional writing" now enjoys quite a vogue, but
I had no idea how pervasive the practice of personal storytelling

has become among our finest writers. I can't help asking myself (although all lives are, by definition, interesting, for what else do we have?): why in heaven's name should I care about the travails of X or Y unless some clear generality about human life and nature emerges thereby? I'm glad that trout fishing defined someone's boyhood, and I'm sad that parental dementia now dominates someone's midlife, but what can we do in life but play the hand we have been dealt?

— Stephen Jay Gould

How the Essayist Acquires Authority

Essays are how we speak to one another in print — caroming thoughts not merely in order to convey a certain packet of information, but with a special edge or bounce of personal character in a kind of public letter. As a writer you multiply yourself, gaining height as though jumping on a trampoline, if you can catch the gist of what other people have also been feeling and clarify it for them. Classic essay subjects, like the flux of friendship, "On Greed," "On Religion," "On Vanity," or solitude, lying, self-sacrifice, can be major-league yet not require Bertrand Russell to handle them. A layman who has diligently looked into something, walking in the mosses of regret after the death of a parent, for instance, may acquire an intangible authority, even without being memorably angry or funny or possessing a beguiling equanimity. *He* cares; therefore, if he has tinkered enough with his words, we do too.

— Edward Hoagland

The Conversational Style

While there is no firmly set, single style for the essayist, styles varying with each particular essayist, the best general description of essayistic style was written in 1827 by William Hazlitt in his essay "Familiar Style." "To write a genuine familiar or truly English style," Hazlitt wrote, "is to write as any one would speak in common conversation who had a thorough command and choice of words, who could discourse with ease, force, and perspicuity, setting aside all pedantic and oratorical flourishes." The style of the essayist is that of an extremely intelligent, highly commonsensical person talking, without stammer and with impressive coherence, to him- or herself and to anyone else who cares to eavesdrop. This self-reflexivity, this notion of talking to oneself, has always seemed to me to mark the essay off from the lecture. The lecturer is always teaching; so, too, frequently is the critic. If the essayist does so, it is usually only indirectly.

— Joseph Epstein

The Essay as Dialogue

Human storytelling was once all breath, the sacred act of telling family stories and tribal histories around a fire. Now a writer must attempt to breathe life into the words on a page, in the hope that the reader will discover something that resonates with his or her own experience. A genuine essay feels less like a monologue than a dialogue between writer and reader. *This is a story I need,* we conclude after reading the opening paragraph. *It will tell me something about the world that I didn't know before, something I sensed but could not articulate.*

An essay that is doing its job feels right. And resonance is the key. To be resonant, the dictionary informs us, is to be "strong and deep in tone, resounding." And to resound means to be filled to the depth with a sound that is sent back to its source. An essay that works is similar; it gives back to the reader a thought, a memory, an emotion made richer by the experience of another. Such an essay may confirm the reader's sense of things, or it may contradict it. But always, and in glorious, mysterious ways that the author cannot control, it begins to belong to the reader.

— Kathleen Norris

The Attractions of Autobiography

Contemporary critical theory lends authority to the autobiographical impulse. As every graduate student knows, only a fool would try to think or bear witness to events objectively anymore, and only an intellectual crook would claim to have done so. There's a line of reasoning that goes like this: writers ought to acknowledge that they are subjective filtering agents and let themselves appear on the page; or, in greater honesty, describe themselves in detail; or, most honest of all, make themselves their main subject matter, since one's own self is the only subject one can really know. Maybe widespread psychotherapy has made literary self-revelation popular. Certainly there are economic reasons. Editors and agents seem to think that the public's hunger for intimate true-life stories has grown large enough to include the private lives of literary figures as well as those of movie stars, mass murderers, and athletes. And the invitation to write about oneself has intrinsic attractions. The subject interests most writers. The research doesn't usually require travel or phone calls or hours in a library. The enterprise *looks* easy.

— Tracy Kidder

The Essayist's Audience

Essays are addressed to a public in which some degree or equity exists between the writer and the reader. Shared knowledge is a necessity, although the information need not be concrete. Perhaps it is more to be thought of as a sharing of the experience of reading certain kinds of texts, texts with omissions and elisions, leaps. The essayist does not stop to identify the common ground; he will not write, "Picasso, the great Spanish painter who lived long in France." On the other hand, essays are about something, something we may not have had reason to study and master, often matters about which we are quite ignorant. Elegance of presentation, reflection made interesting and significant, easily lead us to engage our reading minds with Zulus, herbaceous borders in the English garden, marriage records in eighteenth-century France, Japanese scrolls.

— Elizabeth Hardwick

Essays Start Out in Magazines

Essays end up in books, but they start their lives in magazines. (It's hard to imagine a book of recent but previously unpublished essays.) The perennial comes now mainly in the guise of the topical and, in the short run, no literary form has as great and immediate an impact on contemporary readers. Many essays are discussed, debated, reacted to in a way that poets and writers of fiction can only envy.

— Susan Sontag

On Certain Magazine Interviews

I myself have been interviewed by writers carrying recorders, and as I sit answering their questions, I see them half-listening, nodding pleasantly, and relaxing in the knowledge that the little wheels are rolling. But what they are getting from me (and I assume from other people they talk to) is not the insight that comes from deep probing and perceptive analysis and old-fashioned legwork; it is rather the first-draft drift of my mind, a once-over-lightly dialogue that — while perhaps symptomatic of a society permeated by fast-food computerized bottom-line impersonalized workmanship — too frequently reduces the once-artful craft of magazine writing to the level of talk radio on paper.

— Gay Talese

Listening to People Think

Quoting people verbatim, to be sure, has rarely blended well with my narrative style of writing or with my wish to observe and describe people actively engaged in ordinary but revealing situations rather than to confine them to a room and present them in the passive posture of a monologist. Since my earliest days in journalism, I was far less interested in the exact words that came out of people's mouths than in the essence of their meaning. More important than what people say is what they think, even though the latter may initially be difficult for them to articulate and may require much pondering and reworking within the interviewee's mind — which is what I gently try to prod and stimulate as I query, interrelate, and identify with my subjects as I personally accompany them whenever possible, be it on their errands, their appointments, their aimless peregrinations before dinner or after work. Wherever it is, I try physically to be there in my role as a curious confidant, a trustworthy fellow traveler searching into their interior, seeking to discover, clarify, and finally to describe in words (my words) what they personify and how they think.

— Gay Talese

On the Subjects of Essays

Those with the least gift are most anxious to receive a commission. It seems to them that there lies waiting a topic, a new book, a performance, and that this is known as material. The true prose writer knows there is nothing given, no idea, no text or play seen last evening until an assault has taken place, the forced domination that we call "putting it in your own words." Talking about, thinking about a project bears little relation to the composition; enthusiasm boils down with distressing speed to a paragraph, often one of mischievous banality. To proceed from musing to writing is to feel a robbery has taken place. And certainly there has been a loss; the loss of the smiles and ramblings and discussions so much friendlier to ambition than the cold hardship of writing.

— Elizabeth Hardwick

The Essay's Unlimited Possibilities

The essay is, and has been, all over the map. There's nothing you cannot do with it; no subject matter is forbidden, no structure is proscribed. You get to make up your own structure every time, a structure that arises from the materials and best contains them. The material is the world itself, which, so far, keeps on keeping on. The thinking mind will analyze, and the creative imagination will link instances, and time itself will churn out scenes — scenes unnoticed and lost, or scenes remembered, written, and saved.

In his essay "Home," William Kittredge remembers Jack Ray, his boyhood hero, whom he later hired as a hand on his Oregon ranch. After a bout in jail, Jack Ray would show up in the bunkhouse grinning. "Well, hell, Jack," Kittredge would say. "It's a new day."

"Kid," he would say, "she's a new world every morning."

— Annie Dillard

1

The Personal Voice: Identity, Diversity, Self-Discovery

ANWAR F. ACCAWI

The Telephone

Newspapers and popular magazines indirectly encourage readers to think essays are synonymous with opinion pieces — columns and articles in which writers speak their minds and air their views on topics in the news. But essays can be effective means of storytelling, as Anwar Accawi proves in the following account of his childhood in a tiny village in southern Lebanon. In "The Telephone," Accawi offers an unpretentious description of how the modern world began its intrusion into a timeless and insulated culture, where "there was no real need for a calendar or a watch to keep track of the hours, days, months, and years." As Accawi says of village life: "We lived and loved and toiled and died without ever needing to know what year it was, or even the time of day."

Accawi, who was born in Lebanon in 1943 and came to the United States in 1965, began writing essays as a way to preserve a disappearing culture for his young children who knew nothing of the old country. A teacher at the English Language Institute at the University of Tennessee, Knoxville, he is the author of a memoir, The Boy from the Tower of the Moon *(1999). "The Telephone," which originally appeared in* The Sun *(1997), was one of Accawi's first publications and was selected by Cynthia Ozick for* The Best American Essays, *1998.*

When I was growing up in Magdaluna, a small Lebanese village in the terraced, rocky mountains east of Sidon, time didn't mean much to anybody, except maybe to those who were dying, or those waiting to appear in court because they had tampered with the boundary markers on their land. In those days, there was no real need for a calendar or a watch to keep track of the hours, days, months, and years. We knew what to do and when to do it, just as the Iraqi geese knew when to fly north, driven by the hot wind that blew in from the desert, and the ewes knew when to give birth to wet lambs that stood on long, shaky legs in the chilly March wind and baaed hesitantly, because they were small and cold and did not know where they were or what to do now that they were here. The only timepiece we had need of then was the sun. It rose and set, and the seasons rolled by, and we sowed seed and harvested and ate and played and married our cousins and had babies who got whooping cough and chickenpox — and those children who survived grew up and married *their* cousins and had babies who got whooping cough and chickenpox. We lived and loved and toiled and died without ever needing to know what year it was, or even the time of day.

It wasn't that we had no system for keeping track of time and of the important events in our lives. But ours was a natural — or, rather, a divine — calendar, because it was framed by acts of God. Allah himself set down the milestones with earthquakes and droughts and floods and locusts and pestilences. Simple as our calendar was, it worked just fine for us.

Take, for example, the birth date of Teta Im Khalil, the oldest woman in Magdaluna and all the surrounding villages. When I first met her, we had just returned home from Syria at the end of the Big War and were living with Grandma Mariam. Im Khalil came by to welcome my father home and to take a long, myopic look at his foreign-born wife, my mother. Im Khalil was so old that the skin of her cheeks looked like my father's grimy tobacco pouch, and when I kissed her (because Grandma insisted that I show her old friend affection), it was like kissing a soft suede glove that had been soaked with sweat and then left in a dark closet for a season. Im Khalil's face got me to wondering how old one had to be to look and taste the way she did. So, as soon as she had hobbled off on her cane, I asked Grandma, "How old is Teta Im Khalil?"

Grandma had to think for a moment; then she said, "I've been told that Teta was born shortly after the big snow that caused the roof on the mayor's house to cave in."

"And when was that?" I asked.

"Oh, about the time we had the big earthquake that cracked the wall in the east room."

Well, that was enough for me. You couldn't be more accurate

than that, now, could you? Satisfied with her answer, I went back to playing with a ball made from an old sock stuffed with other, much older socks.

And that's the way it was in our little village for as far back as anybody could remember: people were born so many years before or after an earthquake or a flood; they got married or died so many years before or after a long drought or a big snow or some other disaster. One of the most unusual of these dates was when Antoinette the seamstress and Saeed the barber (and tooth puller) got married. That was the year of the whirlwind during which fish and oranges fell from the sky. Incredible as it may sound, the story of the fish and oranges was true, because men — respectable men, like Abu George the blacksmith and Abu Asaad the mule skinner, men who would not lie even to save their own souls — told and retold that story until it was incorporated into Magdaluna's calendar, just like the year of the black moon and the year of the locusts before it. My father, too, confirmed the story for me. He told me that he had been a small boy himself when it had rained fish and oranges from heaven. He'd gotten up one morning after a stormy night and walked out into the yard to find fish as long as his forearm still flopping here and there among the wet navel oranges.

The year of the fish-bearing twister, however, was not the last remarkable year. Many others followed in which strange and wonderful things happened: milestones added by the hand of Allah to Magdaluna's calendar. There was, for instance, the year of the drought, when the heavens were shut for months and the spring from which the entire village got its drinking water slowed to a trickle. The spring was about a mile from the village, in a ravine that opened at one end into a small, flat clearing covered with fine gray dust and hard, marble-sized goat droppings, because every afternoon the goatherds brought their flocks there to water them. In the year of the drought, that little clearing was always packed full of noisy kids with big brown eyes and sticky hands, and their mothers — sinewy, overworked young women with protruding collarbones and cracked, callused brown heels. The children ran around playing tag or hide-and-seek while the women talked, shooed flies, and awaited their turns to fill up their jars with drinking water to bring home to their napping men and wet babies. There were days when we had to wait from sunup until late afternoon just to fill a small clay jar with precious, cool water.

Sometimes, amid the long wait and the heat and the flies and the smell of goat dung, tempers flared, and the younger women, anxious about their babies, argued over whose turn it was to fill up her jar. And sometimes the arguments escalated into full-blown, knockdown-dragout fights; the women would grab each other by the hair and curse and scream and spit and call each other names that made my ears tingle. We little brown boys who went with our mothers to fetch water loved these fights, because we got to see the women's legs and their colored panties as they grappled and rolled around in the dust. Once in a while, we got lucky and saw much more, because some of the women wore nothing at all under their long dresses. God, how I used to look forward to those fights. I remember the rush, the excitement, the sun dancing on the dust clouds as a dress ripped and a young white breast was revealed, then quickly hidden. In my calendar, that year of drought will always be one of the best years of my childhood, because it was then, in a dusty clearing by a trickling mountain spring, I got my first glimpses of the wonders, the mysteries, and the promises hidden beneath the folds of a woman's dress. Fish and oranges from heaven . . . you can get over that.

But, in another way, the year of the drought was also one of the worst of my life, because that was the year that Abu Raja, the retired cook who used to entertain us kids by cracking walnuts on his forehead, decided it was time Magdaluna got its own telephone. Every civilized village needed a telephone, he said, and Magdaluna was not going to get anywhere until it had one. A telephone would link us with the outside world. At the time, I was too young to understand the debate, but a few men — like Shukri, the retired Turkish-army drill sergeant, and Abu Hanna the vineyard keeper — did all they could to talk Abu Raja out of having a telephone brought to the village. But they were outshouted and ignored and finally shunned by the other villagers for resisting progress and trying to keep a good thing from coming to Magdaluna.

One warm day in early fall, many of the villagers were out in their fields repairing walls or gathering wood for the winter when the shout went out that the telephone-company truck had arrived at Abu Raja's *dikkan*, or country store. There were no roads in those days, only footpaths and dry streambeds, so it took the telephone-company truck almost a day to work its way up the rocky terrain from Sidon — about the same time it took to walk. When the truck came into view, Abu George, who had a huge voice and, before the telephone, was Magdaluna's only long-distance communication system, bellowed the news from his front porch. Everybody dropped what they were doing and ran to Abu Raja's house to see what was happening. Some of the more dignified villagers, however, like Abu Habeeb and Abu Nazim, who had been to big cities like Beirut and Damascus and had seen things like telephones and telegraphs, did not run the way the rest did; they walked with their canes hanging from the crooks of their arms, as if on a Sunday afternoon stroll.

It did not take long for the whole village to assemble at Abu Raja's *dikkan*. Some of the rich villagers, like the widow Farha and the gendarme Abu Nadeem, walked right into the store and stood at the elbows of the two important-looking men from the telephone company, who proceeded with utmost gravity, like priests at Communion, to wire up the telephone. The poorer villagers stood outside and listened carefully to the details relayed to them by the not-so-poor people who stood in the doorway and could see inside.

"The bald man is cutting the blue wire," someone said.

"He is sticking the wire into the hole in the bottom of the black box," someone else added.

"The telephone man with the mustache is connecting two pieces of wire. Now he is twisting the ends together," a third voice chimed in.

Because I was small and unaware that I should have stood outside with the other poor folk to give the rich people inside more room (they seemed to need more of it than poor people did), I wriggled my way through the dense forest of legs to get a firsthand look at the action. I felt like the barefoot Moses, sandals in hand, staring at the burning bush on Mount Sinai. Breathless, I watched as the men in blue, their shirt pockets adorned with fancy lettering in a foreign language, put together a black machine that supposedly would make it possible to talk with uncles, aunts, and cousins who lived more than two days' ride away.

It was shortly after sunset when the man with the mustache announced that the telephone was ready to use. He explained that all Abu Raja had to do was lift the receiver, turn the crank on the black box a few times, and wait for an operator to take his call. Abu Raja, who had once lived and worked in Sidon, was impatient with the telephone man for assuming that he was ignorant. He grabbed the receiver and turned the crank forcefully, as if trying to start a Model T Ford. Everybody was impressed that he knew what to do. He even called the operator by her first name: "Centralist." Within moments, Abu Raja was talking with his brother, a concierge in Beirut. He didn't even have to raise his voice or shout to be heard.

If I hadn't seen it with my own two eyes and heard it with my own two ears, I would not have believed it — and my friend Kameel didn't. He was away that day watching his father's goats, and when he came back to the village that evening, his cousin Habeeb and I told him about the telephone and how Abu Raja had used it to speak with his brother in Beirut. After he heard our report, Kameel made the sign of the cross, kissed his thumbnail, and warned us that lying was a bad sin and would surely land us in purgatory. Kameel believed in Jesus and Mary, and wanted to be a priest when he grew up. He always crossed himself when Habeeb, who was irreverent, and I, who was Presbyterian, were around, even when we were not bearing bad news.

And the telephone, as it turned out, was bad news. With its coming, the face of the village began to change. One of the first effects was the shifting of the village's center. Before the telephone's arrival, the men of the village used to gather regularly at the house of Im Kaleem, a short, middle-aged widow with jet-black hair and a raspy voice that could be heard all over the village, even when she was only whispering. She was a devout Catholic and also the village *shlikki* — whore. The men met at her house to argue about politics and drink coffee and play cards or backgammon. Im Kaleem was not a true prostitute, however, because she did not charge for her services — not even for the coffee and tea (and, occasionally, the strong liquor called arrack) that she served the men. She did not need the money; her son, who was overseas in Africa, sent her money regularly. (I knew this because my father used to read her son's letters to her and take down her replies, as Im Kaleem could not read and write.) Im Kaleem was no slut either — unlike some women in the village — because she loved all the men she entertained, and they loved her, every one of them. In a way, she was married to all the men in the village. Everybody knew it — the wives knew it; the itinerant Catholic priest knew it; the Presbyterian minister knew it — but nobody objected. Actually, I suspect the women (my mother included) did not mind their husbands' visits to Im Kaleem. Oh, they wrung their hands and complained to one another about their men's unfaithfulness, but secretly they were relieved, because Im Kaleem took some of the pressure off them and kept the men out of their hair while they attended to their endless chores. Im Kaleem was also a kind of confessor and troubleshooter, talking sense to those men who were having family problems, especially the younger ones.

Before the telephone came to Magdaluna, Im Kaleem's house was bustling at just about any time of day, especially at night, when its windows were brightly lit with three large oil lamps, and the loud voices of the men talking, laughing, and arguing could be heard in the street below — a reassuring, homey sound. Her house was an island of comfort, an oasis for the weary village men, exhausted from having so little to do.

But it wasn't long before many of those men — the younger ones especially — started spending more of their days and evenings at Abu Raja's *dikkan*. There, they would eat and drink and talk and play checkers and backgammon, and then lean their chairs back against the wall — the signal that they were ready to toss back and forth, like a ball, the latest rumors going around the village. And they were always looking up from their games and drinks and talk to glance at the phone in the corner, as if expecting it to ring any minute and bring news that would change their lives and deliver them from their aimless existence. In the meantime, they smoked cheap, hand-rolled cigarettes, dug dirt out from under their fingernails with big pocketknives, and drank lukewarm sodas they called Kacula, Seffen-Ub, and Bebsi. Sometimes, especially when it was hot, the days dragged on so slowly that the men turned on Abu Saeed, a confirmed bachelor who practically lived in Abu Raja's *dikkan,* and teased him for going around barefoot and unshaven since the Virgin had appeared to him behind the olive press.

The telephone was also bad news for me personally. It took away my lucrative business — a source of much-needed income. Before the telephone came to Magdaluna, I used to hang around Im Kaleem's courtyard and play marbles with the other kids, waiting for some man to call down from a window and ask me to run to the store for cigarettes or arrack, or to deliver a message to his wife, such as what he wanted for supper. There was always something in it for me: a ten- or even a twenty-five-piaster piece. On a good day, I ran nine or ten of those errands, which assured a steady supply of marbles that I usually lost to Sami or his cousin Hani, the basket weaver's boy. But as the days went by, fewer and fewer men came to Im Kaleem's, and more and more congregated at Abu Raja's to wait by the telephone. In the evenings, no light fell from her window onto the street below, and the laughter and noise of the men trailed off and finally stopped. Only Shukri, the retired Turkish-army drill sergeant, remained faithful to Im Kaleem after all the other men had deserted her; he was still seen going into or leaving her house from time to time. Early that winter, Im Kaleem's hair suddenly turned gray, and she got sick and old. Her legs started giving her trouble, making it hard for her to walk. By spring she hardly left her house anymore.

At Abu Raja's *dikkan*, the calls did eventually come, as expected, and men and women started leaving the village the way a hailstorm begins: first one, then two, then bunches. The army took them. Jobs in the cities lured them. And ships and airplanes carried them to such faraway places as Australia and Brazil and New Zealand. My friend Kameel, his cousin Habeeb, and their cousins and my cousins all went away to become ditch diggers and mechanics and butcher-shop boys and deli owners who wore dirty aprons sixteen hours a day, all looking for a better life than the one they had left behind. Within a year, only the sick, the old, and the maimed were left in the village. Magdaluna became a skeleton of its former self, desolate and forsaken, like the tombs, a place to get away from.

Finally, the telephone took my family away, too. My father got a call from an old army buddy who told him that an oil company in southern Lebanon was hiring interpreters and instructors. My father applied for a job and got it, and we moved to Sidon, where I went to a Presbyterian missionary school and graduated in 1962. Three years later, having won a scholarship, I left Lebanon for the United States. Like the others who left Magdaluna before me, I am still looking for that better life.

Reflections and Responses

1. Why do you think Accawi begins his recollections of childhood by focusing on the way the passage of time was measured by the villagers? Does Accawi see the village's attitude toward time in positive or negative ways? How do his word choices and images reflect his position?

2. Consider the way Accawi introduces the telephone into the village. How does he prepare for its appearance? From whose perspective do we view the installation? How are the class lines of the village drawn when the telephone is installed? Finally, why did the telephone turn out to be "bad news" for the village as a whole?

3. How would you assess Accawi's attitude in the final paragraph? How did the telephone personally change his life? Do you think the change was for the worse? Do you think Accawi himself believes it was for the worse? How do you interpret his final sentence?

MARCIA ALDRICH

Hair

Montaigne, the first essayist, would have enjoyed Marcia Aldrich's wonderful meditation on hairstyles and the way they reflect our personal identity. When Montaigne began writing personal essays in the 1570s, he initiated a new style of self-portrayal. He brought his whole body into his writing, inviting his readers to see his essays not simply as thoughts on a page but as an extension of his physical being. Not having (as he put it) an "imposing presence" in actual life, he tried to create one in and through his remarkable essays. A very "physical" writer, he would discuss his looks, height, voice, and complexion, the way he walked, and his habit of scratching the inside of his ears. A persistent self-reviser, Montaigne would also appreciate Aldrich's resistance to a settled style ("a new hairstyle," she says, "will write over the last") and to a coherent philosophy.

Marcia Aldrich is a professor of English who specializes in twentieth-century poetry at Michigan State University. She is the author of a memoir about growing up in the '50s, Girl Rearing *(1998). She is also working on a study of the poet Louise Bogan. "Hair" originally appeared in* The Northwest Review *(1992) and was selected by Joseph Epstein for* The Best American Essays *1993.*

I've been around and seen the Taj Mahal and the Grand Canyon and Marilyn Monroe's footprints outside Grauman's Chinese Theater, but I've never seen my mother wash her own hair. After my mother married, she never washed her own hair again. As a girl and an unmarried woman — yes — but, in my lifetime, she never washed her hair with her own two hands. Upon matrimony, she began weekly treks to the beauty salon where Julie washed and styled her hair. Her appointment on Fridays at two o'clock was never cancelled or rescheduled; it was the bedrock of her week, around which she pivoted and planned. These two hours were indispensable to my mother's routine, to her sense of herself and what, as a woman, she should concern herself with — not to mention their being her primary source of information about all sorts of things she wouldn't otherwise come to know. With Julie my mother discussed momentous decisions concerning hair color and the advancement of age and what could be done about it, hair length and its effect upon maturity, when to perm and when not to perm, the need to proceed with caution when a woman desperately wanted a major change in her life like dumping her husband or sending back her newborn baby and the only change she could effect was a change in her hair. That was what Julie called a "dangerous time" in a woman's life. When my mother spoke to Julie, she spoke in conspiratorial, almost confessional, tones I had never heard before. Her voice was usually tense, on guard, the laughter forced, but with Julie it dropped much lower, the timbre darker than the upper-register shrills sounded at home. And most remarkably, she listened to everything Julie said.

As a child I was puzzled by the way my mother's sense of self-worth and mood seemed dependent upon how she thought her hair looked, how the search for the perfect hairstyle never ended. Just as Mother seemed to like her latest color and cut, she began to agitate for a new look. The cut seemed to have become a melancholy testimony, in my mother's eyes, to time's inexorable passage. Her hair never stood in and of itself; it was always moored to a complex set of needs and desires her hair couldn't in itself satisfy. She wanted her hair to illuminate the relationship between herself and the idea of motion while appearing still, for example. My mother wanted her hair to be fashioned into an event with a complicated narrative past. However, the more my mother attempted to impose a hairstyle pulled from an idealized image of herself, the more the hairstyle seemed to be at odds with my mother. The more the hairstyle became substantial, the more the woman underneath was obscured. She'd riffle through women's magazines and stare for long dreamy hours at a particular woman's coiffure. Then she'd ask my father in an artificially casual voice: "How do you think I'd look with really short hair?" or "Would blonde become me?" My father never committed himself to an opinion. He had learned from long experience that no response he made could turn out well; anything he said would be used against him, if not in the immediate circumstances, down the line, for my mother never forgot anything anyone ever said about her hair. My father's refusal to engage the "hair question" irritated her.

So too, I was puzzled to see that unmarried women washed their own hair, and married women, in my mother's circle at least, by some unwritten dictum never touched their own hair. I began studying before and after photographs of my mother's friends. These photographs were all the same. In the pre-married mode, their hair was soft and unformed. After the wedding, the women's hairstyles bore the stamp of property, looked constructed from grooming talents not their own, hairstyles I'd call produced, requiring constant upkeep and technique to sustain the considerable loft and rigidity — in short, the antithesis of anything I might naively call natural. This was hair no one touched, crushed, or ran fingers through. One poked and prodded various hair masses back into formation. This hair presented obstacles to embrace, the scent of the hair spray alone warded off man, child, and pests. I never saw my father stroke my mother's head. Children whimpered when my mother came home fresh from the salon with a potent do. Just when a woman's life was supposed to be opening out into daily affection, *the* sanctioned affection of husband and children, the women of my mother's circle encased themselves in a helmet of hair not unlike Medusa's.

In so-called middle age, my mother's hair never moved, never blew, never fell in her face: her hair became a museum piece. When she went to bed, she wore a blue net, and when she took short showers, short because, after all, she wasn't washing her hair and she was seldom dirty, she wore a blue plastic cap for the sake of preservation. From one appointment to the next, the only change her hair could be said to undergo was to become crestfallen. Taking extended vacations presented problems sufficiently troublesome to rule out countries where she feared no beauty parlors existed. In the beginning, my parents took overnighters, then week jaunts, and thereby avoided the whole hair dilemma. Extending their vacations to two weeks was eventually managed by my mother applying more hair spray and sleeping sitting up. But after the two week mark had been reached, she was forced to either return home or venture into an unfamiliar salon and subject herself to scrutiny, the kind of scrutiny that leaves no woman unscathed. Then she faced Julie's disapproval, for no matter how expensive and expert the salon, my mother's hair was to be lamented. Speaking just for myself, I had difficulty distinguishing Julie's cunning from the stranger's. In these years my mother's hair looked curled, teased, and sprayed into a waved tossed monument with holes poked through for glasses. She believed the damage done to her hair was tangible proof she had been somewhere, like stickers on her suitcases.

My older sisters have worked out their hair positions differently. My oldest sister's solution has been to fix upon one hairstyle and never change it. She wants to be thought of in a singular fashion. She may vary the length from long to longer, but that is the extent of her alteration. Once, after having her first baby, the "dangerous time" for women, she recklessly cut her hair to just below the ear. She immediately regretted the decision and began growing it back as she walked home from the salon, vowing not to repeat the mistake. Her signature is dark, straight hair pulled heavily off her face in a large silver clip, found at any Woolworth's. When one clip breaks, she buys another just like it. My mother hates the timelessness of my sister's hair. She equates it with a refusal to face growing old. My mother says, "It's immature to wear your hair the same way all your life." My sister replies,

"It's immature to never stop thinking about your hair. If this hairstyle was good enough when I was twenty, it's good enough when I'm forty, if not better."

"But what about change?" my mother asks.

"Change is overrated," my sister says flipping her long hair over her shoulder definitively. "I feel my hair."

My other sister was born with thin, lifeless, nondescript hair: a cross she has had to bear. Even in the baby pictures, the limp strands plastered on her forehead in question marks wear her down. Shame and self-effacement are especially plain in the pictures where she posed with our eldest sister, whose dark hair dominates the frame. She's spent her life attempting to disguise the real state of her hair. Some years she'd focus on style, pulling it back in ponytails so that from the front no one could see there wasn't much hair in the back. She tried artless, even messy styles — as if she had just tied it up any old way before taking a bath or bunched it to look deliberately snarled. There were the weird years punctuated by styles that looked as if she had taken sugar water and lemon juice and squeezed them onto her wet hair and then let them crystallize. The worst style was when she took her hair and piled it on the top of her head in a cone shape and then crimped the ponytail into a zigzag. Personally, I thought she had gone too far. No single approach solved the hair problem, and so now, in maturity, she combines the various phases of attack in hope something will work. She frosts both the grey strands and the pale brown, and then perms for added body and thickness. She's forced to keep her hair short because chemicals do tend to destroy. My mother admires my sister's determination to transform herself, and never more than in my sister's latest assault upon middle age. No one has known for many years nor does anyone remember what the untreated color or texture of either my mother's or my sister's hair might be.

As the youngest by twelve years, there was little to distract Mother's considerable attention from the problem of my hair. I had cowlicks, a remarkable number of them, which like little arrows shot across my scalp. They refused to be trained, to lie down quietly in the same direction as the rest of my hair. One at the front insisted on sticking straight up while two on either side of my ears jutted out seeking sun. The lack of uniformity, the fact that my hair had a mind of its own, infuriated my mother and she saw to it that Julie cut my hair as short as possible in order to curtail its wanton expression. Sitting in the swivel chair before the mirror while Julie snipped, I felt invisible, as if I was unattached to my hair.

Just when I started to menstruate, my mother decided the battle plan needed a change, and presto, the page boy replaced the pixie. Having not outgrown the thicket of cowlicks, Mother bought a spectrum of brightly colored stretch bands to hold my hair back off my face. Then she attached thin pink plastic curlers with snap on lids to the ends of my hair to make them flip up or under, depending on her mood. The stretch bands pressed my hair flat until the very bottom, at which point the ends formed a tunnel with ridges from the roller caps — a point of emphasis, she called it. Coupled with the aquamarine eyeglasses, newly acquired, I looked like an overgrown insect that had none of its kind to bond with.

However, I was not alone. Unless you were the last in a long line of sisters, chances were good that your hair would not go unnoticed by your mother. Each of my best friends was subjected to her mother's hair dictatorship, although with entirely different results. Perry Jensen's mother insisted that all five of her daughters peroxide their hair blonde and pull it back into high ponytails. All the girls' hair turned green in the summer from chlorine. Melissa Matson underwent a look-alike "home perm" with her mother, an experience she never did recover from. She developed a phobic reaction to anything synthetic, which made life very expensive. Not only did mother and daughter have identical tight curls and wear mother-daughter outfits, later they had look-alike nose jobs.

In my generation, many women who survived hair bondage to their mothers now experiment with hairstyles as one would test a new design: to see how it works, what it will withstand, and how it can be improved. Testing requires boldness, for often the style fails dramatically, as when I had my hair cut about a half inch long at the top, and it stood straight up like a tacky shag carpet. I had to live with the results, bear daily witness to the kinks in its design for nine months until strategies of damage control could be deployed. But sometimes women I know create a look that startles in its originality and suggests a future not yet realized.

The women in my family divide into two general groups: those who fasten upon one style, become identified with a look, and are impervious to change, weathering the years steadfastly, and those who, for a variety of reasons, are in the business of transforming themselves. In my sister's case, the quest for perfect hair originates in a need to mask her own appearance; in my mother's case, she wants to achieve a beauty of person unavailable in her own life story. Some women seek transformation, not out of dissatisfaction with themselves, but because hair change is a means of moving along in their lives. These women create portraits of themselves that won't last forever, a new hairstyle will write over the last.

Since my mother dictated my hair, I never took a stand on the hair issue. In maturity, I'm incapable of assuming a coherent or consistent philosophy. I have wayward hair: it's always becoming something else. The moment it arrives at a recognizable style, it begins to undo itself, it grows, the sun colors it, it waves. When one hair pin goes in, another seems to come out. Sometimes I think I should follow my oldest sister — she claims to never give more than a passing thought to her hair and can't see what all the angst is about. She asks, "Don't women have better things to think about than their hair?"

I bite back: "But don't you think hair should reflect who you are?"

"To be honest, I've never thought about it. I don't think so. Cut your hair the same way, and lose your self in something else. You're distracted from the real action."

I want to do what my sister says, but when I walk out into shop-lined streets, I automatically study women's hair and always with the same question: How did they arrive at their hair? Lately, I've been feeling more and more like my mother. I hadn't known how to resolve the dilemma until I found Rhonda. I don't know if I found Rhonda or made her up. She is not a normally trained hair-dresser: she has a different set of eyes, unaffected. One day while out driving around to no place in particular, at the bottom of a hill, I found: "Rhonda's Hair Salon — Don't Look Back" written on a life-size cardboard image of Rhonda. Her shop was on the top of this steep orchard planted hill, on a plateau with a great view that opened out and went on forever. I parked my car at the bottom and walked up. Zigzagging all the way up the hill, leaning against or sticking out from behind the apple trees were more life-sized cardboard likenesses of Rhonda. Except for the explosive sun-bursts in her hair, no two signs were the same. At the bottom, she wore long red hair falling below her knees and covering her entire body like a shawl. As I climbed the hill, Rhonda's hair gradually be-came shorter and shorter, and each length was cut differently, until when I reached the top, her head was shaved and glistening in the sun. I found Rhonda herself out under one of the apple trees wearing running shoes. Her hair was long and red and looked as if it had never been cut. She told me she had no aspira-tions to be a hairdresser, "she just fell into it." "I see hair," she con-tinued, "as an extension of the head and therefore I try to do hair with a lot of thought." Inside there were no mirrors, no swivel chairs, no machines of torture with their accompanying stink. She said, "Nothing is permanent, nothing is forever. Don't feel hampered or hemmed in by the shape of your face or the shape of your past. Hair is vital, sustains mistakes, can be born again. You don't have to marry it. Now tip back and put your head into my hands."

Reflections and Responses

---

1. Consider how Aldrich invites you to see hairstyles in terms of personal identity. Compare the different female members of her family. How does each reflect a different philosophical attitude through her hairstyle? What are they? Why do you think Aldrich left her father out of these reflections?

2. How does Aldrich establish a relationship between hairstyle and writing style? For Aldrich, what do the two have in common? In going through her essay, identify some features of her writing style that also reflect her attitude toward her hair.

3. Reread Aldrich's final paragraph carefully. It's tricky. What do you think is happening? Is "Rhonda" real or fictitious? What makes you think she is real? Alternatively, what makes you think Aldrich made her up? Why do you think Aldrich concluded her essay with this visit to Rhonda's Hair Salon?

JUDITH ORTIZ COFER

Silent Dancing

Nothing rekindles childhood memories better than old photographs or home movies. In this vivid essay, a grainy and poorly focused five-minute home movie of a New Year's Eve party helps a writer capture the spirit of a Puerto Rican community in Paterson, New Jersey. That the movie is fragmented and silent adds to its documentary value and, for a lyrical essayist, it evokes much more than it can possibly reveal. "Even the home movie," Cofer writes, "cannot fill in the sensory details such a gathering left imprinted in a child's brain." Those sensory details — "the flavor of Puerto Rico" — must be supplied through the art of writing.

A professor of English and creative writing at the University of Georgia, Judith Ortiz Cofer has published prize-winning books in a number of genres: a novel, The Line of the Sun *(1989); two poetry collections,* Terms of Survival *(1987) and* Reaching for the Mainland *(1986); two autobiographical books combining prose and poetry,* Silent Dancing *(1990) and* The Latin Deli *(1993); and* An Island Like You: Stories of the Barrio *(1995). She has recently published* The Year of Our Revolution: New and Selected Stories and Poems *(1998) and* Sleeping with One Eye Open: Women Writers and the Art of Survival *(1999). Cofer has received many prestigious awards, including fellowships from the National Endowment for the Arts, the Witter Bynner Foundation for Poetry, and the Bread Loaf Writers' Conference. "Silent Dancing" originally appeared in* The Georgia Review *(1990) and was selected by Joyce Carol Oates for* The Best American Essays *1991. Ms. Cofer courteously supplied the notes to this selection.*

We have a home movie of this party. Several times my mother and I have watched it together, and I have asked questions about the silent revelers

coming in and out of focus. It is grainy and of short duration, but it's a
great visual aid to my memory of life at that time. And it is in color — the
only complete scene in color I can recall from those years.

We lived in Puerto Rico until my brother was born in 1954. Soon
after, because of economic pressures on our growing family, my father joined the United States Navy. He was assigned to duty on a
ship in Brooklyn Yard — a place of cement and steel that was to be
his home base in the States until his retirement more than twenty
years later. He left the Island first, alone, going to New York City
and tracking down his uncle who lived with his family across the
Hudson River in Paterson, New Jersey. There my father found a
tiny apartment in a huge tenement that had once housed Jewish
families but was just being taken over and transformed by Puerto
Ricans, overflowing from New York City. In 1955 he sent for us.
My mother was only twenty years old, I was not quite three, and my
brother was a toddler when we arrived at *El Building,* as the place
had been christened by its newest residents.

My memories of life in Paterson during those first few years are
all in shades of gray. Maybe I was too young to absorb vivid colors
and details, or to discriminate between the slate blue of the winter
sky and the darker hues of the snow-bearing clouds, but that single
color washes over the whole period. The building we lived in was
gray, as were the streets, filled with slush the first few months of my
life there. The coat my father had bought for me was similar in
color and too big; it sat heavily on my thin frame.

I do remember the way the heater pipes banged and rattled,
startling all of us out of sleep until we got so used to the sound that
we automatically shut it out or raised our voices above the racket.
The hiss from the valve punctuated my sleep (which has always
been fitful) like a nonhuman presence in the room — a dragon
sleeping at the entrance of my childhood. But the pipes were also
a connection to all the other lives being lived around us. Having
come from a house designed for a single family back in Puerto
Rico — my mother's extended-family home — it was curious to
know that strangers lived under our floor and above our heads,
and that the heater pipe went through everyone's apartments. (My
first spanking in Paterson came as a result of playing tunes on the
pipes in my room to see if there would be an answer.) My mother

was as new to this concept of beehive life as I was, but she had been given strict orders by my father to keep the doors locked, the noise down, ourselves to ourselves.

It seems that Father had learned some painful lessons about prejudice while searching for an apartment in Paterson. Not until years later did I hear how much resistance he had encountered with landlords who were panicking at the influx of Latinos into a neighborhood that had been Jewish for a couple of generations. It made no difference that it was the American phenomenon of ethnic turnover which was changing the urban core of Paterson, and that the human flood could not be held back with an accusing finger.

"You Cuban?" one man had asked my father, pointing at his name tag on the Navy uniform — even though my father had the fair skin and light-brown hair of his northern Spanish background, and the name Ortiz is as common in Puerto Rico as Johnson is in the U.S.

"No," my father had answered, looking past the finger into his adversary's angry eyes. "I'm Puerto Rican."

"Same shit." And the door closed.

My father could have passed as European, but we couldn't. My brother and I both have our mother's black hair and olive skin, and so we lived in El Building and visited our great-uncle and his fair children on the next block. It was their private joke that they were the German branch of the family. Not many years later that area too would be mainly Puerto Rican. It was as if the heart of the city map were being gradually colored brown — *café con leche* brown. Our color.

The movie opens with a sweep of the living room. It is "typical" immigrant Puerto Rican decor for the time: the sofa and chairs are square and hard-looking, upholstered in bright colors (blue and yellow in this instance), and covered with the transparent plastic that furniture salesmen then were so adept at convincing women to buy. The linoleum on the floor is light blue; if it had been subjected to spike heels (as it was in most places), there were dime-sized indentations all over it that cannot be seen in this movie. The room is full of people dressed up: dark suits for the men, red dresses for the women. When I have asked my mother why most of the women are in red that night, she has shrugged, "I don't remember. Just a coincidence." She doesn't have my obsession for assigning symbolism to everything.

The three women in red sitting on the couch are my mother, my eighteen-year-old cousin, and her brother's girlfriend. The novia *is just up from the Island, which is apparent in her body language. She sits up formally, her dress pulled over her knees. She is a pretty girl, but her posture makes her look insecure, lost in her full-skirted dress, which she has carefully tucked around her to make room for my gorgeous cousin, her future sister-in-law. My cousin has grown up in Paterson and is in her last year of high school. She doesn't have a trace of what Puerto Ricans call* la mancha *(literally, the stain: the mark of the new immigrant — something about the posture, the voice, or the humble demeanor that makes it obvious to everyone the person has just arrived on the mainland). My cousin is wearing a tight, sequined, cocktail dress. Her brown hair has been lightened with peroxide around the bangs, and she is holding a cigarette expertly between her fingers, bringing it up to her mouth in a sensuous arc of her arm as she talks animatedly. My mother, who has come up to sit between the two women, both only a few years younger than herself, is somewhere between the poles they represent in our culture.*

It became my father's obsession to get out of the barrio, and thus we were never permitted to form bonds with the place or with the people who lived there. Yet El Building was a comfort to my mother, who never got over yearning for *la isla.* She felt surrounded by her language: the walls were thin, and voices speaking and arguing in Spanish could be heard all day. *Salsas* blasted out of radios, turned on early in the morning and left on for company. Women seemed to cook rice and beans perpetually — the strong aroma of boiling red kidney beans permeated the hallways.

Though Father preferred that we do our grocery shopping at the supermarket when he came home on weekend leaves, my mother insisted that she could cook only with products whose labels she could read. Consequently, during the week I accompanied her and my little brother to *La Bodega* — a hole-in-the-wall grocery store across the street from El Building. There we squeezed down three narrow aisles jammed with various products. Goya's and Libby's — those were the trademarks that were trusted by *her mamá,* so my mother bought many cans of Goya beans, soups, and condiments, as well as little cans of Libby's fruit juices for us. And she also bought Colgate toothpaste and Palmolive soap. (The final *e* is pronounced in both these products in Spanish, so for many years I believed that they were manufactured on the Island. I remember my surprise at first hearing a commercial on television in which Colgate rhymed with "ate.") We always lingered at La Bodega, for it was there that Mother breathed best, taking in the familiar aromas of the foods she knew from Mamá's kitchen. It was also there that she got to speak to the other women of El Building without violating outright Father's dictates against fraternizing with our neighbors.

Yet Father did his best to make our "assimilation" painless. I can still see him carrying a real Christmas tree up several flights of stairs to our apartment, leaving a trail of aromatic pine. He carried it formally, as if it were a flag in a parade. We were the only ones in El Building that I knew of who got presents on both Christmas day AND *día de Reyes*, the day when the Three Kings brought gifts to Christ and to Hispanic children.

Our supreme luxury in El Building was having our own television set. It must have been a result of Father's guilt feelings over the isolation he had imposed on us, but we were among the first in the barrio to have one. My brother quickly became an avid watcher of Captain Kangaroo and Jungle Jim, while I loved all the series showing families. By the time I started first grade, I could have drawn a map of Middle America as exemplified by the lives of characters in *Father Knows Best*, *The Donna Reed Show*, *Leave It to Beaver*, *My Three Sons*, and (my favorite) *Bachelor Father*, where John Forsythe treated his adopted teenage daughter like a princess because he was rich and had a Chinese houseboy to do everything for him. In truth, compared to our neighbors in El Building, *we* were rich. My father's Navy check provided us with financial security and a standard of life that the factory workers envied. The only thing his money could not buy us was a place to live away from the barrio — his greatest wish, Mother's greatest fear.

In the home movie the men are shown next, sitting around a card table set up in one corner of the living room, playing dominoes. The clack of the ivory pieces was a familiar sound. I heard it in many houses on the Island and in many apartments in Paterson. In Leave It to Beaver, *the Cleavers played bridge in every other episode; in my childhood, the men started every social occasion with a hotly debated round of dominoes. The women would sit around and watch, but they never participated in the games.*

Here and there you can see a small child. Children were always brought to parties and, whenever they got sleepy, were put to bed in the host's bedroom. Babysitting was a concept unrecognized by the Puerto Rican women I knew: a responsible mother did not leave her children with any stranger. And in a culture where children are not considered intrusive, there was no need to leave the children at home. We went where our mother went.

Of my preschool years I have only impressions: the sharp bite of the wind in December as we walked with our parents towards the brightly lit stores downtown; how I felt like a stuffed doll in my heavy coat, boots, and mittens; how good it was to walk into the five-and-dime and sit at the counter drinking hot chocolate. On Saturdays our whole family would walk downtown to shop at the big department stores on Broadway. Mother bought all our clothes at Penney's and Sears, and she liked to buy her dresses at the women's specialty shops like Lerner's and Diana's. At some point we'd go into Woolworth's and sit at the soda fountain to eat.

We never ran into other Latinos at these stores or when eating out, and it became clear to me only years later that the women from El Building shopped mainly in other places — stores owned by other Puerto Ricans or by Jewish merchants who had philosophically accepted our presence in the city and decided to make us their good customers, if not real neighbors and friends. These establishments were located not downtown but in the blocks around our street, and they were referred to generically as *La Tienda, El Bazar, La Bodega, La Botánica.* Everyone knew what was meant. These were the stores where your face did not turn a clerk to stone, where your money was as green as anyone else's.

One New Year's Eve we were dressed up like child models in the Sears catalogue: my brother in a miniature man's suit and bow tie, and I in black patent-leather shoes and a frilly dress with several layers of crinoline underneath. My mother wore a bright-red dress that night, I remember, and spike heels; her long black hair hung to her waist. Father, who usually wore his Navy uniform during his short visits home, had put on a dark civilian suit for the occasion: we had been invited to his uncle's house for a big celebration. Everyone was excited because my mother's brother Hernan — a bachelor who could indulge himself with luxuries — had bought a home movie camera, which he would be trying out that night.

Even the home movie cannot fill in the sensory details such a gathering left imprinted in a child's brain. The thick sweetness of women's perfumes mixing with the ever-present smells of food cooking in the kitchen: meat and plantain *pasteles,* as well as the ubiquitous rice dish made special with pigeon peas — *gandules* — and seasoned with precious *sofrito** sent up from the Island by somebody's mother or smuggled in by a recent traveler. *Sofrito* was one of the items that women hoarded, since it was hardly ever in stock at La Bodega. It was the flavor of Puerto Rico.

The men drank Palo Viejo rum, and some of the younger ones got weepy. The first time I saw a grown man cry was at a New Year's Eve party: he had been reminded of his mother by the smells in the kitchen. But what I remember most were the boiled *pasteles* — plantain or yucca rectangles stuffed with corned beef or other meats, olives, and many other savory ingredients, all wrapped in banana leaves. Everybody had to fish one out with a fork. There was always a "trick" pastel — one without stuffing — and whoever got that one was the "New Year's Fool."

There was also the music. Long-playing albums were treated like precious china in these homes. Mexican recordings were popular, but the songs that brought tears to my mother's eyes were sung by the melancholy Daniel Santos, whose life as a drug addict was the stuff of legend. Felipe Rodríguez was a particular favorite of couples, since he sang about faithless women and brokenhearted men. There is a snatch of one lyric that has stuck in my mind like a needle on a worn groove: *De piedra ha de ser mi cama, de piedra la cabezera . . . la mujer que a mi me quiera . . . ha de quererme de veras. Ay, Ay, Ay, corazón, porque no amas*[†]*. . . .* I must have heard it a thousand times since the idea of a bed made of stone, and its connection to love, first troubled me with its disturbing images.

The five-minute home movie ends with people dancing in a circle — the creative filmmaker must have set it up, so that all of

Author's note — ***sofrito:** A cooked condiment. A sauce composed of a mixture of fatback, ham, tomatoes, and many island spices and herbs. It is added to many typical Puerto Rican dishes for a distinctive flavor.

Author's note — [†]**"De piedra ha de ser . . ."** Lyrics from a popular romantic ballad (called a *bolero* in Puerto Rico). Freely translated: "My bed will be made of stone, of stone also my headrest (or pillow), the woman who (dares to) loves me, will have to love me for real. Ay, Ay, Ay, my heart, why can't you (let me) love. . . ."

them could file past him. It is both comical and sad to watch silent dancing. Since there is no justification for the absurd movements that music provides for some of us, people appear frantic, their faces embarrassingly intense. It's as if you were watching sex. Yet for years, I've had dreams in the form of this home movie. In a recurring scene, familiar faces push themselves forward into my mind's eye, plastering their features into distorted close-ups. And I'm asking them: "Who is she? Who is the old woman I don't recognize? Is she an aunt? Somebody's wife? Tell me who she is."

"See the beauty mark on her cheek as big as a hill on the lunar landscape of her face — well, that runs in the family. The women on your father's side of the family wrinkle early; it's the price they pay for that fair skin. The young girl with the green stain on her wedding dress is *La Novia* — just up from the Island. See, she lowers her eyes when she approaches the camera, as she's supposed to. Decent girls never look at you directly in the face. *Humilde,* humble, a girl should express humility in all her actions. She will make a good wife for your cousin. He should consider himself lucky to have met her only weeks after she arrived here. If he marries her quickly, she will make him a good Puerto Rican–style wife; but if he waits too long, she will be corrupted by the city — just like your cousin there."

"She means me. I do what I want. This is not some primitive island I live on. Do they expect me to wear a black mantilla on my head and go to mass every day? Not me. I'm an American woman, and I will do as I please. I can type faster than anyone in my senior class at Central High, and I'm going to be a secretary to a lawyer when I graduate. I can pass for an American girl anywhere — I've tried it. At least for Italian, anyway — I never speak Spanish in public. I hate these parties, but I wanted the dress. I look better than any of these *humildes* here. *My* life is going to be different. I have an American boyfriend. He is older and has a car. My parents don't know it, but I sneak out of the house late at night sometimes to be with him. If I marry him, even my name will be American. I hate rice and beans — that's what makes these women fat."

"Your *prima** is pregnant by that man she's been sneaking around with. Would I lie to you? I'm your *Tiá Política,†* your great-uncle's

Author's note — *prima: Female cousin.

Author's note — †tía política: Aunt by marriage.

common-law wife — the one he abandoned on the Island to go marry your cousin's mother. *I* was not invited to this party, of course, but I came anyway. I came to tell you that story about your cousin that you've always wanted to hear. Do you remember the comment your mother made to a neighbor that has always haunted you? The only thing you heard was your cousin's name, and then you saw your mother pick up your doll from the couch and say: 'It was as big as this doll when they flushed it down the toilet.' This image has bothered you for years, hasn't it? You had nightmares about babies being flushed down the toilet, and you wondered why anyone would do such a horrible thing. You didn't dare ask your mother about it. She would only tell you that you had not heard her right, and yell at you for listening to adult conversations. But later, when you were old enough to know about abortions, you suspected.

I am here to tell you that you were right. Your cousin was growing an *Americanito* in her belly when this movie was made. Soon after she put something long and pointy into her pretty self, thinking maybe she could get rid of the problem before breakfast and still make it to her first class at the high school. Well, *Niña,** her screams could be heard downtown. Your aunt, her mamá, who had been a midwife on the Island, managed to pull the little thing out. Yes, they probably flushed it down the toilet. What else could they do with it — give it a Christian burial in a little white casket with blue bows and ribbons? Nobody wanted that baby — least of all the father, a teacher at her school with a house in West Paterson that he was filling with real children, and a wife who was a natural blond.

Girl, the scandal sent your uncle back to the bottle. And guess where your cousin ended up? Irony of ironies. She was sent to a village in Puerto Rico to live with a relative on her mother's side: a place so far away from civilization that you have to ride a mule to reach it. A real change in scenery. She found a man there — women like that cannot live without male company — but believe me, the men in Puerto Rico know how to put a saddle on a woman like her. *La Gringa,*† they call her. Ha, ha, ha. *La Gringa* is what she always wanted to be. . . ."

The old woman's mouth becomes a cavernous black hole I fall into. And as I fall, I can feel the reverberations of her laughter. I hear the echoes of her last mocking words: *La Gringa, La Gringa!*

Author's note — ***niña:** Girl.

Author's note — †**La gringa:** Derogatory epithet used here to ridicule a Puerto Rican girl who wants to look like a blonde North American.

And the conga line keeps moving silently past me. There is no music in my dream for the dancers.

When Odysseus visits Hades to see the spirit of his mother, he makes an offering of sacrificial blood, but since all the souls crave an audience with the living, he has to listen to many of them before he can ask questions. I, too, have to hear the dead and the forgotten speak in my dream. Those who are still part of my life remain silent, going around and around in their dance. The others keep pressing their faces forward to say things about the past.

My father's uncle is last in line. He is dying of alcoholism, shrunken and shriveled like a monkey, his face a mass of wrinkles and broken arteries. As he comes closer I realize that in his features I can see my whole family. If you were to stretch that rubbery flesh, you could find my father's face, and deep within *that* face — my own. I don't want to look into those eyes ringed in purple. In a few years he will retreat into silence, and take a long, long time to die. *Move back, Tío,* I tell him. *I don't want to hear what you have to say. Give the dancers room to move. Soon it will be midnight. Who is the New Year's Fool this time?*

Reflections and Responses

1. Consider the idea of "silence" in the essay. Why is it significant that the home movie has no soundtrack? What does Cofer do with that missing element? How does silence contribute to the theme of the essay?

2. What connections does Cofer make between the home movie and her dreams? In what ways is the movie dreamlike? In what ways does the essay become more nightmarish as it proceeds?

3. Consider Cofer's final paragraph. How does it pull together the various strands of the essay?

EDWIDGE DANTICAT

Westbury Court

What do we remember from our childhood? And why do we remember some things vividly, some things not at all, and yet others in some fuzzy in-between? In "Westbury Court," Edwidge Danticat examines the inner work-ings of memory, as she describes a deadly fire that took the lives of two children who lived next door to her in a New York apartment building when she was fourteen. Though vivid in many ways, the memory still leaves her wondering if she recalls the most significant details correctly: "Even now, I question what I remember about the children. Did they really die? Or did their mother simply move away with them after the fire?" She wonders if she is really "struggling to phase them out of [her] memory alto-gether."

Born in Port-au-Prince, Haiti, in 1969, Edwidge Danticat settled with her family in New York at age twelve. She began writing stories as a child and at fourteen she published a short essay about her experiences as a Haitian immigrant in New York. After graduating from Barnard College in Manhattan, she went on to earn an M.F.A. from Brown University. Her books include the novels Breath, Eyes, Memory *(1994) and* The Farm-ing of Bones *(1998); a collection of short stories,* Krik? Krak! *(1995);* After the Dance *(2002), and several compilations of essays. "Westbury Court" originally appeared in* New Letters *and was selected by Alan Lightman for* The Best American Essays *2000.*

When I was fourteen years old, we lived in a six-story brick build-ing in a cul-de-sac off of Flatbush Avenue, in Brooklyn, called West-bury Court. Beneath the building ran a subway station through which rattled the D, M, and Q trains every fifteen minutes or so. Though there was graffiti on most of the walls of Westbury Court, and hills of trash piled up outside, and though the elevator wasn't always there when we opened the door to step inside and the heat and hot water weren't always on, I never dreamed of leaving Westbury Court until the year of the fire.

I was watching television one afternoon when the fire began. I loved television then, especially the afternoon soap operas, my favorite of which was *General Hospital.* I would bolt out of my last high school class every day, pick up my youngest brother, Karl, from day care, and watch *General Hospital* with him on my lap while doing my homework during the commercials. My other two brothers, André and Kelly, would later join us in the apartment, but they preferred to watch cartoons in the back bedroom.

One afternoon while *General Hospital* and afternoon cartoons were on, a fire started in apartment 6E, across the hall. There in that apartment lived our new neighbors, an African-American mother and her two boys. We didn't know the name of the mother, or the names and ages of her boys, but I venture to guess that they were around five and ten years old.

I didn't know a fire had started until two masked, burly firemen came knocking on our door. My brothers and I rushed out into the hallway filled with smoke and were quickly escorted down to the first floor by some other firemen already on our floor. While we ran by, the door to apartment 6E had already been knocked over by the fire squad and inside was filled with bright flames and murky smoke.

All of the tenants of the building who were home at that time were crowded on the sidewalk outside. My brothers and I, it seemed, were the last to be evacuated. Clutching my brothers' hands, I wondered if I had remembered to lock our apartment door. Was there anything valuable we could have taken?

An ambulance screeched to a stop in front of the building, and the two firemen who had knocked on our door came out carrying the pliant and lifeless bodies of the two children from across the hall. Their mother jumped out of the crowd and ran toward them, screaming, "My babies — not my babies," as the children were lowered into the back of the ambulance and transferred into the arms of the emergency medical personnel. The fire was started by the two boys, after their mother had stepped out to pick up some groceries at the supermarket down the street. They had been playing with matches.

(Later my mother would tell us, "See, this is what happens to children who play with matches. Sometimes it is too late to say, 'I shouldn't have.'" My brother Kelly, who was fascinated with fire and liked to hold up a match to the middle of his palm until the light fizzled out, gave up this party trick after the fire.)

We were quiet that afternoon when both our parents came home. We were the closest to the fire in the building, and the most religious of our parents' friends saw it as a miracle that we had escaped safe and sound. When my mother asked how come I, the oldest one, hadn't heard the children scream or hadn't smelled the smoke coming from across the hall, I confessed that I had been watching *General Hospital* and was too consumed in the intricate plot.

(After the fire, my mother had us stay with a family on the second floor for a few months, after school. I felt better not having to be wholly responsible for myself and my brothers, in case something like that fire should ever happen again.)

The apartment across the hall stayed empty for a long time, and whenever I walked past it, a piece of its inner skeleton would squeak, and occasionally burnt wood that might have been hanging by a fragile singed thread would crash down and cause a domino effect of further ruptures, unleashed like those children's last cries, which I had not heard because I had been so wrapped up in the made-up drama of a world where, even though the adults' lives were often in turmoil, the children came home to the welcoming arms of waiting mommies and nannies who served them freshly baked cookies on porcelain plates and helped them to remove their mud-soaked boots, if it was raining, lest they soil the lily-white carpets. But should their boots accidentally sully the carpet, or should their bright yellow raincoats inadvertently drip on the sparkling linoleum, there would be a remedy for that as well. And if their house should ever catch fire, a smart dog or a good neighbor would rescue them just in time, and the fire trucks would come right quick because some attentive neighbor would call them.

Through the trail of voices that came up to comfort us, I heard that the children's mother would be prosecuted for negligence and child abandonment. I couldn't help but wonder, would our parents have suffered the same fate had it been my brothers and me who were killed in the fire?

When they began to repair the apartment across the hall, I would occasionally sneak out to watch the workmen. They were shelling the inside of the apartment and replacing everything from the bedroom closets to the kitchen floors. I never saw the mother of the dead boys again and never heard anything of her fate.

A year later, after the apartment was well polished and painted, two blind Haitian brothers and their sister moved in. They were all musicians and were part of a group called les Frères Parent, the Parent Brothers. Once my parents allowed my brothers and me to come home from school to our apartment, I would always listen carefully for our new tenants, so I'd be the first to know if anything went awry.

What I heard coming from the apartment soon after they moved in was music, "engagé" music, which the brothers were composing to protest against the dictatorship in Haiti, from which they had fled. The Parent Brothers and their sister, Lydie, did nothing but rehearse a cappella most days when they were not receiving religious and political leaders from Haiti and from the Haitian community in New York.

The same year after the fire, a cabdriver who lived down the hall in 6J was killed on a night shift in Manhattan; a good friend of my father's, a man who gave great Sunday afternoon parties in 6F, died of cirrhosis of the liver. One day while my brothers and I were at school and my parents were at work, someone came into our apartment through our fire escape and stole my father's expensive camera. That same year a Nigerian immigrant was shot and killed in front of the building across the street. To appease us, my mother said, "Nothing like that ever happens out of the blue. He was in a fight with someone." It was too troublesome for her to acknowledge that people could die randomly, senselessly, at Westbury Court or anywhere else.

Every day on my way back from school, I hurried past the flowers and candles piled in front of the spot where the Nigerian, whose name I didn't know, had been murdered. Still I never thought I was living in a violent place. It was an elevated castle above a clattering train tunnel, a blind alley where children from our building and the building across the street had erected a common basketball court for hot summer afternoon games, an urban yellow brick road where hopscotch squares dotted the sidewalk next to burned-out, abandoned cars. It was home.

My family and I moved out of Westbury Court three years after the fire. Every once in a while, though, the place came up in conversation, linked to either a joyous or a painful memory. One of the girls who had scalded her legs while boiling a pot of water for her bath during one of those no-heat days got married last year. After the burglar had broken into the house and taken my father's camera, my father — an amateur photography buff — never took another picture.

My family and I often reminisce about the Parent Brothers when we see them in Haitian newspapers or on television; we brag that we knew them when, before one of the brothers became a senator in Haiti and the sister, Lydie, became mayor of one of the better-off Haitian suburbs, Pétion-Ville. We never talk about the lost children.

Even now, I question what I remember about the children. Did they really die? Or did their mother simply move away with them after the fire? Maybe they were not even boys at all. Maybe they were two girls. Or one boy and one girl. Or maybe I am struggling to phase them out of my memory altogether. Not just them, but the fear that their destiny could have so easily been mine and my brothers'.

A few months ago, I asked my mother, "Do you remember the children and the fire at Westbury Court?"

Without missing a flutter of my breath, my mother replied, "Oh those children, those poor children, their poor mother. Sometimes it is too late to say, 'I shouldn't have.'"

Reflections and Responses

1. Consider the way Danticat narrates her essay. What information does she introduce that she would not have known during the incident of the fire? What other methods of telling the story might she have chosen?

2. Why does Danticat emphasize her mother's response to the fire, referring to it at the time and then repeating it later? In what sense is her mother's comment a warning? How do you think Danticat wants us to interpret her mother's comment in the final paragraph?

3. Why do you think that after vividly describing the firefighters carrying out the "lifeless bodies of the two children," Danticat toward the end of the essay wonders whether the children actually did die? What effect does her wondering about this produce? Do you think it leaves the issue open-ended? In light of her questions, how are we to understand the final paragraph?

HENRY LOUIS GATES, JR.

In the Kitchen

In recent years, the memoir has become an attractive genre for many American writers. Once written only toward the close of a career, as a kind of summary of a successful life (Benjamin Franklin's Autobiography *is the leading American prototype), the memoir is today often composed by individuals in early or midcareer. As a result, such memoirs tend to be fashioned around the family, childhood, and the formative years. This is especially true with memoirs that introduce us to cultural worlds we may be unfamiliar with, or, as in the case of Henry Louis Gates, Jr., to acquaint us with a world that has vanished. He begins his celebrated memoir* Colored People *(1994) with an address to his children: "Dear Maggie and Liza: I have written to you because a world into which I was born, a world that nurtured and sustained me, has mysteriously disappeared."*

Henry Louis Gates, Jr., is W. E. B. Du Bois Professor of the Humanities and chair of the Afro-American Studies Department at Harvard University, as well as director of the W. E. B. Du Bois Institute for Afro-American Research at Harvard. He received his Ph.D. in English literature from the University of Cambridge. Well known for his work in recovering black writers from obscurity, Dr. Gates, a "literary archaeologist," has brought to light thousands of previously lost or neglected works of nineteenth-century black literature. Among his books are Figures in Black: Words, Signs, and the Racial Self *(1987);* The Signifying Monkey: A Theory of Afro-American Literary Criticism *(1988);* Loose Canons: Notes on the Culture Wars *(1992); and* Thirteen Ways of Looking at a Black Man *(1997). An essay-chapter of* Colored People, *"In the Kitchen" originally appeared in* The New Yorker *(1994) and was selected by Jamaica Kincaid for* The Best American Essays *1995.*

We always had a gas stove in the kitchen, in our house in Piedmont, West Virginia, where I grew up. Never electric, though using electric became fashionable in Piedmont in the sixties, like using Crest toothpaste rather than Colgate, or watching Huntley and Brinkley rather than Walter Cronkite. But not us: gas, Colgate, and good ole Walter Cronkite, come what may. We used gas partly out of loyalty to Big Mom, Mama's mama, because she was mostly blind and still loved to cook, and could feel her way more easily with gas than with electric. But the most important thing about our gas-equipped kitchen was that Mama used to do hair there. The "hot comb" was a fine-toothed iron instrument with a long wooden handle and a pair of iron curlers that opened and closed like scissors. Mama would put it in the gas fire until it glowed. You could smell those prongs heating up.

I liked that smell. Not the smell so much, I guess, as what the smell meant for the shape of my day. There was an intimate warmth in the women's tones as they talked with my mama, doing their hair. I knew what the women had been through to get their hair ready to be "done," because I would watch Mama do it to herself. How that kink could be transformed through grease and fire into that magnificent head of wavy hair was a miracle to me, and still is.

Mama would wash her hair over the sink, a towel wrapped around her shoulders, wearing just her slip and her white bra. (We had no shower — just a galvanized tub that we stored in the kitchen — until we moved down Rat Tail Road into Doc Wolverton's house, in 1954). After she dried it, she would grease her scalp thoroughly with blue Bergamot hair grease, which came in a short, fat jar with a picture of a beautiful colored lady on it. It's important to grease your scalp real good, my mama would explain, to keep from burning yourself. Of course, her hair would return to its natural kink almost as soon as the hot water and shampoo hit it. To me, it was another miracle how hair so "straight" would so quickly become kinky again the second it even approached some water.

My mama had only a few "clients" whose heads she "did" — did, I think, because she enjoyed it, rather than for the few pennies it brought in. They would sit on one of our red plastic kitchen chairs, the kind with the shiny metal legs, and brace themselves for the process. Mama would stroke that red-hot iron — which by this time had been in the gas fire for half an hour or more — slowly but firmly through their hair, from scalp to strand's end. It made a scorching, crinkly sound, the hot iron did, as it burned its way through kink, leaving in its wake straight strands of hair, standing long and tall but drooping over at the ends, their shape like the top of a heavy willow tree. Slowly, steadily, Mama's hands would transform a round mound of Odetta kink* into a darkened swamp of everglades. The Bergamot made the hair shiny; the heat of the hot iron gave it a brownish-red cast. Once all the hair was as straight as God allows kink to get, Mama would take the well-heated curling iron and twirl the straightened strands into more or less loosely wrapped curls. She claimed that she owed her skill as a hairdresser to the strength in her wrists, and as she worked her little finger would poke out, the way it did when she sipped tea. Mama was a southpaw, and wrote upside down and backward to produce the cleanest, roundest letters you've ever seen.

The "kitchen" she would all but remove from sight with a hand-held pair of shears, bought just for this purpose. Now, the kitchen was the room in which we were sitting — the room where Mama did hair and washed clothes, and where we all took a bath in that galvanized tub. But the word has another meaning, and the kitchen that I'm speaking of is the very kinky bit of hair at the back of your head, where your neck meets your shirt collar. If there was ever a part of our African past that resisted assimilation, it was the kitchen. No matter how hot the iron, no matter how powerful the chemical, no matter how stringent the mashed-potatoes-and-lye formula of a man's "process," neither God nor woman nor Sammy Davis, Jr., could straighten the kitchen. The kitchen was permanent, irredeemable, irresistible kink. Unassimilably African. No matter what you did, no matter how hard you tried, you couldn't de-kink a person's kitchen. So you trimmed it off as best you could.

When hair had begun to "turn," as they'd say — to return to its natural kinky glory — it was the kitchen that turned first (the kitchen around the back, and nappy edges at the temples). When the kitchen started creeping up the back of the neck, it was time to get your hair done again.

*   *   *

*__Odetta kink:__ Odetta Holmes Felious Gorden, the African American folk singer of the 1960s, helped popularize the "afro" hair style. — Ed.

Sometimes, after dark, a man would come to have his hair done. It was Mr. Charlie Carroll. He was very light-complected and had a ruddy nose — it made me think of Edmund Gwenn, who played Kris Kringle in *Miracle on 34th Street*. At first, Mama did him after my brother, Rocky, and I had gone to sleep. It was only later that we found out that he had come to our house so Mama could iron his hair — not with a hot comb or a curling iron but with our very own Proctor-Silex steam iron. For some reason I never understood, Mr. Charlie would conceal his Frederick Douglass–like mane* under a big white Stetson hat. I never saw him take it off except when he came to our house, at night, to have his hair pressed. (Later, Daddy would tell us about Mr. Charlie's most prized piece of knowledge, something that the man would only confide after his hair had been pressed, as a token of intimacy. "Not many people know this," he'd say, in a tone of circumspection, "but George Washington was Abraham Lincoln's daddy." Nodding solemnly, he'd add the clincher: "A white man told me." Though he was in dead earnest, this became a humorous refrain around our house — "a white man told me" — which we used to punctuate especially preposterous assertions.)

My mother examined my daughters' kitchens whenever we went home to visit, in the early eighties. It became a game between us. I had told her not to do it, because I didn't like the politics it suggested — the notion of "good" and "bad" hair. "Good" hair was "straight," "bad" hair kinky. Even in the late sixties, at the height of Black Power, almost nobody could bring themselves to say "bad" for good and "good" for bad. People still said that hair like white people's hair was "good," even if they encapsulated it in a disclaimer, like "what we used to call 'good.'"

Maggie would be seated in her highchair, throwing food this way and that, and Mama would be cooing about how cute it all was, how I used to do just like Maggie was doing, and wondering whether her flinging her food with her left hand meant that she was going to be left-handed like Mama. When my daughter was just about covered with Chef Boyardee Spaghetti-O's, Mama would

---

*__Frederick Douglass–like mane:__ Photographs of Frederick Douglass (1817?–1895), the escaped slave who became a prominent African American writer and abolitionist, show that he had an impressive head of hair. — Ed.

seize the opportunity: wiping her clean, she would tilt Maggie's head to one side and reach down the back of her neck. Sometimes Mama would even rub a curl between her fingers, just to make sure that her bifocals had not deceived her. Then she'd sigh with satisfaction and relief: no kink . . . yet. Mama! I'd shout, pretending to be angry. Every once in a while, if no one was looking, I'd peek, too.

I say "yet" because most black babies are born with soft, silken hair. But after a few months it begins to turn, as inevitably as do the seasons or the leaves on a tree. People once thought baby oil would stop it. They were wrong.

Everybody I knew as a child wanted to have good hair. You could be as ugly as homemade sin dipped in misery and still be thought attractive if you had good hair. "Jesus moss," the girls at Camp Lee, Virginia, had called Daddy's naturally "good" hair during the war. I know that he played that thick head of hair for all it was worth, too.

My own hair was "not a bad grade," as barbers would tell me when they cut it for the first time. It was like a doctor reporting the results of the first full physical he has given you. Like "You're in good shape" or "Blood pressure's kind of high — better cut down on salt."

I spent most of my childhood and adolescence messing with my hair. I definitely wanted straight hair. Like Pop's. When I was about three, I tried to stick a wad of Bazooka bubble gum to that straight hair of his. I suppose what fixed that memory for me is the spanking I got for doing so: he turned me upside down, holding me by my feet, the better to paddle my behind. Little *nigger*, he had shouted, walloping away. I started to laugh about it two days later, when my behind stopped hurting.

When black people say "straight," of course, they don't usually mean literally straight — they're not describing hair like, say, Peggy Lipton's (she was the white girl on *The Mod Squad*), or like Mary's of Peter, Paul & Mary fame; black people call that "stringy" hair. No, "straight" just means not kinky, no matter what contours the curl may take. I would have done *anything* to have straight hair — and I used to try everything, short of getting a process.

Of the wide variety of techniques and methods I came to master in the challenging prestidigitation of the follicle, almost all had two things in common: a heavy grease and the application of pressure. It's not an accident that some of the biggest black-owned companies in the fifties and sixties made hair products. And I tried them all, in search of that certain silken touch, the one that would leave neither the hand nor the pillow sullied by grease.

I always wondered what Frederick Douglass put on *his* hair, or what Phillis Wheatley* put on hers. Or why Wheatley has that rag on her head in the little engraving in the frontispiece of her book. One thing is for sure: you can bet that when Phillis Wheatley went to England and saw the Countess of Huntingdon, she did not stop by the Queen's coiffeur on her way there. So many black people still get their hair straightened that it's a wonder we don't have a national holiday for Madame C. J. Walker, the woman who invented the process of straightening kinky hair. Call it Jheri-Kurled or call it "relaxed," it's still fried hair.

I used all the greases, from sea-blue Bergamot and creamy vanilla Duke (in its clear jar with the orange, white, and green label) to the godfather of grease, the formidable Murray's. Now, Murray's was some *serious* grease. Whereas Bergamot was like oily jello and Duke was viscous and sickly sweet, Murray's was light brown and *hard*. Hard as lard and twice as greasy, Daddy used to say. Murray's came in an orange can with a press-on top. It was so hard that some people would put a match to the can, just to soften the stuff and make it more manageable. Then, in the late sixties, when Afros came into style, I used Afro Sheen. From Murray's to Duke to Afro Sheen: that was my progression in black consciousness.

We used to put hot towels or washrags over our Murray-coated heads, in order to melt the wax into the scalp and the follicles. Unfortunately, the wax also had the habit of running down your neck, ears, and forehead. Not to mention your pillowcase. Another problem was that if you put two palmfuls of Murray's on your head your hair turned white. (Duke did the same thing.) The challenge was to get rid of that white color. Because if you got rid of the white stuff you had a magnificent head of wavy hair. That was the beauty of it: Murray's was so hard that it froze your hair into the wavy style

*__Phillis Wheatley:__ An African-born slave in a prosperous Boston family, Phillis Wheatley (1753?–1784) became America's first major black poet. — Ed.

you brushed it into. It looked really good if you wore a part. A lot of guys had parts *cut* into their hair by a barber, either with the clippers or with a straightedge razor. Especially if you had kinky hair — then you'd generally wear a short razor cut, or what we called a Quo Vadis.

We tried to be as innovative as possible. Everyone knew about using a stocking cap, because your father or your uncle wore one whenever something really big was about to happen, whether sacred or secular: a funeral or a dance, a wedding or a trip in which you confronted official white people. Any time you were trying to look really sharp, you wore a stocking cap in preparation. And if the event was really a big one, you made a new cap. You asked your mother for a pair of her hose, and cut it with scissors about six inches or so from the open end — the end with the elastic that goes up to the top of the thigh. Then you knotted the cut end, and it became a beehive-shaped hat, with an elastic band that you pulled down low on your forehead and down around your neck in the back. To work well, the cap had to fit tightly and snugly, like a press. And it had to fit that tightly because it *was* a press: it pressed your hair with the force of the hose's elastic. If you greased your hair down real good, and left the stocking cap on long enough, voilà: you got a head of pressed-against-the-scalp waves. (You also got a ring around your forehead when you woke up, but it went away.) And then you could enjoy your concrete do. Swore we were bad, too, with all that grease and those flat heads. My brother and I would brush it out a bit in the mornings, so that it looked — well, "natural." Grown men still wear stocking caps — especially older men, who generally keep their stocking caps in their top drawers, along with their cufflinks and their see-through silk socks, their *Maverick* ties, their silk handkerchiefs, and whatever else they prize the most.

A Murrayed-down stocking cap was the respectable version of the process, which, by contrast, was most definitely not a cool thing to have unless you were an entertainer by trade. Zeke and Keith and Poochie and a few other stars of the high school basketball team all used to get a process once or twice a year. It was expensive, and you had to go somewhere like Pittsburgh or D.C. or Uniontown — somewhere where there were enough colored people to support a trade. The guys would disappear, then reappear a day or two later, strutting like peacocks, their hair burned slightly red from the lye base. They'd also wear "rags"— cloths or handkerchiefs — around their heads when they slept or played basketball. Do-rags, they were called. But the result was straight hair, with just a hint of wave. No curl. Do-it-yourselfers took their chances at home with a concoction of mashed potatoes and lye.

The most famous process of all, however, outside of the process Malcolm X describes in his *Autobiography*, and maybe the process of Sammy Davis, Jr., was Nat King Cole's process. Nat King Cole had patent-leather hair. That man's got the finest process money can buy, or so Daddy said the night we saw Cole's TV show on NBC. It was November 5, 1956. I remember the date because everyone came to our house to watch it and to celebrate one of Daddy's buddies' birthdays. Yeah, Uncle Joe chimed in, they can do shit to his hair that the average Negro can't even *think* about — secret shit.

Nat King Cole was *clean*. I've had an ongoing argument with a Nigerian friend about Nat King Cole for twenty years now. Not about whether he could sing — any fool knows that he could — but about whether or not he was a handkerchief head for wearing that patent-leather process.

Sammy Davis, Jr.'s process was the one I detested. It didn't look good on him. Worse still, he liked to have a fried strand dangling down the middle of his forehead, so he could shake it out from the crown when he sang. But Nat King Cole's hair was a thing unto itself, a beautifully sculpted work of art that he and he alone had the right to wear. The only difference between a process and a stocking cap, really, was taste; but Nat King Cole, unlike, say, Michael Jackson, looked *good* in his. His head looked like Valentino's head in the twenties, and some say it was Valentino the process was imitating. But Nat King Cole wore a process because it suited his face, his demeanor, his name, his style. He was as clean as he wanted to be.

I had forgotten all about that patent-leather look until one day in 1971, when I was sitting in an Arab restaurant on the island of Zanzibar surrounded by men in fezzes and white caftans, trying to learn how to eat curried goat and rice with the fingers of my right hand and feeling two million miles from home. All of a sudden, an old transistor radio sitting on top of a china cupboard stopped blaring out its Swahili music and started playing "Fly Me to the Moon," by Nat King Cole. The restaurant's din was not affected at all, but in my mind's eye I saw it: the King's magnificent sleek black tiara. I managed, barely, to blink back the tears.

Reflections and Responses

1. Of what importance is the kitchen to the family's identity? Of what importance is it to African American identity? What does "kitchen" have to do with assimilation?

2. Evaluate Gates's position on processed hair. What are the politics of "good" and "bad" hair? Which kind does Gates most identify himself with? What makes his response difficult to pin down?

3. Read Gates's last paragraph again carefully. What does its setting suggest? What is the concluding paragraph's relation to the essay as a whole? What is Gates's emotional state — and why do you think he feels the way he does about Nat King Cole?

LUCY GREALY

Mirrorings

Survival has become one of the dominant themes of our times. Today's es-
sayists seem to be especially candid about personal pain and more willing to
disclose the details of illnesses and injuries than were essayists in the past.
This literary phenomenon may be stimulated by the public's vast interest in
authentic medical case histories, an interest more popularly manifested in
the growing number of online support groups and numerous television and
film portrayals based on actual cases. One of the finest recent books in this
memoir genre is Lucy Grealy's Autobiography of a Face, *which is re-*
markable not only for its intense level of self-examination but for its elegant
and engaging prose.

    An award-winning poet who lived in New York City, Lucy Grealy (pro-
nounced GRAY-lee) attended the Iowa Writer's Workshop and received fellow-
ships at the Bunting Institute of Radcliffe and the Fine Arts Work Center in
Provincetown. Published in 1994, Autobiography of a Face *was based on*
the essay "Mirrorings," which originally appeared in Harper's *magazine*
and which also won the National Magazine Award. Lucy Grealy, also the
author of As Seen on TV *(2000), died in December 2002. "Mirrorings"*
was selected by Tracy Kidder for The Best American Essays *1994.*

There was a long period of time, almost a year, during which I
never looked in a mirror. It wasn't easy, for I'd never suspected just
how omnipresent are our own images. I began by merely avoiding
mirrors, but by the end of the year I found myself with an acute
knowledge of the reflected image, its numerous tricks and wiles,
how it can spring up at any moment: a glass tabletop, a well-polished
door handle, a darkened window, a pair of sunglasses, a restaurant's otherwise magnificent brass-plated coffee machine sitting
innocently by the cash register.

At the time, I had just moved, alone, to Scotland and was surviving on the dole, as Britain's social security benefits are called. I didn't know anyone and had no idea how I was going to live, yet I went anyway because by happenstance I'd met a plastic surgeon there who said he could help me. I had been living in London, working temp jobs. While in London, I'd received more nasty comments about my face than I had in the previous three years, living in Iowa, New York, and Germany. These comments, all from men and all odiously sexual, hurt and disoriented me. I also had journeyed to Scotland because after more than a dozen operations in the States my insurance had run out, along with my hope that further operations could make any *real* difference. Here, however, was a surgeon who had some new techniques, and here, amazingly enough, was a government willing to foot the bill: I didn't feel I could pass up yet another chance to "fix" my face, which I confusedly thought concurrent with "fixing" my self, my soul, my life.

Twenty years ago, when I was nine and living in America, I came home from school one day with a toothache. Several weeks and misdiagnoses later, surgeons removed most of the right side of my jaw in an attempt to prevent the cancer they found there from spreading. No one properly explained the operation to me, and I awoke in a cocoon of pain that prevented me from moving or speaking. Tubes ran in and out of my body, and because I was temporarily unable to speak after the surgery and could not ask questions, I made up my own explanations for the tubes' existence. I remember the mysterious manner the adults displayed toward me. They asked me to do things: lie still for x-rays, not cry for needles, and so on, tasks that, although not easy, never seemed equal to the praise I received in return. Reinforced to me again and again was how I was "a brave girl" for not crying, "a good girl" for not complaining, and soon I began defining myself this way, equating strength with silence.

Then the chemotherapy began. In the seventies chemo was even cruder than it is now, the basic premise being to poison patients right up to the very brink of their own death. Until this point I almost never cried and almost always received praise in return. Thus I got what I considered the better part of the deal. But now it was like a practical joke that had gotten out of hand. Chemotherapy was a nightmare and I wanted it to stop; I didn't want to be brave anymore. Yet I had grown so used to defining myself as "brave" — i.e., *silent* — that the thought of losing this sense of myself was even more terrifying. I was certain that if I broke down I would be despicable in the eyes of both my parents and the doctors.

The task of taking me into the city for the chemo injections fell mostly on my mother, though sometimes my father made the trip. Overwhelmed by the sight of the vomiting and weeping, my father developed the routine of "going to get the car," meaning that he left the doctor's office before the injection was administered, on the premise that then he could have the car ready and waiting when it was all over. Ashamed of my suffering, I felt relief when he was finally out of the room. When my mother took me, she stayed in the room, yet this only made the distance between us even more tangible. She explained that it was wrong to cry *before* the needle went in; afterward was one thing, but before, that was mere fear, and hadn't I demonstrated my bravery earlier? Every Friday for two and a half years I climbed up onto that big doctor's table and told myself not to cry, and every week I failed. The two large syringes were filled with chemicals so caustic to the vein that each had to be administered very slowly. The whole process took about four minutes; I had to remain utterly still. Dry retching began in the first fifteen seconds, then the throb behind my eyes gave everything a yellow-green aura, and the bone-deep pain of alternating extreme hot and cold flashes made me tremble, yet still I had to sit motionless and not move my arm. No one spoke to me — not the doctor, who was a paradigm of the cold-fish physician; not the nurse, who told my mother I reacted much more violently than many of "the other children"; and not my mother, who, surely overwhelmed by the sight of her child's suffering, thought the best thing to do was remind me to be brave, to try not to cry. All the while I hated myself for having wept before the needle went in, convinced that the nurse and my mother were right, that I was "overdoing it," that the throwing up was psychosomatic, that my mother was angry with me for not being good or brave enough.

Yet each week, two or three days after the injection, there came the first flicker of feeling better, the always forgotten and gratefully rediscovered understanding that to simply be well in my body was the greatest thing I could ask for. I thought other people felt this appreciation and physical joy all the time, and I felt cheated because I was able to feel it only once a week.

Because I'd lost my hair, I wore a hat constantly, but this fooled no one, least of all myself. During this time, my mother worked in a nursing home in a Hasidic community. Hasidic law dictates that married women cover their hair, and most commonly this is done with a wig. My mother's friends were now all willing to donate their discarded wigs, and soon the house seemed filled with them. I never wore one, for they frightened me even when my mother insisted I looked better in one of the few that actually fit. Yet we didn't know how to say no to the women who kept graciously offering their wigs. The cats enjoyed sleeping on them and the dogs playing with them, and we grew used to having to pick a wig up off a chair we wanted to sit in. It never struck us as odd until one day a visitor commented wryly as he cleared a chair for himself, and suddenly a great wave of shame overcame me. I had nightmares about wigs and flushed if I even heard the word, and one night I put myself out of my misery by getting up after everyone was asleep and gathering all the wigs except for one the dogs were fond of and that they had chewed up anyway. I hid all the rest in an old chest.

When you are only ten, which is when the chemotherapy began, two and a half years seem like your whole life, yet it finally did end, for the cancer was gone. I remember the last day of treatment clearly because it was the only day on which I succeeded in not crying, and because later, in private, I cried harder than I had in years; I thought now I would no longer be "special," that without the arena of chemotherapy in which to prove myself no one would ever love me, that I would fade unnoticed into the background. But this idea about *not being different* didn't last very long. Before, I foolishly believed that people stared at me because I was bald. After my hair eventually grew in, it didn't take long before I understood that I looked different for another reason. My face. People stared at me in stores, and other children made fun of me to the point that I came to expect such reactions constantly, wherever I went. School became a battleground.

Halloween, that night of frights, became my favorite holiday because I could put on a mask and walk among the blessed for a few brief, sweet hours. Such freedom I felt, walking down the street, my face hidden! Through the imperfect oval holes I could peer out at other faces, masked or painted or not, and see on those faces nothing but the normal faces of childhood looking back at me, faces I mistakenly thought were the faces everyone else but me saw all the time, faces that were simply curious and ready for fun, not the faces I usually braced myself for, the cruel, lonely, vicious ones I spent every day other than Halloween waiting to see around each corner. As I breathed in the condensed, plastic-scented air under the mask, I somehow thought that I was breathing in normality, that this joy and weightlessness were what the world was composed of, and that it was only my face that kept me from it, my face that was my own mask that kept me from knowing the joy I was sure everyone but me lived with intimately. How could the other children not know it? Not know that to be free of the fear of taunts and the burden of knowing no one would ever love you was all that anyone could ever ask for? I was a pauper walking for a short while in the clothes of the prince, and when the day ended I gave up my disguise with dismay.

I was living in an extreme situation, and because I did not particularly care for the world I was in, I lived in others, and because the world I did live in was dangerous now, I incorporated this danger into my secret life. I imagined myself to be an Indian. Walking down the streets, I stepped through the forest, my body ready for any opportunity to fight or flee one of the big cats that I knew stalked me. Vietnam and Cambodia, in the news then as scenes of catastrophic horror, were other places I walked through daily. I made my way down the school hall, knowing a land mine or a sniper might give themselves away at any moment with the subtle metal click I'd read about. Compared with a land mine, a mere insult about my face seemed a frivolous thing.

In those years, not yet a teenager, I secretly read — knowing it was somehow inappropriate — works by Primo Levi and Elie Wiesel, and every book by a survivor I could find by myself without asking the librarian. Auschwitz, Birkenau: I felt the blows of the capos and somehow knew that because any moment we might be called upon to live for a week on one loaf of bread and some water called soup, the peanut-butter sandwich I found on my plate was nothing less than a miracle, an utter and sheer miracle capable of making me literally weep with joy.

I decided to become a "deep" person. I wasn't exactly sure what this would entail, but I believed that if I could just find the right philosophy, think the right thoughts, my suffering would end. To try to understand the world I was in, I undertook to find out what was "real," and I quickly began seeing reality as existing in the lowest common denominator, that suffering was the one and only dependable thing. But rather than spend all of my time despairing, though certainly I did plenty of that, I developed a form of defensive egomania: I felt I was the only one walking about in the world who understood what was really important. I looked upon people complaining about the most mundane things — nothing on TV, traffic jams, the price of new clothes — and felt joy because I knew how unimportant those things really were and felt unenlightened superiority because other people didn't. Because in my fantasy life I had learned to be thankful for each cold, blanketless night that I survived on the cramped wooden bunks, my pain and despair were a stroll through the country in comparison. I was often miserable, but I knew that to feel warm instead of cold was its own kind of joy, that to eat was a reenactment of the grace of some god whom I could only dimly define, and that to simply be alive was a rare, ephemeral gift.

As I became a teenager, my isolation began. My nonidentical twin sister started going out with boys, and I started — my most tragic mistake of all — to listen to and believe the taunts thrown at me daily by the very boys she and the other girls were interested in. I was a dog, a monster, the ugliest girl they had ever seen. Of all the remarks, the most damaging wasn't even directed at me but was really an insult to "Jerry," a boy I never saw because every day between fourth and fifth periods, when I was cornered by a particular group of kids, I was too ashamed to lift my eyes off the floor. "Hey, look, it's Jerry's girlfriend!" they shrieked when they saw me, and I felt such shame, knowing that this was the deepest insult to Jerry that they could imagine.

When pressed to it, one makes compensations. I came to love winter, when I could wrap up the disfigured lower half of my face in a scarf: I could speak to people and they would have no idea to whom and to what they were really speaking. I developed the bad habit of letting my long hair hang in my face and of always covering my chin and mouth with my hand, hoping it might be mistaken as a thoughtful, accidental gesture. I also became interested in horses and got a job at a rundown local stable. Having those horses to go to each day after school saved my life; I spent all of my time either with them or thinking about them. Completely and utterly repressed by the time I was sixteen, I was convinced that I would never want a boyfriend, not ever, and wasn't it convenient for me, even a blessing, that none would ever want me. I told myself I was free to concentrate on the "true reality" of life, whatever that was. My sister and her friends put on blue eye shadow, blow-dried their hair, and spent interminable hours in the local mall, and I looked down on them for this, knew they were misleading themselves and being overly occupied with the "mere surface" of living. I'd had thoughts like this when I was younger, ten or twelve, but now my philosophy was haunted by desires so frightening I was unable even to admit they existed.

Throughout all of this, I was undergoing reconstructive surgery in an attempt to rebuild my jaw. It started when I was fifteen, two years after chemo ended. I had known for years I would have operations to fix my face, and at night I fantasized about how good my life would finally be then. One day I got a clue that maybe it wouldn't be so easy. An older plastic surgeon explained the process of "pedestals" to me, and told me it would take *ten years* to fix my face. Ten years? Why even bother, I thought; I'll be ancient by then. I went to a medical library and looked up the "pedestals" he talked about. There were gruesome pictures of people with grotesque tubes of their own skin growing out of their bodies, tubes of skin that were harvested like some kind of crop and then rearranged, with results that did not look at all normal or acceptable to my eye. But then I met a younger surgeon, who was working on a new way of grafting that did not involve pedestals, and I became more hopeful and once again began to await the fixing of my face, the day when I would be whole, content, loved.

Long-term plastic surgery is not like in the movies. There is no one single operation that will change everything, and there is certainly no slow unwrapping of the gauze in order to view the final, remarkable result. There is always swelling, sometimes to a grotesque degree, there are often bruises, and always there are scars. After each operation, too frightened to simply go look in the mirror, I developed an oblique method, with several stages. First, I tried to catch my reflection in an overhead lamp: the roundness of the metal distorted my image just enough to obscure details and give no true sense of size or proportion. Then I slowly worked my way up to looking at the reflection in someone's eyeglasses, and from there I went to walking as briskly as possible by a mirror, glancing only quickly. I repeated this as many times as it would take me, passing the mirror slightly more slowly each time until finally I was able to stand still and confront myself.

The theory behind most reconstructive surgery is to take large chunks of muscle, skin, and bone and slap them into the roughly appropriate place, then slowly begin to carve this mess into some sort of shape. It involves long, major operations, countless lesser ones, a lot of pain, and many, many years. And also, it does not always work. With my young surgeon in New York, who with each passing year was becoming not so young, I had two or three soft-tissue grafts, two skin grafts, a bone graft, and some dozen other operations to "revise" my face, yet when I left graduate school at the age of twenty-five I was still more or less in the same position I had started in: a deep hole in the right side of my face and a rapidly shrinking left side and chin, a result of the radiation I'd had as a child and the stress placed upon the bone by the other operations. I was caught in a cycle of having a big operation, one that would force me to look monstrous from the swelling for many months, then having the subsequent revision operations that improved my looks tremendously, and then slowly, over the period of a few months or a year, watching the graft reabsorb back into my body, slowly shrinking down and leaving me with nothing but the scarred donor site the graft had originally come from.

It wasn't until I was in college that I finally allowed that maybe, just maybe, it might be nice to have a boyfriend. I went to a small, liberal, predominantly female school and suddenly, after years of alienation in high school, discovered that there were other people I could enjoy talking to who thought me intelligent and talented. I was, however, still operating on the assumption that no one, not ever, would be physically attracted to me, and in a curious way this shaped my personality. I became forthright and honest in the way that only the truly self-confident are, who do not expect to be rejected, and in the way of those like me, who do not even dare to ask acceptance from others and therefore expect no rejection. I had come to know myself as a person, but I would be in graduate school before I was literally, physically able to use my name and the word "woman" in the same sentence.

Now my friends repeated for me endlessly that most of it was in my mind, that, granted, I did not look like everyone else, but that didn't mean I looked bad. I am sure now that they were right some of the time. But with the constant surgery I was in a perpetual state of transfiguration. I rarely looked the same for more than six months at a time. So ashamed of my face, I was unable even to admit that this constant change affected me; I let everyone who wanted to know that it was only what was inside that mattered, that I had "grown used to" the surgery, that none of it bothered me at all. Just as I had done in childhood, I pretended nothing was wrong, and this was constantly mistaken by others for bravery. I spent a great deal of time looking in the mirror in private, positioning my head to show off my eyes and nose, which were not only normal but quite pretty, as my friends told me often. But I could not bring myself to see them for more than a moment: I looked in the mirror and saw not the normal upper half of my face but only the disfigured lower half.

People still teased me. Not daily, as when I was younger, but in ways that caused me more pain than ever before. Children stared at me, and I learned to cross the street to avoid them; this bothered me, but not as much as the insults I got from men. Their taunts came at me not because I was disfigured but because I was a disfigured *woman*. They came from boys, sometimes men, and almost always from a group of them. I had long, blond hair, and I also had a thin figure. Sometimes, from a distance, men would see a thin blonde and whistle, something I dreaded more than anything else because I knew that as they got closer, their tune, so to speak, would inevitably change; they would stare openly or, worse, turn away quickly in shame or repulsion. I decided to cut my hair to avoid any misconception that anyone, however briefly, might have about my being attractive. Only two or three times have I ever been teased by a single person, and I can think of only one time when I was ever teased by a woman. Had I been a man, would I have had to walk down the street while a group of young women followed and denigrated my sexual worth?

Not surprisingly, then, I viewed sex as my salvation. I was sure that if only I could get someone to sleep with me, it would mean I wasn't ugly, that I was attractive, even lovable. This line of reasoning led me into the beds of several manipulative men who liked themselves even less than they liked me, and I in turn left each short-term affair hating myself, obscenely sure that if only I had been prettier it would have worked — he would have loved me and it would have been like those other love affairs that I was certain "normal" women had all the time. Gradually, I became unable to say "I'm depressed" but could say only "I'm ugly," because the two had become inextricably linked in my mind. Into that universal lie, that sad equation of "if only . . ." that we are all prey to, I was sure that if only I had a normal face, then I would be happy.

The new surgeon in Scotland, Oliver Fenton, recommended that I undergo a procedure involving something called a tissue expander, followed by a bone graft. A tissue expander is a small balloon placed under the skin and then slowly blown up over the course of several months, the object being to stretch out the skin and create room and cover for the new bone. It's a bizarre, nightmarish thing to do to your face, yet I was hopeful about the end results and I was also able to spend the three months that the expansion took in the hospital. I've always felt safe in hospitals: they're the one place I feel free from the need to explain the way I look. For this reason the first tissue expander was bearable — just — and the bone graft that followed it was a success; it did not melt away like the previous ones.

The surgical stress this put upon what remained of my original jaw instigated the deterioration of that bone, however, and it became unhappily apparent that I was going to need the same operation I'd just had on the right side done to the left. I remember my surgeon telling me this at an outpatient clinic. I planned to be traveling down to London that same night on an overnight train, and I barely made it to the station on time, such a fumbling state of despair I was in.

I could not imagine going through it *again,* and just as I had done all my life, I searched and searched through my intellect for a way to make it okay, make it bearable, for a way to *do* it. I lay awake all night on that train, feeling the tracks slip beneath me with an odd eroticism, when I remembered an afternoon from my three months in the hospital. Boredom was a big problem those long afternoons, the days marked by meals and television programs. Waiting for the afternoon tea to come, wondering desperately how I could make time pass, it had suddenly occurred to me that I didn't have to make time pass, that it would do it of its own accord, that I simply had to relax and take no action. Lying on the train, remembering that, I realized I had no obligation to improve my situation, that I didn't have to explain or understand it, that I could just simply let it happen. By the time the train pulled into King's Cross station, I felt able to bear it yet again, not entirely sure what other choice I had.

But there was an element I didn't yet know about. When I returned to Scotland to set up a date to have the tissue expander inserted, I was told quite casually that I'd be in the hospital only three or four days. Wasn't I going to spend the whole expansion time in the hospital? I asked in a whisper. What's the point of that? came the answer. You can just come in every day to the outpatient ward to have it expanded. Horrified by this, I was speechless. I would have to live and move about in the outside world with a giant balloon inside the tissue of my face? I can't remember what I did for the next few days before I went into the hospital, but I vaguely recall that these days involved a great deal of drinking alone in bars and at home.

I had the operation and went home at the end of the week. The only things that gave me any comfort during the months I lived with my tissue expander were my writing and Franz Kafka. I started a novel and completely absorbed myself in it, writing for hours each day. The only way I could walk down the street, could stand the stares I received, was to think to myself, "I'll bet none of them are writing a novel." It was that strange, old, familiar form of egomania, directly related to my dismissive, conceited thoughts of adolescence. As for Kafka, who had always been one of my favorite writers, he helped me in that I felt permission to feel alienated, and to have that alienation be okay, bearable, noble even. In the same way that imagining I lived in Cambodia helped me as a child, I walked the streets of my dark little Scottish city by the sea and knew without doubt that I was living in a story Kafka would have been proud to write.

The one good thing about a tissue expander is that you look so bad with it in that no matter what you look like once it's finally removed, your face has to look better. I had my bone graft and my fifth soft-tissue graft and, yes, even I had to admit I looked better. But I didn't look like me. Something was wrong: was *this* the face I had waited through eighteen years and almost thirty operations for? I somehow just couldn't make what I saw in the mirror correspond to the person I thought I was. It wasn't only that I continued to feel ugly; I simply could not conceive of the image as belonging to me. My own image was the image of a stranger, and rather than try to understand this, I simply stopped looking in the mirror. I perfected the technique of brushing my teeth without a mirror, grew my hair in such a way that it would require only a quick, simple brush, and wore clothes that were simply and easily put on, no complex layers or lines that might require even the most minor of visual adjustments.

On one level I understood that the image of my face was merely that, an image, a surface that was not directly related to any true, deep definition of the self. But I also knew that it is only through appearances that we experience and make decisions about the everyday world, and I was not always able to gather the strength to prefer the deeper world to the shallower one. I looked for ways to find a bridge that would allow me access to both, rather than riding out the constant swings between peace and anguish. The only direction I had to go in to achieve this was to strive for a state of awareness and self-honesty that sometimes, to this day, occasionally rewards me. I have found, I believe, that our whole lives are dominated, though it is not always so clearly translatable, by the question "How do I look?" Take all the many nouns in our lives — car, house, job, family, love, friends — and substitute the personal pronoun "I." It is not that we are all so self-obsessed; it is that all things eventually relate back to ourselves, and it is our own sense of how we appear to the world by which we chart our lives, how we navigate our personalities, which would otherwise be adrift in the ocean of *other* people's obsessions.

One evening toward the end of my year-long separation from the mirror, I was sitting in a café talking to someone — an attractive man, as it happened — and we were having a lovely, engaging conversation. For some reason I suddenly wondered what I looked like to him. What was he *actually* seeing when he saw me? So many times I've asked this of myself, and always the answer is this: a warm, smart woman, yes, but an unattractive one. I sat there in the café and asked myself this old question, and startlingly, for the first time in my life, I had no answer readily prepared. I had not looked in a mirror for so long that I quite simply had no clue as to what I looked like. I studied the man as he spoke; my entire life I had seen my ugliness reflected back to me. But now, as reluctant as I was to admit it, the only indication in my companion's behavior was positive.

And then, that evening in that café, I experienced a moment of the freedom I'd been practicing for behind my Halloween mask all those years ago. But whereas as a child I expected my liberation to come as a result of gaining something, a new face, it came to me now as the result of shedding something, of shedding my image. I once thought that truth was eternal, that when you understood something it was with you forever. I know now that this isn't so, that most truths are inherently unretainable, that we have to work hard all our lives to remember the most basic things. Society is no help; it tells us again and again that we can most be ourselves by looking like someone else, leaving our own faces behind to turn into ghosts that will inevitably resent and haunt us. It is no mistake that in movies and literature the dead sometimes know they are dead only after they can no longer see themselves in the mirror; and as I sat there feeling the warmth of the cup against my palm, this small observation seemed like a great revelation to me. I wanted to tell the man I was with about it, but he was involved in his own topic and I did not want to interrupt him, so instead I looked with curiosity toward the window behind him, its night-darkened glass reflecting the whole café, to see if I could, now, recognize myself.

Reflections and Responses

1. Note how Grealy opens her essay with a description of mirroring objects. Why do you think she begins in this fashion? Why doesn't she start by telling the reader first about her physical condition?

2. How does Grealy introduce images of disguise into her essay? What sort of disguises does she invent? In what ways do Grealy's

discoveries about self-deception and self-honesty apply to all readers, not just those with similar afflictions? How does Grealy extend
those discoveries to others?

3. Consider carefully Grealy's final paragraph. What "small observation" does she make? Why does it seem like a "great revelation"?
Try putting her observation into your own words.

YUSEF KOMUNYAKAA

The Blue Machinery of Summer

The central purpose behind an autobiographical essay can sometimes remain obscure, never explicitly stated by the writer, who may be more interested in self-exploration than full disclosure, more concerned with raising questions than with answering them. Essayists are under no obligation to write only about personal experiences they fully understand. In "The Blue Machinery of Summer," an essay full of questions and "maybes," one of America's foremost poets describes his successes and failures years ago at a summer factory job that forced him to realize the difficulties his education would bring.

Yusef Komunyakaa, who has received numerous honors and awards, including a 1994 Pulitzer Prize for Neon Vernacular, *the 2001 Ruth Lilly Poetry Prize, and a Bronze Star for service as a journalist in Vietnam, was born in Bogalusa, Louisiana, in 1947. His first book of poetry,* Dedications & Other Darkhorses, *appeared in 1977, and subsequent volumes include* Copacetic *(1984),* I Apologize for the Eyes in My Head *(1986),* Dien Cai Dau *(1988),* Magic City *(1992),* Thieves of Paradise *(1998),* Talking Dirty to the Gods *(2000), and* Pleasure Dome: New & Collected Poems, 1975–1999 *(2001). He has written extensively on jazz and in 1999 was elected a Chancellor of the Academy of American Poets. He lives in New York City and is a professor in the Council of Humanities and Creative Writing Program at Princeton University. "The Blue Machinery of Summer" first appeared in* The Washington Post Magazine *and was selected by Kathleen Norris for* The Best American Essays 2001.

"I feel like I'm part of this damn thing," Frank said. He carried himself like a large man even though he was short. A dead cigarette dangled from his half-grin. "I've worked on this machine for twenty-odd years, and now it's almost me."

It was my first day on a summer job at ITT Cannon in Phoenix in 1979. This factory manufactured parts for electronic systems — units that fit into larger, more complex ones. My job was to operate an air-powered punch press. Depending on each item formed, certain dies or templates were used to cut and shape metal plates into designs the engineers wanted.

"I know all the tricks of the trade, big and small, especially when it comes to these punch presses. It seems like I was born riding this hunk of steel."

Frank had a gift for gab, but when the foreman entered, he grew silent and meditative, bent over the machine, lost in his job. The whole day turned into one big, rambunctious dance of raw metal, hiss of steam, and sparks. Foremen strutted about like banty roosters. Women tucked falling curls back into hair nets, glancing at themselves in anything chrome.

This job reminded me of the one I'd had in 1971 at McGraw Edison, also in Phoenix, a year after I returned from Vietnam. Back then, I had said to myself, this is the right setting for a soap opera. Muscle and sex changed the rhythm of this place. We'd call the show "The Line."

I'd move up and down the line, shooting screws into metal cabinets of coolers and air conditioners — one hour for Montgomery Ward or Sears, and the next two hours for a long line of cabinets stamped McGraw Edison. The designs differed only slightly, but made a difference in the selling price later on. The days seemed endless, and it got to where I could do the job with my eyes closed.

In retrospect, I believe I was hyper from the war. I couldn't lay back; I was driven to do twice the work expected — sometimes taking on both sides of the line, giving other workers a hand. I worked overtime two hours before 7 A.M. and one hour after 4 P.M. I learned everything about coolers and air conditioners, and rectified problem units that didn't pass inspection.

At lunch, rather than sitting among other workers, I chose a secluded spot near the mountain of boxed-up coolers to eat my homemade sandwiches and sip iced tea or lemonade. I always had a paperback book in my back pocket: Richard Wright's *Black Boy,*

Albert Camus' *The Fall,* Frantz Fanon's *The Wretched of the Earth,* or C. W. E. Bigsby's *The Black American Writer.* I wrote notes in the margins with a ballpoint. I was falling in love with language and ideas. All my attention went to reading.

When I left the gaze of Arizona's Superstition Mountain and headed for the Colorado Rockies, I wasn't thinking about higher education. Once I was in college, I vowed never to take another job like this, and yet here I was, eight years later, a first-year graduate student at the University of California at Irvine, and working another factory job in Phoenix, hypnotized by the incessant clang of machinery.

Frank schooled me in the tricks of the trade. He took pride in his job and practiced a work ethic similar to the one that had shaped my life early on even though I had wanted to rebel against it. Frank was from Little Rock: in Phoenix, everyone seemed to be from somewhere else except the indigenous Americans and Mexicans.

"If there's one thing I know, it's this damn machine," Frank said. "Sometimes it wants to act like it has a brain of its own, as if it owns me, but I know better."

"Iron can wear any man out," I said.

"Not this hunk of junk. It was new when I came here."

"But it'll still be here when you're long gone."

"Says who?"

"Says iron against flesh."

"They will scrap this big, ugly bastard when I'm gone."

"They'll bring in a new man."

"Are you the new man, whippersnapper? They better hire two of you to replace one of me."

"Men will be men."

"And boys will be boys."

The hard dance held us in its grip.

I spotted Lily Huong the second day in a corner of the wiring department. The women there moved their hands in practiced synchrony, looping and winding color-coded wires with such graceful dexterity and professionalism. Some chewed gum and blew bubbles, others smiled to themselves as if they were reliving the weekend. And a good number talked about the soap operas, naming off the characters as if they were family members or close friends.

Lily was in her own world. Petite, with long black hair grabbed up, stuffed beneath a net and baseball cap, her body was one fluid motion, as if it knew what it was doing and why.

"Yeah, boys will be boys," Frank said.

"What you mean?"

"You're looking at trouble, my friend."

"Maybe trouble is looking for me. And if it is, I'm not running."

"She is nothing but bona fide trouble."

I wonder if she was thinking of Vietnam while she sat bent over the table, or when she glided across the concrete floor as if she were moving through lush grass. Lily? It made me think of waterlily, lotus — how shoots and blooms were eaten in that faraway land. The lotus grows out of decay, in lagoons dark with sediment and rot.

Mornings arrived with the taste of sweet nighttime still in our mouths, when the factory smelled like the deepest ore, and the syncopation of the great heaving presses fascinated me.

The nylon and leather safety straps fit our hands like fingerless gloves and sometimes seemed as if they'd pull us into the thunderous pneumatic vacuum faster than an eye blink. These beasts pulsed hypnotically; they reminded everyone within earshot of terrifying and sobering accidents. The machinery's dance of smooth heft seemed extraordinary, a masterpiece of give-and-take precision. If a foolhardy novice wrestled with one of these metal contraptions, it would suck up the hapless soul. The trick was to give and pull back with a timing that meant the difference between life and death.

"Always use a safety block, one of these chunks of wood. Don't get careless," Frank said. "Forget the idea you can second-guess this monster. Two months ago we had a guy in here named Leo on that hunk of junk over there, the one that Chico is now riding."

"Yeah, and?"

"I don't believe it. It's crazy. I didn't know Leo was a fool. The machine got stuck, he bent down, looked underneath, and never knew his last breath. That monster flattened his head like a pancake."

One morning, I stood at the checkout counter signing out my tools for the day's work and caught a glimpse of Lily out of the corner of my eye. She stopped. Our eyes locked for a moment, and

then she glided on toward her department. Did she know I had
been in 'Nam? Had there been a look in my eyes that had given
me away?"

"You can't be interested in her," Paula said. She pushed her hair
away from her face in what seemed like an assured gesture.

"Why not?" I said.

"She's nothing, nothing but trouble."

"Oh?"

"Anyway, you ain't nobody's foreman."

I took my toolbox and walked over to the punch press. The
buzzer sounded. The gears kicked in. The day started.

After three weeks, I discovered certain social mechanisms ran
the place. The grapevine, long, tangled, and thorny, was merciless.
After a month on the job I had been wondering why Frank disappeared at lunchtime but always made it back just minutes before
the buzzer.

"I bet Frank tells you why he comes back here with a smile on his
mug?" Maria coaxed. She worked as a spot-welder, with most of
her day spent behind heavy black goggles as the sparks danced
around her.

"No."

"Why don't you ask Paula one of these mornings when you're
signing out tools?"

"I don't think so," I said.

"She's the one who puts that grin on his face. They've been tearing up that rooming house over on Sycamore for years."

"Good for them," I said.

"Not if that cop husband of hers come to his senses."

It would have been cruel irony for Frank to work more than
twenty years on the monster and lose his life at the hands of a
mere mortal.

The grapevine also revealed that Lily had gotten on the payroll
because of Rico, who was a foreman on the swing shift. They had
been lovers and he had put in a good word for her. Rico was built
like a lightweight boxer, his eyes bright and alert, always able to
look over the whole room in a single glance. The next news said
Lily was sleeping with Steve, the shipping foreman, who wore western shirts, a silver and turquoise belt buckle, and cowboy boots.
His red Chevy pickup had a steer's horn on the hood. He was tall
and lanky and had been in the Marines, stationed at Khe Sanh.

I wondered about Lily. What village or city had she come from — Chu Chi or Danang, Saigon or Hue? What was her story? Did she still hear the war during sleepless nights? Maybe she had had an American boyfriend, maybe she was in love with a Vietnamese once, a student, and they had intimate moments besides the Perfume River as boats with green and red lanterns passed at dusk. Or maybe she met him on the edge of a rice paddy, or in some half-lit place in Danang a few doors down from the Blue Dahlia.

She looked like so many who tried to outrun past lovers, history. *"She's nothing but trouble . . ."* Had she become a scapegoat? Had she tried to play a game that wasn't hers to play? Didn't anyone notice her black eye one week, the corner of her lip split the next?

I told myself I would speak to her. I didn't know when, but I would.

The women were bowed over their piecework.

As a boy I'd make bets with myself, and as a man I was still making bets, and sometimes they left me in some strange situations.

"In New Guinea those Fuzzy Wuzzies saved our asses," Frank said. "They're the smartest people I've ever seen. One moment almost in the Stone Age, and the next they're zooming around in our jeeps and firing automatic weapons like nobody's business. They gave the Japanese hell. They were so outrageously brave it still hurts to think about it."

I wanted to tell him about Vietnam, a few of the things I'd witnessed, but I couldn't. I could've told him about the South Vietnamese soldiers who were opposites of Frank's heroes.

I gazed over toward Lily.

Holding up one of the doodads — we were stamping out hundreds hourly — I said to Frank, "Do you know what this is used for?"

"No. Never crossed my mind."

"You don't know? How many do you think you've made?"

"God only knows."

"And you don't know what they're used for?"

"No."

"How much does each sell for?"

"Your guess is as good as mine. I make 'em. I don't sell 'em."

He's right, I thought. Knowing wouldn't change these workers' lives. This great symphony of sweat, oil, steel, rhythm, it all made a strange kind of sense.

"These are used in the firing mechanisms of grenade launch-
ers," I said as I scooped up a handful. "And each costs the government almost eighty-five dollars."

The buzzer sounded.

In the cafeteria, most everybody sat in their usual clusters. A few
of the women read magazines — *True Romance, Tan, TV Guide,
Reader's Digest* — as they nibbled at sandwiches and sipped Cokes.
One woman was reading her Bible. I felt like the odd man out as I
took my paperback from my lunch pail: a Great Books Foundation
volume, with blue-white-black cover and a circle around *GB*. My
coworkers probably thought I was reading the same book all summer long, or that it was a religious text. I read Voltaire, Hegel, and
Darwin.

Voltaire spoke to me about Equality:

> All the poor are not unhappy. The greater number are born in that state,
> and constant labor prevents them from too sensibly feeling their situa-
> tion; but when they do strongly feel it, then follow wars such as these of
> the popular party against the Senate at Rome, and those of the peasantry
> in Germany, England and France. All these wars ended sooner or later in
> the subjection of the people, because the great have money, and money
> in a state commands everything: I say in a state, for the case is different
> between nation and nation. That nation makes the best use of iron will al-
> ways subjugate another that has more gold but less courage.

Maybe I didn't want to deal with those images of 'Nam still in my
psyche, ones that Lily had rekindled.

"You catch on real fast, friend," Frank said. "It is hard to teach a
man how to make love to a machine. It's almost got to be in your
blood. If you don't watch out, you'll be doing twenty in this sweat-
box too. Now mark my word."

I wanted to tell him about school. About some of the ideas filling my head. Lily would smile, but she looked as if she were gazing
through me.

One morning in early August, a foreman said they needed me to
work on a special unit. I was led through the security doors. The
room was huge, and the man working on the big, circular-dome
object seemed small and insignificant in the voluminous space.
Then I was shaking hands with the guy they called Dave the Lathe.

Almost everyone had a nickname here, as in the Deep South, where, it turned out, many of the workers were from. The nicknames came from the almost instinctual impulse to make language a game of insinuation.

Dave was from Paradise, California. He showed me how to polish each part, every fixture and pin. The work led to painstaking tedium. Had I posed too many questions? Was that why I was working this job?

Here everything was done by hand, with patience and silence. The room was air-conditioned. Now the clang of machines and whine of metal being cut retreated into memory. Behind this door Dave the Lathe was a master at shaping metals, alloyed with secrets, a metal that could be smoothed but wouldn't shine, take friction and heat out of this world. In fact, it looked like a fine piece of sculpture designed aeronautically, that approached perfection. Dave the Lathe had been working on this nose cone for a spacecraft for more than five months.

Dave and I seldom talked. Lily's face receded from my thoughts. Now I stood across from Dave the Lathe, thinking about two women in my class back at the University of California with the same first name. One was from New York. She had two reproductions of French nudes over her bed and was in love with Colette, the writer. The other woman was part Okinawan from Honolulu. If we found ourselves in a room alone, she always managed to disengage herself. We had never had a discussion, but here she was, undressing in my mind. At that moment, standing a few feet from Dave the Lathe, I felt that she and I were made for each other but she didn't know it yet.

I told Dave that within two weeks I'd return to graduate school. He wished me luck in a tone that suggested he knew what I'd planned to say before I said it.

"Hey, college boy!" Maria shouted across the cafeteria. "Are you in college or did you do time like Frank says?" I wanted the impossible, to disappear.

Lily's eyes caught mine. I still hadn't told her I felt I'd left part of myself in her country. Maria sat down beside me. I fished out the ham sandwich, but left Darwin in the lunch box. She said, "You gonna just soft-shoe in here and then disappear, right?"

"No. Not really."

"*Not really,* he says," she mocked.

"Well."

"Like a lousy lover who doesn't tell you everything. Doesn't tell the fine print."

"Well."

"Cat got your tongue, college boy?"

"Are you talking to me or somebody else?"

"Yeah, you! Walk into somebody's life and then turn into a ghost. A one-night stand."

"I didn't think anyone needed to know."

"I suppose you're too damn good to tell us the truth."

She stood up, took her lunch over to another table, sat down, and continued to eat. I didn't know what to say. I was still learning.

There's good silence. There's bad silence. Growing up in rural Louisiana, along with four brothers and one sister, I began to cultivate a life of the imagination. I traveled to Mexico, Africa, and the Far East. When I was in elementary school and junior high, sometimes I knew the answers to questions, but I didn't dare raise my hand. Boys and girls danced up and down, waving their arms, with right and wrong answers. It was hard for me to chance being wrong. Also, I found it difficult to share my feelings; but I always broke the silence and stepped in if someone was being mistreated.

Now, as I sat alone, looking out the window of a Greyhound bus at 1 A.M., I felt like an initiate who had gotten cold feet and was hightailing it back to some privileged safety zone. I began to count the figures sprawled on the concrete still warm from the sun's weight on the city. There seemed to be an uneasy equality among destitutes: indigenous Americans, Mexicans, a few blacks and whites. Eleven. Twelve. I thought, a massacre of the spirit.

The sounds of the machines were still inside my head. The clanging punctuated by Frank's voice: "Are you ready to will your body to this damn beast, my friend?"

"No, Frank. I never told you I am going to college," I heard myself saying. Did education mean moving from one class to the next? My grandmothers told me again and again that one could scale a mountain with a good education. But could I still talk to them, to my parents, my siblings? I would try to live in two worlds —

at the very least. That was now my task. I never wanted again to feel that my dreams had betrayed me.

Maybe the reason I hadn't spoken to Lily was I didn't want to talk about the war. I hadn't even acknowledged to my friends that I'd been there.

The bus pulled out, headed for L.A. with its headlights sweeping like slow yellow flares across drunken faces, as if images of the dead had followed Lily and me from a distant land only the heart could bridge.

Reflections and Responses

1. What images does Komunyakaa use early in his essay to link the assembly-line work, the machinery, and sexuality? Why do you think he wants to establish these links?

2. Why do you think Komunyakaa informs us about his reading? What kind of books does he seem to prefer? Why do you think he includes a long quotation from Voltaire in an essay that is almost entirely personal?

3. How does Komunyakaa present himself in this essay? How does he portray the way his fellow workers relate to him? How does he relate to his fellow workers? What role does Lily Huong play in the essay? What sense do you make of his final conversation with Maria toward the end of the essay? What is she saying about him? How do her comments link up with the sexual themes introduced early in the essay?

REBECCA MCCLANAHAN

Book Marks

Anyone who's ever bought a used book (perhaps eventually this one) has found traces of a previous reader who marked up the volume in various ways — through marginal comments, underlining, doodles, and even an occasional personal note. Sometimes the presence of the other reader still lingers in food or beverage stains, handy bookmarks such as a fast-food receipt, or even forgotten letters or photographs that once marked a pause in the reading. In "Book Marks," Rebecca McClanahan contemplates the presence of someone whose life is suggested by marginal notes scribbled in a library book. As she plays detective and tries to imagine the person who previously borrowed the book, she recollects various stages of her own life as it moved in and out of books that became closely associated with relatives, schoolmates, husbands, and lovers. McClanahan weaves these episodes together, revealing how arbitrary the lines can be that we conventionally draw between life and literature.

Rebecca McClanahan lives in New York City and has published four books of poetry (most recently Naked as Eve*) and two books on writing:* Word Painting: A Guide to Writing More Descriptively *(1999) and* Write Your Heart Out *(2001). She has received the Carter Prize for the essay from* Shenandoah, *a Pushcart award in fiction, and the Wood Prize from* Poetry *magazine. A collection of personal essays,* The Riddle Song and Other Mysteries, *appeared in 2002. Her work is included in* The Best American Poetry 1998. *First published in* Southern Review, *"Book Marks" was selected by Kathleen Norris for* The Best American Essays 2001.

I am worried about the woman. I am afraid she might hurt herself, perhaps has already hurt herself — there's no way to know which of the return dates stamped on the book of poetry was hers. The book, Denise Levertov's *Evening Train,* belongs to the New York City Public Library. I checked it out yesterday and can keep it for three weeks. Ever since my husband and I moved to the city several months ago, I've been homesick for my books, the hundreds of volumes stored in my brother's basement. I miss having them near me, running my hands over their spines, recalling when and where I acquired each one, and out of what need.

There's no way to know for certain that the phantom library patron is a woman, but all signs point in that direction. On one page is a red smear that looks like lipstick, and between two other pages, lying like a bookmark, is a long, graying hair. The underlinings, which may or may not have been made by the woman, are in pencil — pale, tentative marks I study carefully, reverently, the way an archaeologist traces a fossil's delicate imprint. The rest is dream, conjecture, the making of *my* story. It's a weird obsession, I know, studying other readers' leavings and guessing the lives lived beneath. Even as my reasonable mind is having its say (*This makes no sense. How can you assume? The marks could have been made by anyone, for any reason, over any period of time . . .*), my other self is leaving on its own journey. I've always been a hungry reader, what one friend calls a "selfish reader." But is there any other kind? Don't we all read to answer our own needs, to complete the lives we've begun, to point us toward some light?

Some of the underlinings in *Evening Train* have been partially erased (eraser crumbles have gathered in the center seams), as if the woman reconsidered her first responses or tried to cover her tracks. The markings do not strike me as those of a defiant woman but rather of one who has not only taken her blows but feels she might deserve them. She has underlined "serviceable heart" in one poem; in another, "Grey-haired, I have not grown wiser." If she exists, I would like to sit down with this woman. We seem to have a lot in common. We chose the same book, we both wear red lipstick, and though I am not so honest (the gray in my hair is hidden beneath an auburn rinse), I am probably her age or thereabouts.

And from what she has left behind on the pages of Levertov's poems, it appears that our hearts have worn down in the same places. This is the part that worries me. Though my heart has mended, for the time being at least, hers seems to be in the very act of breaking. A present-tense pain pulses through each marked-up poem, and the further I read, the clearer it becomes what she is considering. I want to reach through the pages and lead her out.

My interest in marginalia, reading between the lines, began when I was an evening student at a college in California, still living with my parents but working days to help pay my expenses. It was a lonely time. Untethered from the rock-hard rituals of high school, I'd been set adrift, floating between adolescence and Real Life, a place I'd heard about that both terrified and seduced me. As a toddler, I'd been one of those milkily content clingers who must be pulled away from the nipple; eighteen years later I was still reluctant to leave my mother's side.

My siblings had no such trouble. An older sister had married and left home, a brother was away at college, and my younger siblings, in various stages of adolescent rebellion, had struck out on their own. As for my friends, most had left to study at faraway colleges; the few who stayed, taking jobs at the local bank or training to be dental assistants, seemed even more remote than those who had left. Whatever had held us together in high school — intramural sports, glee club, the senior-class play — was light-years away. As was the boy who'd promised to marry me someday. He'd found someone else, and though part of me had always known that's how that book would end (we'd never progressed beyond kissing), nevertheless his leaving was the first hairline crack in my serviceable heart.

My only strike at independence was the paycheck I earned typing invoices at a printing shop. Though I reluctantly accepted my father's offer to pay tuition costs, I insisted on buying my own textbooks. I could afford only used ones, and the more *used* the book, the cheaper it was. Some had passed through several hands; the multiple marked-through names and phone numbers on the flyleaves bore witness to this fact. At first I was put off by the previous owners' underlinings, marginal comments, bright yellow highlighted sections, sophomoric doodlings and obscenities. Worse still were the unintentional markings — coffee stains, dried pizza sauce, cigarette burns.

After a while, however, I became accustomed to the markings. I even began to welcome them. Since I didn't live on campus or have college buddies — I worked all day, then went straight home after class — I appreciated the company the used books offered. I imagined the boy who had splattered pizza sauce across the map of South America. Was he lonely too? Had he eaten the pizza alone, in his tiny dorm room, while memorizing Bolivia's chief exports? What about the girl who had misspelled *orgasm* (using two *s*'s) in the margins of John Donne's "The Canonization"? Had she ever said the word aloud? Was she a virgin like me?

The used texts served practical purposes as well. In the case of difficult subject matter (which, for me, meant political science, chemistry, and botany), it was as though I had engaged a private tutor, someone to sit at my elbow and guide me through each lesson, pointing out important concepts, underlining the principles that would show up on next week's exam. The marked-up textbook was my portable roommate, someone to sit up nights with me, to quiz me with questions I didn't know enough to ask.

Not since I was a child sharing a room with Great-Aunt Bessie, an inveterate reader, had I had a reading partner. Bessie and I would sit up late in our double bed and read mysteries and westerns aloud. We'd take turns, each reading a chapter a night, and at the end, right before Bessie removed her dentures and switched off the light (she was a disciplined reader, always stopping at the end of a chapter), right before she slipped her embroidered handkerchief into the book to mark our place, we would discuss our reactions to what we had read and make predictions about how the story would turn. Because of Aunt Bessie, I never saw books as dead, finished texts. They were living, breathing entities, unexplored territories into which we would venture the next night, and the next. Anything could happen, and we would be present when it did.

Years later, carrying this lesson into my first college class, I was amazed at what I encountered: rows of bleary-eyed students slumped around me, their limp hands spread across Norton anthologies. Most never ventured into the territory Bessie and I had explored. This stymied me, that people could read a poem by Shelley or Keats or Sylvia Plath and not want to live inside it, not want to add their words to the ones on the page. Looking back on my college literature texts, I can trace the journey of those years.

In the margins of Wordsworth's sonnets, beside the lines "The world is too much with us; late and soon, / Getting and spending, we lay waste our powers," I can chart my decision to quit my day job and pursue my studies full-time, even if it meant borrowing from the savings account I'd been feeding each payday. "I am done with this," I wrote in blue ink, meaning the commerce of getting and spending, the laying waste of powers I'd yet to discover.

And in the underlined sections of Gerard Manley Hopkins's poems, I can trace the ecstasy of my first spiritual awakening ("I caught this morning morning's minion"), made all the more ecstatic since, because I was unable to understand his elliptical syntax with my *mind,* I was forced to take it in through the rhythms of my body. This was a new music for me. My heart was no longer metaphorical. It beat rapidly in my chest, my temples, in my pale, veined wrists. Suddenly, within Hopkins's lines, I was breaking in new places: "here / Buckle! And the fire that breaks from thee then, a billion / Times told lovelier, more dangerous."

At the time I encountered those lines, I had no knowledge of the fire that awaited me in the eyes of a young man I'd yet to meet. I saw myself vaguely, like a character in one of the books I fell asleep with each night. In dreams I drank black coffee at street cafés, lay beneath the branches of the campus oaks, or wandered late at night, as Whitman's narrator had wandered, looking up "in perfect silence at the stars." In daylight, I pulled another used book from the shelf and fell into its pages. Could it be that Rilke's injunction, "You must change your life," was aimed at me? I highlighted it in yellow, then wrote in the margin, in bright blue indelible ink, "THIS MEANS *YOU!*"

Had I chosen to resell these books to the campus bookstore (I didn't; they had become part of me), their new owners might one day have read my underlinings, my marginal scribblings, and wondered at the person who left such a trail. "She needs to get more sun," they might have thought, if they could deduce I was a *she.* Maybe they would have worried about me the way I now worry about the gray-haired woman. They might even have responded, as I sometimes do, with an answering note. It might have gone on and on like that, a serial installment of marginalia, each new reader adding his own twist to Hopkins or Wordsworth — or to me, the phantom whose pages they were turning.

When life interrupts, you close the book. Or perhaps you leave it open, facedown on the bed or table, to mark your place. Aunt Bessie taught me never to do this. "You'll break its spine," she said, running her age-spotted hands across the book's cover, and the tenderness in her gesture made me ashamed that I'd ever considered such violence. After that I took to dog-earing pages, but after a while even that seemed too violent. Now, whenever I encounter a dog-eared page, I smooth its wounded edge.

Aunt Bessie used embroidered handkerchiefs to mark her place, though to me they seemed unnecessary since she always stopped at the end of a chapter. Some readers are like that. They regulate their reading, fitting books neatly into their lives the way some people schedule exercise or sex: five poems, twenty laps. One of my friends always stops after twenty-five pages so she can easily remember where she left off. Though I admire such discipline, I've never been able to accomplish it. I fall into books the way I fall into lust — wholly, hungrily. Often the book disappoints, or I disappoint. The first flush cools and the words grow tired and dull, or I grow tired and dull and slam the book shut. Occasionally, though, I keep reading, and lust ripens slowly into love, and I want to stay right there, at the lamplit table or in the soft, worn chair, until the last page is turned.

Then suddenly, always unexpectedly, life interferes; it is what life does best. It usually happens in mid-paragraph, sometimes even mid-sentence — a kind of biblio-interruptus — and I grab something to mark my place. Though I own many beautiful bookmarks, they are never there when I need them. So I reach for whatever is close at hand. A newspaper clipping, the phone bill, my bourbon-fossiled cocktail napkin, a note from a friend, the grocery list. Once I plucked a protruding feather from the sofa cushion where I rested my head, once I used a maple leaf that had blown in through the patio door, once I even pulled a hair from my head.

Looking back on my nineteenth year, I am amazed at how easily I closed the books I'd been living inside. What replaced them were the poems the young man handed me across a restaurant table. "Pretty Brown-Haired Girl" was the title of one; "Monday Rain" another. Some were written in German, and I used my secondhand Cassell's dictionary to translate them. The poems were not good —

I remember thinking this even then — but they were the first love poems anyone had ever written for me. I ran my fingers across the words. I folded the papers, put them into my pocket, and later that night unfolded them on my bedside table. Already the poems were in my head, every ragged line break and rhyme.

At twenty-one he had one of those faces that might have looked old all along. His hair was retreating prematurely, exposing a forehead with furrows already deeply plowed. But his eyes were bright blue, center-of-a-flame blue, simultaneously cool and hot. He wore faded jeans and a rugged woolen jacket and drove a motorcycle; his mouth tasted of cigarettes. Plus he could quote Wordsworth, which weakened me even more. He was independently brilliant, a part-time student with no declared major, taking classes in subjects like German and astronomy and horticulture — nothing that fit together to form anything like a formal degree. "Come into the light of things," he teased. "Let nature be your teacher."

Nature taught me so much over the next year that it was all I could do to attend classes, let alone sit up nights with pencil in hand, scribbling notes in the margins of textbooks. He'd moved into his own apartment, and his marks were all over me — his mouth on my forehead, his tongue on my neck, my belly, the smell of his cigarettes in my hair. All else fell away. When an occasional misgiving surfaced I pushed it down. I had reason to doubt that I was his only brown-haired girl, the only one to whom he wrote poems. But I hushed the voice of reason, even when it spoke directly into my ear.

My parents disapproved of him, and though Aunt Bessie had moved back to her Midwest childhood home, I was certain she would have disapproved too. I *knew* Carolyn did. She'd told me so, in the same loving yet blatantly forthright tone she'd used on me since I was small. Carolyn was my mother's best friend, and had served as a kind of alternate mother for me as long as I could remember. Perhaps *mother* is the wrong word; *mentor* may come closer. She was a librarian who not only loved books but believed in them, even more so than Aunt Bessie. Carolyn believed that books could change our lives, could save us from ourselves.

My mother also loved books, but while she was raising her six children — sometimes single-handedly, when my pilot father was overseas — she put reading aside. I cannot recall, during those

years, ever seeing my mother sit down, except to play a game of
Monopoly or Old Maid, or to sew our Halloween costumes or
Easter dresses. Certainly not to read. Late at night, when my father
was away and she couldn't sleep, perhaps she switched on the light
beside their double bed and opened a book, probably her Bible, a
beautiful burgundy-leather King James my father had given her
early in their marriage and that she kept close at hand. I loved to
feel the cover and the onionskin pages that were tipped in gold
and totally free of marginalia. The only mark I could find was a
handwritten notation on the flyleaf. "Deuteronomy 29:29. The secret things belong unto the Lord our God: but those things which
are revealed belong unto us and to our children for ever."

Over the years Carolyn gave me many books that she felt I
needed to read at particular stages of my life. Some she'd bought
on her travels; some had belonged to her mother; some had been
gifts. She shared my passion for hand-me-downs, and never apolo-
gized for giving me used books. "Words don't go bad," she'd say,
"like cheese. Read everything you can get your hands on. Live inside them." On the subject of my newfound love, she was adamant:
"You're too young to give it all up for a man." Carolyn had married
an older, stable, kind man who adored her yet allowed the space
her inquiring mind demanded. "I'm afraid you're going to lose
yourself," she told me. "Besides," she added, almost as an af-
terthought, "I don't trust him."

"You won't be able to put it down," booksellers claim as they ring
up your purchase. But of course you do, you must. The oven timer
goes off, the children come in from school, your plane lands, the
nurse calls your name, your lover kisses the back of your neck,
your heavy eyes close in sleep. By the time you return to the
book — if you return — you will be changed, will not be the same
person you were ten days, or ten years, before. Life is a river, and
you can't step into the same book twice.

One night after we'd made love, he lit a cigarette and leaned
back onto the pillows. "I'm in trouble," he said. "There's this girl."
Smoke floated around his eyes; he blinked, fanned the air. "*Was*
this girl. It's over, but she's been calling. She says she's pregnant."
Something hot flashed through my head, then was gone. All I
could think was *He will marry her, and I will lose him.*

"There's this place in Mexico City," he continued. "It's nine hundred dollars for everything, to fly her there and back. I have two hundred."

I had seen the word *abortion* in biology textbooks, but I had never uttered it. In 1969, even at the crest of the free-love movement, it was not a legal option. I had fourteen hundred dollars in my savings account, all that was left of nearly two years of typing invoices at the print shop. Each Friday I had taken the little vinyl passbook to the bank window, where the cashier recorded the deposit, half of my paycheck.

"I'll get the rest," I said, surprising even myself.

"I can't ask you to do that."

My next line was from a movie. Something out of the forties. I should have been wearing a hat with a feather. We should have been in a French café: "You're not asking. I'm offering."

"I'll make it up to you," he said.

To this day I can't recall if he repaid me. The passbook shows no record of the money being replaced. Within a year we were married, and what was left of my savings was pooled into a joint account. There was little money and much to buy — a dinette table, a TV stand, a couch. One night he suddenly sat straight up on that couch. "I'll bet she was lying all along," he said, as though continuing a conversation started just seconds before. "Maybe she just wanted a trip to Mexico. She probably spent the whole time on the beach." I wanted to believe him. I hoped the girl *had* spent the weekend on the sand. I hoped she'd gotten a tan. But I knew she hadn't lied. I knew because of what had been set into motion since I'd handed over the money. The shadow over our marriage had first approached in the bank's parking lot, had lengthened and darkened with each month, and has never completely lifted.

The girl's name is Barbara. She had blue eyes and long brown hair, and she lived in Garden Grove with her parents. She had a lisp. That's all he ever told me. The rest has been written in daylight imaginings and in dreams: Barbara and I are sitting beneath a beach umbrella reading books and sipping tall, cool drinks. The ocean is crashing in the distance, and the child crawling the space between our knees is a girl. She is a harlequin, seamed down the center. Not one eyelash, one fingernail, one cell of the child is his. She is the two best halves of Barbara and me, sewn with perfectly spaced stitches: this is the story I write.

*   *   *

Studying the markings in *Evening Train*, I surmise that the gray-haired woman is an honest reader, unashamed to admit her ignorance. She has drawn boxes around difficult words — *epiphanies, antiphonal, tessellations, serrations* — and placed a question mark above each box. Maybe she's merely an eager learner, the kind who sets small tasks for herself; she will go directly to the dictionary and find these words. Or maybe someone — her husband, her lover, whoever broke her serviceable heart — also criticized her vocabulary. It was too small or too large. She asked too many questions.

In the poem about the breaking heart, she has underlined "in surface fissures" and "a web / of hairline fractures." She probably didn't even notice the fissures at first. Maybe, she guessed, this webbing is the necessary landscape of every marriage, each act of love. But reading on, I sense that more has been broken than a metaphorical heart. She has circled the entire poem "The Batterers," about a man who, after beating a woman, dresses her wounds and, in so doing, begins to love her again. "Why had he never / seen, before, what she was? / What if she stops breathing?" I tell myself *I* wouldn't have stayed in that kind of situation. As it is, I'll never know. He never hit me, though one night, desperate for attention, I begged him to. (How do we live with the knowledge of our past selves?) He'd come home late, at two or three o'clock, with no explanation. Earlier in the evening, returning from a night class and looking for clues to his absence, I'd found a woman's jacket behind a chair. It smelled foreign yet familiar — her musky perfume mingled with the memory of his cigarettes. They had been here together, in our apartment. He had not touched me in weeks.

When his fist finally flew, it landed on the door of the filing cabinet where I kept my class notes, term papers, and poetry drafts. This should not have surprised me. For months he'd been angry that I'd returned to school. "What are you trying to prove?" he'd ask. "Where do you think this is going to get you? Just listen to yourself, can't you just hear yourself?" Though I still worked part-time at the print shop, he spent whole days on the assembly line, drilling holes into bowling balls. Anything to make ends meet. He was hoping, beyond logic, that as a married man with a full-time job, he would be saved from Vietnam. He was terrified; his draft number was low.

The force of the blow was audible: a thud, a crack. Loose sheets flew from the top of the cabinet. He cried out, then brought the fist to his mouth. Surely it was broken, I thought. I rushed toward him, but he held up his other hand to block me. Time slowed. White paper fluttered around me like birds. I stared at his hand, and something went out of me, I could feel it, a sucking force, tidal, pulling me out of myself. Then the moment was over. He turned and walked away, his wounded fist still pressed to his mouth, his blue eyes filling. I knelt on the floor and began to gather the papers. My eyes were dry, my vision clear. This is what hurt the most: the clarity of the moment, its sharp focus. Each black word, on each scattered page, distinct and singular.

Two years ago, when Carolyn was dying, when she could count the remaining months on her fingers, she wrote from her home in Virginia, asking me to come as soon as possible to help her sort through her books. "You can have whatever you want," she said. "The only thing I ask is that you don't cry. Just pretend it's a book sale. Come early, stay late. And go home with your arms full."

It took two full afternoons. Too weak to stand, Carolyn sat on a little stool, pointing and nodding, directing me shelf by shelf. Each row called forth a memory. Her life's story unfolded book by book. She told me she was glad she'd lived long enough to see a grandchild safely into the world. She was glad I had a found a husband who was good to me, this time, and she wished me all the happiness she had known. When my car could hold no more books, she handed me a large envelope and explained that one of her jobs as assistant librarian had been to check the returned books before reshelving them. The envelope was labeled in Carolyn's scrawl: *Woodrow Wilson Public Library, Things Found in Books.* "You'd be surprised at what people use as bookmarks," she said.

When I got home, I emptied the envelope onto the floor, amazed at what spilled out. Bits and pieces of strangers' lives, hundreds of markers of personal histories. Love letters, folded placemats, envelopes, sympathy cards, valentines, handwritten recipes, train tickets, report cards, newspaper clippings, certificates of achievement, bills, receipts, religious tracts, swimming-pool passes, scratch-and-sniff perfume ads, canceled tickets for the bullfight, bar coasters, rice paper, happy money. Studying the bookmarks, I slid into each stranger's life, wondering which book he had checked out and whether he had finished it. What calls us away from books, then back to them?

When I am in pain, I *devour* books, often stripping the words of conceptual and metaphorical context and digging straight for the meat. The gray-haired woman seems to be doing the same thing, taking each word personally, *too* personally, as if Levertov had written them just for her, to guide her toward some terrible action. Certainly this wasn't the poet's intention, yet the more I study the markings, the more I fear what the woman is considering. In "Dream Instruction" she has underlined, twice, "gradual stillness," but appears to have missed entirely the "blessing" in the line that follows. The marks in "Contraband" are even more alarming. I want to take the woman by the hand and remind her of the poem's symbolic level, a level that's nearly impossible to see when you are in pain. Contraband, I would tell her, represents the Tree of Knowledge, the tree of reason, and the fruit is the words we stuff into our mouths, and yes, that fruit might indeed be "toxic in large quantities; fumes / swirled in our heads and around us," but those lines are not a prescription for suicide. There are other ways to live with knowledge.

For instance, you can leave, gather up what remains of yourself and set off on a journey much like the journey of faith Levertov writes of. Or, if that proves too difficult, you can send your self off on its own, wave goodbye, step back into childhood's shoes and refuse to go one step further. You can cut off your hair, take the pills the doctors prescribe and beg for more, then lose yourself daily in a gauzy sleep, surrounded by the books that have become your only food. His deferment dream did not materialize, so you have followed him to a military base where you know no one. Vietnam is still a possibility. Your heart is divided: you dread the orders yet pray for them. If they come, you will be able to retreat honorably to your parents' home. In the meantime, you have the pills and the books and the bed grown huge by his nightly absence — he is sleeping elsewhere now, with someone else, and he no longer even tries to hide it.

If you're lucky, one night your hand will find the phone, and if you are doubly lucky and have a mother like mine, she will arrive early the next day, having driven hundreds of miles alone in a car large enough to hold several children. Though she is a quiet woman who rarely interferes, in this case she will make an exception. She will locate your husband, demand that he come home, now, and when he does (this is where the details get fuzzy, you have sent yourself off somewhere), together they will lift you into the backseat of her big car and rush you to the emergency room, where the attending physician will immediately direct you to the psychiatric wing.

I would remember none of this part, which is a blessing. Had I recalled the details of the breakdown, I might have felt compelled to tell the story too soon, to anyone who would listen: strangers on buses, prospective employers, longtime family friends, men I met in bars or churches (for months I would search both places, equally, for comfort). "There's no need to tell," my mother said after my release, and she would repeat this many times, long after I was out of danger. Though I've finally decided, after nearly thirty years, to tell, I still hear her words in my head: "You don't need any more hurt. It's no one's business but yours."

This is my mother's way. Though she freely gives to anyone in need — food, comfort, time, love — there is a part of herself, the heart's most enclosed, tender core, that she guards like a secret. In this way, and others, I would like to be more like her. Less needy, more protective of private fears and desires. Less prone to look back, more single-minded in forward resolve. Though I had re-hearsed his leaving for months, when he finally went, for good this time (isn't it strange how we use *good* to mean *final?*), I was devas-tated, terrified to imagine my future. "What should I do," I begged my mother. "What would you do?" I don't know what I expected her to say. My mother has never been one to give advice. Experi-ence, in her view, is not transferable. It is not an inheritance you pass on to your children, no matter how much you wish you could.

If her words held no answer, I decided, then I would read her life. Certainly there were worlds it could teach me. She had left her parents and the family farm to follow her husband from one mili-tary base to the next; waited out his long absences; buried one child and raised six others; watched as loved ones suffered di-vorces, financial ruin, alcoholism, depression, life-threatening ill-nesses and accidents; nursed them through their last years. "Take me with you," I begged, meaning back home, to *her* home, to the nest she and my father had made.

My mother remembers this as one of the painful moments of her life. "I wanted more than anything to say yes," she recalls. "But I knew if I did, you'd never find your way. It was time you found your own way." So she took my face in her hands and said *no*. No, I could not follow her, I could not come back home. Then she helped me pack my suitcase, and, so I would not be alone, so I would be safe if worse once again came to worst, she made me a plane reservation to my brother's town in South Carolina. Half a world away, or so it seemed to me.

The narrator of Levertov's *Evening Train* sets off on a journey too, and though I suspect that the luggage and racks of the book's title poem are intended to be metaphorical, I cannot help but feel the heft of the bags, the steel slickness of the racks. And as I study the phantom woman's markings, it seems clear that, like mine, her journey required a real ticket on a real train or plane, and that by the time she arrived at the poem called "Arrived," she had already sat alone in a room with "Chairs, / sofa, table, a cup —" and begun the inventory of her life. Was she, like the poem's narrator, unable to call forth the face of the one she had left, who had left her? Why else mark these lines: "the shape / of his head, or / color of his eyes appear / at moments, but I can't / assemble feature with feature"?

In my pain, I prayed for such moments of forgetfulness. How pleasant it would be not to recall his hands, his tanned, furrowed forehead, the flame-cool blue of his eyes. My only release was to stuff my brain with cotton. That's how it felt when I took the pills. Though they no longer had the power to put me to sleep, they lifted me to a place of soundlessness and ether. I thought of T. S. Eliot's hollow men, their heads filled with straw. The image of scarecrows was comforting, as were thoughts of helium balloons, slow-floating dirigibles, and anything submerged in water. I was an aquarium, enclosed. Amniotic silence surrounded me hour after hour, and then suddenly—*What's that noise?*, I'd think, startled, amazed to discover it was my own breath in my lungs, my heart thumping, the blood thrumming in my ears.

When this happened, when I was brought back to myself, I'd think, *No, please not that.* I had forgotten for a while that I was alive, that there were hands at the ends of my arms, fingers that could burn themselves on the gas stove, the iron, the teakettle's steam. The world was too much with me. Why bother? (*This is the way the world ends . . .*) I fell back into bed, finding comfort in Eliot, and

later in Job. The New Testament was stuffed too full of promise
and light, but Old Testament sufferings were redemptive, though
not in the traditional sense of the word. I was long past questioning why a loving God would destroy Job's house and cattle, afflict
him with boils all over his body, and kill his children. The worst is
yet to come, I thought — and almost said, aloud, to Job. Happiness
is what you should be fearing. Why waste your breath talking back
to God, calling out for salvation? The cure might be worse than
the disease. If God answers, out of the whirlwind and the chaos
of destruction, beware of what will be given: healing, forgiveness,
six thousand camels, a thousand she-asses, seven sons and three
daughters, each fairer than the next, your life overflowing, another high place from which to fall.

I didn't want to live, but I couldn't imagine dying. How to gather
the energy? I didn't own a gun and could see no way to get one. I
had no courage for knives. Pills seemed an easy way out; I tried,
but my stomach refused to accept them. Over the next weeks I
started taking long drives on country roads, staring at the yellow
lines and thinking how easy it would be to pull the wheel to the
left, into the oncoming truck, which was heavy enough, I was sure,
to bear the impact without killing its driver. (I didn't want to kill
anyone, not even myself. I just wanted not to live. There's a difference.) Or better yet, pull the wheel to the right, into that stand of
pine trees.

What terrified me was not the thought of the mangled metal,
the row of wounded trunks, or even of the sheet pulled over me —
a gesture that seemed almost a kindness, something a loved one
would do. What terrified me that late summer day was the sudden
greenness of the trees, the way their beauty insinuated itself into
my vision — peripherally at first, vaguely, and without my consent.
I blinked to stop what felt like tears, which I hadn't tasted for so
long I'd forgotten that they were made of salt, that they were something my body was producing on its own, long after I thought I
had shut down. O.K., I said to the steering wheel, the padded dashboard, the pines. If I can think of five reasons not to die, I won't.

When I got back to my room, I pulled from the pages of Eliot a
blank prescription refill form I'd been using as a bookmark. I
found a pencil in the nightstand, one without an eraser, I recall. I
remember thinking that I couldn't go back on what I'd written,

couldn't retrace my steps if I made a mistake. I turned the form over and numbered the blank side — 1, 2, 3, 4, 5 — with a black period after each, as if preparing to take a spelling test. It was the first time I'd put pencil to paper since I'd left California. I thought for a while, then wrote beside number one, "My parents," immediately wishing I'd split them into "Mother" and "Dad" so that I could have filled two lines. Then to my surprise the next four blanks filled quickly, and my hand was adding numbers and more numbers to accommodate the names of my siblings, my nieces and nephews, the handful of friends I still claimed and even the ones who were gone. I filled the back of the form and probably could have filled another, but I didn't want to try, I couldn't bear any more just yet — the stab of joy, the possibility.

As months passed, the world slowly continued to make itself known, appearing in small, merciful gestures, as if not wishing to startle: voices, a pair of hands, golden leaf-shadow, a suggestion of sky. Then one morning, for no reason I can recall, the world lifted her veil and showed her whole self. She looked strangely familiar — yes, I thought, it's all coming back. Put on shoes, brush teeth, smile into the mirror, pour orange juice into a glass. *This is the way the world begins. This is the way the world begins. This is the way.*

I smooth the center seam of *Evening Train* and run my hands over the marked-up lines. Poems can be dangerous places in which to venture, alone, and I'm not sure the woman is ready for "After Mindwalk." She has underlined "panic's black cloth falling / over our faces, over our breath." Please don't, I want to say. Don't do it, don't drink it, don't eat that apple. I want to tell her about the pine trees, the list, Mother and Bessie and Carolyn and Wordsworth and Hopkins and Job. Look, I'd say, pointing to the footnote. See, *Mindwalk* was a film by Bernt Capra, it's not a real place; don't worry. It's about Pascal and the Void. It doesn't have to be about you. But it is, of course. That's why she is not only reading the book but writing one of her own as well, with each scratch of the pencil. The printed words are Levertov's, but the other poem is the woman's — written in the margins, in the small boxes that cage the words she cannot pronounce, in the crumbled erasures, in the question marks floating above the lines. Wait up, I want to say — a crazy thought, but I can't help myself. Wait up; I want to tell you something.

Reflections and Responses

1. How do the marginal notes of others that McClanahan finds in various books affect her? What general responses do they provoke in her? What connection do they have with loneliness and the need for companionship? How are markings connected with love and sexuality?

2. "I never saw books as dead, finished texts," McClanahan writes. "They were living breathing, entities. . . ." How does she throughout the essay blur the boundaries between books and people, herself included? How are books like people, and people like books? How do lines from poems intersect with her own life? What does she find so intriguing about *Evening Train,* the volume of Denise Levertov's poetry she borrowed from the library?

3. Consider the way McClanahan shapes her essay. Although it tells the story of her life, it does not proceed in an orderly chronological fashion. Go back through the essay and try putting events into a narrative timeline, starting with the earliest episodes and ending with her present time. How different does the essay seem when reassembled? Why do you think McClanahan chose to structure the essay in just the way she did?

JOHN MCPHEE

Silk Parachute
As originally appeared in *The New Yorker*

Personal memoirs can be hundreds of pages long or — like this one — very short. Whether long or short, they are fueled by the writer's recollection of evocative details. In "Silk Parachute," John McPhee constructs a complex miniature memoir around a number of details concerning his relationship with his mother; some of the details he claims he cannot vouch for and others he alleges he can. The reader is invited to wonder why he vividly recalls certain moments and denies any recollection of others: "The assertion is absolutely false that when I came home from high school with an A-minus she demanded an explanation for the minus."

One of America's most celebrated nonfiction writers, John McPhee was born in Princeton, New Jersey, in 1931 and is the author of numerous award-winning books. His first book, A Sense of Where You Are, *is a profile of basketball star Bill Bradley and appeared in 1965. He has published nearly a book every year since then, all of them with the same publisher, Farrar, Straus & Giroux. Although his subjects range from sports to science, McPhee has written extensively in the fields of nature and geology. Two of McPhee's recent books are* Annals of the Former World *(2000) and* The Founding Fish *(2002). He has been a staff writer for* The New Yorker *magazine since 1965 and a professor of journalism at Princeton University since 1975. "Silk Parachute" originally appeared in* The New Yorker *and was selected by Cynthia Ozick for* The Best American Essays 1998.

When your mother is ninety-nine years old, you have so many memories of her that they tend to overlap, intermingle, and blur. It is extremely difficult to single out one or two, impossible to remember any that exemplify the whole.

It has been alleged that when I was in college she heard that I had stayed up all night playing poker and wrote me a letter that used the word "shame" forty-two times. I do not recall this.

I do not recall being pulled out of my college room and into the church next door.

It has been alleged that on December 24, 1936, when I was five years old, she sent me to my room at or close to 7 P.M. for using four-letter words while trimming the Christmas tree. I do not recall that.

The assertion is absolutely false that when I came home from high school with an A-minus she demanded an explanation for the minus.

It has been alleged that she spoiled me with protectionism, because I was the youngest child and therefore the most vulnerable to attack from overhead — an assertion that I cannot confirm or confute, except to say that facts don't lie.

We lived only a few blocks from the elementary school and routinely ate lunch at home. It is reported that the following dialogue and ensuing action occurred on January 22, 1941:

"Eat your sandwich."

"I don't want to eat my sandwich."

"I made that sandwich, and you are going to eat it, Mister Man. You filled yourself up on penny candy on the way home, and now you're not hungry."

"I'm late. I have to go. I'll eat the sandwich on the way back to school."

"Promise?"

"Promise."

Allegedly, I went up the street with sandwich in my hand and buried it in a snowbank in front of Dr. Wright's house. My mother, holding back the curtain in the window of the side door, was watching. She came out in the bitter cold, wearing only a light dress, ran to the snowbank, dug out the sandwich, chased me up Nassau Street,* and rammed the sandwich down my throat, snow

---

*__Nassau Street:__ Princeton's main street. — Ed.

and all. I do not recall any detail of that story. I believe it to be a total fabrication.

There was the case of the missing Cracker Jack at Lindel's corner store. Flimsy evidence pointed to Mrs. McPhee's smallest child. It has been averred that she laid the guilt on with the following words: "'Like mother, like son' is a saying so true, the world will judge largely of mother by you." It has been asserted that she immediately repeated that proverb three times, and also recited it on other occasions too numerous to count. I have absolutely no recollection of her saying that about the Cracker Jack or any other controlled substance.

We have now covered everything even faintly unsavory that has been reported about this person in ninety-nine years, and even those items are a collection of rumors, half-truths, prevarications, false allegations, inaccuracies, innuendos, and canards.

This is the mother who — when Alfred Knopf* wrote her twenty-two-year-old son a letter saying, "The readers' report in the case of your manuscript would not be very helpful, and I think might discourage you completely" — said, "Don't listen to Alfred Knopf. Who does Alfred Knopf think he is, anyway? Someone should go in there and k-nock his block off." To the best of my recollection, that is what she said.

I also recall her taking me, on or about March 8, my birthday, to the theater in New York every year, beginning in childhood. I remember those journeys as if they were today. I remember *A Connecticut Yankee*. Wednesday, March 8, 1944. Evidently, my father had written for the tickets, because she and I sat in the last row of the second balcony. Mother knew what to do about that. She gave me for my birthday an elegant spyglass, sufficient in power to bring the Connecticut Yankee back from Vermont. I sat there watching the play through my telescope, drawing as many guffaws from the surrounding audience as the comedy on the stage.

On one of those theater days — when I was eleven or twelve — I asked her if we could start for the city early and go out to La Guardia Field to see the comings and goings of airplanes. The temperature was well below the freeze point and the March winds were so blustery that the wind-chill factor was forty below zero. Or seemed to be. My mother figured out how to take the subway to a

*Alfred Knopf: founder of the prominent New York publishing house that bears his name; the "K" is sounded. — Ed.

stop in Jackson Heights and a bus from there — a feat I am unable to duplicate to this day. At La Guardia, she accompanied me to the observation deck and stood there in the icy wind for at least an hour, maybe two, while I, spellbound, watched the DC-3s coming in on final, their wings flapping in the gusts. When we at last left the observation deck, we went downstairs into the terminal, where she bought me what appeared to be a black rubber ball but on closer inspection was a pair of hollow hemispheres hinged on one side and folded together. They contained a silk parachute. Opposite the hinge, each hemisphere had a small nib. A piece of string wrapped round and round the two nibs kept the ball closed. If you threw it high into the air, the string unwound and the parachute blossomed. If you sent it up with a tennis racket, you could put it into the clouds. Not until the development of the ten-megabyte hard disk would the world ever know such a fabulous toy. Folded just so, the parachute never failed. Always, it floated back to you — silkily, beautifully — to start over and float back again. Even if you abused it, whacked it really hard — gracefully, lightly, it floated back to you.

Reflections and Responses

1. Note the style of McPhee's opening paragraphs. Why do you think he repeats the phrase "It has been alleged . . ."? What does the tone of the phrase suggest, along with such words as *reported, assertion,* and *averred*? Who do you imagine has made the assertions and allegations?

2. Why is McPhee careful to say that he can't recall some details and events yet specifically remembers others? Can you detect any differences between what he recalls and what he doesn't?

3. Given its title role and its final emphasis, the silk parachute McPhee's mother bought for him at La Guardia Airport is clearly the essay's dominant image. How does McPhee enlarge its significance? What do you think the parachute represents?

DANIELLE OFRI

Merced

*Essays of self-discovery frequently follow a narrative arc as the writer details
the process of moving from a state of innocence or unawareness to one of experience or enlightenment. The process usually conforms to the following pattern:
"At point A one thinks or understands X, but by point B one is now aware of
Y." Danielle Ofri's narrative convincingly shows that this can be the case
even if one starts out at point A thinking she has all the answers. Such essays—and this one is no exception—often conclude with an "epiphany." Irish
novelist James Joyce first used this ancient religious term in a modern literary
sense to describe the sudden flash of insight or the unexpected illumination
that can transform our lives. "Merced" takes us inside today's medical profession while it grapples with what becoming a doctor means, intellectually and
spiritually. It should be required reading for all pre-med students.*

Danielle Ofri, M.D., Ph.D. is the author of Singular Intimacies: Becoming a Doctor at Bellevue *(Beacon, 2003). Ofri is editor-in-chief
and co-founder of the* Bellevue Literary Review, *and associate chief editor of the award-winning medical textbook,* The Bellevue Guide to Outpatient Medicine. *Her stories have appeared in both literary and medical
journals, as well as in several anthologies. She is an attending physician
at Bellevue Hospital and on the faculty of New York University School of
Medicine. She lives in New York City with her husband and two children.
Her essay "Merced" received the* Missouri Review *Editor's Prize and was
selected by Stephen Jay Gould for* The Best American Essays 2002, *and
another of her essays was selected by Oliver Sacks for* Best American Science Writing 2003.

For this is the end of examinations
For this is the beginning of testing
For Death will give the final examination and everyone will pass

   —John Stone, *Gaudeamus Igitur*

"This is a case of a twenty-three-year-old Hispanic female without significant past medical history who presented to Bellevue Hospital complaining of a headache." The speaker droned on with the details of the case that I knew so well. I leaned back in my chair, anticipating the accolades that were going to come. After all, in a roundabout way I'd made the diagnosis. I was the one who had had the idea to send the Lyme test in the first place.

Mercedes had been to two other ERs before showing up at Bellevue three weeks ago. I'd only been doing sick call that day because one of the other residents had twisted his knee playing volleyball. She was a classic aseptic meningitis, the kind that you'd send home with aspirin and some chicken soup, but the ER had decided to admit her to the hospital. Her CT scan was normal, and the spinal tap just showed a few lymphocytes, but the ER always overreacts. They gave her IV antibiotics even though there was no hint of the life-threatening bacterial meningitis.

One of the emergency room docs had scrawled something about "bizarre behavior" on the chart, then given her a stat dose of acyclovir. Another ridiculous ER maneuver; this patient had no signs of herpes encephalitis.

I'll admit that I was a little cocky that day. But I was just two months short of finishing residency, and I knew a lot more medicine than those ER guys. I chewed them out for admitting Mercedes and made a big show of canceling the acyclovir order.

When I met Mercedes that first day, she was sleeping on a stretcher in a corner of the ER. I had to wake her up to take the history, but after a few shakes she was completely lucid. With her plump cheeks and wide brown eyes, she didn't even look seventeen, much less twenty-three. The sleeves of her pink sweatshirt were pushed up past her elbows. A gold cross with delicate filigree was partly obscured by the folds of the sweatshirt.

"Doctor, you have to believe me," she said, pulling herself up on the stretcher. "I've never been sick a day in my life. It's only this past month that I've been getting these headaches. They come almost every day, and aspirin doesn't do anything. I came to the ER yesterday, but they said, 'You got nothin', lady,' and just gave me a couple of Tylenols." Dark, mussed curls spilled over her pink shirt. While she spoke, one hand wove itself absent-mindedly in and out of the locks.

"So, what made you come back today?" I asked.

"This headache, it didn't go away. And then my arm. It got all pins and needles for a few minutes. Just a couple of minutes, but now it's fine." Mercedes smiled slightly, and two tiny dimples flickered in her cheeks. "I guess they got tired of me complaining, so they decided to let me stay."

I did a thorough physical exam, spending extra time on the neurologic part. I checked every reflex I could think of: biceps, triceps, brachoradialis, patellar, plantar. I examined all twelve cranial nerves. Everything seemed normal. I tried to do all the obscure neurological tests I could remember from *Bates's Guide to Physical Examination and History Taking,* but nothing seemed amiss, and the patient was certainly not behaving bizarrely.

From talking to her, I learned that Mercedes was a single mother with two children, aged three and four. She lived with her own mother but still maintained a close relationship with the father of her children. She worked as a preschool teacher in upper Manhattan. She'd been born in Puerto Rico, but since moving to the United States at age two had never left the country.

I questioned her extensively about possible exposure to viruses or atypical organisms: travel to the countryside, recent illnesses, recent vaccinations, outbreaks of sickness at her preschool, HIV risk factors, contact with pets, consumption of poorly cooked fish or meat, all of which she denied.

Based on her history and physical exam, I concluded that she had garden-variety aseptic meningitis. The ER staff, with their usual sledgehammer approach to medical care, had overdone it with intravenous antibiotics and acyclovir. Mercedes didn't even need to stay in the hospital, but she'd already been officially admitted, and the administrative folks would have a conniption if I sent a patient home just two hours after checking in.

Just to show the ER docs how real academic medicine was done, I wrote up an extensive admission note for Mercedes, detailing all the rare causes of aseptic meningitis listed in *Harrison's Principles of Internal Medicine.* Paragraph after paragraph elucidated my clinical logic; it was a textbook example of orderly scientific thinking. And I printed neatly, so it would be easy for anyone perusing the chart to read.

There was an extra tube of Mercedes's cerebrospinal fluid in my pocket, so I decided to send it for a couple of rare tests, including a Lyme titre. What the heck, I thought. This is a teaching institution. We're supposed to waste some money on exotic tests in order to learn. Besides, it would really impress the attending on rounds tomorrow when I would blithely nod my head at each diagnosis he'd ask about.

Rickettsia? "Got it."

Sarcoid? "Covered."

Coxsackie virus? "Sent it."

Toxoplasmosis? "Already there."

Lupus? "Done."

The ER docs might just toss a pile of medications at anyone who walked in the door, but here in the Department of Medicine, we utilized our diagnostic acumen.

The next morning during rounds, just as I was dazzling the crowd with my erudite analysis of Mercedes's case, the nurses called me urgently to her room. Mercedes was on the floor with her clothes off, hair askew, babbling incoherently. Her IV had been pulled out, and her body was splattered with blood. Completely disoriented, she fought us vociferously as we tried to help her back to bed.

Thirty minutes later she was entirely back to normal, with no recollection of the event. I was absolutely dumbfounded. What the hell had just happened?

Immediately I repeated a CT scan and spinal tap, but the results were no different than they'd been the day before. The neurologist felt Mercedes's behavior might have represented a seizure of the temporal lobe. The herpes virus has a predilection for the temporal lobe, so this episode might have been a sign of herpes encephalitis. Regretting my earlier haughtiness toward the ER staff, I restarted the acyclovir.

Mercedes was transferred to the neurology service for management of herpes encephalitis, and I was transferred off the ward when the other resident's knee got better. I was happy to get back to my cushy dermatology elective.

A week later, still smarting from missing the herpes encephalitis diagnosis, I tracked down the intern to see how Mercedes was doing. "Hey, did you hear the news?" he asked. "That herpes encephalitis patient really had Lyme disease. The test just came back positive yesterday."

Lyme disease? The test that I had sent came back positive? I was exhilarated. This would be the most fascinating diagnosis on the medical wards. Who would have suspected that a New York City dweller would have a disease carried by deer ticks in the forest? But hey, it was a careful diagnostic evaluation of the patient, and my thoroughness had paid off.

Soon everybody was talking about the case of Lyme meningitis in our inner-city hospital. The head of my residency program became interested and suggested I plan a seminar on Lyme disease. I set about obtaining all the details of Mercedes's case and searched the medical literature for current articles on Lyme disease.

Meanwhile, Mercedes was started on the appropriate medication for Lyme. She'd been discharged home and was finishing her three-week course of antibiotics with daily shots in the clinic.

Today the case was being presented at neurology grand rounds. I wasn't a participant in this particular conference, but I didn't care. I sat back and listened to speaker after speaker comment on the "incredible diagnosis" that had been made. My bulging Mercedes/ Lyme folder sat on my lap as I took mental notes, preparing for my own presentation in the Department of Medicine two weeks from now. Residency would be over at the end of next month. I had been here ten years, from the beginning of medical school through my Ph.D. and then my residency. Ten years of medical training! But now it was truly paying off. Ten years of the scientific approach to medicine had prepared me for this case. Ten years of emphasis on careful analysis of data — whether it be of receptor binding assays in the lab or signs and symptoms in a patient — had taught me how to establish a hypothesis and reach a logical conclusion. This was the academic way that ensured the highest-quality medical care.

Our attendings were always pointing out medical disasters that occurred "out in the community" when the doctors in charge were not academic physicians. Doctors who didn't keep up with the latest medical journals — doctors who, without diligent and thoughtful analysis, ordered any old test or prescribed any fancy packaged medicine marketed by the pharmaceutical companies — could seriously harm or even kill their patients. Mercedes was lucky to have come to an academic medical center rather than to a community hospital, where her diagnosis would have been missed entirely.

Mercedes's case was presented in elaborate detail. There was a sense of triumph in the air: a patient had come to us sick, exhibiting mysterious symptoms. With the combined clinical acumen of the internists, neurologists, radiologists, infectious disease specialists, lab technicians, and nursing staff of this academic medical center, we had plumbed the unknown and come up with the diagnosis.

I let the neurologists prattle on and on. I didn't need any official praise here at the neurology conference; I'd have my moment in the limelight in two weeks at my presentation. Anyway, I knew that it had been my decision to send the initial Lyme test. If it wasn't for that Lyme test, the diagnosis would never have been made, and this whole panel of esteemed experts would not be sitting in this room patting their own backs. What a fantastic case for my residency training to culminate in. Maybe I should submit this to the *New England Journal of Medicine!*

Someone had invited Mercedes to the conference, and she sat in the back listening quietly. I watched her from my vantage point in the corner. She looked wonderful — no hint of the illness that had caused that bizarre episode on her second hospital day. Her long, curly brown hair was lustrous against her olive skin. She looked perfectly healthy. I smiled proudly. What a true success story.

I went to say hello to Mercedes at the end of the conference, but she had no recollection of me or of her initial days in the hospital. Her family, however, recognized me and thanked me for her early care. I shook Mercedes's hand heartily and congratulated her on her recovery. Her hand was warm and plump and her handshake reassuringly healthy. The conference lasted all Friday afternoon. I was looking forward to a relaxing weekend, because Monday was "switch day," and I'd be going to the intensive care unit. Though I loved the ICU, I knew I'd have no free time for the entire month. I'd be working thirty-six-hour shifts every three days, which added up to only one free Saturday for the entire month. But I knew I could make it — it was the last month of my residency, and on June 30 it would all be over. In fact, the ICU was a great way to end. I'd work like a maniac and then be done with everything. Since I wasn't starting a fellowship, I'd have the whole summer ahead of me to enjoy.

Monday morning our new team gathered in the ICU. There was a crackle in the air from all the different machines breathing life into our critically ill patients. We rounded on all of our new patients as a tightly organized team, talking in easy jargon, with no need to translate for anyone. At each bedside was a computer loaded with data for each patient. We raced each other to calculate arterial alveolar gradients and oxygen extraction ratios. We reeled off ventilator management strategies, debating the relative values of positive endexpiratory pressure versus continuous positive airway pressure. I marveled at how easy it all was. For an intern, or even a second-year resident, the ICU was a terrifying place, especially the first day. But now I took it all in stride. Just another twelve sick patients on ventilators with arterial lines and Swans. Let 'em crash; let 'em code; I could handle it. That's what ten years of Bellevue training does for you.

That evening I was home alone, gathering my thoughts about my new set of patients. It was only Monday, but it was clear it was going to be an exciting month. My residency was going to end in style. Our team would get this ICU into top shape.

I ran down my list of patients. Whom could we improve? There was that lady in bed 3, on two different antibiotics for an abdominal abscess. Maybe she could use a third. But that could wait until tomorrow. And the guy in bed 12 with esophageal cancer. His family had been vacillating on the DNR. I'd call the brother first thing in the morning.

The old guy in bed 5 who'd stroked out last month — left side not moving, already demented from Alzheimer's. I wasn't sure if his ventilator settings were optimized; his peak pressures had been fluctuating. If I could get the latest blood-gas results, I could make the adjustments over the phone and then see his new numbers before rounds in the morning. Why wait until tomorrow if I could keep that patient one step ahead? I propped my feet up on my couch and tore open a bag of chile-and-lime tortilla chips. One hand dialed the phone while the other plunged into the bag.

Instead of the clerk who usually answers the phone, George, one of the other residents, happened to answer. We chatted for a while about how much fun the ICU was — what a great way to end residency. We discussed the ventilator management of bed 5 and agreed to lower flow rate but increase the tidal volume. I asked how his first night on call was going.

"What a night," George said. "We've been incredibly busy. One cardiac arrest, one septic shock. But my third admission is the most interesting."

"Really," I said. "What did you get?"

"It's a surprise. Something rare. But you'll see on tomorrow's rounds."

"C'mon, George," I said between chomps of chips. "Give me a hint."

"It's a good one. You ain't never seen this before."

"Listen, I covered for you on your anniversary last March. You owe me one." I pestered him some more, and he finally relented. In a conspiratorially low voice, to tantalize my curiosity, he said, "Read up on Lyme meningitis for rounds tomorrow."

The chips and chili turned to sawdust in my mouth. "That's strange," I said. "I just had a case of Lyme meningitis three weeks ago." I could feel the muscles in my neck tightening. My throat began to constrict. Please, God, don't let it be the same person. Don't let it be Mercedes.

"Yep, that's the one," George said.

Mercedes? In the ICU? I had just seen her on Friday, and she was fine. How could she be in the ICU on Monday? I jammed the telephone against my ear, struggling to absorb the story that was being transmitted.

On Saturday, George told me, Mercedes had experienced another headache. On Sunday her headache worsened, so she came to the ER. Nothing was found on physical exam, and she was sent home with a diagnosis of "postmeningitic headache," a frequent phenomenon.

On Monday, this afternoon, she had complained of the "worst headache of her life," accompanied by nausea and vomiting. She returned to the ER, and this time she was admitted to the hospital. The doctors who spoke with her said she was able to give a coherent history of her recent treatment and again had a perfectly normal neurological exam. Nonetheless, they sent her for a CT scan of her head.

The CT scan lasted about fifteen minutes. When the technician went to help her out of the scanner, he found her unresponsive. A code was called, but by the time the code team arrived, her pupils were already fixed and dilated, a sign of irreversible brain swelling. She was brought to the ICU, where a hole was drilled in her skull in an attempt to relieve the pressure, but it was too late.

Steroids were given to decrease the inflammation. Antibiotics of every stripe were administered. Various maneuvers to lower her intracranial pressure were attempted — artificially increasing her breathing rate, angling the bed to keep her head above her feet, infusing massive doses of osmotic diuretics — but none worked. Now she lay in bed 10 of the ICU, her breathing maintained by a ventilator . . . brain dead.

Tests for tuberculosis, lupus, syphilis, vasculitis, and other inflammatory diseases were performed, and all were negative.

"Could this all be from the Lyme?" I stammered into the phone.

"Nah," George replied. "We sent another Lyme titre, and it came back negative. This ain't Lyme. The first Lyme was a false positive." His voice faded for a minute as he told one of the nurses to suction bed 4.

How could a young woman whom we had presumably cured, who had been so alive and healthy three days ago, be brain dead now?

I could not absorb the story as it was relayed to me over the phone. How could she be brain dead? I had been there on Friday. I had touched her and felt her warm and alive skin just seventy-two hours ago. It couldn't be the same person.

I stormed back and forth in the two cramped rooms of my Manhattan apartment. Eventually I called a pulmonologist I knew and paged two of my residency colleagues, but the case didn't make any sense to them either. I called my nonmedical friends, just to calm myself, but the very act of converting all of the clinical terminology into lay language frustrated me unbearably. I tore my textbooks off the shelves, ripping through the indexes for answers. I upended the contents of my Mercedes/Lyme folder, scouring the fine print in the scientific papers, hurling them aside when they proved useless.

Lyme in the inner city? How could I have been so stupid? So what did she have? Mercedes had received treatment for everything when she'd been in the hospital the first time: acyclovir for herpes encephalitis, regular antibiotics for bacterial meningitis, full treatment for Lyme. All the other tests were negative.

This could not be happening. This Mercedes George had told me about could not be the same as the Friday Mercedes who'd smiled at me when I shook her hand. The Friday Mercedes was real. This Monday Mercedes was just a case report over the phone.

I knew that there was nothing I could do. The neurosurgeons were already there, and the head of the infectious disease unit had personally examined Mercedes. She was already receiving the best nursing and medical care available. Everything would still be the same on morning rounds a few hours from now. Also, if I went in at this late hour I might be overstepping my bounds by insinuating that George's care was inadequate. Besides, once the pupils are fixed and dilated, everyone knows that there is nothing else to do.

But it was now two A.M. I couldn't sit still, and I'd run out of friends whom I could call at that hour. I tried to convince myself that it would be for the greater good of all my patients if I just calmed down and got a good night of sleep so I could function in the morning. But my hands wouldn't stop trembling, and I had already eaten all the chocolate I could unearth in my apartment. I had to see Mercedes with my own eyes.

I pulled on an old pair of scrubs and set off on First Avenue. The street was quiet; even the homeless had gone off somewhere to sleep. The gloomy brick behemoths of the old Bellevue buildings cast spooky shadows in the moonlight. The decaying TB sanatorium and mental hospital menaced from behind the tall cast-iron gates. The dusky ivy on the brick buildings made the walls look moist and velvety. Scalloped columns in an abandoned courtyard poked eerily out of the ground, like portals into some dark netherworld. I waded through the midnight heaviness, my feet only vaguely aware of the sidewalk beneath them. By the faint lights in the garden in front of Bellevue, I could just see the dark shadows that were the birdbath and fountain.

Inside the hospital building it was brightly lit. I squinted at the shock of light as I walked down the long white hallways, past the closed coffee shop, past the darkened candy store, past the sleepy security guard. Upstairs, the wards were alive with the night shift: orderlies wheeling newly admitted patients from the ER to their rooms, night float interns replacing IVs, clerks taking coffee breaks, nurses giving late-night doses of medicines. I felt blurry from the incongruity of it all. The Mercedes I had seen on Friday had disappeared, and another patient, all but dead, had been substituted. How could normal hospital life go on when such unearthly metamorphosis was occurring in its midst?

From the ICU doorway I saw George addressing Mercedes's family and friends, who were gathered around bed 10. I edged in closer, but the bed was obscured by the people standing around it. George was trying vainly to explain the finality of the situation. Mercedes's mother and two sisters were sobbing openly. Her brother stood motionless, bewildered. Some friends clustered around the sisters, hugging them and weeping. The aunt was pleading through her tears, "Isn't there another medication to try? Can't she be transferred to another hospital that has some experimental treatment for this? Don't you have an expert here who knows more?"

George escaped from the family when he caught sight of me and pulled me aside at the nurses' desk. He didn't seem surprised that I was standing in the ICU at two-thirty A.M. on a noncall night. "I've been trying for hours to explain her condition to them, but they just won't accept it. They know you from before. Maybe you can convince them."

I hovered by the supply cart, gathering my courage. In the surreal penumbra of the night ICU, the family appeared like a landscape: a range of backs, with shadowed peaks and dips, surrounded a central canyon. The fluorescent lights from the bed glinted up off their faces, creating awkward silhouettes and oddly sculpted ravines. I crept closer to the rocky-looking human formation, hoping that no one would notice me. Though queasy with nervousness, I was drawn forward by the light. I had to see what was on the other side of them. The air seemed to thin as I neared, and I had to work harder to breathe. My stomach rebelled, and I placed a hand on it to keep it down. A rivulet of yellowish green light seeped from between the mother and one of the cousins. I peered between them, into the crack of light, to see what lay in bed 10.

It was Mercedes, the one that I knew, with luminous cheeks and luxurious black hair cascading on the pillow. Her eyelids were softly closed, and the dark lashes rested in delicate parallel lines upon her olive cheeks. Her gold filigree cross floated on the plump, unblemished skin of her neck. Her respirations were calm and even, thanks to the ventilator. Apart from the breathing tube, she looked like a beautiful, healthy woman who was only sleeping.

From the electronic monitors overhead, though, a different story was evident. The red line that indicated the pressure inside Mercedes's head was undulating menacingly at the edge of the screen, nearly off the scale entirely. Despite all of the medical interventions, her brain was swelling inside the solid walls of her skull. A pressure chamber was roiling inside those unforgiving cranial bones, driving the base of her brain out the bottom of her skull. The respiratory center of her brain was already destroyed by the relentless onslaught. The cardiac center would soon follow.

Her brother noticed me standing behind the crowd, and the whole family turned to me. Nobody said anything, but I could feel their desperation. I was still trying to convince myself that this was the same Mercedes, this beautiful, sleeping woman whom we had so triumphantly diagnosed with Lyme disease. And all because I'd sent that damn test.

The intracranial pressure alarm clanged overhead, forcing me to look again at the ominous red line. It was creeping upward inexorably, mocking my ten years of training, my ludicrous Lyme test. It was all over. Mercedes's brain was slipping out, and I had no way to catch it.

I gazed at the nine people standing before me with their swollen eyes and tear-stained cheeks. How could I get them to believe that it was hopeless? I wanted to explain how brain death is different from a persistent vegetative state, where the cardiac and respiratory centers in the brain are intact. The body can breathe and pump blood for a long time, even if a person is unconscious, but brain death is different. Brain death is death. The body can no longer carry out the most basic functions. Even on a ventilator, the person cannot "live" for very long.

The family waited for words, but I could only stare at Mercedes. I wished I weren't a doctor. I wanted the freedom to hold false hope. Usually when I've had to explain to a family that a patient is dying, the patient graciously assists me by looking the part. They are pale or emaciated, or in pain, or struggling for breath: they look like death. But Mercedes refused to play along. Serenely she

lay, as beautiful as she'd been three days ago: no scars from repeated IVs and blood draws, no skin ulcers from prolonged immo-
bility, no dull coating of the skin from weeks of not seeing the sun.
No, she looked steadfastly alive.

There is no gray area in brain death, though. Mercedes's apparent vitality was just an illusion, created by the ventilator and the
short duration of her condition. In a day or two her body would
swell up and her skin would grow dusky. The cardiac center of her
brain would be smothered by the persistent intracranial swelling,
and her heart would finally give out. Then she would look like the
death that we know.

The hospital chaplain arrived, a rotund, balding Catholic priest
whom I had seen around the hospital but never met. A Bellevue
ID card and a wooden crucifix dangled from his neck. He slowly
made his way around the bed, touching each family member, offering tissues, murmuring softly. I could see the family members
relax ever so slightly at his touch. With his pudgy white hands, he
seemed to spread soft dapples of comfort. His job looked so much
more palatable than mine.

He glanced at me from across the bed, where he was standing
with one of the sisters, and he must have seen a tear welling up in
my eye. He circled back to where I stood and silently reached out
his arm and rested it on my shoulder. My stethoscope twisted off
my neck onto the floor as I leaned into his black tunic and began
to cry. His arms circled around me, and my body reacted to that
touch, unraveling and letting go. I collapsed deeper into his chest,
sobbing and sobbing. I prayed that I would regain my composure
so I could give the medical explanation that I had been dispatched
to deliver. But I could not. The family stared with quiet amaze-
ment as I cried uncontrollably in the arms of a strange priest. One
of the sisters left Mercedes's side and came to me. She stroked my
back, her fingers running along my hair. I only bawled louder.

Unable to stop, I mumbled something incoherent and dashed
out of the ICU, stumbling over my stethoscope on the floor. I escaped into a deserted conference room, where I sat hunched over
in the dark, crying. The sobs hacked out of me in dry, ragged
spasms as I fought for breath.

I couldn't understand why I was crying so hard. I did not know
Mercedes or her family very well. I had only by chance cared for

her on the first two days of her admission, and again only by
chance happened to telephone the ICU tonight for an unrelated
reason. I could so easily have missed one or both parts of her story,
but fate had me present at both ends.

Only seventy-two hours ago we doctors had celebrated our
prowess in saving her life. We had been so self-congratulatory
about our diagnosis. Were we being punished for our hubris? I
cried for Mercedes. I cried for her family and her two little children. I cried for all the patients who had died during my years at
Bellevue. I cried for the death of my belief that intellect conquers
all.

When I ran out of tears and stamina, I limped back to the ICU
and said quiet, embarrassed goodbyes to Mercedes's family. The
older sister handed me my stethoscope. She took my hand, looked
me straight in the eye, and said "thank you" with such sincerity
that I felt guilty. Her sister was dying, and instead of me comforting her, she was giving comfort to me.

I walked out of Bellevue in a daze. It was raining and I didn't
have an umbrella. Dawn hadn't yet risen over the East River, but
the air was lighter. I was exhausted, but felt strangely relieved.
That uncontrollable nervous energy had finally abated, and the
drenching rain felt cleansing.

I stayed up the rest of the night and wrote down as much about
Mercedes as I could remember. For the first time in my ten years
of medical training, sleep did not interest me.

The next day the ICU was utter chaos. Neurosurgeons, neurologists, infectious disease specialists, internists, ethicists, social workers, and nursing leaders were all packed into the ICU, intrigued
and horrified by the confounding case.

Mercedes's aunt was adamant about not turning the ventilator
off. She threatened a lawsuit and tried to intimidate the medical
team by flaunting her close friendship with a district attorney. I
doubted she really thought we were giving Mercedes substandard
care, but her panicky desperation made her willing to do anything
to prevent Mercedes's death.

The reality was that the family had no say in such a decision, because Mercedes was brain dead. The ventilator was merely breathing oxygen into a dead body. But the ICU staff agreed that we

could delay the moment of turning it off until everyone in the family had come to accept it.

Mercedes's entire extended family was camped out in the ICU. The nurses had long since given up enforcing the two-visitors-at-a-time rule. There was a young man in the terminal throes of AIDS in bed 8. He also possessed a huge, distraught Hispanic family. In the middle of everything, the organ transplant team slipped in, coolly evaluating Mercedes for possible organ donation. They sat in the corner reviewing her chart and making endless phone calls. In the end they could find no hospital to accept her organs, because of the unknown cause of her demise.

By nine that night, we had finally convinced the aunt that there was no more to do. With everyone at the bedside, we turned the ventilator off, and the breathing stopped. Mercedes was really dead.

Three weeks later I completed my internal medicine residency. My ten years at Bellevue had finally ended. There was little pomp as I limped out of the ICU all alone on a rainy Sunday morning after my final thirty-six-hour shift. Bed 2 was coding, but somebody else was taking care of it.

My body drooped with exhaustion, and my soul felt drained, aching for rest. I couldn't think of anything except unloading these 206 bones into a soft, warm, horizontal bed. I couldn't imagine opening a newspaper tomorrow, much less starting a fellowship or a job, as most of my colleagues were doing. I needed repose.

I knew that I had to get out of Bellevue, even if for just a little while — away from residency, away from training, away from death. I didn't know exactly what I wanted to do, but I knew I had to do something different.

I signed up with a locum tenens agency that would allow me to do short-term medical jobs anywhere in the country — after a two-month summer break, of course. I planned to work only one month at a time and then travel as far as the money would take me. I wanted to go to Central America to see the native countries of so many of my patients at Bellevue. I wanted to learn the language that had prevented me from communicating with them. And I had to write down my stories from Bellevue.

I purchased a laptop computer that fit into my backpack. I

stocked up on as many novels as I could carry and canceled my subscription to the *New England Journal of Medicine* for a full year.

But Mercedes continued to haunt me. For the next two years, between my travels and my locum assignments, I cornered every neuropathologist who could spare a moment to listen. I faxed her case history to experts at different medical centers and hounded them with phone calls, but no one had an answer for me. Mercedes's autopsy was performed at the New York City medical examiner's office, in the basement of the building where I'd stood as a nervous first-year medical student watching my first autopsy ten long years ago. I remembered the spacious, echoing room. I envisioned Mercedes's unblemished body stretched out on a metal table with the troughs around it to catch the blood. I wondered if the rubber-aproned pathology residents looked at her and saw a sleeping beauty. But the autopsy was "unrevealing," and every test was negative or "nondiagnostic." The medical examiner eventually signed the case out as "unknown etiology."

What will Mercedes's children think of the medical profession, I've often wondered. Their mother, of whom they'll have only dim recollections, died mysteriously, and the doctors never knew why. I wanted to go to them and apologize for our shortcomings, our limited intellect, our inadequate tools, the false pride that led us down the wrong path, our utter failure. But they are in their own world, being raised by a loving extended family.

And while I was intellectually frustrated, I felt strangely emotionally complete. That night in the ICU with Mercedes was excruciatingly painful, but it was also perhaps my most authentic experience as a doctor. Something was sad. And I cried. Simple logic, but so rarely adhered to in the high-octane world of academic medicine. Standing in the ICU, the chaplain's arms around me, surrounded by Mercedes's family, I felt like a person. Not like a physician or a scientist or an emissary from the world of rational logic, but just a person. Like each of the other persons who were locked in that tight circle around bed 10. There was a strength in that circle that I'd never felt from my colleagues or my professors. A strength that allowed me to relinquish the tense determination for intellectual mastery that had so supported me as a doctor. After years of toning those muscles, it was a deliriously aching relief to let them go slack.

And it didn't turn me away from medicine; it enticed me. I did need a break, but I knew that I would come back. I still wanted to learn more and be a smarter doctor, but I also wanted to be in this world populated with living, breathing, feeling people. I wanted to be in this sacred zone that was alive with real feelings, theirs and mine. I didn't know why I had initially entered the field of medicine ten years ago, but I now knew why I wanted to stay.

Reflections and Responses

1. Although "Merced" moves pretty much in a straightforward, day-by-day narrative, Ofri doesn't begin quite at the beginning. Where does she start her story, and why do you think she decides to start there? How does starting the way she does help her establish her point?

2. Note the frequent appearance of medical terms and abbreviations. Note, too, that Ofri rarely defines or glosses terms that a general reader would not be expected to know. Why do you think she does this? How does it affect your reading of the essay? What advantages does she gain by not defining all the terms and jargon? How much comes through in context?

3. What does Ofri learn from her experience with Mercedes? Why is the experience so important to her? How do you respond to Ofri's conclusion: were you hoping to learn what exactly caused Mercedes's death? How does Ofri handle the lack of that information?

SCOTT RUSSELL SANDERS

The Inheritance of Tools

A heritage is not only ethnic or cultural; it can also be a code of behavior, a system of manners, or even the practical skills that grandparents and parents often pass along to their children. In this widely reprinted personal essay, a writer, upon hearing of his father's sudden death, is reminded of the tools and techniques he inherited from his grandfather and father, which he in turn is now passing along to his own children. Though these tools and techniques have literally to do with carpentry, they take on extra duty in this finely crafted essay in which the hand tools themselves become equivalent to works of art: "I look at my claw hammer, the distillation of a hundred generations of carpenters, and consider that it holds up well beside those other classics—Greek vases, Gregorian chants, Don Quixote, *barbed fish hooks, candles, spoons."*

Scott Russell Sanders is the author of more than a dozen books of fiction, science fiction, essays, and nonfiction; these include Stone Country *(1985),* The Paradise of Bombs *(1987),* Secrets of the Universe *(1991),* Staying Put *(1993),* Hunting for Hope: A Father's Journeys *(1998), and* The Force of Spirit *(2001).* Writing from the Center *(1994) is a volume of essays about living and working in the Midwest. The recipient of many prestigious writing awards and fellowships, Sanders is a professor of English at Indiana University. "The Inheritance of Tools" originally appeared in* The North American Review *(1986) and was selected by* Gay Talese for The Best American Essays *1987.*

At just about the hour when my father died, soon after dawn one February morning when ice coated the windows like cataracts, I banged my thumb with a hammer. Naturally I swore at the hammer, the reckless thing, and in the moment of swearing I thought of what my father would say: "If you'd try hitting the nail it would go in a whole lot faster. Don't you know your thumb's not as hard as that hammer?" We both were doing carpentry that day, but far apart. He was building cupboards at my brother's place in Oklahoma; I was at home in Indiana, putting up a wall in the basement to make a bedroom for my daughter. By the time my mother called with news of his death — the long distance wires whittling her voice until it seemed too thin to bear the weight of what she had to say — my thumb was swollen. A week or so later a white scar in the shape of a crescent moon began to show above the cuticle, and month by month it rose across the pink sky of my thumbnail. It took the better part of a year for the scar to disappear, and every time I noticed it I thought of my father.

The hammer had belonged to him, and to his father before him. The three of us have used it to build houses and barns and chicken coops, to upholster chairs and crack walnuts, to make doll furniture and bookshelves and jewelry boxes. The head is scratched and pockmarked, like an old plowshare that has been working rocky fields, and it gives off the sort of dull sheen you see on fast creek water in the shade. It is a finishing hammer, about the weight of a bread loaf, too light, really, for framing walls, too heavy for cabinet work, with a curved claw for pulling nails, a rounded head for pounding, a fluted neck for looks, and a hickory handle for strength.

The present handle is my third one, bought from a lumberyard in Tennessee, down the road from where my brother and I were helping my father build his retirement house. I broke the previous one by trying to pull sixteen-penny nails out of floor joists — a foolish thing to do with a finishing hammer, as my father pointed out. "You ever hear of a crowbar?" he said. No telling how many handles he and my grandfather had gone through before me. My grandfather used to cut down hickory trees on his farm, saw them into slabs, cure the planks in his hayloft, and carve handles with a drawknife. The grain in hickory is crooked and knotty, and therefore tough, hard to split, like the grain in the two men who owned this hammer before me.

After proposing marriage to a neighbor girl, my grandfather used this hammer to build a house for his bride on a stretch of river bottom in northern Mississippi. The lumber for the place, like the hickory for the handle, was cut on his own land. By the day of the wedding he had not quite finished the house, and so right after the ceremony he took his wife home and put her to work. My grandmother had worn her Sunday dress for the wedding, with a fringe of lace tacked on around the hem in honor of the occasion. She removed this lace and folded it away before going out to help my grandfather nail siding on the house. "There she was in her good dress," he told me some fifty-odd years after that wedding day, "holding up them long pieces of clapboard while I hammered, and together we got the place covered up before dark." As the family grew to four, six, eight, and eventually thirteen, my grandfather used this hammer to enlarge his house room by room, like a chambered nautilus expanding its shell.

By and by the hammer was passed along to my father. One day he was up on the roof of our pony barn nailing shingles with it, when I stepped out the kitchen door to call him for supper. Before I could yell, something about the sight of him straddling the spine of that roof and swinging the hammer caught my eye and made me hold my tongue. I was five or six years old, and the world's commonplaces were still news to me. He would pull a nail from the pouch at his waist, bring the hammer down, and a moment later the *thunk* of the blow would reach my ears. And that is what had stopped me in my tracks and stilled my tongue, that momentary gap between seeing and hearing the blow. Instead of yelling from the kitchen door, I ran to the barn and climbed two rungs up the ladder — as far as I was allowed to go — and spoke quietly to my father. On our walk to the house he explained that sound takes time to make its way through air. Suddenly the world seemed larger, the air more dense, if sound could be held back like any ordinary traveler.

By the time I started using this hammer, at about the age when I discovered the speed of sound, it already contained houses and mysteries for me. The smooth handle was one my grandfather had made. In those days I needed both hands to swing it. My father would start a nail in a scrap of wood, and I would pound away until I bent it over.

"Looks like you got ahold of some of those rubber nails," he would tell me. "Here, let me see if I can find you some stiff ones." And he would rummage in a drawer until he came up with a fistful of more cooperative nails. "Look at the head," he would tell me. "Don't look at your hands, don't look at the hammer. Just look at the head of that nail and pretty soon you'll learn to hit it square."

Pretty soon I did learn. While he worked in the garage cutting dovetail joints for a drawer or skinning a deer or tuning an engine, I would hammer nails. I made innocent blocks of wood look like porcupines. He did not talk much in the midst of his tools, but he kept up a nearly ceaseless humming, slipping in and out of a dozen tunes in an afternoon, often running back over the same stretch of melody again and again, as if searching for a way out. When the humming did cease, I knew he was faced with a task requiring great delicacy or concentration, and I took care not to distract him.

He kept scraps of wood in a cardboard box — the ends of two-by-fours, slabs of shelving and plywood, odd pieces of molding — and everything in it was fair game. I nailed scraps together to fashion what I called boats or houses, but the results usually bore only faint resemblance to the visions I carried in my head. I would hold up these constructions to show my father, and he would turn them over in his hands admiringly, speculating about what they might be. My cobbled-together guitars might have been alien spaceships, my barns might have been models of Aztec temples, each wooden contraption might have been anything but what I had set out to make.

Now and again I would feel the need to have a chunk of wood shaped or shortened before I riddled it with nails, and I would clamp it in a vise and scrape at it with a handsaw. My father would let me lacerate the board until my arm gave out, and then he would wrap his hand around mine and help me finish the cut, showing me how to use my thumb to guide the blade, how to pull back on the saw to keep it from binding, how to let my shoulder do the work.

"Don't force it," he would say, "just drag it easy and give the teeth a chance to bite."

As the saw teeth bit down, the wood released its smell, each kind with its own fragrance, oak or walnut or cherry or pine — usually pine because it was the softest, easiest for a child to work. No matter how weathered or gray the board, no matter how warped and cracked, inside there was this smell waiting, as of something freshly baked. I gathered every smidgen of sawdust and stored it away in coffee cans, which I kept in a drawer of the workbench. When I did not feel like hammering nails, I would dump my sawdust on the concrete floor of the garage and landscape it into highways and farms and towns, running miniature cars and trucks along miniature roads. Looming as huge as a colossus, my father worked over and around me, now and again bending down to inspect my work, careful not to trample my creations. It was a landscape that smelled dizzyingly of wood. Even after a bath my skin would carry the smell, and so would my father's hair, when he lifted me for a bedtime hug.

I tell these things not only from memory but also from recent observation, because my own son now turns blocks of wood into nailed porcupines, dumps cans full of sawdust at my feet and sculpts highways on the floor. He learns how to swing a hammer from the elbow instead of the wrist, how to lay his thumb beside the blade to guide a saw, how to tap a chisel with a wooden mallet, how to mark a hole with an awl before starting a drill bit. My daughter did the same before him, and even now, on the brink of teenage aloofness, she will occasionally drag out my box of wood scraps and carpenter something. So I have seen my apprenticeship to wood and tools reenacted in each of my children, as my father saw his own apprenticeship renewed in me.

The saw I use belonged to him, as did my level and both of my squares, and all four tools had belonged to his father. The blade of the saw is the bluish color of gun barrels, and the maple handle, dark from the sweat of hands, is inscribed with curving leaf designs. The level is a shaft of walnut two feet long, edged with brass and pierced by three round windows in which air bubbles float in oil-filled tubes of glass. The middle window serves for testing if a surface is horizontal, the others for testing if a surface is plumb or vertical. My grandfather used to carry this level on the gun rack behind the seat in his pickup, and when I rode with him I would turn around to watch the bubbles dance. The larger of the two squares is called a framing square, a flat steel elbow, so beat up and tarnished you can barely make out the rows of numbers that show how to figure the cuts on rafters. The smaller one is called a try square, for marking right angles, with a blued steel blade for the shank and a brass-faced block of cherry for the head.

I was taught early on that a saw is not to be used apart from a square: "If you're going to cut a piece of wood," my father insisted, "you owe it to the tree to cut it straight."

Long before studying geometry, I learned there is a mystical virtue in right angles. There is an unspoken morality in seeking the level and the plumb. A house will stand, a table will bear weight, the sides of a box will hold together, only if the joints are square and the members upright. When the bubble is lined up between two marks etched in the glass tube of a level, you have aligned yourself with the forces that hold the universe together. When you miter the corners of a picture frame, each angle must be exactly forty-five degrees, as they are in the perfect triangles of Pythagoras, not a degree more or less. Otherwise the frame will hang crookedly, as if ashamed of itself and of its maker. No matter if the joints you are cutting do not show. Even if you are butting two pieces of wood together inside a cabinet, where no one except a wrecking crew will ever see them, you must take pains to ensure that the ends are square and the studs are plumb.

I took pains over the wall I was building on the day my father died. Not long after that wall was finished — paneled with tongue-and-groove boards of yellow pine, the nail holes filled with putty and the wood all stained and sealed — I came close to wrecking it one afternoon when my daughter ran howling up the stairs to announce that her gerbils had escaped from their cage and were hiding in my brand new wall. She could hear them scratching and squeaking behind her bed. Impossible! I said. How on earth could they get inside my drum-tight wall? Through the heating vent, she answered. I went downstairs, pressed my ear to the honey-colored wood, and heard the *scritch scritch* of tiny feet.

"What can we do?" my daughter wailed. "They'll starve to death, they'll die of thirst, they'll suffocate."

"Hold on," I soothed. "I'll think of something."

While I thought and she fretted, the radio on her bedside table delivered us the headlines: Several thousand people had died in a city in India from a poisonous cloud that had leaked overnight from a chemical plant. A nuclear-powered submarine had been launched. Rioting continued in South Africa. An airplane had been hijacked in the Mediterranean. Authorities calculated that several thousand homeless people slept on the streets within sight of the Washington Monument. I felt my usual helplessness in the face of all these calamities. But here was my daughter, weeping because her gerbils were holed up in a wall. This calamity I could handle.

"Don't worry," I told her. "We'll set food and water by the heating vent and lure them out. And if that doesn't do the trick, I'll tear the wall apart until we find them."

She stopped crying and gazed at me. "You'd really tear it apart? Just for my gerbils? The wall?" Astonishment slowed her down only for a second, however, before she ran to the workbench and began tugging at drawers, saying, "Let's see, what'll we need? Crowbar. Hammer. Chisels. I hope we don't have to use them — but just in case."

We didn't need the wrecking tools. I never had to assault my handsome wall, because the gerbils eventually came out to nibble at a dish of popcorn. But for several hours I studied the tongue-and-groove skin I had nailed up on the day of my father's death, considering where to begin prying. There were no gaps in that wall, no crooked joints.

I had botched a great many pieces of wood before I mastered the right angle with a saw, botched even more before I learned to miter a joint. The knowledge of these things resides in my hands and eyes and the webwork of muscles, not in the tools. There are machines for sale — powered miter boxes and radial arm saws, for instance — that will enable any casual soul to cut proper angles in boards. The skill is invested in the gadget instead of the person who uses it, and this is what distinguishes a machine from a tool. If I had to earn my keep by making furniture or building houses, I suppose I would buy powered saws and pneumatic nailers; the need for speed would drive me to it. But since I carpenter only for my own pleasure or to help neighbors or to remake the house around the ears of my family, I stick with hand tools. Most of the ones I own were given to me by my father, who also taught me how to wield them. The tools in my workbench are a double inheritance, for each hammer and level and saw is wrapped in a cloud of knowing.

All of these tools are a pleasure to look at and to hold. Merchants would never paste NEW NEW NEW! signs of them in stores. Their designs are old because they work, because they serve their purpose well. Like folk songs and aphorisms and the grainy bits of language, these tools have been pared down to essentials. I look at my claw hammer, the distillation of a hundred generations of carpenters, and consider that it holds up well beside those other classics — Greek vases, Gregorian chants, *Don Quixote,* barbed fish hooks, candles, spoons. Knowledge of hammering stretches back to the earliest humans who squatted beside fires, chipping flints. Anthropologists have a lovely name for those unworked rocks that served as the earliest hammers. "Dawn stones," they are called. Their only qualification for the work, aside from hardness, is that they fit the hand. Our ancestors used them for grinding corn, tapping awls, smashing bones. From dawn stones to this claw hammer is a great leap in time, but no great distance in design or imagination.

On that iced-over February morning when I smashed my thumb with the hammer, I was down in the basement framing the wall that my daughter's gerbils would later hide in. I was thinking of my father, as I always did whenever I built anything, thinking how he would have gone about the work, hearing in memory what he would have said about the wisdom of hitting the nail instead of my thumb. I had the studs and plates nailed together all square and trim, and was lifting the wall into place when the phone rang upstairs. My wife answered, and in a moment she came to the basement door and called down softly to me. The stillness in her voice made me drop the framed wall and hurry upstairs. She told me my father was dead. Then I heard the details over the phone from my mother. Building a set of cupboards for my brother in Oklahoma, he had knocked off work early the previous afternoon because of cramps in his stomach. Early this morning, on his way into the kitchen of my brother's trailer, maybe going for a glass of water, so early that no one else was awake, he slumped down on the linoleum and his heart quit.

For several hours I paced around inside my house, upstairs and down, in and out of every room, looking for the right door to open and knowing there was no such door. My wife and children followed me and wrapped me in arms and backed away again, circling and staring as if I were on fire. Where was the door, the door, the door? I kept wondering. My smashed thumb turned purple and throbbed, making me furious. I wanted to cut it off and rush outside and scrape away the snow and hack a hole in the frozen earth and bury the shameful thing.

I went down into the basement, opened a drawer in my workbench, and stared at the ranks of chisels and knives. Oiled and sharp, as my father would have kept them, they gleamed at me like teeth. I took up a clasp knife, pried out the longest blade, and tested the edge on the hair of my forearm. A tuft came away cleanly, and I saw my father testing the sharpness of tools on his own skin, the blades of axes and knives and gouges and hoes, saw the red hair shaved off in patches from his arms and the backs of his hands. "That will cut bear," he would say. He never cut a bear with his blades, now my blades, but he cut deer, dirt, wood. I closed the knife and put it away. Then I took up the hammer and went back to work on my daughter's wall, snugging the bottom plate against a chalk line on the floor, shimming the top plate against the joists overhead, plumbing the studs with my level, making sure before I drove the first nail that every line was square and true.

Reflections and Responses

1. Consider the way Sanders opens the essay. Given the significance of his father's death, why does he mention his injured thumb in the same sentence? Why is this a relevant detail? How does it figure later in the essay?

2. Note the many concrete references to carpentry in the essay. In what ways is the language of tools and carpentry related to other aspects of life? Why is there "a mystical virtue in right angles"?

3. In rereading the essay, try to reconstruct the chronology of the February day that Sanders's father died. First, consider how Sanders constructs his narrative. Why does he deviate from a straightforward, hour-by-hour account? Why, for example, does he introduce the story about his daughter's gerbils? In what ways does that anecdote deepen the essay's theme?

AMY TAN

Mother Tongue

For many American students, the language spoken at home is far different from the one spoken in school. For that reason, many students learn to switch back and forth between two languages, the one they use with their family and the one required for their education. Such switching, however, need not be confining or demoralizing. Rather, it can enhance one's sensitivity to language and can even be creatively enabling, as the Chinese American novelist Amy Tan suggests in this charming personal essay. "Language is the tool of my trade," Tan writes. "And I use them all — all the Englishes I grew up with."

Born into a Chinese family that had recently arrived in California, Amy Tan began writing as a child and after graduation from college worked for several years as a freelance business writer. In the mid-eighties, she began writing fiction, basing much of her work on family stories. She is the author of several best-selling novels: The Joy Luck Club *(1989), which was a finalist for both the National Book Award and National Book Critics Circle Award and was made into a motion picture directed by Wayne Wang,* The Kitchen God's Wife *(1991),* The Hundred Secret Senses *(1995), and* The Bonesetter's Daughter *(2000). In 1992 she published a popular children's book,* The Moon Lady. *"Mother Tongue" originally appeared in the* Threepenny Review *(1990) and was selected by Joyce Carol Oates for* The Best American Essays 1991.

I am not a scholar of English or literature. I cannot give you much more than personal opinions on the English language and its variations in this country or others.

I am a writer. And by that definition, I am someone who has always loved language. I am fascinated by language in daily life. I spend a great deal of my time thinking about the power of language — the way it can evoke an emotion, a visual image, a complex idea, or a simple truth. Language is the tool of my trade. And I use them all — all the Englishes I grew up with.

Recently, I was made keenly aware of the different Englishes I do use. I was giving a talk to a large group of people, the same talk I had already given to half a dozen other groups. The nature of the talk was about my writing, my life, and my book, *The Joy Luck Club*. The talk was going along well enough, until I remembered one major difference that made the whole talk sound wrong. My mother was in the room. And it was perhaps the first time she had heard me give a lengthy speech, using the kind of English I have never used with her. I was saying things like, "The intersection of memory upon imagination" and "There is an aspect of my fiction that relates to thus-and-thus"— a speech filled with carefully wrought grammatical phrases, burdened, it suddenly seemed to me, with nominalized forms, past perfect tenses, conditional phrases, all the forms of standard English that I had learned in school and through books, the forms of English I did not use at home with my mother.

Just last week, I was walking down the street with my mother, and I again found myself conscious of the English I was using, the English I do use with her. We were talking about the price of new and used furniture and I heard myself saying this: "Not waste money that way." My husband was with us as well, and he didn't notice any switch in my English. And then I realized why. It's because over the twenty years we've been together I've often used that same kind of English with him, and sometimes he even uses it with me. It has become our language of intimacy, a different sort of English that relates to family talk, the language I grew up with.

So you'll have some idea of what this family talk I heard sounds like, I'll quote what my mother said during a recent conversation which I videotaped and then transcribed. During this conversation, my mother was talking about a political gangster in Shanghai who had the same last name as her family's, Du, and how the gangster in his early years wanted to be adopted by her family, which was rich by comparison. Later, the gangster became more powerful, far richer than my mother's family, and one day showed up at my mother's wedding to pay his respects. Here's what she said in part:

"Du Yusong having business like fruit stand. Like off the street kind. He is Du like Du Zong — but not Tsung-ming Island people. The local people call putong, the river east side, he belong to that side local people. That man want to ask Du Zong father take him in like become own family. Du Zong father wasn't look down on him, but didn't take seriously, until that man big like become a mafia. Now important person, very hard to inviting him. Chinese way, came only to show respect, don't stay for dinner. Respect for making big celebration, he shows up. Mean gives lots of respect. Chinese custom. Chinese social life that way. If too important won't have to stay too long. He come to my wedding. I didn't see, I heard it. I gone to boy's side, they have YMCA dinner. Chinese age I was nineteen."

You should know that my mother's expressive command of English belies how much she actually understands. She reads the *Forbes* report, listens to *Wall Street Week,* converses daily with her stockbroker, reads all of Shirley MacLaine's books with ease — all kinds of things I can't begin to understand. Yet some of my friends tell me they understand 50 percent of what my mother says. Some say they understand 80 to 90 percent. Some say they understand none of it, as if she were speaking pure Chinese. But to me, my mother's English is perfectly clear, perfectly natural. It's my mother tongue. Her language, as I hear it, is vivid, direct, full of observation and imagery. That was the language that helped shape the way I saw things, expressed things, made sense of the world.

Lately, I've been giving more thought to the kind of English my mother speaks. Like others, I have described it to people as "broken" or "fractured" English. But I wince when I say that. It has always bothered me that I can think of no way to describe it other than "broken," as if it were damaged and needed to be fixed, as if it lacked a certain wholeness and soundness. I've heard other terms used, "limited English," for example. But they seem just as bad, as if everything is limited, including people's perceptions of the limited English speaker.

I know this for a fact, because when I was growing up, my mother's "limited" English limited *my* perception of her. I was ashamed of her English. I believed that her English reflected the quality of what she had to say. That is, because she expressed them imperfectly her thoughts were imperfect. And I had plenty of empirical evidence to support me: the fact that people in department stores, at banks, and at restaurants did not take her seriously, did not give her good service, pretended not to understand her, or even acted as if they did not hear her.

My mother has long realized the limitations of her English as well. When I was fifteen, she used to have me call people on the phone to pretend I was she. In this guise, I was forced to ask for information or even to complain and yell at people who had been rude to her. One time it was a call to her stockbroker in New York. She had cashed out her small portfolio and it just so happened we were going to go to New York the next week, our very first trip outside California. I had to get on the phone and say in an adolescent voice that was not very convincing, "This is Mrs. Tan."

And my mother was standing in the back whispering loudly, "Why he don't send me check, already two weeks late. So mad he lie to me, losing me money."

And then I said in perfect English, "Yes, I'm getting rather concerned. You had agreed to send the check two weeks ago, but it hasn't arrived."

Then she began to talk more loudly. "What he want, I come to New York tell him front of his boss, you cheating me?" And I was trying to calm her down, make her be quiet, while telling the stockbroker, "I can't tolerate any more excuses. If I don't receive the check immediately, I am going to have to speak to your manager when I'm in New York next week." And sure enough, the following week there we were in front of this astonished stockbroker, and I was sitting there red-faced and quiet, and my mother, the real Mrs. Tan, was shouting at his boss in her impeccable broken English.

We used a similar routine just five days ago, for a situation that was far less humorous. My mother had gone to the hospital for an appointment, to find out about a benign brain tumor a CAT scan had revealed a month ago. She said she had spoken very good English, her best English, no mistakes. Still, she said, the hospital did not apologize when they said they had lost the CAT scan and she had come for nothing. She said they did not seem to have any sympathy when she told them she was anxious to know the exact diagnosis, since her husband and son had both died of brain tumors. She said they would not give her any more information until the next time and she would have to make another appointment for that. So she said she would not leave until the doctor called her daughter. She wouldn't budge. And when the doctor finally called her daughter, me, who spoke in perfect English — lo and behold — we had assurances the CAT scan would be found, promises that a conference call on Monday would be held, and apologies for any suffering my mother had gone through for a most regrettable mistake.

I think my mother's English almost had an effect on limiting my possibilities in life as well. Sociologists and linguists probably will tell you that a person's developing language skills are more influenced by peers. But I do think that the language spoken in the family, especially in immigrant families which are more insular, plays a large role in shaping the language of the child. And I believe that it affected my results on achievement tests, IQ tests, and the SAT. While my English skills were never judged as poor, compared to math, English could not be considered my strong suit. In grade school I did moderately well, getting perhaps B's, sometimes B-pluses, in English and scoring perhaps in the sixtieth or seventieth percentile on achievement tests. But those scores were not good enough to override the opinion that my true abilities lay in math and science, because in those areas I achieved A's and scored in the ninetieth percentile or higher.

This was understandable. Math is precise; there is only one correct answer. Whereas, for me at least, the answers on English tests were always a judgment call, a matter of opinion and personal experience. Those tests were constructed around items like fill-in-the-blank sentence completion, such as, "Even though Tom was ____, Mary thought he was ____." And the correct answer always seemed to be the most bland combinations of thoughts, for example, "Even though Tom was shy, Mary thought he was charming," with the grammatical structure "even though" limiting the correct answer to some sort of semantic opposites, so you wouldn't get answers like, "Even though Tom was foolish, Mary thought he was ridiculous." Well, according to my mother, there were very few limitations as to what Tom could have been and what Mary might have thought of him. So I never did well on tests like that.

The same was true with word analogies, pairs of words in which you were supposed to find some sort of logical, semantic relationship — for example, "*Sunset* is to *nightfall* as ____ is to ____." And here you would be presented with a list of four possible pairs, one of which showed the same kind of relationship: *red* is to *stoplight, bus* is to *arrival, chills* is to *fever, yawn* is to *boring.* Well, I could never think that way. I knew what the tests were asking, but I could not block out of my mind the images already created by the first pair, "*sunset* is to *nightfall*" — and I would see a burst of colors against a darkening sky, the moon rising, the lowering of a curtain of stars. And all the other pairs of words — red, bus, stoplight, boring — just threw up a mass of confusing images, making it impossible for me to sort out something as logical as saying: "A sunset precedes nightfall" is the same as "a chill precedes a fever." The only way I would have gotten that answer right would have been to imagine an associative situation, for example, my being disobedient and staying out past sunset, catching a chill at night, which turns into feverish pneumonia as punishment, which indeed did happen to me.

I have been thinking about all this lately, about my mother's English, about achievement tests. Because lately I've been asked, as a writer, why there are not more Asian Americans represented in American literature. Why are there few Asian Americans enrolled in creative writing programs? Why do so many Chinese students go into engineering? Well, these are broad sociological questions I can't begin to answer. But I have noticed in surveys — in fact, just last week — that Asian students, as a whole, always do significantly better on math achievement tests than in English. And this makes me think that there are other Asian-American students whose English spoken in the home might also be described as "broken" or "limited." And perhaps they also have teachers who are steering them away from writing and into math and science, which is what happened to me.

Fortunately, I happen to be rebellious in nature and enjoy the challenge of disproving assumptions made about me. I became an English major my first year in college, after being enrolled as pre-med. I started writing nonfiction as a freelancer the week after I was told by my former boss that writing was my worst skill and I should hone my talents toward account management.

But it wasn't until 1985 that I finally began to write fiction. And at first I wrote using what I thought to be wittily crafted sentences, sentences that would finally prove I had mastery over the English language. Here's an example from the first draft of a story that later made its way into *The Joy Luck Club,* but without this line: "That was my mental quandary in its nascent state." A terrible line, which I can barely pronounce.

Fortunately, for reasons I won't get into today, I later decided I should envision a reader for the stories I would write. And the reader I decided upon was my mother, because these were stories about mothers. So with this reader in mind — and in fact she did read my early drafts — I began to write stories using all the Englishes I grew up with: the English I spoke to my mother, which for lack of a better term might be described as "simple"; the English she used with me, which for lack of a better term might be described as "broken"; my translation of her Chinese, which could certainly be described as "watered down"; and what I imagined to be her translation of her Chinese if she could speak in perfect English, her internal language, and for that I sought to preserve the essence, but neither an English nor a Chinese structure. I wanted to capture what language ability tests can never reveal: her intent, her passion, her imagery, the rhythms of her speech and the nature of her thoughts.

Apart from what any critic had to say about my writing, I knew I had succeeded where it counted when my mother finished reading my book and gave me her verdict: "So easy to read."

Reflections and Responses

1. What "Englishes" did Amy Tan grow up with? Why does she feel uncomfortable with the term "broken English"? Why do you think she still uses that term toward the end of her essay?

2. What point is Tan making about language tests? Why did she perform less well on them than she did on math and science? In her opinion, what aspects of language do the tests fail to take into account?

3. Tan cites a sentence — "That was my mental quandary in its nascent state" — that she deleted from *The Joy Luck Club*. What do you think she dislikes about that sentence? What kind of English does it represent? Does it or doesn't it demonstrate a "mastery" of the English language?

2

The Attentive Mind: Observation, Reflection, Insight

RUDOLPH CHELMINSKI

Turning Point

FROM SMITHSONIAN

Warning: As you read this essay, your palms may begin to sweat and your stomach tighten, for it contains a breathtaking account of one of the most astonishing acrobatic feats ever performed. Few people today remember the name of Philippe Petit, the daring, enigmatic character who at the age of twenty-five mesmerized New Yorkers early one August morning by walking and dancing on a high wire he had secretly strung across the tops of the twin towers of the World Trade Center. In "Turning Point," Rudolph Chelminski recounts his visit with Petit at the top of the 1,360-foot-high South Tower just a few weeks before it would be destroyed by the 9/11 attacks. As Chelminski observes, Petit's feat was far more than a stunt or daredevil routine but instead represented "a creative statement of true theater, as valid as ballet or modern dance."

Rudolph Chelminski is a freelance writer living in France. Formerly a Life *magazine staff correspondent in Paris and Moscow, he has written for numerous major American and French publications, including* Life, Time, Fortune, People, Money, Playboy, Geo, Town & Country, Reader's Digest, Smithsonian, Signature, Saturday Review, Wired, Reporter, France Today, Le Monde, *and others. He is author of four books and has never won a single prize. Except, Chelminski says, the best one of all: having managed for more than thirty years to support himself and family as a freelancer. "Turning Point" first appeared in* Smithsonian *and was selected by Stephen Jay Gould for* The Best American Essays *2002.*

What turned the tide of public regard [for the World Trade Center] was not the bigness of the place but the way it could be momentarily captured by fanciful gestures on a human scale. It was the French high-wire artist Philippe Petit crossing between the towers on a tight-rope in 1974 . . .

—*The New York Times*, September 13, 2001

Was it only twenty-seven years ago? It seems a lifetime, or two, has passed since that August morning in 1974 when Philippe Petit, a slim, young Frenchman, upstaged Richard Nixon by performing one of the few acts more sensational — in those faraway times — than resigning the presidency of the United States.

A week before his twenty-sixth birthday, the nimble Petit clandestinely strung a cable between the not-yet-completed Twin Towers, already dominating lower Manhattan's skyline, and for the better part of an hour walked back and forth over the void, demonstrating his astonishing obsession to one hundred thousand or so wide-eyed gawkers gathered so far below.

I missed that performance, but last summer, just two weeks before the 1,360-foot-tall towers would come to symbolize a ghastly new reality, I persuaded Petit to accompany me to the top and show me how he did it and, perhaps, explain why. I was driven by a long-standing curiosity. Ever since reading about his exploit in New York, I had felt a kind of familiarity with this remarkable fellow. Years before, I had watched him at close range and much lower altitude, in another city on the other side of the pond.

In the 1960s, the Montparnasse area of Paris was animated by a colorful fauna of celebrities, eccentrics, and artistic characters. On any given day, you might run into Giacometti walking bent forward like one of his skinny statues, Raymond Duncan (Isadora's brother) in his goofy sandals and Roman toga, or Jean-Paul Sartre morosely seeking the decline of capitalism in the Communist daily, *L'Humanité*. And after nightfall, if you hung around long enough, you were almost certain to see Philippe Petit.

When he might appear was anyone's guess, but his hangouts were pretty well known: the corner of Rue de Buci and Boulevard St. Germain; the sidewalk outside Les Deux Magots, or directly under the terrace windows of La Coupole. Silent and mysterious, this skinny, pasty-faced kid dressed in black would materialize unannounced on his unicycle, a shock of pale blond hair escaping from under a battered top hat. He would draw a circle of white chalk on the sidewalk, string a rope between two trees, hop up onto it, and, impassive and mute as a carp, go into an improvised show that combined mime, juggling, prestidigitation, and the precarious balancing act of loose-rope walking. After an hour or so he would pass the hat and, as wordlessly as he had arrived, disappear into the night.

Then, on a drizzly morning in June 1971, the kid in black suddenly showed up dancing on a barely perceptible wire between the massive towers of Notre Dame Cathedral. For nearly three hours, he walked back and forth, mugged, saluted, and juggled Indian clubs while angry gendarmes waited for him to come down. When he finally did, they arrested him for disturbing the peace.

Disturbing the peace was a good part of what it was all about, of course, because Petit was out to prove something. Notre Dame was his first great coup, the sensational stunt that was to become his trademark. It was also his first declaration of status: he was not a mere street entertainer but a performer, an artiste. Ever since that June morning, he has dedicated himself to demonstrating his passionate belief that the high wire — his approach to the high wire, that is — transcends the cheap hype of circus "daredevil" routines to become a creative statement of true theater, as valid as ballet or modern dance.

Getting that point across has never been easy. After gratifying Petit with a few front-page pictures, the French establishment gave a Gallic shrug, dismissed him as a youthful crank, and returned to more serious matters — like having lunch and talking politics. There was a very interesting story to be told about this young loner who had learned the art of the *funambule* (literally, "rope walker") all by himself as a teenager, but the Parisian press ignored it. Within a couple of days, his Notre Dame stunt was largely forgotten.

Stung, Petit resolved to take his art elsewhere and began a long vagabondage around the world, returning to Paris for brief spells before setting off again. Traveling as light as a medieval minstrel and living hand to mouth, he carried his mute personage from city to city, juggling for his supper. None of his onlookers could know that back in his tiny Parisian studio — a rented broom closet he had somehow converted into a dwelling — he had a folder marked "projects."

Two years after the Notre Dame caper, the skinny figure in black appeared with his balancing pole between the gigantic northern pylons of the Sydney Harbour Bridge in Australia. Petit had strung his cable there just as furtively as he had done at Notre Dame, but this time the police reacted with brainless if predictable fury, attempting to force him down by cutting one of his cavalettis, the lateral guy ropes that hold a sky walker's cable steady. Flung a foot up in the air when the cavaletti sprang free, Petit managed to land square on the cable and keep his balance. He came in and was manacled, led to court, and found guilty of the usual crimes. The owner of a Sydney circus offered to pay his $250 fine in return for a tightrope walk two days later over the lions' cage.

And then came the World Trade Center. Petit had been planning it ever since he was nineteen when, in a dentist's waiting room, he saw an article with an artist's rendering of the gigantic towers planned for New York's financial district. ("When I see three oranges I juggle," he once said, "and when I see two towers I walk.") He ripped the article from the magazine and slipped it into his projects file.

The World Trade Center would be the ultimate test of Petit's fanatically meticulous planning. For Notre Dame and Sydney, he had copied keys to open certain locks, picked others, and hacksawed his way through still others in order to sneak his heavy material up into place for the sky walk. But New York presented a much more complicated challenge. The World Trade Center buildings were fearfully higher than anything he had ever tackled, making it impossible to set up conventional cavalettis. And how to get a cable across the 140-foot gap between the South and North Towers, anyway, in the face of omnipresent security crews?

There was one factor in Petit's favor: the buildings were still in the final stages of construction, and trucks were regularly delivering all sorts of material to the basement docks, to be transferred to a freight elevator and brought up to the floors by workers of all descriptions. Wearing hard hats, Petit and an accomplice hauled his gear to the top of the South Tower (his walking cable passed off as antenna equipment) while two other friends similarly made their way to the roof of the North Tower, armed with a bow and arrow and a spool of stout fishing line. Come nightfall, they shot the arrow and line across the 140-foot gap between the towers. Petit retrieved the line, pulled it over until he was in possession of the stronger nylon cord attached to it, then tied on the heavy rope that would be used to carry his steel walking cable over to the other side.

As Petit paid out the rope and then the cable, gravity took over. The cable ran wild, shooting uncontrollably through his hands and snaking down the side of the giant building before coming up short with a titanic *thwonk!* at the steel beam to which Petit had anchored it. On the North Tower, holding fast to the other end of the heavy rope, his friends were pulled perilously close to the roof's edge. Gradually, the four regained control and spent the rest of the night hours pulling the cable up, double-cinching the anchor points, getting it nearly level, tensioning it to three tons with a ratchet, and finally attaching a set of nearly horizontal cavalettis to the buildings. At a few minutes past seven A.M., August 7, 1974, just as the first construction workers were arriving on the rooftop, Petit seized his balancing pole and stepped out over the void.

The conditions weren't exactly ideal. Petit had not slept for forty-eight hours, and now he saw that the hurry-up rigging job he had carried out in the dark had resulted in a cable that zigzagged where the improvised cavalettis joined it. Sensitive to wind, temperature, and any sway of the buildings, it was so alive — swooping, rolling, and twisting. At slightly more than twenty-six feet, his balancing pole was longer and heavier — fifty-five pounds — than any he had ever used before. Greater weight meant greater stability, but such a heavy load is hard enough to tote around on terra firma, let alone on a thin wire in midair at an insane altitude. It would require an uncommon debauch of nervous energy, but energy was the one thing Petit had plenty of.

With his eyes riveted to the edge of the far tower — wire walkers aren't supposed to look down — Petit glided his buffalo-hide slippers along the cable, feeling his way until he was halfway across. He knelt, put his weight on one knee, and swung his right arm free. This was his "salute," the signature gesture of the high-wire artist. Each has his own, and each is an individual trademark creation. Arising, he continued to the North Tower, hopped off the wire, double-checked the cable's anchoring points, made a few adjustments, and hopped back on.

By now traffic had stopped in the environs of Wall Street, and Petit could already hear the first police and ambulance sirens as he nimbly set forth again. Off he went, humming and mumbling to himself, puffing grunts of concentration at tricky moments. Halfway across, he steadied, halted, then knelt again. And then, God in heaven, he lay down, placing his spine directly atop the cable and resting the balancing pole on his stomach. Breathless, in Zen-like calm, he lay there for a long moment, contemplating the red-eyed seabird hovering motionless above him.

Time to get up. But how do you do it, I asked Petit as we stood together on the roof of the South Tower, when the only thing between you and certain death is a cable under your body and fifty-five extra pounds lying on your belly?

"All the weight on the right foot," he replied with a shrug. "I draw my right foot back along the cable and move the balancing bar lower down below my belt. I get a little lift from the wire, because it is moving up and down. Then I do a sit-up and rise to a standing position, with all the weight on my right foot. It takes some practice."

He got up. Unable to resist the pleasure of seeing New York at his feet, he caressed the side of the building with a glance and slowly panned his eyes all the way down to the gridlocked traffic below. Then he flowed back to the South Tower. "I could hear the horns of cars below me," he recalled, relishing the memory. "I could hear the applause too. The *rumeur* [clamor] of the crowd rose up to me from four hundred meters below. No other show person has ever heard a sound like that."

Now, as he glided along north to south, a clutch of police officers, rescue crews, and security men hovered with arms outstretched to pull him in. But Petit hadn't finished. Inches from their grasp, he did a wire walker's turnaround, slipping his feet 180 degrees and swinging his balancing bar around to face in the other direction. He did his elegant "torero's" walk and his "promenader's" walk; he knelt; he did another salute; he sat in casual repose, lord of his domain; he stood and balanced on one foot.

After seven crossings and forty-five minutes of air dancing, it began to rain. For his finale he ran along the cable to give himself up. "Running, ah! ah!" he had written in one of his early books. "That's the laughter of the wire walker." Then he ran into the arms of waiting police.

Petit's astonishing star turn created a sensation the likes of which few New Yorkers had ever seen. Years later, the art critic Calvin Tompkins was still so impressed by what Petit had done that he wrote in *The New Yorker:* "He achieved the almost unimaginable feat of investing the World Trade Center . . . with a thrilling and terrible beauty."

Ever resourceful, Petit worked out a deal with the Manhattan district attorney. In lieu of punishment or fine, and as penance for his artistic crime, he agreed to give a free performance in Central Park. The following week he strung a 600-foot wire across Turtle Pond, from a tree on one side to Belvedere Castle on the other. And this time he nearly fell. He was wearing the same walking slippers and using the same balancing pole, but security was relaxed among the fifteen thousand people who had come to watch him perform, and kids began climbing and jumping on his cavalettis. The wire twitched, and suddenly he felt himself going beyond the point of return.

But he didn't go all the way down. Instinctively squirming as he dropped, he hooked a leg over the wire. Somehow, he managed to swing himself back up, get vertical, and carry on with the performance. The crowd applauded warmly, assuming it was all part of the act, but Petit doesn't enjoy the memory. Falling is the wire walker's shame, he says, and due only to a lack of concentration.

In the years since his World Trade Center triumph, Petit has disdainfully turned away all offers to profit from it. "I could have become a millionaire," he told me. "Everyone was after me to endorse their products, but I was not going to walk a wire dressed in a hamburger suit, and I was not going to say I succeeded because I was wearing such and such a shirt." Continuing to operate as a stubbornly independent freelance artist, he has organized and starred in more than seventy performances around the world, all without safety nets. They have included choreographed strolls across the Louisiana Superdome in New Orleans, between the towers of the Laon Cathedral in France, and a "Peace Walk" between the Jewish and Arab quarters of Jerusalem. In 1989, on the bicentennial of the French Revolution, he took center stage in Paris — legally and officially this time — by walking the 2,300-foot gap between the Trocadéro esplanade on the Right Bank, over the Seine, and up to the second tier of the Eiffel Tower.

Today, at fifty-two, Petit is somewhat heavier than in his busking days in Paris, and his hair has turned a reddish blond, but neither his energy nor his overpowering self-confidence has waned in the least. He shares a pleasantly rustic farmhouse at the edge of the Catskills near Woodstock, New York, with his longtime companion, Kathy O'Donnell, daughter of a former Manhattan publishing executive. She handles the planning, producing, problem-solving, and money-raising aspects of Petit's enterprises while they both think up new high-wire projects and he painstakingly prepares them. Petit supplements his income from performances with, among other things, book royalties and fees from giving lectures and workshops.

His preferred place of study is his New York City office. Knowing what an artiste he is, you would not expect to find him in an ordinary building, and you would be right. Petit hangs out at the Cathedral of St. John the Divine, the world's biggest Gothic cathedral, at Amsterdam Avenue and 112th Street. His office is a balustraded aerie in the cathedral's triforium, the narrow gallery high above the vast nave. Behind a locked entryway, up a suitably medieval spiral staircase and then down a stone passageway, the rare visitor to his domain comes upon a sturdy door bearing a small framed sign: *Philippe Petit, Artist in Residence.* Behind that door, stowed as neatly as a yacht's navigational gear, lie his treasures: thousands of feet of rope coiled just so, all manner of rigging and tensioning equipment, floor-to-ceiling archives, maps and models of past and future walk projects, and shelves upon shelves of technical and reference books.

It was another of his coups that got him there. In 1980 he offered to walk the length of the nave to raise funds for the cathedral's building program. He was sure he had the perfect occasion for it: Ascension Day. The cathedral's then dean, the ebullient James Parks Morton, famous for his support of the arts, was enthusiastic, but his board of trustees vetoed the idea as too dangerous. Petit sneaked a cable crosswise over the nave and did his walk anyway. Once again the police came to arrest him, but Morton spoiled their day by announcing that Petit was artist in residence and the cathedral was his workplace. And so he came to be.

Over the years, taking his title seriously, Petit reciprocated by carrying out a dozen wire walks inside and outside the cathedral. He figures that by now he has raised half a million dollars for the still uncompleted cathedral's building program, and enjoys pointing out the small stone carving of a wire walker niched in among the saints in the main portal. "It is high art," Morton says of Petit's work. "There is a documented history of wire walkers in cathedrals and churches. It's not a new idea, but his walk here was his first in an American cathedral."

Sometimes after six P.M., when the lights go out, the big front door slams shut, and the cathedral closes down for the night, Petit is left alone in the mineral gloom of St. John with his writing, sketches, calculations, chess problems, poetry, and reveries. The comparison to Quasimodo is immediate and obvious, of course, but unlike Notre Dame's famous hunchback, Petit wants nothing more than to be seen, in the ever greater, more ambitious, and spectacular shows that fill his dreams. One night after he took me up to his cathedral office, he gazed longingly at a print of the Brooklyn Bridge — what a walk that could be! But there is, he assured me, plenty more in his projects file. A walk on Easter Island, from the famous carved heads to the volcano. Or the half-mile stretch over open water between the Sydney Harbour Bridge and the celebrated Opera House.

Even more than all these, though, there is one walk — *the* walk, the ultimate, the masterpiece — that has filled his dreams for more than a decade. It's the Grand Canyon. Prospecting in the heart of the Navajo nation by air in 1988, Petit discovered the ideal spot for crowning his career: a ruggedly beautiful landscape off the road from Flagstaff to Grand Canyon Village, where a noble mesa soars at the far end of a 1,200-foot gap from the canyon's edge. The gap is deeper than it is wide, 1,600 feet straight down to the Little Colorado River.

Petit's eyes glowed as he went through the mass of blueprints, maps, drawings, and models he has produced over all the years of planning the Canyon Walk. Only one thing is missing: money. Twice now, the money people have backed out at the last minute.

But none of that seemed to matter when I spoke to Petit a few days after the September 11 catastrophe struck. He could scarcely find words for his sorrow at the loss of so many lives, among them people he knew well — elevator operators, tour guides, maintenance workers. "I feel my house has been destroyed," he said. "Very often I would take family and friends there. It was my pride as a poet and a lover of beautiful things to show as many people as possible the audacity of those impossible monoliths."

Haunted, as we all are, by the images of the towers in their final moments, Petit told me it was his hope that they would be remembered not as they appeared then but as they were on that magical August day more than a generation ago, when he danced between them on a wire and made an entire city look up in awe. "In a very small way I helped frame them with glory," he said, "and I want to remember them in their glory."

Reflections and Responses

1. Chelminski begins his essay by setting the context for an interview with Petit. He says that he persuaded Petit "to accompany me to the top and show me how he did it and, perhaps, explain why." What does Chelminski learn from Petit? Why do you think he places so little of the interview in dialogue format? How does he use the information he receives from Petit? In your opinion, does Petit give him an explanation of *why* he did what he did?

2. Chelminski had clearly begun to work on this essay and interview before the surprise attack on the World Trade Center. How do you think the devastation of the towers affected Chelminski's essay? How different would it be had the attacks never occurred? What connection does Chelminski see between Petit's feat and the Twin Towers? How is that connection supported by the way he concludes his essay?

3. Compare "Turning Point" with the next essay in this section, Annie Dillard's "The Stunt Pilot." In what ways are the two essays similar? How does each author construct a profile? How does each author use terms from art to describe their subjects' exploits?

ANNIE DILLARD

The Stunt Pilot

*Creative expression can take many forms; it need not refer only to literature,
painting, or music. We can find creativity in craft and design, in the movements of dancers and athletes, and even — as the following essay reveals — in
the aerobatics of a stunt pilot. Observing the breathtaking dives and spins,
the "loops and arabesques" of a celebrated pilot, Annie Dillard is struck by
their resemblance to artistic expression. She finds in the pilot's use of space a
new kind of beauty, one that seems to encompass all the arts — poetry, painting, music, sculpture: "The black plane dropped spinning, and flattened
out spinning the other way; it began to carve the air into forms that built
wildly and musically on each other and never ended."*

*Annie Dillard is one of America's preeminent essayists, someone for
whom, as she puts it, the essay is not an occasional piece but her "real
work." Her many award-winning books of essays and nonfiction include*
Pilgrim at Tinker Creek, *which won the Pulitzer Prize for General Nonfiction in 1975,* Holy the Firm *(1977),* Living by Fiction *(1982),*
Teaching a Stone to Talk *(1982),* An American Childhood *(1987),*
The Writing Life *(1989), and* For the Time Being *(1999). Dillard
has taught creative writing at Wesleyan University in Middletown, Connecticut, since 1979. In 1992, she published her first novel,* The Living.
"The Stunt Pilot" originally appeared in Esquire *(1989) and was selected by Justin Kaplan for* The Best American Essays 1990.

Dave Rahm lived in Bellingham, Washington, north of Seattle.
Bellingham, a harbor town, lies between the alpine North Cascade
Mountains and the San Juan Islands in Haro Strait above Puget
Sound. The latitude is that of Newfoundland. Dave Rahm was a
stunt pilot, the air's own genius.

In 1975, with a newcomer's willingness to try anything once, I attended the Bellingham Air Show. The Bellingham airport was a wide clearing in a forest of tall Douglas firs; its runways suited small planes. It was June. People wearing blue or tan zipped jackets stood loosely on the concrete walkways and runways outside the coffee shop. At that latitude in June, you stayed outside because you could, even most of the night, if you could think up something to do. The sky did not darken until ten o'clock or so, and it never got very dark. Your life parted and opened in the sunlight. You tossed your dark winter routines, thought up mad projects, and improvised everything from hour to hour. Being a stunt pilot seemed the most reasonable thing in the world; you could wave your arms in the air all day and night, and sleep next winter.

I saw from the ground a dozen stunt pilots; the air show scheduled them one after the other, for an hour of aerobatics. Each pilot took up his or her plane and performed a batch of tricks. They were precise and impressive. They flew upside down, and straightened out; they did barrel rolls, and straightened out; they drilled through dives and spins, and landed gently on a far runway.

For the end of the day, separated from all other performances of every sort, the air show director had scheduled a program titled "Dave Rahm." The leaflet said that Rahm was a geologist who taught at Western Washington University. He had flown for King Hussein in Jordan. A tall man in the crowd told me Hussein had seen Rahm fly on a visit the king made to the United States; he had invited him to Jordan to perform at ceremonies. Hussein was a pilot, too. "Hussein thought he was the greatest thing in the world."

Idly, paying scant attention, I saw a medium-sized, rugged man dressed in brown leather, all begoggled, climb in a black biplane's open cockpit. The plane was a Bücker Jungman, built in the thirties. I saw a tall, dark-haired woman seize a propeller tip at the plane's nose and yank it down till the engine caught. He was off; he climbed high over the airport in his biplane, very high until he was barely visible as a mote, and then seemed to fall down the air, diving headlong, and streaming beauty in spirals behind him.

The black plane dropped spinning, and flattened out spinning the other way; it began to carve the air into forms that built wildly and musically on each other and never ended. Reluctantly, I started paying attention. Rahm drew high above the world an inexhaustibly glorious line; it piled over our heads in loops and arabesques. It was like a Saul Steinberg* fantasy; the plane was the pen. Like Steinberg's contracting and billowing pen line, the line Rahm spun moved to form new, punning shapes from the edges of the old. Like a Klee[†] line, it smattered the sky with landscapes and systems.

The air show announcer hushed. He had been squawking all day, and now he quit. The crowd stilled. Even the children watched dumbstruck as the slow, black biplane buzzed its way around the air. Rahm made beauty with his whole body; it was pure pattern, and you could watch it happen. The plane moved every way a line can move, and it controlled three dimensions, so the line carved massive and subtle slits in the air like sculptures. The plane looped the loop, seeming to arch its back like a gymnast; it stalled, dropped, and spun out of it climbing; it spiraled and knifed west on one side's wings and back east on another; it turned cartwheels, which must be physically impossible; it played with its own line like a cat with yarn. How did the pilot know where in the air he was? If he got lost, the ground would swat him.

Rahm did everything his plane could do: tailspins, four-point rolls, flat spins, figure eights, snap rolls, and hammerheads. He did pirouettes on the plane's tail. The other pilots could do these stunts too, skillfully, one at a time. But Rahm used the plane inexhaustibly, like a brush marking thin air.

His was pure energy and naked spirit. I have thought about it for years. Rahm's line unrolled in time. Like music, it split the bulging rim of the future along its seam. It pried out the present. We watchers waited for the split-second curve of beauty in the present to reveal itself. The human pilot, Dave Rahm, worked in the cockpit right at the plane's nose; his very body tore into the future for us and reeled it down upon us like a curling peel.

*__Saul Steinberg:__ Contemporary artist (b. 1914) who also created numerous covers for *The New Yorker* magazine. — Ed.

[†]__Klee:__ Paul Klee (1879–1940), a Swiss artist known for his highly distinctive abstract paintings. — Ed.

Like any fine artist, he controlled the tension of the audience's longing. You desired, unwittingly, a certain kind of roll or climb, or a return to a certain portion of the air, and he fulfilled your hope slantingly, like a poet, or evaded it until you thought you would burst, and then fulfilled it surprisingly, so you gasped and cried out.

The oddest, most exhilarating and exhausting thing was this: he never quit. The music had no periods, no rests or endings; the poetry's beautiful sentence never ended; the line had no finish; the sculptured forms piled overhead, one into another without surcease. Who could breathe, in a world where rhythm itself had no periods?

It had taken me several minutes to understand what an extraordinary thing I was seeing. Rahm kept all that embellished space in mind at once. For another twenty minutes I watched the beauty unroll and grow more fantastic and unlikely before my eyes. Now Rahm brought the plane down slidingly, and just in time, for I thought I would snap from the effort to compass and remember the line's long intelligence; I could not add another curve. He brought the plane down on a far runway. After a pause, I saw him step out, an ordinary man, and make his way back to the terminal.

The show was over. It was late. Just as I turned from the runway, something caught my eye and made me laugh. It was a swallow, a blue-green swallow, having its own air show, apparently inspired by Rahm. The swallow climbed high over the runway, held its wings oddly, tipped them, and rolled down the air in loops. The inspired swallow. I always want to paint, too, after I see the Rembrandts. The blue-green swallow tumbled precisely, and caught itself and flew up again as if excited, and looped down again, the way swallows do, but tensely, holding its body carefully still. It was a stunt swallow.

I went home and thought about Rahm's performance that night, and the next day, and the next.

I had thought I knew my way around beauty a little bit. I knew I had devoted a good part of my life to it, memorizing poetry and focusing my attention on complexity of rhythm in particular, on force, movement, repetition, and surprise, in both poetry and prose. Now I had stood among dandelions between two asphalt runways in Bellingham, Washington, and begun learning about beauty. Even the Boston Museum of Fine Arts was never more inspiriting than this small northwestern airport on this time-killing Sunday afternoon in June. Nothing on earth is more gladdening than knowing we must roll up our sleeves and move back the boundaries of the humanly possible once more.

Later I flew with Dave Rahm; he took me up. A generous geographer, Dick Smith, at Western Washington University, arranged it, and came along. Rahm and Dick Smith were colleagues at the university. In geology, Rahm had published two books and many articles. Rahm was handsome in a dull sort of way, blunt-featured, wide-jawed, wind-burned, keen-eyed, and taciturn. As anyone would expect. He was forty. He wanted to show me the Cascade Mountains; these enormous peaks, only fifty miles from the coast, rise over nine thousand feet; they are heavily glaciated. Whatcom County has more glaciers than the lower forty-eight states combined; the Cascades make the Rocky Mountains look like hills. Mount Baker is volcanic, like most Cascade peaks. That year, Mount Baker was acting up. Even from my house at the shore I could see, early in the morning on clear days, volcanic vapor rise near its peak. Often the vapor made a cloud that swelled all morning and hid the snows. Every day the newspapers reported on Baker's activity: Would it blow? (A few years later, Mount St. Helens did blow.)

Rahm was not flying his trick biplane that day, but a faster enclosed plane, a single-engine Cessna. We flew from a bumpy grass airstrip near my house, out over the coast and inland. There was coastal plain down there, but we could not see it for clouds. We were over the clouds at five hundred feet and inside them too, heading for an abrupt line of peaks we could not see. I gave up on everything, the way you do in airplanes; it was out of my hands. Every once in a while Rahm saw a peephole in the clouds and buzzed over for a look. "That's Larsen's pea farm," he said, or "That's Nooksack Road," and he changed our course with a heave.

When we got to the mountains, he slid us along Mount Baker's flanks sideways.

Our plane swiped at the mountain with a roar. I glimpsed a

windshield view of dirty snow traveling fast. Our shaking, swooping belly seemed to graze the snow. The wings shuddered; we peeled away and the mountain fell back and the engines whined. We felt flung, because we were in fact flung; parts of our faces and internal organs trailed pressingly behind on the curves. We came back for another pass at the mountain, and another. We dove at the snow headlong like suicides; we jerked up, down, or away at the last second, so late we left our hearts, stomachs, and lungs behind. If I forced myself to hold my heavy head up against the G's,* and to raise my eyelids, heavy as barbells, and to notice what I saw, I could see the wrinkled green crevasses cracking the glaciers' snow.

Pitching snow filled all the windows, and shapes of dark rock. I had no notion which way was up. Everything was black or gray or white except the fatal crevasses; everything made noise and shook. I felt my face smashed sideways and saw rushing abstractions of snow in the windshield. Patches of cloud obscured the snow fleetingly. We straightened out, turned, and dashed at the mountainside for another pass, which we made, apparently, on our ear, an inch or two away from the slope. Icefalls and cornices jumbled and fell away. If a commercial plane's black box, such as the FAA painstakingly recovers from crash sites, could store videotapes as well as pilots' last words, some videotapes would look like this: a mountainside coming up at the windows from all directions, ice and snow and rock filling the screen up close and screaming by.

Rahm was just being polite. His geographer colleague wanted to see the fissure on Mount Baker from which steam escaped. Everybody in Bellingham wanted to see that sooty fissure, as did every geologist in the country; no one on earth could fly so close to it as Rahm. He knew the mountain by familiar love and feel, like a face; he knew what the plane could do and what he dared to do.

When Mount Baker inexplicably let us go, he jammed us into cloud again and soon tilted. "The Sisters!" someone shouted, and I saw the windshield fill with red rock. This mountain looked infernal, a drear and sheer plane of lifeless rock. It was red and sharp; its gritty blades cut through the clouds at random. The mountain was quiet. It was in shade. Careening, we made sideways passes at these brittle peaks too steep for snow. Their rock was full of iron,

*G's: A measure of gravitational force. — Ed.

somebody shouted at me then or later; the iron had rusted, so they were red. Later, when I was back on the ground, I recalled that, from a distance, the two jagged peaks called the Twin Sisters looked translucent against the sky; they were sharp, tapered, and fragile as arrowheads.

I talked to Rahm. He was flying us out to the islands now. The islands were fifty or sixty miles away. Like many other people, I had picked Bellingham, Washington, by looking at an atlas. It was clear from the atlas that you could row in the salt water and see snow-covered mountains; you could scale a glaciated mountainside with an ice ax in August, skirting green crevasses two hundred feet deep, and look out on the islands in the sea. Now, in the air, the clouds had risen over us; dark forms lay on the glinting water. There was almost no color to the day, just blackened green and some yellow. I knew the islands were forested in dark Douglas firs the size of skyscrapers. Bald eagles scavenged on the beaches; robins the size of herring gulls sang in the clearings. We made our way out to the islands through the layer of air between the curving planet and its held, thick clouds.

"When I started trying to figure out what I was going to do with my life, I decided to become an expert on mountains. It wasn't much to be, it wasn't everything, but it was something. I was going to know everything about mountains from every point of view. So I started out in geography." Geography proved too pedestrian for Rahm, too concerned with "how many bushels of wheat an acre." So he ended up in geology. Smith had told me that geology departments throughout the country used Rahm's photographic slides — close-ups of geologic features from the air.

"I used to climb mountains. But you know, you can get a better feel for a mountain's power flying around it, flying all around it, than you can from climbing it tied to its side like a flea."

He talked about his flying performances. He thought of the air as a line, he said. "This end of the line, that end of the line — like a rope." He improvised. "I get a rhythm going and stick with it." While he was performing in a show, he paid attention, he said, to the lighting. He didn't play against the sun. That was all he said about what he did.

In aerobatic maneuvers, pilots pull about seven positive G's on some stunts and six negative G's on others. Some gyrations push;

others pull. Pilots alternate the pressures carefully, so they do not gray out or black out.

Later I learned that some stunt pilots tune up by wearing gravity boots. These are boots made to hook over a doorway; wearing them, you hang in the doorway upside down. It must startle a pilot's children to run into their father or mother in the course of their home wanderings — the parents hanging wide-eyed, upside down in the doorway like a bat.

We were landing; here was the airstrip on Stuart Island — that island to which Ferrar Burn was dragged by the tide. We put down, climbed out of the plane, and walked. We wandered a dirt track through fields to a lee shore where yellow sandstone ledges slid into the sea. The salt chuck, people there called salt water. The sun came out. I caught a snake in the salt chuck; the snake, eighteen inches long, was swimming in the green shallows.

I had a survivor's elation. Rahm had found Mount Baker in the clouds before Mount Baker found the plane. He had wiped it with the fast plane like a cloth and we had lived. When we took off from Stuart Island and gained altitude, I asked if we could turn over — could we do a barrel roll? The plane was making a lot of noise, and Dick Smith did not hear any of this, I learned later. "Why not?" Rahm said, and added surprisingly, "It won't hurt the plane." Without ado he leaned on the wheel and the wing went down and we went somersaulting over it. We upended with a roar. We stuck to the plane's sides like flung paint. All the blood in my body bulged on my face; it piled between my skull and skin. Vaguely I could see the chrome sea twirling over Rahm's head like a baton, and the dark islands sliding down the skies like rain.

The G's slammed me into my seat like thugs and pinned me while my heart pounded and the plane turned over slowly and compacted each organ in turn. My eyeballs were newly spherical and full of heartbeats. I seemed to hear a crescendo; the wing rolled shuddering down the last 90 degrees and settled on the flat. There were the islands, admirably below us, and the clouds, admirably above. When I could breathe, I asked if we could do it again, and we did. He rolled the other way. The brilliant line of the sea slid up the side window bearing its heavy islands. Through the shriek of my blood and the plane's shakes I glimpsed the line of the sea over the windshield, thin as a spear. How in performance did Rahm keep track while his brain blurred and blood roared in his ears without ceasing? Every performance was a tour de force and a show of will, a *Machtspruch*.* I had seen the other stunt pilots straighten out after a trick or two; their blood could drop back and the planet simmer down. An Olympic gymnast, at peak form, strings out a line of spins ten stunts long across a mat, and is hard put to keep his footing at the end. Rahm endured much greater pressure on his faster spins using the plane's power, and he could spin in three dimensions and keep twirling till he ran out of sky room or luck.

When we straightened out, and had flown straightforwardly for ten minutes toward home, Dick Smith, clearing his throat, brought himself to speak. "What was that we did out there?"

"The barrel rolls?" Rahm said. "They were barrel rolls." He said nothing else. I looked at the back of his head; I could see the serious line of his cheek and jaw. He was in shirtsleeves, tanned, strong-wristed. I could not imagine loving him under any circumstance; he was alien to me, unfazed. He looked like GI Joe. He flew with that matter-of-fact, bored gesture pilots use. They click overhead switches and turn dials as if only their magnificent strength makes such dullness endurable. The half circle of wheel in their big hands looks like a toy they plan to crush in a minute; the wiggly stick the wheel mounts seems barely attached.

A crop-duster pilot in Wyoming told me the life expectancy of a crop-duster pilot is five years. They fly too low. They hit buildings and power lines. They have no space to fly out of trouble, and no space to recover from a stall. We were in Cody, Wyoming, out on the north fork of the Shoshone River. The crop duster had wakened me that morning flying over the ranch house and clearing my bedroom roof by half an inch. I saw the bolts on the wheel assembly a few feet from my face. He was spraying with pesticide the plain old grass. Over breakfast I asked him how long he had been dusting crops. "Four years," he said, and the figure stalled in the air between us for a moment. "You know you're going to die at it someday," he added. "We all know it. We accept that; it's part of it."

***Machtspruch:** German, meaning "power speech." — Ed.

I think now that, since the crop duster was in his twenties, he accepted only that he had to say such stuff; privately he counted on skewing the curve.

I suppose Rahm knew the fact too. I do not know how he felt about it. "It's worth it," said the early French aviator Mermoz. He was Antoine de Saint-Exupéry's friend. "It's worth the final smashup."

Rahm smashed up in front of King Hussein, in Jordan, during a performance. The plane spun down and never came out of it; it nosedived into the ground and exploded. He bought the farm. I was living then with my husband out on that remote island in the San Juans, cut off from everything. Battery radios picked up the Canadian Broadcasting Company out of Toronto, half a continent away; island people would, in theory, learn if the United States blew up, but not much else. There were no newspapers. One friend got the Sunday *New York Times* by mail boat on the following Friday. He saved it until Sunday and had a party, every week; we all read the Sunday *Times* and no one mentioned that it was last week's.

One day, Paul Glenn's brother flew out from Bellingham to visit; he had a seaplane. He landed in the water in front of the cabin and tied up to our mooring. He came in for coffee, and he gave out news of this and that, and — Say, did we know that stunt pilot Dave Rahm had cracked up? In Jordan, during a performance: he never came out of a dive. He just dove right down into the ground, and his wife was there watching. "I saw it on CBS News last night." And then — with a sudden sharp look at my filling eyes — "What, did you know him?" But no, I did not know him. He took me up once. Several years ago. I admired his flying. I had thought that danger was the safest thing in the world, if you went about it right.

Later, I found a newspaper. Rahm was living in Jordan that year; King Hussein invited him to train the aerobatics team, the Royal Jordanian Falcons. He was also visiting professor of geology at the University of Jordan. In Amman that day he had been flying a Pitt Special, a plane he knew well. Katy Rahm, his wife of six months, was sitting beside Hussein in the viewing stands, with her daughter. Rahm died performing a Lomcevak combined with a tail slide and hammerhead. In a Lomcevak, the pilot brings the plane up on a slant and pirouettes. I had seen Rahm do this: the falling plane twirled slowly like a leaf. Like a ballerina, the plane seemed to hold its head back stiff in concentration at the music's slow, painful beauty. It was one of Rahm's favorite routines. Next the pilot flies straight up, stalls the plane, and slides down the air on his tail. He brings the nose down — the hammerhead — kicks the engine, and finishes with a low loop.

It is a dangerous maneuver at any altitude, and Rahm was doing it low. He hit the ground on the loop; the tail slide had left him no height. When Rahm went down, King Hussein dashed to the burning plane to pull him out, but he was already dead.

A few months after the air show, and a month after I had flown with Rahm, I was working at my desk near Bellingham, where I lived, when I heard a sound so odd it finally penetrated my concentration. It was the buzz of an airplane, but it rose and fell musically, and it never quit; the plane never flew out of earshot. I walked out on the porch and looked up: it was Rahm in the black and gold biplane, looping all over the air. I had been wondering about his performance flight: could it really have been so beautiful? It was, for here it was again. The little plane twisted all over the air like a vine. It trailed a line like a very long mathematical proof you could follow only so far, and then it lost you in its complexity. I saw Rahm flying high over the Douglas firs, and out over the water, and back over farms. The air was a fluid, and Rahm was an eel.

It was as if Mozart could move his body through his notes, and you could walk out on the porch, look up, and see him in periwig and breeches, flying around in the sky. You could hear the music as he dove through it; it streamed after him like a contrail.

I lost myself; standing on the firm porch, I lost my direction and reeled. My neck and spine rose and turned, so I followed the plane's line kinesthetically. In his open-cockpit black plane, Rahm demonstrated curved space. He slid down ramps of air, he vaulted and wheeled. He piled loops in heaps and praised height. He unrolled the scroll of air, extended it, and bent it into Möbius strips; he furled line in a thousand new ways, as if he were inventing a script and writing it in one infinitely recurring utterance until I thought the bounds of beauty must break.

From inside, the looping plane had sounded tinny, like a kazoo. Outside, the buzz rose and fell to the Doppler effect as the plane looped near or away. Rahm cleaved the sky like a prow and tossed out time left and right in his wake. He performed for forty minutes; then he headed the plane, as small as a wasp, back to the airport inland. Later I learned Rahm often practiced acrobatic flights over this shore. His idea was that if he lost control and was going to go down, he could ditch in the salt chuck, where no one else would get hurt.

If I had not turned two barrel rolls in an airplane, I might have fancied Rahm felt good up there, and playful. Maybe Jackson Pollock felt a sort of playfulness, in addition to the artist's usual deliberate and intelligent care. In my limited experience, painting, unlike writing, pleases the senses while you do it, and more while you do it than after it is done. Drawing lines with an airplane, unfortunately, tortures the senses. Jet bomber pilots black out. I knew Rahm felt as if his brain were bursting his eardrums, felt that if he let his jaws close as tight as centrifugal force pressed them, he would bite through his lungs.

"All virtue is a form of acting," Yeats said. Rahm deliberately turned himself into a figure. Sitting invisible at the controls of a distant airplane, he became the agent and the instrument of art and invention. He did not tell me how he felt when we spoke of his performance flying; he told me instead that he paid attention to how his plane and its line looked to the audience against the lighted sky. If he had noticed how he felt, he could not have done the work. Robed in his airplane, he was as featureless as a priest. He was lost in his figural aspect like an actor or a king. Of his flying, he had said only, "I get a rhythm and stick with it." In its reticence, this statement reminded me of Veronese's* "Given a large canvas, I enhanced it as I saw fit." But Veronese was ironic, and Rahm was not; he was as literal as an astronaut; the machine gave him tongue.

When Rahm flew, he sat down in the middle of art and strapped himself in. He spun it all around him. He could not see it himself. If he never saw it on film, he never saw it at all — as if Beethoven could not hear his final symphonies not because he was deaf but because he was inside the paper on which he wrote. Rahm must have felt it happen, that fusion of vision and metal, motion and idea. I think of this man as a figure, a college professor with a Ph.D. upside down in the loud band of beauty. What are we here for? *Propter chorum*, the monks say: for the sake of the choir.

"Purity does not lie in separation from but in deeper pene-

Veronese: Paolo Veronese (1528–1588), famous Venetian painter. — Ed.

tration into the universe," Teilhard de Chardin* wrote. It is hard to imagine a deeper penetration into the universe than Rahm's last dive in his plane, or than his inexpressible wordless selfless line's inscribing the air and dissolving. Any other art may be permanent. I cannot recall one Rahm sequence. He improvised. If Christo† wraps a building or dyes a harbor, we join his poignant and fierce awareness that the work will be gone in days. Rahm's plane shed a ribbon in space, a ribbon whose end unraveled in memory while its beginning unfurled as surprise. He may have acknowledged that what he did could be called art, but it would have been, I think, only in the common misusage, which holds art to be the last extreme of skill. Rahm rode the point of the line to the possible; he discovered it and wound it down to show. He made his dazzling probe on the run. "The world is filled, and filled with the Absolute," Teilhard de Chardin wrote. "To see this is to be made free."

Reflections and Responses

1. How does Dillard establish a connection between stunt piloting and artistic performance? Identify the various moments in her essay when she makes such a connection. What do these moments have in common? What images do they share?

2. Note that Dillard doesn't wait until the very end of her essay to introduce Rahm's death. Why do you think she avoids this kind of climax? What advantage does this give her?

3. "The Stunt Pilot" also appears as an untitled chapter in Dillard's book *The Writing Life*. Why is this an appropriate context for the essay? What does the essay tell us about expression and composition?

---

*Teilhard de Chardin: Pierre Teilhard de Chardin (1881–1953), a noted paleontologist and Catholic priest whose most famous book, *The Phenomenon of Man*, attempts to bridge the gap between science and religion. — Ed.

†Christo: A contemporary Bulgarian artist known for staging spectacular environmental effects. — Ed.

GRETEL EHRLICH

Spring

"Recuperation is like spring," writes Gretel Ehrlich in a lyrical essay that sensitively charts the changes both within a Wyoming season and a woman's psyche. A model of the modern reflective essay, her meditation on her slow recovery from pneumonia and the death of a young rancher branches out into thoughts about time and space, sex and death, dream and reality, cosmology and Jurassic landscapes. As she considers the way life and thought move between the linear and the circular, particle and wave, she shapes her essay accordingly, at some moments pursuing a narrative, at others following the trail of an image: "In March I'm ramshackle, weak in the knees, giddy, dazzled by broken-backed clouds, the passing of Halley's comet, the on-and-off strobe of sun."

Ehrlich is the author of The Solace of Open Spaces *(1985),* Wyoming Stories *(1986),* Heart Mountain *(1988),* Islands, the Universe, Home *(1991),* Arctic Heart: A Poem Cycle *(1992),* A Match to the Heart *(1994),* Questions of Heaven: The Chinese Journeys of an American Buddhist *(1997), and* This Cold Heaven: Seven Seasons in Greenland *(2001). Her essays have appeared in* Harper's, The Atlantic, Time, The New York Times, *and many other national periodicals. She divides her time between the central coast of California and Wyoming. "Spring" originally appeared in* Antaeus *(1986) and was selected by Gay Talese for* The Best American Essays *1987.*

We have a nine-acre lake on our ranch and a warm spring that feeds it all winter. By mid-March the lake ice begins to melt where the spring feeds in, and every year the same pair of mallards come ahead of the others and wait. Though there is very little open water they seem content. They glide back and forth through a thin estuary, brushing watercress with their elegant folded wings, then tip end-up to eat and, after, clamber onto the lip of ice that retreats, hardens forward, and retreats again.

Mornings, a transparent pane of ice lies over the meltwater. I peer through and see some kind of waterbug — perhaps a leech — paddling like a sea turtle between green ladders of lakeweed. Cattails and sweetgrass from the previous summer are bone dry, marked with black mold spots, and bend like elbows into the ice. They are swords that cut away the hard tenancy of winter. At the wide end a mat of dead waterplants has rolled back into a thick, impregnable breakwater. Near it, bubbles trapped under the ice are lenses focused straight up to catch the coming season.

It's spring again and I wasn't finished with winter. That's what I said at the end of summer too. I stood on the twenty-foot-high haystack and yelled "No!" as the first snow fell. We had been up since four in the morning picking the last bales of hay from the oatfield by hand, slipping under the weight of them in the mud, and by the time we finished the stack, six inches of snow had fallen.

It's spring but I was still cataloguing the different kinds of snow: snow that falls dry but is rained on; snow that melts down into hard crusts; wind-driven snow that looks blue; powder snow on hardpack on powder — a Linzertorte of snow. I look up. The troposphere is the seven-to-ten-mile-wide sleeve of air out of which all our weather shakes. A bank of clouds drives in from the south. Where in it, I wonder, does a snowflake take on its thumbprint uniqueness? Inside the cloud where schools of flakes are flung this way and that like schools of fish? What gives the snowflake its needle, plate, column, branching shapes — the battering wind or the dust particles around which water vapor clings?

Near town the river ice breaks up and lies stacked in industrial-sized hunks — big as railway cars — on the banks, and is flecked black by wheeling hurricanes of newly plowed topsoil. That's how I feel when winter breaks up inside me: heavy, onerous, upended, inert against the flow of water. I had thought about ice during the cold months too. How it is movement betrayed, water seized in the moment of falling. In November, ice thickened over the lake like a cataract, and from the air looked like a Cyclops, one bad eye. Under its milky spans over irrigation ditches, the sound of water running south was muffled. One solitary spire of ice hung noise-lessly against dark rock at the Falls as if mocking or mirroring the broom-tail comet on the horizon. Then, in February, I tried for words not about ice, but words hacked from it — the ice at the end of the mind, so to speak — and failed.

Those were winter things and now it is spring, though one name can't describe what, in Wyoming, is a three-part affair: false spring, the vernal equinox, and the spring when flowers come and the grass grows.

Spring means restlessness. The physicist I've been talking to all winter says if I look more widely, deeply, and microscopically all at once I might see how springlike the whole cosmos is. What I see as order and stillness — the robust, time-bound determinacy of my life — is really a mirage suspended above chaos. "There's a lot of random jiggling going on all the time, everywhere," he tells me. Winter's tight sky hovers. Under it, the hayfields are green, then white, then green growing under white. The confinement I've felt since November resembles the confinement of subatomic parti-cles, I'm told. A natural velocity finally shows itself. The particle moves; it becomes a wave.

The sap rises in trees and in me and the hard knot of persever-ance I cultivated to meet winter dissipates; I walk away from the obsidian of bitter nights. Now, when snow comes, it is wet and heavy, but the air it traverses feels light. I sleep less and dream not of human entanglements, but of animals I've never seen: a cater-pillar fat as a man's thumb, made of linked silver tubes, has two heads — one human, one a butterfly's.

Last spring at this time I was coming out of a bout with pneumo-nia. I went to bed on January first and didn't get up until the end of February. Winter was a cocoon in which my gagging, basso cough shook the dark figures at the end of my bed. Had I read too much Hemingway? Or was I dying? I'd lie on my stomach and look out. Nothing close up interested me. All engagements of mind — the circumlocutions of love interests and internal gossip — ap-peared false. Only my body was true. And my body was trying to close down, go out the window without me.

I saw things out there. Our ranch faces south down a long tree-less valley whose vanishing point is two gray hills, folded one in front of the other like two hands, and after that — space, cerulean air, clouds like pleated skirts, and red mesas standing up like breaching whales in a valley three thousand feet below. Afternoons, our young horses played, rearing up on back legs and pawing oh so carefully at each other, reaching around, ears flat back, nipping manes and withers. One of those times their falsetto squeals looped across the pasture and hung on frozen currents of air. But when I tried to ingest their sounds of delight, I found my lungs had no air.

It was thirty-five below zero that night. Our plumbing froze, and because I was very weak my husband had to bundle me up and help me to the outhouse. Nothing close at hand seemed to register with me: neither the cold nor the semicoziness of an uninsulated house. But the stars were lurid. For a while I thought I saw the horses, dead now, and eating each other, and spinning round and round in the ice of the air.

My scientist friends talk with relish about how insignificant we humans are when placed against the time-scale of geology and the cosmos. I had heard it a hundred times, but never felt it truly. As I lay in bed, the black room was a screen through which some part of my body traveled, leaving the rest behind. I thought I was a sun flying over a barge whose iron holds soaked me up until I became rust floating on a bright river.

A ferocious loneliness took hold of me. I felt spring-inspired desire, a sense of trajectory, but no interception was in sight. In fact, I wanted none. My body was a parenthetical dash laid against a landscape so spacious it defied space as we know it — space as a membrane — and curved out of time. That night a luscious, creamy fog rolled in, like a roll of fat, hugging me, but it was snow.

Recuperation is like spring: dormancy and vitality collide. In any year I'm like a bear, a partial hibernator. During January thaws I stick my nose out and peruse the frozen desolation as if reading a book whose language I don't know. In March I'm ramshackle, weak in the knees, giddy, dazzled by broken-backed clouds, the passing of Halley's comet, the on-and-off strobe of sun. Like a sheepherder I X out each calendar day as if time were a forest through which I could clear-cut a way to the future. My physicist friend straightens me out on this point too. The notion of "time passing," like a train through a landscape, is an illusion, he says. I hold the Big Ben clock taken from a dead sheepherder's wagon and look at it. The clock measures intervals of time, not the speed of time, and the calendar is a scaffolding we hang as if time were rushing water we could harness. Time-bound, I hinge myself to a linear bias — cause and effect all laid out in a neat row — and in this we learn two things: blame and shame.

Julius Caesar had a sense of humor about time. The Roman calendar with its calends, nones, and ides — counting days — changed according to who was in power. Caesar serendipitously added days, changed the names of certain months, and when he was through, the calendar was so skewed that January fell in autumn.

Einsteinian time is too big for even Julius Caesar to touch. It stretches and shrinks and dilates. In fact, it is the antithesis of the mechanistic concept we've imposed on it. Time, indecipherable from space, is not one thing but an infinity of space-times, overlapping, interfering, wavelike. There is no future that is not now, no past that is not now. Time includes every moment.

It's the ides of March today.

I've walked to a hill a mile from the house. It's not really a hill but a mountain slope that heaves up, turns sideways, and comes down again, straight down to a foot-wide creek. Everything I can see from here used to be a flatland covered with shallow water. "Used to be" means several hundred million years ago, and the land itself was not really "here" at all, but part of a continent floating near Bermuda. On top is a fin of rock, a marine deposition created during Jurassic times by small waves moving in and out slapping the shore.

I've come here for peace and quiet and to see what's going on in this secluded valley, away from ranch work and sorting corrals, but what I get is a slap on the ass by a prehistoric wave, gains and losses in altitude and aridity, outcrops of mud composed of rotting volcanic ash that fell continuously for ten thousand years a hundred million years ago. The soils are a geologic flag — red, white, green, and gray. On one side of the hill, mountain mahogany gives off a scent like orange blossoms; on the other, colonies of sagebrush root wide in ground the color of Spanish roof tiles. And it still looks like the ocean to me. "How much truth can a man stand, sitting by the ocean, all that perpetual motion," Mose Allison, the jazz singer, sings.

The wind picks up and blusters. Its fat underbelly scrapes the uneven ground, twisting like taffy toward me, slips up over the mountain, and showers out across the Great Plains. The sea smell it carried all the way from Seattle has long since been absorbed by pink gruss — the rotting granite that spills down the slopes of the Rockies. Somewhere over the Midwest the wind slows, tangling in the hair of hardwood forests, and finally drops into the corridors of the cities, past Manhattan's World Trade Center, ripping free again as it crosses the Atlantic's green swell.

Spring jitterbugs inside me. Spring *is* wind, symphonic and billowing. A dark cloud pops like a blood blister over me, letting hail down. It comes on a piece of wind that seems to have widened the sky, comes so the birds have something to fly on.

A message reports to my brain but I can't believe my eyes. The sheet of wind had a hole in it: an eagle just fell out of the sky. It fell as if down the chute of a troubled airplane. Landed, falling to one side as if a leg were broken. I was standing on the hill overlooking the narrow valley that had been a seashore 170 million years ago, whose sides had lifted like a medic's litter to catch up this eagle now.

She hops and flaps seven feet of wing and closes them down and sways. She had come down (on purpose?) near a dead fawn whose carcass had recently been feasted upon. When I walked closer, all I could see of the animal was a ribcage rubbed red with fine tissue and the decapitated head lying peacefully against sagebrush, eyes closed.

At twenty yards the eagle opened her wings halfway and rose up, her whole back lengthening and growing stiff. At forty feet she looked as big as a small person. She craned her neck, first to one side, then the other, and stared hard. She's giving me the eagle eye, I thought.

Friends who have investigated eagles' nests have literally feared for their lives. It's not that they were in danger of being pecked to death but, rather, grabbed. An eagle's talons are a powerful jaw. Their grip is so strong the talons can slice down through flesh to bone in one motion.

But I had come close only to see what was wrong, to see what I could do. An eagle with a bum leg will starve to death. Was it broken, bruised, or sprained? How could I get close enough to know? I approached again. She hopped up in the air, dashing the critical distance between us with her great wings. Best to leave her alone, I decided. My husband dragged a road-killed deer up the mountain slope so she could eat, and I brought a bucket of water. Then we turned toward home.

A golden eagle is not golden but black with yellow spots on the neck and wings. Looking at her, I had wondered how feathers came to be, how their construction — the rachis, vane, and quill — is unlike anything else in nature.

Birds are glorified flying lizards. The remarkable feathers that, positioned together, are like hundreds of smaller wings, evolved from reptilian scales. Ancestral birds had thirteen pairs of cone-shaped teeth that grew in separate sockets like a snake's, rounded ribs, and bony tails. Archaeopteryx was half bird, half dinosaur who glided instead of flying; ichthyornis was a fish-bird, a relative of the pelican; diatryma was a giant, seven feet tall with a huge beak and wings so absurdly small they must have been useless, though later the wingbone sprouted from them. *Aquila chrysaëtos*, the modern golden eagle, has seven thousand contour feathers, no teeth, and weighs about eight pounds.

I think about the eagle. How big she was, how each time she spread her wings it was like a thought stretching between two seasons.

Back at the house I relax with a beer. At 5:03 the vernal equinox occurs. I go outside and stand in the middle of a hayfield with my eyes closed. The universe is restless but I want to feel celestial equipoise: twelve hours of daylight, twelve of dark, and the earth ramrod straight on its axis. In celebration I straighten my posture in an effort to resist the magnetic tilt back into dormancy, spiritual and emotional reticence. Far to the south I imagine the equatorial sash, now nose to nose with the sun, sizzling like a piece of bacon, then the earth slowly tilting again.

In the morning I walk up to the valley again. I glass both hillsides, back and forth through the sagebrush, but the eagle isn't there. The hindquarters of the road-killed deer have been eaten. Coyote tracks circle the carcass. Did they have eagle for dinner too?

Afternoon. I return. Far up on the opposite hill I see her, flapping and hopping to the top. When I stop, she stops and turns her head. Her neck is the plumbline on which earth revolves. Even at two hundred yards, I can feel her binocular vision zeroing in; I can feel the heat of her stare.

Later, I look through my binoculars at all sorts of things. I'm seeing the world with an eagle eye. I glass the crescent moon. How jaded I've become, taking the moon at face value only, forgetting the charcoal, shaded backside, as if it weren't there at all.

That night I dream about two moons. One is pink and spins fast; the other is an eagle's head, farther away and spinning in the opposite direction. Slowly, both moons descend and then it is day.

At first light I clamber up the hill. Now the dead deer my husband brought is only a hoop of ribs, two forelegs, and hair. The eagle is not here or along the creek or on either hill. I go to the hill and sit. After a long time an eagle careens out from the narrow slit of the red-walled canyon whose creek drains into this valley. Surely it's the same bird. She flies by. I can hear the bone-creak and whoosh of air under her wings. She cocks her head and looks at me. I smile. What is a smile to her? Now she is not so much flying as lifting above the planet, far from me.

Late March. The emerald of the hayfields brightens. A flock of gray-capped rosy finches who overwintered here swarms a leafless apple tree, then falls from the smooth boughs like cut grass. The tree was planted by the Texan who homesteaded this ranch. As I walk past, one of the boughs, shaped like an undulating dragon, splits off from the trunk and falls.

Space is an arena in which the rowdy particles that are the building blocks of life perform their antics. All spring, things fall; the general law of increasing disorder is on the take. I try to think of what it is to be a cause without an effect, an effect without a cause. To abandon time-bound thinking, the use of tenses, the temporally related emotions of impatience, expectation, hope, and fear. But I can't. I go to the edge of the lake and watch the ducks. Like them, my thinking rises and falls on the same water.

Another day. Sometimes when I'm feeling small-minded I take a plane ride over Wyoming. As we take off I feel the plane's resistance to accepting air under its wings. Is this how an eagle feels? Ernst Mach's* principle tells me that an object's resistance against being accelerated is not the intrinsic property of matter, but a measure of its interaction with the universe; that matter has inertia only because it exists in relation to other matter.

Airborne, then, I'm not aloof but in relation to everything —

*Ernst Mach: Austrian physicist and philosopher (1838–1916). — Ed.

like Wallace Stevens's floating eagle for whom the whole, intricate Alps is a nest. We fly southeast from Heart Mountain across the Big Horn River, over the long red wall where Butch Cassidy trailed stolen horses, across the high plains to Laramie. Coming home the next day, we hit clouds. Turbulence, like many forms of trouble, cannot always be seen. We bounce so hard my arms sail helplessly above my head. In evolution, wingbones became arms and hands; perhaps I'm de-evolving.

From ten thousand feet I can see that spring is only half here: the southern part of the state is white, the northern half is green. Land is also time. The greening of time is a clock whose hands are blades of grass moving vertically, up through the fringe of numbers, spreading across the middle of the face, sinking again as the sun moves from one horizon to the other. Time doesn't go anywhere; the shadow of the plane, my shadow, moves across it.

To sit on a plane is to sit on the edge of sleep where the mind's forge brightens into incongruities. Down there I see disparate wholenesses strung together and the string dissolving. Mountains run like rivers; I fly through waves and waves of chiaroscuro light. The land looks bare but is articulate. The body of the plane is my body, pressing into spring, pressing matter into relation with matter. Is it even necessary to say the obvious? That spring brings on surges of desire? From this disinterested height I say out loud what Saint Augustine wrote: "My love is my weight. Because of it I move."

Directly below us now is the fine old Wyoming ranch where Joel, Mart, Dave, Hughy, and I have moved thousands of head of cattle. Joel's father, Smokey, was one of two brothers who put the outfit together. They worked hard, lived frugally, and even after Fred died, Smokey did not marry until his late fifties. As testimony to a long bachelorhood, there is no kitchen in the main house. The cookhouse stands separate from all the other buildings. In back is a bedroom and bath, which have housed a list of itinerant cooks ten pages long.

Over the years I've helped during roundup and branding. We'd rise at four. Smokey, now in his eighties, cooked flapjacks and boiled coffee on the wood cookstove. There was a long table. Joel and Smokey always sat at one end. They were lookalikes, both skin-and-bones tall with tipped-up dark eyes set in narrow faces. Stern and vigilant, Smokey once threw a young hired hand out of the cookhouse because he hadn't grained his saddle horse after a long day's ride. "On this outfit we take care of our animals first," he said. "Then if there's time, we eat."

Even in his early twenties, Joel had his father's dignity and razor-sharp wit. They both wore white Stetsons identically shaped. Only their hands were different: Joel had eight fingers and one thumb — the other he lost while roping.

Eight summers ago my parents visited their ranch. We ate a hearty meal of homemade whiskey left over from Prohibition days, steaks cut from an Angus bull, four kinds of vegetables, watermelon, ice cream, and pie. Despite a thirteen-year difference in our ages, Smokey wanted Joel and me to marry. As we rose from the meal, he shook my father's hand. "I guess you'll be my son's father-in-law," he said. That was news to all of us. Joel's face turned crimson. My father threw me an astonished look, cleared his throat, and thanked his host for the fine meal.

One night Joel did come to my house and asked me if I would take him into my bed. It was a gentlemanly proposition — doffed hat, moist eyes, a smile almost grimacing with loneliness. "You're an older woman. Think of all you could teach me," he said jauntily, but with a blush. He stood ramrod straight waiting for an answer. My silence turned him away like a rolling wave and he drove to the home ranch, spread out across the Emblem Bench thirty-five miles away.

The night Joel died I was staying at a writer's farm in Missouri. I had fallen asleep early, then awakened suddenly, feeling claustrophobic. I jumped out of bed and stood in the dark. I wanted to get out of there, drive home to Wyoming, and I didn't know why. Finally, at seven in the morning, I was able to sleep. I dreamed about a bird landing, then lifting out of a tree along a river bank. That was the night Joel's pickup rolled. He was found five hours after the accident occurred — just about daylight — and died on the way to the hospital.

Now I'm sitting on a fin of Gypsum Springs rock looking west. The sun is setting. What I see are three gray cloud towers letting rain down at the horizon. The sky behind these massifs is gilded gold, and long fingers of land — benches where the Hunt Oil Company's Charolais cattle graze — are pink. Somewhere over Joel's grave the sky is bright. The road where he died shines like a dash in a Paul

Klee painting. Over my head, it is still winter: snow so dry it feels like Styrofoam when squeezed together, tumbles into my lap. I think about flying and falling. The place in the sky where the eagle fell is dark, as if its shadow had burned into the backdrop of rock — Hiroshima style. Why does a wounded eagle get well and fly away; why do the head wounds of a young man cut him down? Useless questions.

Sex and death are the riddles thrown into the hopper, thrown down on the planet like hailstones. Where one hits the earth, it makes a crater and melts, perhaps a seed germinates, perhaps not. If I dice life down into atoms, the trajectories I find are so wild, so random, anything could happen: life or nonlife. But once we have a body, who can give it up easily? Our own or others'? We check our clocks and build our beautiful narratives, under which indeterminacy seethes.

Sometimes, lying in bed, I feel like a flounder with its two eyes on one side pointing upward into nothingness. The casings of thought rattle. Then I realize there are no casings at all. Is it possible that the mind, like space, is finite, but has no boundaries, no center or edge? I sit cross-legged on old blankets. My bare feet strain against the crotch of my knees. Time is between my toes, it seems. Just as morning comes and the indigo lifts, the leaflessness of the old apple tree looks ornate. Nothing in this world is plain.

"Every atom in your body was once inside a star," another physicist says, but he's only trying to humor me. Not all atoms in all kinds of matter are shared. But who wouldn't find that idea appealing? Outside, shadows trade places with a sliver of sun that trades places with shadow. Finally the lake ice goes and the water — pale and slate blue — wears its coat of diamonds all day. The mallards number twenty-six pairs now. They nest on two tiny islands and squabble amicably among themselves. A Pacific storm blows in from the south like a jibsail reaching far out, backhanding me with a gust of something tropical. It snows into my mouth, between my breasts, against my shins. Spring teaches me what space and time teach me: that I am a random multiple; that the many fit together like waves; that my swell is a collision of particles. Spring is a kind of music, a seething minor, a twelve-tone scale. Even the odd harmonies amassed only lift up to dissolve.

Spring passes harder and harder and is feral. The first thunder cracks the sky into a larger domain. Sap rises in obdurateness. For the first time in seven months, rain slants down in a slow pavane — sharp but soft — like desire, like the laying on of hands. I drive the highway that crosses the wild-horse range. Near Emblem I watch a black studhorse trot across the range all alone. He travels north, then turns in my direction as if trotting to me. Now, when I dream of Joel, he is riding that horse and he knows he is dead. One night he rides to my house, all smiles and shyness. I let him in.

Reflections and Responses

1. What does the author's physicist friend contribute to the essay? How does particle physics enter into Ehrlich's thinking? Would you say that she is scientific or nonscientific in her approach to nature?

2. Of what significance to Ehrlich's theme is the eagle with the "bum leg"? Consider carefully the passage in which she describes the eagle. What thoughts does the incident prompt? Why is it important that the eagle is hurt?

3. Much of Ehrlich's essay deals with time. Aside from her philosophical reflections on the subject, how does she mark the passage of time in the essay? Can you reconstruct her chronological outline? What is the time of the essay's opening, and how does it proceed? Of what importance is Wyoming's "three-part" spring to her structure?

ANNE FADIMAN

Mail

Anne Fadiman's "Mail" grows out of a long literary tradition. Such essays, with their attention to everyday detail, their casual humor, intellectual curiosity, occasional idiosyncratic stance, and mixture of information, criticism, and entertainment, were once known as "familiar" essays. That literary designation disappeared more than a half-century ago; in fact, Fadiman's father, the distinguished American essayist, Clifton Fadiman, noted this disappearance back in 1955 when he wrote "A Gentle Dirge for the Familiar Essay." The "familiar" essay took its name from the essayist's use of ordinary topics — such familiar subjects as taking walks or observing facial expressions or table manners — and from an agreeable style or tone that was neither too formal or too informal. Unlike today's confessional or autobiographically oriented personal essays, the familiar essay had a subject other than the self, though the writer usually approached the subject from a decidedly personal perspective. In "Mail," Anne Fadiman looks at a new phenomenon that has become familiar to millions — electronic mail — and ruminates on its relation to her father's old-fashioned habits of letter writing and even the history of the postal service. Along the way, she raises some significant questions about modern technology and the price we sometimes pay for its efficiency and convenience.

Anne Fadiman is editor of The American Scholar. *Her book* The Spirit Catches You and You Fall Down *won the National Book Critics Circle Award for general nonfiction.* Ex Libris *is a collection of essays on reading and language. A winner of the National Magazine Award for reporting, she has contributed articles and essays to* Civilization, The New Yorker, Harper's, *and* The New York Times, *among other publications. She lives in western Massachusetts and teaches writing at Smith College. "Mail" originally appeared in* The American Scholar

and was selected by Kathleen Norris for The Best American Essays
2001.

Some years ago, my parents lived at the top of a steep hill. My father kept a pair of binoculars on his desk with which, like a pirate
captain hoisting his spyglass to scan the horizon for treasure ships,
he periodically inspected the mailbox to see if the flag had been
raised. When it finally went up, he trudged down the driveway and
opened the extra-large black metal box, purchased by my mother
in the same accommodating spirit with which some wives buy their
husbands extra-large trousers. The day's load — a mountain of letters and about twenty pounds of review books packed in Jiffy bags,
a few of which had been pierced by their angular contents and
were leaking what my father called "mouse dirt"—was always
tightly wedged. But he was a persistent man, and after a brief show
of resistance the mail would surrender, to be carried up the hill in
a tight clinch and dumped onto a gigantic desk. Until that moment, my father's day had not truly begun.

His desk was made of steel, weighed more than a refrigerator,
and bristled with bookshelves and secret drawers and sliding pan-
els and a niche for a cedar-lined humidor. (He believed that cigar-
smoking and mail-reading were natural partners, like oysters and
Muscadet.) I think of it as less a writing surface than a mail-sorting
table. He hated Sundays and holidays because there was nothing
new to spread on it. Vacations were taxing, the equivalent of
forced relocations to places without food. His homecomings were
always followed by day-long orgies of mail-opening — feast after
famine — at the end of which all the letters were answered; all the
bills were paid; the outgoing envelopes were affixed with stamps
from a brass dispenser heavy enough to break your toe; the books
and manuscripts were neatly stacked; and the empty Jiffy bags
were stuffed into an extra-large copper wastebasket, cheering con-
firmation that the process of postal digestion was complete.

"One of my unfailing minor pleasures may seem dull to more
energetic souls: opening the mail," he once wrote.

Living in an advanced industrial civilization is a kind of near-conquest
over the unexpected. . . . Such efficiency is of course admirable. It does
not, however, by its very nature afford scope to that perverse human
trait, still not quite eliminated, which is pleased by the accidental. Thus

to many tame citizens like me the morning mail functions as the voice of the unpredictable and keeps alive for a few minutes a day the keen sense of the unplanned and the unplannable. The letter opener is an instrument that has persisted from some antique land of chance and adventure into our ordered world of the perfectly calculated.

What chance and adventure might the day's haul contain? My brother asked him, when he was in his nineties, what kind of mail he liked best. "In my youth," he replied, "a love letter. In middle age, a job offer. Today, a check." (That was false cynicism, I think. His favorite letters were from his friends.) Whatever the accidental pleasure, it could not please until it arrived. Why were deliveries so few and so late (he frequently grumbled), when, had he lived in central London in the late seventeenth century, he could have received his mail between ten and twelve times a day?

We get what we need. In 1680, London had mail service nearly every hour because there were no telephones. If you wished to invite someone to tea in the afternoon, you could send him a letter in the morning and receive his reply before he showed up at your doorstep. Postage was one penny.

If you wished to send a letter to another town, however, delivery was less reliable and postage was gauged on a scale of staggering complexity. By the mid-1830s,

> the postage on a single letter delivered within eight miles of the office where it was posted was . . . twopence, the lowest rate beyond that limit being fourpence. Beyond fifteen miles it became fivepence; after which it rose a penny at a time, but by irregular augmentation, to one shilling, the charge for three hundred miles. There was as a general rule an additional charge of a half penny on a letter crossing the Scotch border; while letters to or from Ireland had to bear, in addition, packet rates, and rates for crossing the bridges over the Conway and the Menai.

So wrote Rowland Hill, the greatest postal reformer in history, who in 1837 devised a scheme to reduce and standardize postal rates and to shift the burden of payment from the addressee to the sender.

Until a few years ago I had no idea that if you sent a letter out of town — and if you weren't a nobleman, a member of Parliament, or other VIP who had been granted the privilege of free postal franking — the postage was paid by the recipient. This dawned on

me when I was reading a biography of Charles Lamb, whose employer, the East India House, allowed clerks to receive letters gratis
until 1817: a substantial perk, sort of like being able to call your
friends on your office's 800 number. (Lamb, who practiced stringent economies, also wrote much of his personal correspondence
on company stationery. His most famous letter to Wordsworth,
for instance — the one in which he refers to Coleridge as "an
Archangel a little damaged" — is inscribed on a page whose heading reads "Please to state the Weights and Amounts of the following Lots.")

Sir Walter Scott liked to tell the story of how he had once had to
pay "five pounds odd" in order to receive a package from a young
New York lady he had never met: an atrocious play called *The
Cherokee Lovers,* accompanied by a request to read it, correct it,
write a prologue, and secure a producer. Two weeks later another
large package arrived for which he was charged a similar amount.
"Conceive my horror," he told his friend Lord Melville, "when out
jumped the same identical tragedy of *The Cherokee Lovers,* with a
second epistle from the authoress, stating that, as the winds had
been boisterous, she feared the vessel entrusted with her former
communication might have foundered, and therefore judged it
prudent to forward a duplicate." Lord Melville doubtless found
this tale hilarious, but Rowland Hill would have been appalled. He
had grown up poor, and, as Christopher Browne notes in *Getting
the Message,* his splendid history of the British postal system, "Hill
had never forgotten his mother's anxiety when a letter with a high
postal duty was delivered, nor the time when she sent him out to
sell a bag of clothes to raise 3s for a batch of letters."

Hill was a born Utilitarian who, at the age of twelve, had been so
frustrated by the irregularity of the bell at the school where his father was principal that he had instituted a precisely timed bell-
ringing schedule. In 1837 he published a report called "Post
Office Reform: Its Importance and Practicability." Why, he argued,
should legions of accountants be employed to figure out the
Byzantine postal charges? Why should Britain's extortionate postal
rates persist when France's revenues had risen, thanks to higher
mail volume, after its rates were lowered? Why should postmen
waste precious time waiting for absent addressees to come home
and pay up? A national Penny Post was the answer, with postage
paid by the senders, "using a bit of paper . . . covered at the back

with a glutinous wash, which the bringer might, by the application of a little moisture, attach to the back of the letter."

After much debate, Parliament passed a postal reform act in 1839. On January 10, 1840, Hill wrote in his diary, "Penny Postage extended to the whole kingdom this day! . . . I guess that the number despatched to-night will not be less than 100,000, or more than three times what it was this day twelve-months. If less I shall be disappointed." On January 11, he wrote, "The number of letters despatched exceeded all expectation. It was 112,000, of which all but 13,000 or 14,000 were prepaid." In May, after experimentation to produce a canceling ink that could not be surreptitiously removed, the Post Office introduced the Penny Black, bearing a profile of Queen Victoria: the first postage stamp. The press, pondering the process of cancellation, fretted about the "untoward disfiguration of the royal person," but Victoria became an enthusiastic philatelist, and renounced the royal franking privilege for the pleasure of walking to the local post office from Balmoral Castle to stock up on stamps and gossip with the postmaster. When Rowland Hill — by that time, *Sir* Rowland Hill — retired as Post Office Secretary in 1864, *Punch* asked, "SHOULD ROWLAND HILL have a Statue? Certainly, if OLIVER CROMWELL should. For one is celebrated for cutting off the head of a bad King, and the other for sticking on the head of a good Queen."

The Penny Post, wrote Harriet Martineau, "will do more for the circulation of ideas, for the fostering of domestic affections, for the humanizing of the mass generally, than any other single measure that our national wit can devise." It was incontrovertible proof, in an age that embraced progress on all fronts ("the means of locomotion and correspondence, every mechanical art, every manufacture, every thing that promotes the convenience of life," as Macaulay put it in a typical gush of national pride), that the British were the most civilized people on earth. Ancient Syrian runners, Chinese carrier pigeons, Persian post riders, Egyptian papyrus bearers, Greek *hemerodromes*, Hebrew dromedary riders, Roman equestrian relays, medieval monk-messengers, Catalan *troters*, international couriers of the House of Thurn and Taxis, American mail wagons — what could these all have been leading up to, like an ever-ascending staircase, but the Victorian postal system?

And yet (to raise a subversive question), might it be possible that, whatever the profit in efficiency, there may have been a literary cost associated with the conversion from payment by addressee to payment by sender? If you knew that your recipient would have to bear the cost of your letter, wouldn't courtesy motivate you to write an extra-good one? On the other hand, if you paid for it yourself, wouldn't you be more likely to feel you could get away with "Having a wonderful time, wish you were here"?

I used to think my father's attachment to the mail was strange. I now feel exactly the way he did. I live in an apartment building and, with or without binoculars, I cannot see my mailbox, one of thirteen dinky aluminum cells bolted to the lobby wall. The mail usually comes around four in the afternoon (proving that the postal staircase that reached its highest point with Rowland Hill has been descending ever since), which means that at around three, *just in case*, I'm likely to visit the lobby for the first of several reconnaissance missions. There's no flag, but over the years my fingers have become postally sensitive, and I can tell if the box is full by giving it the slightest of pats. If there's a hint of convexity — it's very subtle, nothing as obvious, let us say, as the bulge of a can that might harbor botulism — I whip out my key with the same excitement with which my father set forth down his driveway.

There the resemblance ends. The thrill of the treasure hunt is followed all too quickly by the glum realization that the box contains only four kinds of mail: (1) junk, (2) bills, (3) work, and (4) letters that I will read with enjoyment, place in a folder labeled "To Answer," leave there for a geologic interval, and feel guilty about. The longer they languish, the more I despair of my ability to live up to the escalating challenge of their response. It is a truism of epistolary psychology that, for example, a Christmas thank-you note written on December 26 can say any old thing, but if you wait until February, you are convinced that nothing less than *Middlemarch* will do.

In October of 1998 I finally gave in and signed up for e-mail. I had resisted for a long time. My husband and I were proud of our retrograde status. Not only did we lack a modem, but we didn't have a car, a microwave, a Cuisinart, an electric can opener, a cellular phone, a CD player, or cable television. It's hard to give up that sort of backward image; I worried that our friends wouldn't have enough to make fun of. I also worried that learning how to use e-mail would be like learning how to program our VCR, an unsuccessful project that had confirmed what excellent judgment we had shown in not purchasing a car, etc.

As millions of people had discovered before me, e-mail was fast. Sixteenth-century correspondents used to write "Haste, haste, haste, for lyfe, for lyfe, haste!" on their most urgent letters; my "server," a word that conjured up a delicious sycophancy, treated *every* message as if someone's life depended on it. Not only did it get there instantly, caromed in a series of analog cyberpackets along the nodes of the Internet and reconverted to digital form via its recipient's modem. (I do not understand a word of what I just wrote, but that is immaterial. Could the average Victorian have diagrammed the mail coach route from Swansea to Tunbridge Wells?) More important, I *answered* e-mail fast — almost always on the day it arrived. No more guilt! I used to think I did not like to write letters. I now realize that what I didn't like was folding the paper, sealing the envelope, looking up the address, licking the stamp, getting in the elevator, crossing the street, and dropping the letter in the postbox.

At first I made plenty of mistakes. I clicked on the wrong icons, my attachments didn't stick, and, not having learned how to file addresses, I sent an X-rated message to my husband (I thought) at gcolt@aol.com instead of georgecolt@aol.com. I hope Gerald or Gertrude found it flattering. But the learning curve was as steep as my father's driveway, and pretty soon I was batting our fifteen or twenty e-mails a day in the time it had once taken me to avoid answering a single letter. My box was nearly always full — no waiting, no binoculars, no convexity checks, no tugging — and when it wasn't, the reason was not that the mail hadn't *arrived*, it was that it hadn't been *sent*. I began to look forward every morning to the festive green arrow with which AT&T WorldNet welcomed me into my father's "antique land of chance and adventure." Would I be invited to purchase Viagra, lose thirty pounds, regrow my thinning hair, obtain electronic spy software, get an EZ loan, retire in three years, or win a Pentium III 500 MHz computer (presumably in order to receive such messages even faster)? Or would I find a satisfying little clutch of friendly notes whose responses could occupy me until I awoke sufficiently to tackle something that required intelligence? As Hemingway wrote to Fitzgerald, describing the act of letter-writing: "Such a swell way to keep from working and yet feel you've done something."

My computer, without visible distension, managed to store a flood tide of mail that in nonvirtual form would have silted up my office to the ceiling. This was admirable. And when I wished to commune with my friend Charlie, who lives in Taipei, not only could I disregard the thirteen-hour time difference, but I was billed the same amount as if I had dialed his old telephone number on East 22nd Street. The German critic Bernhard Siegert has observed that the breakthrough concept behind Rowland Hill's Penny Post was "to think of all Great Britain as a single city, that is, no longer to give a moment's thought to what had been dear to Western discourse on the nature of the letter from the beginning: the idea of distance." E-mail is a modern Penny Post: the world is a single city with a single postal rate.

Alas, our Penny Post, like Hill's, comes at a price. If the transfer of postal charges from sender to recipient was the first great de-motivator in the art of letter-writing, e-mail was the second. "It now seems a good bet," Adam Gopnik has written, "that in two hundred years people will be reading someone's collected e-mail the way we read Edmund Wilson's diaries or Pepys's letters." Maybe — but will what they read be any good? E-mails are brief. (One doesn't blather; an overlong message might induce carpal tunnel syndrome in the recipient from excessive pressure on the Down arrow.) They are also — at least the ones I receive — frequently devoid of capitalization, minimally punctuated, and creatively spelled. E-mail's greatest strength — speed — is also its Achilles' heel. In effect, it's always December 26; you are not expected to write *Middlemarch,* and therefore you don't.

In a letter to his friend William Unwin, written on August 6, 1780, William Cowper noted that "a Letter may be written upon any thing or Nothing." This observation is supported by the index of *The Faber Book of Letters, 1578–1939.* Let us examine some entries from the *d* section:

damnation, 87
dances and entertainments, 33, 48, 59, 97, 111, 275
dentistry, 220
depressive illness, 81, 87

I have never received an e-mail on any of these topics. Instead, I am informed that *Your browser is not Y2K-compliant. Your son left his Pokémon turtle under our sofa. Your column is 23 lines too long.* Important pieces of news, but, as Lytton Strachey (one of the all-time great letter writers) pointed out, "No good letter was ever written to convey information, or to please its recipient: it may achieve both these results incidentally; but its fundamental purpose is to express the personality of its writer." *But wait!* you pipe up. *Someone just e-mailed me a joke!* So she did, but wasn't the personality of the sender slightly muffled by the fact that she forwarded it from an e-mail *she* received, and sent it to seventeen additional addressees?

I also take a dim, or perhaps a buffaloed, view of electronic slang. Perhaps I should view it as a linguistic milestone, as historic as the evolution of Cockney rhyming slang in the 1840s. But will the future generations who reopen our hard drives be stirred by the eloquence of the e-acronyms recommended by a Web site on "netiquette"?

BTDT	been there done that
FC	fingers crossed
IITYWTMWYBMAD	if I tell you what this means will you buy me a drink?
MTE	my thoughts exactly
ROTFL	rolling on the floor laughing
RTFM	read the f——— manual
TAH	take a hint
TTFN	ta-ta for now

Or by the "emoticons," otherwise known as "smileys"— punctuational images, read sideways — that "help readers interpret the e-mail writer's attitude and tone"?

:-)	ha ha
:-(	boo hoo
(-:	I am left-handed
%-)	I have been staring at a green screen for 15 hours straight

```
 :-&    I am tongue-tied
 {:-)   I wear a toupee
 :-[    I am a vampire
 :-F    I am a bucktoothed vampire with one tooth missing
=l:-)=  I am Abraham Lincoln
```

"We are of a different race from the Greeks, to whom beauty was everything," wrote Thomas Carlyle, a Victorian progress-booster. "Our glory and our beauty arise out of our inward strength, which makes us victorious over material resistance." We have achieved a similar victory of efficiency over beauty. I wouldn't give up e-mail if you paid me, but I'd feel a pang of regret if the epistolary novels of the future were to revolve around such messages as

Subject: **R U Kidding?**
From: Clarissa Harlowe <claha@virtue.com>
To: Robert Lovelace <lovelaceandlovegirlz@vice.com

hi bob, TAH. if u think i'm gonna run off w/ u, :-F. do u really think i'm that kind of girl?? if you're looking 4 a trollop, CLICK HERE NOW: http://www.hotpix.html. TTFN.

I own a letter written by Robert Falcon Scott, the polar explorer, to G. T. Temple, Esq., who helped procure the footgear for Scott's first Antarctic expedition. The date is February 26, 1901. The envelope and octavo stationery have black borders because Queen Victoria had died in January. The paper is yellowed, the handwriting is messy, and the stamp bears the Queen's profile — and the denomination ONE PENNY. I bought the letter many years ago because, unlike a Cuisinart, which would have cost about the same, it was something I believed I could not live without. I could never feel that way about an e-mail.

I also own my father's old wastebasket, which now holds my own empty Jiffy bags. Several times a day I use his stamp dispenser; it is tarnished and dinged, but still capable of unspooling its contents with a singular smoothness. And my file cabinets hold hundreds of his letters, the earliest written in his sixties in small, crabbed handwriting, the last in his nineties, after he lost much of his sight, penned with a Magic Marker in huge capital letters. I hope my children will find them someday, as Hart Crane once found his grandmother's love letters in the attic,

pressed so long
Into a corner of the roof
That they are brown and soft,
And liable to melt as snow.

Reflections and Responses

1. Note the perspective from which Anne Fadiman opens her essay. Can you find other sections of the essay that you think could also have served as a beginning? Why do you think she doesn't begin with the earliest time and end in the present?

2. A portion of the essay is taken up by her brief history of the British postal system. How does she integrate this information into the essay? What associations does she make between that history and our present system of communication? How is her movement between various time periods reflected in the way she crafts her sentences? Find examples of how she constructs single sentences that link various eras.

3. What specific images does Fadiman use to contrast her father's time with her own? How does she evaluate each era? What aspects of her father's time does she appear to prefer? How does she avoid being completely nostalgic about the past? In what ways does Fadiman's essay resemble Scott Russell Sander's "The Inheritance of Tools"?

IAN FRAZIER

A Lovely Sort of Lower Purpose

In the middle of the eighteenth century the great English essayist, Samuel
Johnson, regularly published a series of essays known as The Idler. *The*
title was carefully chosen; from Montaigne on, essayists have traditionally
cultivated a leisurely pace and written many pieces in praise of idleness or
what in today's terms would be called "hanging out" and "fooling around."
In "A Lovely Sort of Lower Purpose," Ian Frazier revisits this time-tested
topic and, in his inimitable fashion, celebrates the virtues of doing nothing.
Frazier warns us, however, that this virtue is rapidly declining as our rest-
less society continually finds ways to make everything busy, useful, and
purposeful. As Frazier suggests, the terrible question grown-ups often ask
children, "What are you doing*?" now haunts us all.*

Besides several collections of humorous essays and two award-winning
books of nonfiction, Family *(1994) and* Great Plains *(1989), Ian Fra-*
zier has published On the Rez *(1999), a look at life on a reservation,*
and The Fish's Eye *(2002), a collection of his fishing essays. His writing*
has appeared in The New Yorker, Outside, The Atlantic Monthly,
and many other magazines. Frazier was the guest editor of The Best
American Essays 1997. *"A Lovely Sort of Lower Purpose" originally ap-*
peared in Outside *magazine and was selected by Edward Hoagland for*
The Best American Essays 1999.

As kids, my friends and I spent a lot of time out in the woods. "The
woods" was our part-time address, destination, purpose, and excuse. If I went to a friend's house and found him not at home, his
mother might say, "Oh, he's out in the woods," with a tone of airy
acceptance. It's similar to the tone people sometimes use nowadays

to tell me that someone I'm looking for is on the golf course or at the hairdresser's or at the gym, or even "away from his desk." The combination of vagueness and specificity in the answer gives a sense of somewhere romantically incommunicado. I once attended an awards dinner at which Frank Sinatra was supposed to appear, and when he didn't, the master of ceremonies explained that Frank had called to say he was "filming on location." Ten-year-olds suffer from a scarcity of fancy-sounding excuses to do whatever they feel like for a while. For us, saying we were "out in the woods" worked just fine.

We sometimes told ourselves that what we were doing in the woods was exploring. Exploring was a more prominent idea back then than it is today. History, for example, seemed to be mostly about explorers, and the semirural part of Ohio where we lived still had a faint recollection of being part of the frontier. At the town's two high schools, the sports teams were the Explorers and the Pioneers. Our explorations, though, seemed to have less system than the historic kind: something usually came up along the way. Say we began to cross one of the little creeks plentiful in the second-growth forests we frequented and found that all the creek's moisture had somehow become a shell of milk-white ice about eight inches above the now-dry bed. No other kind of ice is as satisfying to break. The search for the true meridian would be postponed while we spent the afternoon breaking the ice, stomping it underfoot by the furlong, and throwing its bigger pieces like Frisbees to shatter in excellent, war-movie-type fragmentation among the higher branches of the trees.

Stuff like that — throwing rocks at a fresh mudflat to make craters, shooting frogs with slingshots, making forts, picking blackberries, digging in what we were briefly persuaded was an Indian burial mound — occupied much of our time in the woods. Our purpose there was a higher sort of un-purpose, a free-form aimlessness that would be beyond me now. Once as we tramped for miles along Tinker's Creek my friend Kent told me the entire plot of two Bob Hope movies, *The Paleface* and *Son of Paleface*, which he had just seen on a double bill. The joke-filled monotony of his synopsis went well with the soggy afternoon, the muddy water, the endless tangled brush. (Afterward, when I saw the movies themselves, I found a lot to prefer in Kent's version.) The woods

were ideal for those trains of thought that involved tedium and
brooding. Often when I went by myself I would climb a tree and
just sit.

I could list a hundred pointless things we did in the woods.
Climbing trees, though, was a common one. Often we got "lost"
and had to climb a tree to get our bearings. If you read a story in
which someone does that successfully, be skeptical; the topmost
branches are usually too skinny to hold weight, and we could never
climb high enough to see anything except other trees. There were
four or five trees that we visited regularly — tall beeches, easy to
climb and comfortable to sit in. We spent hours at a time in trees,
afflicting the best perches with so many carved-in names, hearts,
arrows, and funny sayings from the comic strips that we ran out of
room for more.

It was in a tree, too, that our days of fooling around in the woods
came to an end. By then some of us had reached seventh grade
and had begun the bumpy ride of adolescence. In March, the
month when we usually took to the woods again after winter, two
friends and I set out to go exploring. Right away, we climbed
a tree, and soon were indulging in the spurious nostalgia of
kids who have only short pasts to look back upon. The "remember whens" faltered, finally, and I think it occurred to all three of
us at the same time that we really were rather big to be up in
a tree. Some of us had started wearing unwoodsy outfits like short-
sleeved madras shirts and penny loafers, even after school. Soon
there would be the spring dances on Friday evenings in the high
school cafeteria. We looked at the bare branches around us re-
ceding into obscurity, and suddenly there was nothing up there
for us. Like Adam and Eve, we saw our own nakedness, and
that terrible grown-up question "What are you *doing?*" made us
ashamed.

We went back to the woods eventually — and when I say "we," I'm
speaking demographically, not just of my friends and me. Millions
of us went back, once the sexual and social business of early adulthood had been more or less sorted out. But significantly, we
brought that same question with us. Now we had to be seriously
doing — racing, strengthening, slimming, traversing, collecting,
achieving, catching-and-releasing. A few parts per million of

our concentrated purpose changed the chemistry of the whole outdoors. Even those rare interludes of actually doing nothing in the woods took on a certain fierceness as we reinforced them with personal dramas, usually of a social or sexual kind: the only way we could justify sitting motionless in an A-frame cabin in the north woods of Michigan, for example, was if we had just survived a really messy divorce.

"What are you *doing*?" The question pursues me still. When I go fishing and catch no fish, the idea that it's fun simply to be out on the river consoles me for not one second. I must catch fish; and if I do, I must then catch more and bigger fish. On a Sunday afternoon last summer I took my two young children fishing with me on a famous trout stream near my house. My son was four and my daughter was eight, and I kidded myself that in their company I would be able to fish with my usual single-minded mania. I suited up in my waders and tackle-shopful of gear and led my kids from the parking area down toward the water. On the way, however, we had to cross a narrow, shallow irrigation ditch dating from when this part of the valley had farms. Well, the kids saw that little ditch and immediately took off their shoes and waded in and splashed and floated pine cones. My son got an inexplicable joy from casting his little spinning rod far over the ditch into the woods and reeling the rubber casting weight back through the trees. My daughter observed many tent caterpillars — a curse of yard-owners that year — falling from bushes into the ditch and floating helplessly along, and she decided to rescue them. She kept watching the water carefully, and whenever she spotted a caterpillar she swooped down and plucked it out and put it carefully on the bank. I didn't have the heart to drag the kids away, and as I was sitting in all my fishing gear beside the unlikely trickle, a fly fisherman about my age and just as geared-up came along. He took me in at a glance, noticed my equipment and my idleness, and gave a small but unmistakable snort of derision. I was offended, but I understood how he felt as he and his purpose hurried on by.

Here, I'd like to consider a word whose meaning has begun to drift like a caterpillar on a stream. That word is *margin*. Originally its meaning — the blank space around a body of type or the border of a piece of ground — had neutral connotations. But its adjective form, *marginal,* now has a negative tinge. Marginal people or

places or activities are ones that don't quite work out, don't sufficiently account of themselves in the economic world. From the adjective sprouted a far-fetched verb, *marginalize,* whose meaning is
only bad. To be marginalized is to be a victim, and to marginalize
someone else is an act of exclusion that can cost you tenure. Today's so-called marginal people are the exact equivalents, etymo-
logically, of the old-time heathens. A heathen was a savage, wild,
un-Christian person who lived out on a heath. The heath was the
margin of Christendom. No one today would ever use the word
heathen except ironically, but we call certain people and activities
marginal without a hint of irony all the time.

I've never been on a heath, but to judge from accounts of coal-
smogged London in the days when *heathen* was in vogue, a
windswept place full of heather and salmon streams sounds like
the better place to be. And if the modern version of the margin is
somewhere in western Nebraska, and the un-margin, the coveted
red-hot center, is a site like Rodeo Drive, I wouldn't know which to
choose. We need both, but especially as the world gets more
jammed up, we need margins. A book without margins is impossible to read. And marginal behavior can be the most important
kind. Every purpose-filled activity we pursue in the woods began as
just fooling around. The first person to ride his bicycle down a
mountain trail was doing a decidedly marginal thing. The margin
is where you can try out odd ideas that you might be afraid to
admit to with people looking on. Scientists have a term for research carried on with no immediate prospects of economic gain:
"blue-sky research." Marginal places are the blue-sky research
zones of the outdoors.

Unfortunately, there are fewer and fewer of them every day.
Now a common fate of a place on the margin is to have a convenience store or a windowless brick building belonging to a telephone company built on it. Across the country, endless miles of
exurbia now overlap and spill into one another with hardly a margin at all. There's still a lot of open space out there, of course, but
usually it's far enough from home that just getting to it requires
purpose and premeditation. As the easy-to-wander-into hometown
margins disappear, a certain kind of wandering becomes endangered too.

On the far west side of the small western city where I live, past
the town-killer discount stores, is an open expanse of undeveloped

ground. Its many acres border the Bitterroot River, and its far end abuts a fence surrounding a commercial gravel pit. It is a classic marginal, anything-goes sort of place, and at the moment I prefer it to just about anywhere I know.

Army reservists sometimes drive tanks there on weekends. The camouflaged behemoths slithering across the ground would make my skin crawl if I didn't suspect that the kids driving them were having such a good time. The dirt-bike guys certainly are, as they zip all over, often dawn to dusk, exuberantly making a racket. Dads bring their kids to this place to fly kites and model airplanes, people in a converted school bus camp there for weeks on end, coin-shooters cruise around with metal detectors, hunters just in off the river clean game, college kids party and leave heaps of cigarette butts and beer cans and occasionally pieces of underwear. I fish there, of course, but remarkably I don't always feel I have to. Sometimes I also pick up the trash, and I pull my kids around on a sled in the winter, and I bring friends just off the plane to sit on the riverbank and drink wine and watch the sunset.

Soon, I'm sure, Development will set its surveyor's tripod on this ground and make it get with one program or another. Rumblings of this have already begun to sound in the local newspaper. I foresee rows of condominiums, or an expansion of the gravel pit, or a public park featuring hiking trails and grim pieces of exercise equipment every twenty yards. That last choice, in all its worthy banality, somehow is the most disheartening of all. A plan will claim the empty acres and erase the spotted knapweed and the tank tracks and the beer-can heaps. The place's possibilities, which at the moment are approximately infinite, will be reduced to merely a few. And those of uncertain purpose will have to go elsewhere when they feel like doing nothing in particular, just fooling around.

Reflections and Responses

1. What do you think Frazier means by a "lower purpose"? What would a higher purpose be? Give a few examples of lower-purpose activities that appear in the essay.

2. What is Frazier opposed to in this essay? Do you think he opposes all kinds of purposeful activity? Explain in your own words what he objects to.

3. Why is the idea of margins important to the development of his essay? How has the term taken on negative meanings? Why does Frazier want to retain the word's other meanings? How do Frazier's final three paragraphs illustrate his use of the word *marginal*?

EDWARD HOAGLAND

Heaven and Nature

Speculation, says Edward Hoagland at the conclusion of this intensely reflective essay, is "a high-risk activity." Since speculation is at the heart of the genre, he might have added that to write essays is essentially to take risks. Intellectual, emotional, and literary security are not attractive goals for personal essayists like Hoagland, whose work often explores the outer edges of personality and social behavior. In "Heaven and Nature," he penetrates territory that most people would prefer to skirt around: the inclination to commit suicide. As usual, his approach is deeply personal and yet remarkably inclusive.

Hoagland, whom John Updike has called "the best essayist" of his generation, is the author of five books of fiction, two travel books, and numerous essay collections, including The Courage of Turtles *(1971),* Walking the Dead Diamond River *(1973),* Red Wolves and Black Bears *(1976), and* The Tugman's Passage *(1982). In 1988, he published* Heart's Desire, *a collection of what he considered his best essays from twenty years of writing. Another collection of essays,* Balancing Acts, *appeared in 1992 and was followed by* Tigers and Ice *(1999) and a memoir,* Compass Points: How I Lived *(2001). He is the general editor of the Penguin Nature Library and is a member of the American Academy of Arts and Letters. "Heaven and Nature" originally appeared in* Harper's Magazine *(1988) and was selected by Geoffrey Wolff for* The Best American Essays *1989.*

A friend of mine, a peaceable soul who has been riding the New York subways for thirty years, finds himself stepping back from the tracks once in a while and closing his eyes as the train rolls in. This, he says, is not only to suppress an urge to throw himself in front of it but because every couple of weeks an impulse rises in him to push a stranger onto the tracks, any stranger, thus ending his own life too. He blames this partly on apartment living, "pigeonholes without being able to fly."

It is profoundly startling not to trust oneself after decades of doing so. I don't dare keep ammunition in my country house for a small rifle I bought secondhand two decades ago. The gun had sat in a cupboard in the back room with the original box of .22 bullets under the muzzle all that time, seldom fired except at a few apples hanging in a tree every fall to remind me of my army training near the era of the Korean War, when I'd been considered quite a marksman. When I bought the gun I didn't trust either my professional competence as a writer or my competence as a father as much as I came to, but certainly believed I could keep myself alive. I bought it for protection, and the idea that someday I might be afraid of shooting myself with the gun would have seemed inconceivable — laughable.

One's fifties can be giddy years, as anybody fifty knows. Chest pains, back pains, cancer scares, menopausal or prostate complications are not the least of it, and the fidelities of a lifetime, both personal and professional, may be called into question. Was it a mistake to have stuck so long with one's marriage, and to have stayed with a lackluster well-paying job? (Or *not* to have stayed and stuck?) People not only lose faith in their talents and their dreams or values; some simply tire of them. Grow tired, too, of the smell of fried-chicken grease, once such a delight, and the cold glutinosity of ice cream, the boredom of beer, the stop-go of travel, the hiccups of laughter, and of two rush hours a day, then the languor of weekends, of athletes as well as accountants, and even the frantic birdsong of spring — red-eyed vireos that have been clocked singing twenty-two thousand times in a day. Life is a matter of cultivating the six senses, and an equilibrium with nature and what I think of as its subdivision, human nature, trusting no one completely but almost everyone at least a little; but this is easier said than done.

More than thirty thousand Americans took their own lives last year, men mostly, with the highest rate being among those older than sixty-five. When I asked a friend why three times as many men kill themselves as members of her own sex, she replied with sudden anger, "I'm not going to go into the self-indulgence of men." They won't bend to failure, she said, and want to make themselves memorable. Suicide is an exasperating act as often as it is pitiable. "Committing" suicide is in bad odor in our culture even among those who don't believe that to cash in your chips ahead of time and hand back to God his gifts to you is a blasphemous sin. We the living, in any case, are likely to feel accused by this person who "voted with his feet." It appears to cast a subversive judgment upon the social polity as a whole that what was supposed to work in life — religion, family, friendship, commerce, and industry — did not, and furthermore it frightens the horses in the street, as Shaw's friend Mrs. Patrick Campbell once defined wrongful behavior.

Many suicides inflict outrageous trauma, burning permanent injuries in the minds of their children, though they may have joked beforehand only of "taking a dive." And sometimes the gesture has a peevish or cowardly aspect, or seems to have been senselessly shortsighted as far as an outside observer can tell. There are desperate suicides and crafty suicides, people who do it to cause others trouble and people who do it to save others trouble, deranged exhibitionists who yell from a building ledge and close-mouthed, secretive souls who swim out into the ocean's anonymity. Suicide may in fact be an attempt to escape death, shortcut the dreadful deteriorating processes, abort one's natural trajectory, elude "the ruffian on the stairs," in A. E. Housman's phrase for a cruelly painful, anarchic death — make it neat and not messy. The deed can be grandiose or self-abnegating, vindictive or drably mousy, rationally plotted or plainly insane. People sidle toward death, intent upon outwitting their own bodies' defenses, or they may dramatize the chance to make one last, unambiguous, irrevocable decision, like a captain scuttling his ship — death before dishonor — leaping toward oblivion through a curtain of pain, like a frog going down the throat of a snake. One man I knew hosted a quietly affectionate evening with several unknowing friends on the night before he swallowed too many pills. Another waved an apologetic goodbye to a bystander on a bridge. Seldom shy ordinarily, and rarely considerate, he turned shy and apologetic in the last moment of life. Never physically inclined, he made a great vault toward the ice on the Mississippi.

In the army, we wore dog tags with a notch at one end by which these numbered pieces of metal could be jammed between our teeth, if we lay dead and nameless on a battlefield, for later sorting. As "servicemen" our job would be to kill people who were pointed out to us as enemies, or make "the supreme sacrifice" for a higher good than enjoying the rest of our lives. Life was very much a possession, in other words — not only God's, but the soldier's own to dispose of. Working in an army hospital, I frequently did handle dead bodies, but this never made me feel I would refuse to kill another man whose uniform was pointed out to me as being inimical, or value my life more tremulously and vigilantly. The notion of dying for my country never appealed to me as much as dying free-lance for my ideas (in the unlikely event that I *could* do that), but I was ready. People were taught during the 1940s and 1950s that one should be ready to die for one's beliefs. Heroes were revered because they had deliberately chosen to give up their lives. Life would not be worth living under the tyranny of an invader and Nathan Hale apparently hadn't paused to wonder whether God might not have other uses for him besides being hung. Nor did the pilot Colin Kelly hesitate before plunging his plane into a Japanese battleship, becoming America's first well-publicized hero in World War II.

I've sometimes wondered why people who know that they are terminally ill, or who are headed for suicide, so very seldom have paused to take a bad guy along with them. It is lawless to consider an act of assassination, yet hardly more so, really, than suicide is regarded in some quarters (or death itself, in others). Government bureaucracies, including our own, in their majesty and as the executors of laws, regularly weigh the pros and cons of murdering foreign antagonists. Of course the answer is that most individuals are fortunately more timid as well as humbler in their judgment than government officialdom, but beyond that, when dying or suicidal, they no longer care enough to devote their final energies to doing good works of any kind — Hitler himself in their gunsights they would have passed up. Some suicides become so crushed and despairing that they can't recognize the consequences of anything they do, and it's not primarily vindictiveness that wreaks such havoc upon their survivors but their derangement from ordinary life.

Courting the idea is different from the real impulse. "When he begged for help, we took him and locked him up," another friend of mine says, speaking of her husband. "Not till then. Wishing to be out of the situation you are in — feeling helpless and unable to cope — is not the same as wishing to be dead. If I actually wished to be dead, even my children's welfare would have no meaning."

You might think the ready option of divorce available lately would have cut suicide rates, offering an escape to battered wives, lovelorn husbands, and other people in despair. But it doesn't work that way. When the number of choices people have increases, an entire range of possibilities opens up. Suicide among teenagers has almost quadrupled since 1950, although the standard of comfort that their families enjoy is up. Black Americans, less affluent than white Americans, have had less of a rise in suicides, and the rate among them remains about half of that for whites.

Still, if a fiftyish fellow with fine teeth and a foolproof pension plan, a cottage at the beach and the Fourth of July weekend coming up, kills himself, it seems truculent. We would look at him bafflingly if he told us he no longer likes the Sturm und Drang of banging fireworks.

Then stay at your hideaway! we'd argue with him.

"Big mouths eat little mouths. Nature isn't 'timeless.' Whole lives are squeezed into three months or three days."

What about your marriage?

"She's become more mannish than me. I loved women. I don't believe in marriage between men."

Remarry, then!

"I've gone impotent, and besides, when I see somebody young and pretty I guess I feel like dandling her on my knee."

Marriage is friendship. You can find someone your own age.

"I'm tired of it."

But how about your company?—a widows-and-orphans stock that's on the cutting edge of the silicon frontier? That's interesting.

"I know what wins. It's less and less appetizing."

You're not scared of death anymore?

"It interests me less than it did."

What are you so sick of? The rest of us keep going.

"I'm tired of weathermen and sportscasters on the screen. Of being patient and also of impatience. I'm tired of the president, whoever the president happens to be, and sleeping badly, with forty-eight half-hours in the day — of breaking two eggs every morning and putting sugar on something. I'm tired of the drone of my own voice, but also of us jabbering like parrots at each other — of all our stumpy ways of doing everything."

You're bored with yourself?

"That's an understatement. I'm maybe the least interesting person I know."

But to kill yourself?

"You know, it's a tradition, too," he remarks quietly, not making so bold as to suggest that the tradition is an honorable one, though his tone of voice might be imagined to imply this. "I guess I've always been a latent maverick."

Except in circumstances which are themselves a matter of life and death, I'm reluctant to agree with the idea that suicide is not the result of mental illness. No matter how reasonably the person appears to have examined his options, it goes against the grain of nature for him to destroy himself. And any illness that threatens his life changes a person. Suicidal thinking, if serious, can be a kind of death scare, comparable to suffering a heart attack or undergoing a cancer operation. One survives such a phase both warier and chastened. When — two years ago — I emerged from a bad dip into suicidal speculation, I felt utterly exhausted and yet quite fearless of ordinary dangers, vastly afraid of myself but much less scared of extraneous eventualities. The fact of death may not be tragic; many people die with a bit of a smile that captures their mouths at the last instant, and most people who are revived after a deadly accident are reluctant to be brought to life, resisting resuscitation, and carrying back confusing, beamish, or ecstatic memories. But the same impetuosity that made him throw himself out of the window might have enabled the person to love life all the more if he'd been calibrated somewhat differently at the time of the emergency. Death's edge is so abrupt and near that many people who expect a short and momentary dive may be astounded to find that it is bottomless and change their minds and start to scream when they are only halfway down.

Although my fright at my mind's anarchy superseded my fear of death in the conventional guise of automobile or airplane crashes, heart seizures, and so on, nightmares are more primitive and in my dreams I continued to be scared of a death not sought after — dying from driving too fast and losing control of the car, breaking through thin ice while skating and drowning in the cold, or falling off a cliff. When I am tense and sleeping raggedly, my worst nightmare isn't drawn from anxious prep school memories or my stint in the army or the bad spells of my marriages or any other of adulthood's vicissitudes. Nothing else from the past half century has the staying power in my mind of the elevated-train rides that my father and I used to take down Third Avenue to the Battery in New York City on Sunday afternoon when I was three or four or five so I could see the fish at the aquarium. We were probably pretty good companions in those years, but the wooden platforms forty feet up shook terribly as trains from both directions pulled in and out. To me they seemed worse than rickety — ready to topple. And the roar was fearful, and the railings left large gaps for a child to fall through, after the steep climb up the slat-sided, windy, shaking stairway from street level. It's a rare dream, but several times a year I still find myself on such a perch, without his company or anybody else's, on a boyish or a grown-up's mission, when the elevated platform begins to rattle desperately, seesaw, heel over, and finally come apart, disintegrate, while I cling to struts and trusses.

My father, as he lay dying at home of bowel cancer, used to enjoy watching Tarzan reruns on the children's hour of television. Like a strong green vine, they swung him far away from his deathbed to a world of skinny-dipping and friendly animals and scenic beauty linked to the lost realities of his adolescence in Kansas City. Earlier, when he had still been able to walk without much pain, he'd paced the house for several hours at night, contemplating suicide, I expect, along with other anguishing thoughts, regrets, remembrances, and yearnings, while the rest of us slept. But he decided to lie down and die the slower way. I don't know how much of that decision was for the sake of his wife and children, how much was because he didn't want to be a "quitter," as he sometimes put it, and how much was due to his believing that life belongs to God (which I'm not even sure he did). He was not a churchgoer after his thirties. He had belonged to J. P. Morgan's church, St. George's, on Stuyvesant Square — Morgan was a hero of his — but when things went a little wrong for him at the Wall Street law firm he worked for and he changed jobs and moved out to the suburbs, he became a skeptic on religious matters, and gradually, in the absence of faith of that previous kind, he adhered to a determined allegiance to the social order. Wendell Willkie or Dwight D. Eisenhower instead of

J. P. Morgan became the sort of hero he admired, and suicide would have seemed an act of insurrection against the laws and conventions of the society, internationalist-Republican, that he believed in. I was never particularly afraid that I might plan a suicide, swallowing a bunch of pills and keeping them down — only of what I think of as being Anna Karenina's kind of death. This most plausible self-killing in all of literature is frightening because it was unwilled, regretted at midpoint, and came as a complete surprise to Anna herself. After rushing impulsively, in great misery, to the Moscow railway station to catch a train, she ended up underneath another one, dismayed, astonished, and trying to climb out from under the wheels even as they crushed her. Many people who briefly verge on suicide undergo a mental somersault for a terrifying interval during which they're upside down, their perspective topsy-turvy, skidding, churning; and this is why I got rid of the bullets for my .22.

Nobody expects to trust his body overmuch after the age of fifty. Incipient cataracts or arthritis, outlandish snores, tooth-grinding, ankles that threaten to turn, are part of the game. But not to trust one's *mind?* That's a surprise. The single attribute that older people were sure to have (we thought as boys) was a stodgy dependability, a steady temperance or caution. Adults might be vain, unimaginative, pompous, and callous, but they did have their affairs tightly in hand. It was not till my thirties that I began to know friends who were in their fifties on equal terms, and I remember being amused, piqued, irritated, and slightly bewildered to learn that some of them still felt as marginal or rebellious or in a quandary about what to do with themselves for the next dozen years as my contemporaries were likely to. That close to retirement, some of them harbored a deep-seated contempt for the organizations they had been working for, ready to walk away from almost everybody they had known and the efforts and expertise of whole decades with very little sentiment. Nor did twenty years of marriage necessarily mean more than two or three — they might be just as ready to walk away from that also, and didn't really register it as twenty years at all. Rather, life could be about to begin all over again. "Bummish" was how one man described himself, with a raffish smile — "Lucky to have a roof over my head" — though he'd just put a child through Yale. He was quitting his job and claimed with exasperation that his wife still cried for her mother in her sleep, as if they'd never been married.

The great English traveler Richard Burton quoted an Arab proverb that speaks for many middle-aged men of the old-fashioned variety: "Conceal thy Tenets, thy Treasure, and thy Traveling." These are serious matters, in other words. People didn't conceal their tenets in order to betray them, but to fight for them more opportunely. And except for kings and princelings, concealing whatever treasure one had went almost without saying. As for travel, a man's travels were also a matter of gravity. Travel was knowledge, ambiguity, dalliances or misalliances, divided loyalty, forbidden thinking; and besides, someday he might need to make a run for it and go to ground someplace where he had made some secret friends. Friends of mine whose husbands or whose wives have died have been quite startled afterward to discover caches of money or traveler's checks concealed around the house, or a bundle of cash in a safe deposit box.

Burton, like any other desert adage-spinner and most individuals over fifty, would have agreed to an addition so obvious that it wasn't included to begin with: "Conceal thy Illnesses." I can remember how urgently my father worried that word would get out, after a preliminary operation for his cancer. He didn't want to be written off, counted out of the running at the corporation he worked for and in other enclaves of competition. Men often compete with one another until the day they die; comradeship consists of rubbing shoulders jocularly with a competitor. As breadwinners, they must be considered fit and sound by friend as well as foe, and so there's lots of truth to the most common answer I heard when asking why three times as many men as women kill themselves: "They keep their troubles to themselves"; "They don't know how to ask for help." Men greet each other with a sock on the arm, women with a hug, and the hug wears better in the long run.

I'm not entirely like that, and I discovered that when I confided something of my perturbation to a woman friend she was likely to keep telephoning me or mailing cheery postcards, whereas a man would usually listen with concern, communicate his sympathy, and maybe intimate that he had pondered the same drastic course of action himself a few years back and would end up respecting my decision either way. Open-mindedness seems an important attribute to a good many men, who pride themselves on being objective, hearing all sides of an issue, on knowing that truth and honesty do not

always coincide with social dicta, and who may even cherish a sub-
terranean outlaw streak that, like being ready to violently defend
one's family, reputation, and country, is by tradition male.

Men, being so much freer than women in society, used to feel
they had less of a stake in the maintenance of certain churchly
conventions and enjoyed speaking irreverently about various social truisms, including even the principle that people ought to die
on schedule, not cutting in ahead on their assigned place in line.
Contemporary women, after their triumphant irreverence during
the 1960s and 1970s, cannot be generalized about so easily, however. They turn as skeptical and saturnine as any man. In fact,
women attempt suicide more frequently, but favor pills or other
methods, whereas two-thirds of the men who kill themselves have
used a gun. In 1985, 85 percent of suicides by means of firearms
were done by men. An overdose of medication hasn't the same finality. It may be reversible if the person is discovered quickly, or
be subject to benign miscalculation to start with. Even if it works,
perhaps it can be fudged by a kindly doctor in the record-keeping.
Like an enigmatic drowning or a single-car accident that baffles
the suspicions of the insurance company, a suicide by drugs can be
a way to avoid making a loud statement, and merely illustrate the
final modesty of a person who didn't wish to ask for too much of
the world's attention.

Unconsummated attempts at suicide can strike the rest of us as
self-pitying and self-aggrandizing, or plaintive plea-bargaining —
"childish," we say, though actually the suicide of children is ghastly
beyond any stunt of self-mutilation an adult may indulge in because of the helplessness that echoes through the act. It would be
hard to define chaos better than as a world where children decide
that they don't want to live.

Love is the solution to all dilemmas, we sometimes hear, and in
those moments when the spirit bathes itself in beneficence and
manages to transcend the static of personalities rubbing fur off of
each other, indeed it is. Without love nothing matters, Paul told
the Corinthians, a mystery which, if true, has no ready Darwinian
explanation. Love without a significant sexual component and for
people who are unrelated to us serves little practical purpose. It
doesn't help us feed our families, win struggles, thrive and prosper. It distracts us from the ordinary business of sizing people up

and making a living, and is not even conducive to intellectual observation, because instead of seeing them, we see right through
them to the bewildered child and dreaming adolescent who inhabited their bodies earlier, the now-tired idealist who fell in love
and out of love, got hired and quit, hired and fired, bought cars and
wore them out, liked black-eyed Susans, blueberry muffins, and
roosters crowing — liked roosters crowing better than skyscrapers
but now likes skyscrapers better than roosters crowing. As swift as
thought, we select the details that we need to see in order to be
able to love them.

Yet at other times we'll dispense with these same poignancies
and choose only their grunginess to look at, their pinched mouths
and shifty eyes, their thirst for gin at noon and indifference to
their kids, their greed for the best tidbit on the buffet table and
penchant for poking their penises up the excretory end of other
human beings. I tend to gaze quite closely at the faces of priests I
meet on the street to see if a lifetime of love has marked them noticeably. Real serenity or asceticism I no longer expect, and I take
for granted the beefy calm that frequently goes with Catholic
celibacy, but I am watching for the marks of love and often see
mere resignation or tenacity.

Many men are romantics, likely to plunge, go for broke, take action in a spirit of exigency rather than waiting for the problem to
resolve itself. Then, on the contrary, still as romantics, they may
drift into despairing passivity, stare at the TV all day long, and
binge with a bottle. Women too may turn frenetic for a while and
then throw up their hands; but though they may not seem as
grandiosely fanciful and romantic at the outset, they are more
often believers — at least I think they tend to believe in God or in
humanity, the future, and so on. We have above us the inviting
eternity of "the heavens," if we choose to look at it, lying on our
backs in the summer grass under starlight, some of which had left
its source before mankind became man. But because we live in our
heads more than in nature nowadays, even the summer sky is a
mine field for people whose memories are mined. With the sky
no longer humbling, the sunshine only a sort of convenience, and
no godhead located anywhere outside our own heads, every problem may seem insolubly interlocked. When the telephone has

become impossible to answer at home, sometimes it finally becomes impossible to stride down the gangplank of a cruise ship in Mombasa too, although no telephones will ring for you there.

But if escapist travel is ruled out in certain emergencies, surely you can *pray?* Pray, yes; but to whom? That requires a bit of preparation. Rarely do people obtain much relief from praying if they haven't stood in line awhile to get a visa. It's an appealing idea that you can just *go,* and in a previous era perhaps you could have, like on an old-fashioned shooting safari. But it's not so simple now. What do you believe in? Whom are you praying to? What are you praying for? There's no crèche on the courthouse lawn; you're not supposed to adhere exactly even to what your parents had believed. Like psychotherapy, praying takes time, even if you know which direction to face when you kneel.

Love is powerfully helpful when the roof falls in — loving other people with a high and hopeful heart and as a kind of prayer. Yet that feat too requires new and sudden insights or long practice. The beatitude of loving strangers as well as friends — loving them on sight with a leap of empathy and intuition — is a form of inspiration, edging, of course, in some cases toward madness, as other states of beatitude can do. But there's no question that a genuine love for the living will stymie suicidal depressions not chemical in origin. Love is an elixir, changing the life of the lover like no other. And many of us have experienced this — a temporary lightening of our leery, prickly disapproval of much of the rest of the world when at a wedding or a funeral of shared emotion, or when we have fallen in love.

Yet the zest for life of those unusual men and women who make a great zealous success of living is due more often in good part to the craftiness and pertinacity with which they manage to overlook the misery of others. You can watch them watch life beat the stuffing out of the faces of their friends and acquaintances, yet they themselves seem to outwit the dense delays of social custom, the tedious tick-tock of bureaucratic obfuscation, accepting loss and age and change and disappointment without suffering punctures in their stomach lining. Breathlessness or strange dull pains from their nether organs don't nonplus them. They fret and doubt in moderation, and love a lobster roast, squeeze lemon juice on living clams on the half shell to prove that the clams are alive, laugh as robins tussle a worm out of the ground or a kitten flees a dog. Like the problem drinkers, pork eaters, and chain smokers who nevertheless finish out their allotted years, succumbing to a stroke at a nice round biblical age when the best vitamin-eating vegetarian has long since died, their faces become veritable walnuts of fine character, with the same smile lines as the rarer individual whose grin has been affectionate all of his life.

We spend our lives getting to know ourselves, yet wonders never cease. During my adolescent years my states of mind, though undulant, seemed seamless; even when I was unhappy no cracks or fissures made me wonder if I was a danger to myself. My confidence was such that I treaded the slippery lips of waterfalls, fought forest fires, drove ancient cars cross-country night and day, and scratched the necks of menagerie leopards in the course of various adventures which enhanced the joy of being alive. The chemistry of the mind, because unfathomable, is more frightening. In the city, I live on the waterfront and occasionally will notice an agitated-looking figure picking his way along the pilings and string-pieces of the timbered piers nearby, staring at the sliding whorls on the surface of the Hudson as if teetering over an abyss. Our building, across the street, seems imposing from the water and over the years has acted as a magnet for a number of suicides — people who have dreaded the clammy chill, the onerous smothering essential to their first plan. One woman climbed out after jumping in and took the elevator to the roof (my neighbors remember how wringing wet she was) and leapt off, banging window ledges on the way down, and hit with the whap of a sack of potatoes, as others have.

Yet what is more remarkable than that a tiny minority of souls reach a point where they entrust their bodies to the force of gravity is that so few of the rest of us splurge an hour of a summer day gazing at the trees and sky. How many summers do we *have?* One sees prosperous families in the city who keep plants in their apartment windows that have grown so high they block the sunlight and appear to be doing the living for the tenants who are bolted inside. But beauty is nobody's sure salvation: not the beauty of a swimming hole if you get a cramp, and not the beauty of a woman if she doesn't care for you. The swimming hole looks inviting under the blue sky, with its amber bottom, green sedges sticking up in the shallows, and curls of gentle current over a waterlogged basswood tree two feet beneath the surface near the brook that feeds it. Come back at dusk, however, and the pond turns black — as dark as death, or on the contrary, a restful dark, a dark to savor. Take it as you will.

People with sunny natures do seem to live longer than people who are nervous wrecks; yet mankind didn't evolve out of the animal kingdom by being unduly sunny-minded. Life was fearful and phantasmagoric, supernatural and preternatural, as well as encompassing the kind of clockwork regularity of our well-governed day. It had numerous superstitious (from the Latin, "standing over") elements, such as we are likely to catch a whiff of only when we're peering at a dead body. And it was not just our optimism but our pessimistic premonitions, our dark moments as a species, our irrational, frightful speculations, our strange mutations upon the simple theme of love, and our sleepless, obsessive inventiveness — our dread as well as our faith — that made us human beings. Staking one's life on the more general good came to include risking suicide also. Brilliant, fecund people sometimes kill themselves.

"Joy to the world . . . Let heaven and nature sing, and heaven and nature sing. . . Repeat the sounding joy . . . " The famous Christmas carol invokes not only glee but unity: heaven with nature, not always a Christian combination. It's a rapturous hymn, and no one should refuse to surrender to such a pitch of revelation when it comes. But the flip side of rapture can be a riptide of panic, of hysterical gloom. Our faces are not molded as if joy were a preponderant experience. (Nor is a caribou's or a thrush's.) Our faces in repose look stoic or battered, and people of the sunniest temperament sometimes die utterly unstrung, doubting everything they have ever believed in or have done.

Let heaven and nature sing! the hymn proclaims. But *is* there such harmony? Are God and Mother Nature really the same? Are they even compatible? And will we risk burning our wings if we mount high enough to try to see? I've noticed that woods soil in Italy smells the same as woods soil in New England when you pick up a handful of it and enjoy its aromas — but is God there the same? It can be precarious to wonder. I don't rule out suicide as being unthinkable for people who have tried to live full lives, and don't regard it as negating the work and faith and satisfaction and fun and even ecstasy they may have known before. In killing himself a person acknowledges his failures during a time span when perhaps heaven and earth had caught him like a pair of scissors — but not his life span. Man is different from animals in that he speculates, a high-risk activity.

Reflections and Responses

1. Hoagland's position on suicide is noticeably complex. Where do you think he ultimately stands on the issue? Do you think he would say, for example, that individuals have the moral right to take their own lives if they believe it is necessary to do so? Can you identify an instance in the essay in which you can pin down Hoagland's position? If not, why not?

2. Why do you think Hoagland devotes so much attention to the differences between men and women when it comes to suicide? Do you think those differences are significant? Would you say they are natural or cultural?

3. What do you make of the dialogue Hoagland reports on pages 214–215? Do you think it is a transcription of an actual dialogue? If so, who is the person being interviewed? If not, what is Hoagland's purpose in creating it?

ANN HODGMAN

No Wonder They Call Me a Bitch

Whether gently funny or savagely comic, the humorous essay has one of the longest traditions in the history of the essay genre. Decades ago, in the days of James Thurber, E. B. White, Robert Benchley, Dorothy Parker, and S. J. Perelman, the American essay thrived on an urbane wit and humor. For whatever reasons (political correctness? sensitivity? entrenched academic seriousness?), our era seems less accommodating to funny essays. There are far fewer humor magazines now, and the periodicals that ordinarily feature humor include less of it than they once did. Today's best-known humor writers usually work within the restrictions of 750-word newspaper columns and seldom expand the literary possibilities of humor as did S. J. Perelman, who died in 1979. Still, every now and then a humorous essay — like Ann Hodgman's deliciously comic tidbit — finds its way into The Best American Essays. *Reminiscent of Perelman's zany investigations, Hodgman's courageous essay pushes self-education past the point most of us would go.*

A former contributing editor to Spy *magazine, Ann Hodgman is the author of* Beat This! *(1993), a cookbook, several humor books, including* True Tiny Tales of Terror *(1982), and more than forty children's books, including a six-book series for middle-schoolers called* My Babysitter Is a Vampire *(1991). Among her most recent books are* Hard Times for Cats *(1992),* Addams Family Values *(1993),* Children of the Night: Dark Triumph *(1997), and* One Bite Won't Kill You *(1999). "No Wonder They Call Me a Bitch" originally appeared in* Spy *(1989) and was selected by Justin Kaplan for* The Best American Essays 1990.

I've always wondered about dog food. Is a Gaines-burger really like a hamburger? Can you fry it? Does dog food "cheese" taste like real cheese? Does Gravy Train actually make gravy in the dog's bowl, or is that brown liquid just dissolved crumbs? And exactly what *are* by-products?

Having spent the better part of a week eating dog food, I'm sorry to say that I now know the answers to these questions. While my dachshund, Shortie, watched in agonies of yearning, I gagged my way through can after can of stinky, white-flecked mush and bag after bag of stinky, fat-drenched nuggets. And now I understand exactly why Shortie's breath is so bad.

Of course, Gaines-burgers are neither mush nor nuggets. They are, rather, a miracle of beauty and packaging — or at least that's what I thought when I was little. I used to beg my mother to get them for our dogs, but she always said they were too expensive. When I finally bought a box of cheese-flavored Gaines-burgers — after 20 years of longing — I felt deliciously wicked.

"Dogs love real beef," the back of the box proclaimed proudly. "That's why Gaines-burgers is the only beef burger for dogs with real beef and no meat by-products!" The copy was accurate: meat by-products did not appear in the list of ingredients. Poultry by-products did, though — right there next to preserved animal fat.

One Purina spokesman told me that poultry by-products consist of necks, intestines, undeveloped eggs and other "carcass remnants," but not feathers, heads or feet. When I told him I'd been eating dog food, he said, "Oh, you're kidding! Oh no!" (I came to share his alarm when, weeks later, a second Purina spokesman said that Gaines-burgers *do* contain poultry heads and feet — but *not* undeveloped eggs.)

Up close my Gaines-burger didn't much resemble chopped beef. Rather, it looked — and felt — like a single long, extruded piece of redness that had been chopped into segments and formed into a patty. You could make one at home if you had a Play-Doh Fun Factory.

I turned on the skillet. While I waited for it to heat up I pulled out a shred of cheese-colored material and palpated it. Again, like Play-Doh, it was quite malleable. I made a little cheese bird out of it; then I counted to three and ate the bird.

There was a horrifying rush of cheddar taste, followed immediately by the dull tang of soybean flour — the main ingredient in Gaines-burgers. Next I tried a piece of red extrusion. The main difference between the meat-flavored and cheese-flavored extrusions is one of texture. The "cheese" chews like fresh Play-Doh, whereas the "meat" chews like Play-Doh that's been sitting out on a rug for a couple of hours.

Frying only turned the Gaines-burger black. There was no melting, no sizzling, no warm meat smells. A cherished childhood illusion was gone. I flipped the patty into the sink, where it immediately began leaking rivulets of red dye.

As alarming as the Gaines-burgers were, their soy meal began to seem like an old friend when the time came to try some *canned* dog foods. I decided to try the Cycle foods first. When I opened them, I thought about how rarely I use can openers these days, and I was suddenly visited by a long-forgotten sensation of can-opener distaste. *This* is the kind of unsavory place can openers spend their time when you're not watching! Every time you open a can of, say, Italian plum tomatoes, you infect them with invisible particles of by-product.

I had been expecting to see the usual homogeneous scrapple inside, but each can of Cycle was packed with smooth, round, oily nuggets. As if someone at Gaines had been tipped off that a human would be tasting the stuff, the four Cycles really were different from one another. Cycle-1, for puppies, is wet and soyish. Cycle-2, for adults, glistens nastily with fat, but it's passably edible — a lot like some canned Swedish meatballs I once got in a care package at college. Cycle-3, the "lite" one, for fatties, had no specific flavor; it just tasted like dog food. But at least it didn't make me fat.

Cycle-4, for senior dogs, had the smallest nuggets. Maybe old dogs can't open their mouths as wide. This kind was far sweeter than the other three Cycles — almost like baked beans. It was also the only one to contain "dried beef digest," a mysterious substance that the Purina spokesman defined as "enzymes" and my dictionary defined as "the products of digestion."

Next on the menu was a can of Kal-Kan Pedigree with Chunky Chicken. Chunky chicken? There were chunks in the can, certainly — big, purplish-brown chunks. I forked one chunk out (by now I was becoming more callous) and found that while it had no discernible chicken flavor, it wasn't bad except for its texture — like meat loaf with ground-up chicken bones.

In the world of canned dog food, a smooth consistency is a

sign of low quality — lots of cereal. A lumpy, frightening, bloody, stringy horror is a sign of high quality — lots of meat. Nowhere in the world of wet dog foods was this demonstrated better than in the fanciest I tried — Kal Kan's Pedigree Select Dinners. These came not in a can but in a tiny foil packet with a picture of an imperious Yorkie. When I pulled open the container, juice spurted all over my hand, and the first chunk I speared was trailing a long gray vein. I shrieked and went instead for a plain chunk, which I was able to swallow only after taking a break to read some suddenly fascinating office equipment catalogs. Once again, though, it tasted no more alarming than, say, canned hash.

Still, how pleasant it was to turn to *dry* dog food! Gravy Train was the first I tried, and I'm happy to report that it really does make a "thick, rich, real beef gravy" when you mix it with water. Thick and rich, anyway. Except for a lingering rancid-fat flavor, the gravy wasn't beefy, but since it tasted primarily like tap water, it wasn't nauseating either.

My poor dachshund just gets plain old Purina Dog Chow, but Purina also makes a dry food called Butcher's Blend that comes in Beef, Bacon & Chicken flavor. Here we see dog food's arcane semiotics at its best: a red triangle with a *T* stamped into it is supposed to suggest beef; a tan curl, chicken; and a brown *S*, a piece of bacon. Only dogs understand these messages. But Butcher's Blend does have an endearing slogan: "Great Meaty Tastes — without bothering the Butcher!" *You know, I wanted to buy some meat, but I just couldn't bring myself to bother the butcher. . . .*

Purina O.N.E. ("Optimum Nutritional Effectiveness") is targeted at people who are unlikely ever to worry about bothering a tradesperson. "We chose chicken as a primary ingredient in Purina O.N.E. for several reasonings," the long, long essay on the back of the bag announces. Chief among these reasonings, I'd guess, is the fact that chicken appeals to people who are — you know — *like us*. Although our dogs do nothing but spend 18-hour days alone in the apartment, we still want them to be *premium* dogs. We want them to cut down on red meat, too. We also want dog food that comes in a bag with an attractive design, a subtle typeface and no kitschy pictures of slobbering golden retrievers.

Besides that, we want a list of the Nutritional Benefits of our dog food — and we get it on O.N.E. One thing I especially like about this list is its constant references to a dog's "hair coat," as in "Beef tallow is good for the dog's skin and hair coat." (On the other hand, beef tallow merely provides palatability, while the dried beef digest in Cycle provides palatability *enhancement*.)

I hate to say it, but O.N.E. was pretty palatable. Maybe that's because it has about 100 percent more fat than, say, Butcher's Blend. Or maybe I'd been duped by the packaging; that's been known to happen before.

As with people food, dog snacks taste much better than dog meals. They're better-looking too. Take Milk-Bone Flavor Snacks. The loving-hands-at-home prose describing each flavor is colorful; the writers practically choke on their own exuberance. Of bacon they say, "It's so good, your dog will think it's hot off the frying pan." Of liver: "The only taste your dog wants more than liver — is even more liver!" Of poultry: "All those farm fresh flavors deliciously mixed in one biscuit. Your dog will bark with delight!" And of vegetable: "Gardens of taste! Specially blended to give your dog that vegetable flavor he wants — but can rarely get!"

Well, I may be a sucker, but advertising *this* emphatic just doesn't convince me. I lined up all seven flavors of Milk-Bone Flavor Snacks on the floor. Unless my dog's palate is a lot more sensitive than mine — and considering that she steals dirty diapers out of the trash and eats them, I'm loath to think it is — she doesn't detect any more difference in the seven flavors than I did when I tried them.

I much preferred Bonz, the hard-baked, bone-shaped snack stuffed with simulated marrow. I liked the bone part, that is; it tasted almost exactly like the cornmeal it was made of. The mock-marrow inside was a bit more problematic: in addition to looking like the sludge that collects in the treads of my running shoes, it was bursting with tiny hairs.

I'm sure you have a few dog food questions of your own. To save us time, I've answered them in advance.

Q. Are those little cans of Mighty Dog actually branded with the sizzling word BEEF, *the way they show in the commercials?*

A. You should know by now that that kind of thing never happens.

Q. Does chicken-flavored dog food taste like chicken-flavored cat food?

A. To my surprise, chicken cat food was actually a little better — more chickeny. It tasted like inferior canned pâté.

Q. Was there any dog food that you just couldn't bring yourself to try?

A. Alas, it was a can of Mighty Dog called Prime Entree with Bone Marrow. The meat was dark, dark brown, and it was surrounded by gelatin that was almost black. I knew I would die if I tasted it, so I put it outside for the raccoons.

Reflections and Responses

1. What is Ann Hodgman making fun of? Is the essay a satire on dog food products alone or does she have other targets?

2. Of what importance is the "packaging" of dog food? How does Hodgman use the packaging language for comic effect?

3. Consider the advertising language that Hodgman cites. According to the ads, what similarities exist between the eating habits of dogs and people? What has Hodgman learned from her experiment?

BARRY LOPEZ

The Stone Horse

Great works of art do not always hang in museums, accessible to anyone who cares to see them. When Barry Lopez wanted to see a mysterious stone horse carved perhaps some four hundred years ago by the Quechan people, his journey took him far off the beaten track. What he finds in the deserts of southern California near the Mexican border is the kind of large ground carving (an intaglio) that some think was intended as a sign to extraterrestrials. But, upon seeing the horse, Lopez does not believe it was "meant to be seen by gods in the sky above" nor does he think it can even be properly appreciated by an aerial photograph. How we see this work of art, Lopez suggests, is as important as what we see. And how we see it requires the journey to it.

One of America's most distinguished nonfiction writers, Lopez is the author of Arctic Dreams, *which won the National Book Award in 1986, and* Of Wolves and Men, *which won the John Burroughs Medal in 1979. His other publications include* Desert Notes *(1979),* River Notes *(1979),* Winter Count *(1981),* Crossing Open Ground *(1988),* Coyote Love *(1989),* The Rediscovery of North America *(1990),* Field Notes *(1994), and* Lessons from the Wolverine *(1997). He has also recently published* About This Life: Journeys on the Threshold of Memory *(1998). He received an award for fiction from the Friends of American Writers in 1982 and the Award in Literature from the American Academy and Institute of Arts and Letters in 1986. "The Stone Horse" originally appeared in* Antaeus *(1986) and was selected by Gay Talese for* The Best American Essays 1987.

I

The deserts of southern California, the high, relatively cooler and wetter Mojave and the hotter, dryer Sonoran to the south of it, carry the signatures of many cultures. Prehistoric rock drawings in the Mojave's Coso Range, probably the greatest concentration of petroglyphs in North America, are at least three thousand years old. Big-game-hunting cultures that flourished six or seven thousand years before that are known from broken spear tips, choppers, and burins left scattered along the shores of great Pleistocene lakes, long since evaporated. Weapons and tools discovered at China Lake may be thirty thousand years old; and worked stone from a quarry in the Calico Mountains is, some argue, evidence that human beings were here more than 200,000 years ago.

Because of the long-term stability of such arid environments, much of this prehistoric stone evidence still lies exposed on the ground, accessible to anyone who passes by — the studious, the acquisitive, the indifferent, the merely curious. Archaeologists do not agree on the sequence of cultural history beyond about twelve thousand years ago, but it is clear that these broken bits of chalcedony, chert, and obsidian, like the animal drawings and geometric designs etched on walls of basalt throughout the desert, anchor the earliest threads of human history, the first record of human endeavor here.

Western man did not enter the California desert until the end of the eighteenth century, 250 years after Coronado brought his soldiers into the Zuni pueblos in a bewildered search for the cities of Cibola. The earliest appraisals of the land were cursory, hurried. People traveled *through* it, en route to Santa Fe or the California coastal settlements. Only miners tarried. In 1823 what had been Spain's became Mexico's, and in 1848 what had been Mexico's became America's; but the bare, jagged mountains and dry lake beds, the vast and uniform plains of creosote bush and yucca plants, remained as obscure as the northern Sudan until the end of the nineteenth century.

Before 1940 the tangible evidence of twentieth-century man's passage here consisted of very little — the hard tracery of travel corridors; the widely scattered, relatively insignificant evidence of mining operations; and the fair expanse of irrigated fields at the desert's periphery. In the space of a hundred years or so the wagon roads were paved, railroads were laid down, and canals and high-tension lines were built to bring water and electricity across the desert to Los Angeles from the Colorado River. The dark mouths of gold, talc, and tin mines yawned from the bony flanks of desert ranges. Dust-encrusted chemical plants stood at work on the lonely edges of dry lake beds. And crops of grapes, lettuce, dates, alfalfa, and cotton covered the Coachella and Imperial valleys, north and south of the Salton Sea, and the Palo Verde Valley along the Colorado.

These developments proceeded with little or no awareness of earlier human occupations by cultures that preceded those of the historic Indians — the Mojave, the Chemehuevi, the Quechan. (Extensive irrigation began actually to change the climate of the Sonoran Desert, and human settlements, the railroads, and farming introduced many new, successful plants into the region.)

During World War II, the American military moved into the desert in great force, to train troops and to test equipment. They found the clear weather conducive to year-round flying, the dry air and isolation very attractive. After the war, a complex of training grounds, storage facilities, and gunnery and test ranges was permanently settled on more than three million acres of military reservations. Few perceived the extent or significance of the destruction of the aboriginal sites that took place during tank maneuvers and bombing runs or in the laying out of highways, railroads, mining districts, and irrigated fields. The few who intuited that something like an American Dordogne Valley lay exposed here were (only) amateur archaeologists; even they reasoned that the desert was too vast for any of this to matter.

After World War II, people began moving out of the crowded Los Angeles basin into homes in Lucerne, Apple, and Antelope valleys in the western Mojave. They emigrated as well to a stretch of resort land at the foot of the San Jacinto Mountains that included Palm Springs, and farther out to old railroad and military towns like Twentynine Palms and Barstow. People also began exploring the desert, at first in military-surplus jeeps and then with a variety of all-terrain and off-road vehicles that became available in the 1960s. By the mid-1970s, the number of people using such vehicles for desert recreation had increased exponentially. Most came and went in innocent curiosity; the few who didn't wreaked a havoc all out of proportion to their numbers. The disturbance of previously isolated archaeological sites increased by an order of magnitude. Many sites were vandalized before archaeologists, themselves late to the desert, had any firm grasp of the bounds of human history in the desert. It was as though in the same moment an Aztec library had been discovered intact various lacunae had begun to appear.

The vandalism was of three sorts: the general disturbance usually caused by souvenir hunters and by the curious and the oblivious; the wholesale stripping of a place by professional thieves for black-market sale and trade; and outright destruction, in which vehicles were actually used to ram and trench an area. By 1980, the Bureau of Land Management estimated that probably 35 percent of the archaeological sites in the desert had been vandalized. The destruction at some places by rifles and shotguns, or by power winches mounted on vehicles, was, if one cared for history, demoralizing to behold.

In spite of public education, land closures, and stricter law enforcement in recent years, the BLM estimates that, annually, about 1 percent of the archaeological record in the desert continues to be destroyed or stolen.

II

A BLM archaeologist told me, with understandable reluctance, where to find the intaglio. I spread my Automobile Club of Southern California map of Imperial County out on his desk, and he traced the route with a pink felt-tip pen. The line crossed Interstate 8 and then turned west along the Mexican border.

"You can't drive any farther than about here," he said, marking a small X. "There's boulders in the wash. You walk up past them."

On a separate piece of paper he drew a route in a smaller scale that would take me up the arroyo to a certain point where I was to cross back east, to another arroyo. At its head, on higher ground just to the north, I would find the horse.

"It's tough to spot unless you know it's there. Once you pick it up . . ." He shook his head slowly, in a gesture of wonder at its existence.

I waited until I held his eye. I assured him I would not tell anyone else how to get there. He looked at me with stoical despair, like a man who had been robbed twice, whose belief in human beings was offered without conviction.

I did not go until the following day because I wanted to see it at

dawn. I ate breakfast at four A.M. in El Centro and then drove
south. The route was easy to follow, though the last section of road
proved difficult, broken and drifted over with sand in some spots.
I came to the barricade of boulders and parked. It was light
enough by then to find my way over the ground with little trouble.
The contours of the landscape were stark, without any masking
vegetation. I worried only about rattlesnakes.

I traversed the stone plain as directed, but, in spite of the frank-
ness of the land, I came on the horse unawares. In the first moment of recognition I was without feeling. I recalled later being
startled, and that I held my breath. It was laid out on the ground
with its head to the east, three times life size. As I took in its outline I felt a growing concentration of all my senses, as though my
attentiveness to the pale rose color of the morning sky and other
peripheral images had now ceased to be important. I was aware
that I was straining for sound in the windless air, and I felt the uneven pressure of the earth hard against my feet. The horse, out-
lined in a standing profile on the dark ground, was as vivid before
me as a bed of tulips.

I've come upon animals suddenly before, and felt a similar tension, a precipitate heightening of the senses. And I have felt the inexplicable but sharply boosted intensity of a wild moment in the
bush, where it is not until some minutes later that you discover the
source of electricity— the warm remains of a grizzly bear kill, or
the still moist tracks of a wolverine.

But this was slightly different. I felt I had stepped into an unoc-
cupied corridor. I had no familiar sense of history, the temporal
structure in which to think: this horse was made by Quechan people three hundred years ago. I felt instead a headlong rush of images: people hunting wild horses with spears on the Pleistocene
veld of southern California; Cortés riding across the causeway into
Montezuma's Tenochtitlán; a short-legged Comanche, astride his
horse like some sort of ferret, slashing through cavalry lines of
young men who rode like farmers; a hoof exploding past my face
one morning in a corral in Wyoming. These images had the weight
and silence of stone.

When I released my breath, the images softened. My initial feeling, of facing a wild animal in a remote region, was replaced with a
calm sense of antiquity. It was then that I became conscious, like

an ordinary tourist, of what was before me, and thought: this horse
was probably laid out by Quechan people. But when? I wondered.
The first horses they saw, I knew, might have been those that came
north from Mexico in 1692 with Father Eusebio Kino. But Cocopa
people, I recalled, also came this far north on occasion, to fight
with their neighbors, the Quechan. And *they* could have seen
horses with Melchior Díaz, at the mouth of the Colorado River in
the fall of 1540. So, it could be four hundred years old. (No one in
fact knows.)

I still had not moved. I took my eyes off the horse for a moment
to look south over the desert plain into Mexico, to look east past its
head at the brightening sunrise, to situate myself. Then, finally, I
brought my trailing foot slowly forward and stood erect. Sunlight
was running like a thin sheet of water over the stony ground and it
threw the horse into relief. It looked as though no hand had ever
disturbed the stones that gave it its form.

The horse had been brought to life on ground called desert
pavement, a tight, flat matrix of small cobbles blasted smooth by
sand-laden winds. The uniform, monochromatic blackness of the
stones, a patina of iron and magnesium oxides called desert var-
nish, is caused by long-term exposure to the sun. To make this type
of low-relief ground glyph, or intaglio, the artist either selectively
turns individual stones over to their lighter side or removes areas
of stone to expose the lighter soil underneath, creating a negative
image. This horse, about eighteen feet from brow to rump and
eight feet from withers to hoof, had been made in the latter way,
and its outline was bermed at certain points with low ridges of
stone a few inches high to enhance its three-dimensional qualities.
(The left side of the horse was in full profile; each leg was extended at 90 degrees to the body and fully visible, as though seen
in three-quarter profile.)

I was not eager to move. The moment I did I would be back in
the flow of time, the horse no longer quivering in the same way before me. I did not want to feel again the sequence of quotidian
events — to be drawn off into deliberation and analysis. A human
being, a four-footed animal, the open land. That was all that was
present — and a "thoughtless" understanding of the very old desires bearing on this particular animal: to hunt it, to render it, to
fathom it, to subjugate it, to honor it, to take it as a companion.

What finally made me move was the light. The sun now filled the shallow basin of the horse's body. The weighted line of the stone berm created the illusion of a mane and the distinctive roundness of an equine belly. The change in definition impelled me. I moved to the left, circling past its rump, to see how the light might flesh the horse out from various points of view. I circled it completely before squatting on my haunches. Ten or fifteen minutes later I chose another view. The third time I moved, to a point near the rear hooves, I spotted a stone tool at my feet. I stared at it a long while, more in awe than disbelief, before reaching out to pick it up. I turned it over in my left palm and took it between my fingers to feel its cutting edge. It is always difficult, especially with something so portable, to rechannel the desire to steal.

I spent several hours with the horse. As I changed positions and as the angle of the light continued to change I noticed a number of things. The angle at which the pastern carried the hoof away from the ankle was perfect. Also, stones had been placed within the image to suggest at precisely the right spot the left shoulder above the foreleg. The line that joined thigh and hock was similarly accurate. The muzzle alone seemed distorted — but perhaps these stones had been moved by a later hand. It was an admirably accurate representation, but not what a breeder would call perfect conformation. There was the suggestion of a bowed neck and an undershot jaw, and the tail, as full as a winter coyote's, did not appear to be precisely to scale.

The more I thought about it, the more I felt I was looking at an individual horse, a unique combination of generic and specific detail. It was easy to imagine one of Kino's horses as a model, or a horse that ran off from one of Coronado's columns. What kind of horses would these have been? I wondered. In the sixteenth century the most sought-after horses in Europe were Spanish, the offspring of Arabian stock and Barbary horses that the Moors brought to Iberia and bred to the older, eastern European strains brought in by the Romans. The model for this horse, I speculated, could easily have been a palomino, or a descendant of horses trained for lion hunting in North Africa.

A few generations ago, cowboys, cavalry quartermasters, and draymen would have taken this horse before me under consideration and not let up their scrutiny until they had its heritage fixed to their satisfaction. Today, the distinction between draft and harness horses is arcane knowledge, and no image may come to mind for a blue roan or a claybank horse. The loss of such refinement in everyday conversation leaves me unsettled. People praise the Eskimo's ability to distinguish among forty types of snow but forget the skill of others who routinely differentiate between overo and tobiano pintos. Such distinctions are made for the same reason. You have to do it to be able to talk clearly about the world.

For parts of two years I worked as a horse wrangler and packer in Wyoming. It is dim knowledge now; I would have to think to remember if a buckskin was a kind of dun horse. And I couldn't throw a double-diamond hitch over a set of panniers — the packer's basic tie-down — without guidance. As I squatted there in the desert, however, these more personal memories seemed tenuous in comparison with the sweep of this animal in human time. My memories had no depth. I thought of the Hittite cavalry riding against the Syrians 3,500 years ago. And the first of the Chinese emperors, Ch'in Shih Huang, buried in Shensi Province in 210 B.C. with thousands of life-size horses and soldiers, a terra-cotta guardian army. What could I know of what was in the mind of whoever made this horse? Was there some racial memory of it as an animal that had once fed the artist's ancestors and then disappeared from North America? And then returned in this strange alliance with another race of men?

Certainly, whoever it was, the artist had observed the animal very closely. Certainly the animal's speed had impressed him. Among the first things the Quechan would have learned from an encounter with Kino's horses was that their own long-distance runners — men who could run down mule deer — were no match for this animal.

From where I squatted I could look far out over the Mexican plain. Juan Bautista de Anza passed this way in 1774, extending El Camino Real into Alta California from Sinaloa. He was followed by others, all of them astride the magical horse; *gente de razón*, the people of reason, coming into the country of *los primitivos*. The horse, like the stone animals of Egypt, urged these memories upon me. And as I drew them up from some forgotten corner of my mind — huge horses carved in the white chalk downs of southern England by an Iron Age people; Spanish horses rearing and wheeling in fear before alligators in Florida — the images seemed tethered before me. With this sense of proportion, a memory of my own — the morning I almost lost my face to a horse's hoof — now had somewhere to fit.

I rose up and began to walk slowly around the horse again. I had taken the first long measure of it and was now looking for a way to depart, a new angle of light, a fading of the image itself before the rising sun, that would break its hold on me. As I circled, feeling both heady and serene at the encounter, I realized again how strangely vivid it was. It had been created on a barren bajada between two arroyos, as nondescript a place as one could imagine. The only plant life here was a few wands of ocotillo cactus. The ground beneath my shoes was so hard it wouldn't take the print of a heavy animal even after a rain. The only sounds I heard here were the voices of quail.

The archaeologist had been correct. For all its forcefulness, the horse is inconspicuous. If you don't care to see it you can walk right past it. That pleases him, I think. Unmarked on this bleak shoulder of the plain, the site signals to no one; so he wants no protective fences here, no informative plaque, to act as beacons. He would rather take a chance that no motorcyclist, no aimless wanderer with a flair for violence and a depth of ignorance, will ever find his way here.

The archaeologist had given me something before I left his office that now seemed peculiar — an aerial photograph of the horse. It is widely believed that an aerial view of an intaglio provides a fair and accurate depiction. It does not. In the photograph the horse looks somewhat crudely constructed; from the ground it appears far more deftly rendered. The photograph is of a single moment, and in that split second the horse seems vaguely impotent. I watched light pool in the intaglio at dawn; I imagine you could watch it withdraw at dusk and sense the same animation I did. In those prolonged moments its shape and so, too, its general character changed — noticeably. The living quality of the image, its immediacy to the eye, was brought out by the light-in-time, not, at least here, in the camera's frozen instant.

Intaglios, I thought, were never meant to be seen by gods in the sky above. They were meant to be seen by people on the ground, over a long period of shifting light. This could even be true of the huge figures on the Plain of Nazca in Peru, where people could walk for the length of a day beside them. It is our own impatience that leads us to think otherwise.

This process of abstraction, almost unintentional, drew me gradually away from the horse. I came to a position of attention at the edge of the sphere of its influence. With a slight bow I paid my respects to the horse, its maker, and the history of us all, and departed.

III

A short distance away I stopped the car in the middle of the road to make a few notes. I could not write down what I was thinking when I was with the horse. It would have seemed disrespectful, and it would have required another kind of attention. So now I patiently drained my memory of the details it had fastened itself upon. The road I'd stopped on was adjacent to the All American Canal, the major source of water for the Imperial and Coachella valleys. The water flowed west placidly. A disjointed flock of coots, small, dark birds with white bills, was paddling against the current, foraging in the rushes.

I was peripherally aware of the birds as I wrote, the only movement in the desert, and of a series of sounds from a village a half-mile away. The first sounds from this collection of ramshackle houses in a grove of cottonwoods were the distracted dawn voices of dogs. I heard them intermingled with the cries of a rooster. Later, the high-pitched voices of children calling out to each other came disembodied through the dry desert air. Now, a little after seven, I could hear someone practicing on the trumpet, the same rough phrases played over and over. I suddenly remembered how as children we had tried to get the rhythm of a galloping horse with hands against our thighs, or by fluttering our tongues against the roofs of our mouths.

After the trumpet, the impatient calls of adults summoning children. Sunday morning. Wood smoke hung like a lens in the trees. The first car starts — a cold eight-cylinder engine, of Chrysler extraction perhaps, goosed to life, then throttled back to murmur through dual mufflers, the obbligato music of a shade-tree mechanic. The rote bark of mongrel dogs at dawn, the jagged outcries of men and women, an engine coming to life. Like a thousand villages from West Virginia to Guadalajara.

I finished my notes — where was I going to find a description of the horses that came north with the conquistadors? Did their manes come forward prominently over the brow, like this one's, like the forelocks of Blackfeet and Assiniboin men in nineteenth-century paintings? I set the notes on the seat beside me.

The road followed the canal for a while and then arced north, toward Interstate 8. It was slow driving and I fell to thinking how the desert had changed since Anza had come through. New plants and animals — the MacDougall cottonwood, the English house sparrow, the chukar from India — have about them now the air of the native-born. Of the native species, some — no one knows how many — are extinct. The populations of many others, especially the animals, have been sharply reduced. The idea of a desert impoverished by agricultural poisons and varmint hunters, by off-road vehicles and military operations, did not seem as disturbing to me, however, as this other horror, now that I had been those hours with the horse. The vandals, the few who crowbar rock art off the desert's walls, who dig up graves, who punish the ground that holds intaglios, are people who devour history. Their self-centered scorn, their disrespect for ideas and images beyond their ken, create the awful atmosphere of loose ends in which totalitarianism thrives, in which the past is merely curious or wrong.

I thought about the horse sitting out there on the unprotected plain. I enumerated its qualities in my mind until a sense of its vulnerability receded and it became an anchor for something else. I remembered that history, a history like this one, which ran deeper than Mexico, deeper than the Spanish, was a kind of medicine. It permitted the great breadth of human expression to reverberate, and it did not urge you to locate its apotheosis in the present.

Each of us, individuals and civilizations, has been held upside down like Achilles in the River Styx. The artist mixing his colors in the dim light of Altamira; an Egyptian ruler lying still now, wrapped in his byssus,* stored against time in a pyramid; the faded Dorset culture of the Arctic; the Hmong and Samburu and Walbiri of historic time; the modern nations. This great, imperfect stretch of human expression is the clarification and encouragement, the urging and the reminder, we call history. And it is inscribed

*byssus: Ancient cloth. — Ed.

everywhere in the face of the land, from the mountain passes of the Himalayas to a nameless bajada in the California desert.

Small birds rose up in the road ahead, startled, and flew off. I prayed no infidel would ever find that horse.

Reflections and Responses

1. Lopez divides his essay into three parts. How does each of these parts differ? What purpose does each serve?

2. Examine Lopez's choice of words. When does he introduce technical terms into the essay? Go through the essay and identify the various technical terms. From what diverse disciplines are they drawn? How do these terms affect your response to both the author and his subject?

3. When this essay originally appeared, it included no photographs of the carving. Why do you think that decision was made? What distortions would photography introduce? What would a photograph *not* be able to show us? What is Lopez's attitude toward photography in this instance?

JOYCE CAROL OATES

They All Just Went Away

The essay has long been the perfect form for the reflective mind. In the hands of a great writer, the process of reflection can be stimulated by a single incident or image and then veer off in so many different directions that, by the end of the essay, the reader is amazed at how much ground has been covered. "They All Just Went Away" does everything a superb reflective essay can do because it moves from the personal eccentricities of a lonely young girl who finds herself drawn to abandoned houses and desolate families into a consideration of American art, class boundaries, sexual abuse, and strange erotic attachments. It is not a cheerful or placid piece of writing, however. "As I am not drawn to art that makes me feel good, comfortable, or at ease," Joyce Carol Oates writes, "so I am not drawn to essays that 'smile,' except in the context of larger, more complex ambitions."

One of the country's most distinguished authors, Joyce Carol Oates has published over two dozen novels and numerous collections of poems, plays, short stories, criticism, and essays. Equipped with her work alone, the scholar and essayist Henry Louis Gates, Jr., claimed, a future archaeologist could "easily piece together the whole postwar America." The recipient of countless literary awards, she was at thirty-one the youngest writer ever to receive the prestigious National Book Award for fiction, when her novel them *was chosen in 1969. She currently teaches writing at Princeton University. Among her most recent works of fiction are* Man Crazy *(1997),* The Collector of Hearts *(1998),* My Heart Laid Bare *(1998),* Broke Heart Blues *(1999),* Blonde *(2000), and* Big Mouth and Ugly Girl *(2001). "They All Just Went Away" originally appeared in* The New Yorker *(1995) and was selected by Geoffrey C. Ward for* The Best American Essays 1996.

I must have been a lonely child. Until the age of twelve or thirteen, my most intense, happiest hours were spent tramping desolate fields, woods, and creek banks near my family's farmhouse in Millersport, New York. No one knew where I went. My father, working most of the day at Harrison's, a division of General Motors in Lockport, and at other times preoccupied, would not have asked; if my mother asked, I might have answered in a way that would deflect curiosity. I was an articulate, verbal child. Yet I could not have explained what drew me to the abandoned houses, barns, silos, corncribs. A hike of miles through fields of spiky grass, across outcroppings of shale as steeply angled as stairs, was a lark if the reward was an empty house.

Some of these houses had been inhabited as "homes" fairly recently — they had not yet reverted to the wild. Others, abandoned during the Depression, had long since begun to rot and collapse, engulfed by vegetation (trumpet vine, wisteria, rose of Sharon, willow) that elsewhere, on our property for instance, was kept neatly trimmed. I was drawn to both kinds of houses, though the more recently inhabited were more forbidding and therefore more inviting.

To push open a door into such silence: the absolute emptiness of a house whose occupants have departed. Often, the crack of broken glass underfoot. A startled buzzing of flies, hornets. The slithering, ticklish sensation of a garter snake crawling across floorboards.

Left behind, as if in haste, were remnants of a lost household. A broken toy on the floor, a baby's bottle. A rain-soaked sofa, looking as if it has been gutted with a hunter's skilled knife. Strips of wallpaper like shredded skin. Smashed crockery, piles of tin cans; soda, beer, whiskey bottles. An icebox, its door yawning open. Once, on a counter, a dirt-stiffened rag that, unfolded like precious cloth, revealed itself to be a woman's cheaply glamorous "see-through" blouse, threaded with glitter-strips of gold.

This was a long time ago, yet it is more vivid to me than anything now.

This was when I was too young to think *the house is the mother's body, you have been expelled and are forbidden now to reenter.*

Always, I was prepared to see a face at a high, empty window. A woman's hand uplifted in greeting, or in warning. *Hello! Come in! Stay away! Run! Who are you?* A movement in the corner of my eye: the blurred motion of a person passing through a doorway, or glimpsed through a window. There might be a single shriek of laughter from a barn — piercing as a bird's cry. Murmurous, teasing voices confused with wind rippling through tall, coarse, gone-to-seed grass. Voices that, when you pause to listen, fade immediately and are gone.

The sky in such places of abandonment was always of the hue and brightness of tin, as if the melancholy rural poverty of tin roofs reflected upward.

A house: a structural arrangement of space, geometrically laid out to provide what are called rooms, these divided from one another by verticals and horizontals called walls, ceilings, floors. The house contains the home but is not identical with it. The house anticipates the home and will very likely survive it, reverting again simply to house when home (that is, life) departs. For only where there is life can there be home.

I have never found the visual equivalent of these abandoned farmhouses of upstate New York, of northern Erie County, in the area of the long, meandering Tonawanda Creek and the Barge Canal. You think most immediately of the canvases of Edward Hopper: those dreamily stylized visions of a lost America, houses never depicted as homes, and human beings, if you look closer, never depicted as other than mannequins. For Hopper is not a realist but a surrealist. His dreams are of the ordinary, as if, even in imagination, the artist were trapped in an unyielding daylight consciousness. There seems almost a kind of rage, a revenge against such restraints, in Hopper's studied, endlessly repeated *simplicity.* By contrast, Charles Burchfield, with his numerous oils and watercolors — frequently of upstate New York landscapes, houses, and farms — rendered the real as visionary and luminous, suffused with a Blakean rapture and a kind of radical simplicity, too. Then there are the shimmering New England barns, fields, and skies of our contemporary Wolf Kahn — images evoked by memory, almost on the verge of dissolution. But the "real" — what assaults the eye before the eye begins its work of selection — is never on the verge of dissolution, still less of appropriation. The real is raw, jarring, unexpected, sometimes trashy, sometimes luminous. Above all, the real is arbitrary. For to be a realist (in art or in life) is to acknowledge that all things might be other than they are. That there is no design, no intention, no aesthetic or moral or teleological imprimatur but, rather, the equivalent of Darwin's great vision of a blind, purposeless, ceaseless evolutionary process that yields no "products"—only temporary strategies against extinction.

Yet, being human, we think, To what purpose these broken-off things, if not to be gathered up, at last, in a single ecstatic vision?

There is a strange and profound and unknowable reality to these abandoned houses where jealously guarded, even prized possessions have become mere trash: windowpanes long ago smashed, and the spaces where they had been festooned with cobwebs, and cobwebs brushing against your face, catching in your hair like caresses. The peculiar, dank smell of wood rot and mildew, in one of the houses I most recall that had partly burned down, the smell of smoke and scorch, in early summer pervading even the lyric smell of honeysuckle — these haunting smells, never, at the time of experiencing, given specific sources, names.

Where a house has been abandoned — unworthy of being sold to new tenants, very likely seized by the county for default on taxes and the property held in escrow — you can be sure there has been a sad story. There have been devastated lives. Lives to be spoken of pityingly. How they went wrong. Why did she marry him, why did she stay with him? Just desperate people. Ignorant. Poor white trash. Runs in the family. A wrong turn.

Shall I say for the record that ours was a happy, close-knit, and unextraordinary family for our time, place, and economic status? Yet what was vividly real in the solid-built old farmhouse that contained my home (my family consisted of my father, mother, younger brother, grandfather, and grandmother, who owned the property — a slow-failing farm whose principal crop had become Bartlett pears by the time I was a girl) was of far less significance to me than what was real elsewhere. A gone-to-seed landscape had an authority that seemed to me incontestable: the powerful authority of silence in houses from which the human voice had vanished. For the abandoned house contained the future of any house — the lilac tree pushing through the rotted veranda, hornets' nests beneath eaves, windows smashed by vandals, human excrement left to dry on a parlor floor once scrubbed on hands and knees.

The abandoned, the devastated, was the profound experience, whereas involvement in family life — the fever, the bliss, the abrasions, the infinite distractions of human love — was so clearly temporary. Like a television screen upon which antic images (at this time, in the fifties, minimally varying gradations of gray) appear fleetingly and are gone.

I have seemed to suggest that the abandoned houses were all distant from our house, but in fact the one that had been partly gutted by fire — which I will call the Weidel house — was perhaps a half mile away. If you drove, turning right off Transit Road, which was our road, onto the old Creek Road, it would have been a distance of a mile or more, but if you crossed through our back potato field and through the marshy woods which no one seemed to own, it was a quick walk.

The Weidels' dog, Slossie, a mixed breed with a stumpy, energetic tail and a sweet disposition, sand-colored, rheumy-eyed, as hungry for affection as for the scraps we sometimes fed her, trotted over frequently to play with my brother and me. Though, strictly speaking, Slossie was not wanted at our house. None of the Weidels were wanted.

The "Weidel house," it would be called for years. The "Weidel property." As if the very land — which the family had not owned in any case, but only rented, partly with county-welfare support — were somehow imprinted with that name, a man's identity. Or infamy.

For tales were told of the father who drank, beat and terrorized his family, "did things to" his daughters, and finally set the house on fire and fled and was arrested, disappearing forever from the proper, decent life of our community. There was no romance in Mr. Weidel, whom my father knew only slightly and despised as a drinker, and as a wife- and child-beater. Mr. Weidel was a railway worker in Lockport, or perhaps an ex-railway worker, for he seemed to work only sporadically, though he always wore a railwayman's cap. He and his elder sons were hunters, owning a shotgun among them and one or two deer rifles. His face was broad, fair, vein-swollen, with a look of flushed, alcoholic reproach. He was tall and heavyset, with graying black whiskers that sprouted like quills. His eyes had a way of swerving in their sockets, seeking you out when you could not slip away quickly enough. *H'lo there, little*

Joyce! Joycie! Joycie Oates, h'lo! He wore rubber boots that flapped, un-buckled, about his feet.

Mrs. Weidel was a faded-pretty, apologetic woman with a body that seemed to have become bloated, as with a perpetual preg-nancy. Her bosom had sunk to her waist. Her legs were encased, sausagelike, in flesh-colored support hose. *How can that woman live with him? That pig.* There was disdain, disgust, in this frequent re-frain. *Why doesn't she leave him? Did you see that black eye? Did you hear them the other night? Take the girls away, at least.* It was thought that she could, for Mrs. Weidel was the only one in the family who seemed to work at all regularly. She was hired for seasonal canning in a tomato factory in lower Lockport and may have done house-cleaning in the city.

A shifting household of relatives and rumored "boarders" lived in the Weidel house. There were six Weidel children, four sons and two daughters. Ruth was a year older than I, and Dorothy two years younger. There was an older brother of Mr. Weidel's, who walked with a cane and was said to be an ex-convict, from Attica. The eldest Weidel son, Roy, owned a motorcycle, and friends of his often visited, fellow bikers. There were loud parties, frequent dis-putes, and tales of Mr. Weidel's chasing his wife with a butcher knife, a claw hammer, the shotgun, threatening to "blow her head off." Mrs. Weidel and the younger children fled outdoors in terror and hid in the hayloft. Sheriff's deputies drove out to the house, but no charges were ever pressed against Mr. Weidel. Until the fire, which was so public that it couldn't be denied.

There was the summer day — I was eleven years old — that Mr. Weidel shot Slossie. We heard the poor creature yelping and whim-pering for what seemed like hours. When my father came home from work, he went to speak to Mr. Weidel, though my mother begged him not to. By this time, the dog had dragged herself be-neath the Weidels' house to die. Mr. Weidel was furious at the in-trusion, drunk, defensive — Slossie was his goddam dog, he said, she'd been getting in the way, she was "old." But my father con-vinced him to put the poor dog out of her misery. So Mr. Weidel made one of his sons drag Slossie out from beneath the house, and he straddled her and shot her a second time, and a third, at close range. My father, who'd never hunted, who'd never owned a gun, backed off, a hand over his eyes.

Afterward, my father would say of that day that walking away from that drunken son of a bitch with a rifle in his hands was about the hardest thing he'd ever done. He'd expected a shot between his shoulders.

The fire was the following year, around Thanksgiving.

After the Weidels were gone from Millersport and the house stood empty, I discovered Slossie's grave. I'm sure it was Slossie's grave. It was beyond the dog hutch, in the weedy back yard, a sunken patch of earth measuring about three feet by four with one of Mrs. Weidel's big whitewashed rocks at the head.

Morning glories grew in clusters on the posts of the front porch. Mrs. Weidel had planted hollyhocks, sunflowers, and trumpet vine in the yard. Tough, weedlike flowers that would survive for years.

It had been said of Ruth and her sister Dorothy that they were "slow." Yet Ruth was never slow to fly into a rage when she was teased by neighborhood boys or by her older brothers. She waved her fists and stammered obscenities, words that stung like hail. Her face darkened with blood, and her full, thick lips quivered with a strange sort of pleasure. How you loved to see Ruth Weidel fly into one of her rages; it was like holding a lighted match to flammable material.

The Weidel house was like any other rundown woodframe house, said by my grandfather to have been "thrown up" in the 1920s. It had no cellar, only a concrete-block foundation — an emptiness that gradually filled with debris. It had an upstairs with several small bedrooms. There was no attic. No insulation. Steep, almost vertical stairs. The previous tenant had started to construct a front porch of raw planks, never completed or painted. (Though Mrs. Weidel added "touches" to the porch — chairs, a woven-rush rug, geraniums in flowerpots.) The roof of the house was made of sheets of tin, scarred and scabbed like skin, and the front was covered in simulated-brick asphalt siding pieced together from lumberyard scraps. All year round, a number of the windows were covered in transparent duct tape and never opened. From a distance, the house was the fading dun color of a deer's winter coat.

Our house had an attic and a cellar and a deep well and a solid cement foundation. My father did all the carpentry on our house, most of the shingling, the painting, the masonry. I would not know until I was an adult that he'd come from what's called a "broken home" himself—what an image, luridly visual, of a house literally broken, split in two, its secrets spilled out onto the ground for all to see, like entrails.

My mother, unlike Mrs. Weidel, had time to houseclean. It was a continuous task, a mother's responsibility. My mother planted vegetables, strawberries, beds of flowers. Petunias and pansies and zinnias. Crimson peonies that flowered for my birthday, in mid-June.

I remember the night of the fire vividly, as if it had been a festive affair to which I'd been invited.

There was the sound of a siren on the Creek Road. There were shouts, and an astonishing burst of flame in the night, in the direction of the Weidel house. The air was moist, and reflected and magnified the fire, surrounding it like a nimbus. My grandparents would claim there had never been such excitement in Millersport, and perhaps that was true. My father dressed hurriedly and went to help the firefighters, and my mother and the rest of us watched from upstairs windows. The fire began at about 1 A.M., and it would be past 4 A.M. before my seven-year-old brother and I got back to bed.

Yet what was so exciting an event was, in fact, an ending, with nothing to follow. Immediately afterward, the Weidels disappeared from Millersport and from our lives. It was said that Mr. Weidel fled "as a fugitive" but was captured and arrested the next day, in Buffalo. The family was broken up, scattered, the younger children placed in foster homes. That quickly, the Weidels were gone.

For a long time, the smell of wood smoke, scorch, pervaded the air of Millersport, the fresh, damp smell of earth sullied by its presence. Neighbors complained that the Weidel house should be razed at the county's expense, bulldozed over, and the property sold. But nothing was done for years. Who knows why? When I went away to college, the old falling-down house was still there.

How swiftly, in a single season, a human habitation can turn wild. The bumpy cinder driveway over which the eldest Weidel son had ridden his motorcycle was soon stippled with tall weeds.

What had happened to Roy Weidel? It was said he'd joined the navy. No, he had a police record and could not have joined the navy. He'd disappeared. Asked by the police to give a sworn statement about the night of his father's "arson," he'd panicked and fled.

Signs were posted — NO TRESPASSING, THIS PROPERTY CONDEMNED BY ERIE CO. — and they, too, over a period of months, became shabby and faded. My parents warned me never to wander onto the Weidel property. There was a well with a loose-fitting cover, among other dangers. As if *I* would fall into a well! I smiled to think how little my parents knew me. How little anyone knew me.

Have I said that my father never struck his children, as Mr. Weidel struck his? And did worse things to them, to the girls sometimes, it was whispered. Yes, and Mrs. Weidel, who seemed so soft and apologetic and sad, she too had beaten the younger children when she'd been drinking. County social workers came around to question neighbors, and spread the story of what they learned along the way.

In fact, I may have been disciplined, spanked, a few times. Like most children, I don't remember. I remember Mr. Weidel spanking his children until they screamed (though I wasn't a witness, was I?), but I don't remember being spanked by my parents, and in any case, if I was, it was no more than I deserved.

I'd seen Mr. Weidel urinating once at the roadside. The loose-flying skein of the kerosene he'd flung around the house before setting the fire must have resembled the stream of his urine, transparent and glittering. But they laughed, saying Mr. Weidel had been too drunk, or too careless, to have done an adequate job of sprinkling kerosene through the downstairs of the house. Wasn't it like him, such a slovenly job. Only part of the house had burned, a wall of the kitchen and an adjoining woodshed.

Had Mr. Weidel wanted to burn his family alive in their beds? Mrs. Weidel testified no, they'd all been awake, they'd run out into the yard before the fire began. They'd never been in any danger, she swore. But Mr. Weidel was indicted on several counts of attempted murder, along with other charges.

For so many years the Weidel house remained standing. There was something defiant about it, like someone who has been mortally wounded but will not die. In the weedy front yard, Mrs. Weidel's display of whitewashed rocks and plaster-of-Paris gnomes and the clay pedestal with the shiny blue glass ball disappeared from view within a year or so. Brambles grew everywhere. I forced myself to taste a small bitter red berry but spat it out, it made my mouth pucker so.

What did it mean that Erie County had "condemned" the Weidel property? The downstairs windows were carelessly boarded over, and both the front and rear doors were unlocked, collapsing on their hinges. Broken glass underfoot and a sickish stench of burn, mildew, decay. Yet there were "touches"—on what remained of a kitchen wall, a Holstein calendar from a local feed store, a child's crayon drawing. Upstairs, children's clothes, socks and old shoes heaped on the floor. I recognized with a thrill of repugnance an old red sweater of Ruth's, angora-fuzzy. There were broken Christmas tree ornaments, a naked pink plastic doll. Toppled bedsprings, filthy mattresses streaked with yellow and rust-colored stains. The mattresses looked as if they'd been gutted, their stuffing strewn about. The most terrible punishment, I thought, would be to be forced to lie down on such a mattress.

I thought of Mrs. Weidel, her swollen, blackened eyes, her bruised face. Shouts and sirens in the night, the sheriff's patrol car. But no charges filed. The social worker told my mother how Mrs. Weidel had screamed at the county people, insisting her husband hadn't done anything wrong and shouldn't go to jail. The names she'd called them! Unrepeatable.

She was the wife of that man, they'd had babies together. The law had no right to interfere. The law had nothing to do with them.

As a woman and as a writer, I have long wondered at the wellsprings of female masochism. Or what, in despair of a more subtle, less reductive phrase, we can call the congeries of predilections toward self-hurt, self-erasure, self-repudiation in women. These predilections are presumably "learned"—"acquired"—but perhaps also imprinted in our genes, of biological necessity, neurophysiological fate, predilections that predate culture. Indeed, may shape culture. Do not say, "Yes, but these are isolated, peripheral examples. These are marginal Americans, uneducated. They tell us nothing about ourselves." They tell us everything about ourselves, and even the telling, the exposure, is a kind of cutting, an inscription in the flesh.

Yet what could possibly be the evolutionary advantage of self-hurt in the female? Abnegation in the face of another's cruelty? Acquiescence to another's will? This loathsome secret that women do not care to speak of, or even acknowledge.

Two or three years later, in high school, twelve miles away in a consolidated district school to which, as a sophomore, I went by school bus, Ruth Weidel appeared. She was living now with relatives in Lockport. She looked, at sixteen, like a woman in her twenties; big-breasted, with full, strong thighs and burnished-brown hair inexpertly bleached. Ruth's homeroom was "special education," but she took some classes with the rest of us. If she recognized me, in our home economics class, she was careful to give no sign.

There was a tacit understanding that "something had happened" to Ruth Weidel, and her teachers treated her guardedly. Ruth was special, the way a handicapped person is special. She was withdrawn, quiet; if still prone to violent outbursts of rage, she might have been on medication to control it. Her eyes, like her father's, seemed always about to swerve in their sockets. Her face was round, fleshy, like a pudding, her nose oily-pored. Yet she wore lipstick, she was "glamorous" — almost. In gym class, Ruth's large breasts straining against her T-shirt and the shining rippled muscles and fatty flesh of her thighs were amazing to us; we were so much thinner and less female, so much younger.

I believed that I should protect Ruth Weidel, so I told none of the other students about her family. Even to Ruth, for a long time I pretended not to know who she was. I can't explain how Ruth could have possibly believed me, yet this seems to have been so. Quite purposefully, I befriended Ruth. I thought her face would lose its sallow hardness if she could be made to smile, and so it became a kind of challenge to me to induce Ruth Weidel to smile. She was lonely and miserable at school, and flattered by my attention. For so few "normal" girls sought out "specialed" girls. At first she may have been suspicious, but by degrees she became trusting. I thought of Slossie: trust shows in the eyes.

I sat with Ruth at lunch in the school cafeteria and eventually I asked her about the house on the old Creek Road, and she lied bluntly, to my face, insisting that an uncle of hers had owned that house. She'd only visited a few times. She and her family. I asked,

"How did the fire start?" and Ruth said, slowly, each word sucked like a pebble in the mouth, "Lightning. Lightning hit it. One night in a storm." I asked, "Are you living with your mother now, Ruth?" and Ruth shrugged, and made a face, and said, "She's OK. I see her sometimes." I asked about Dorothy. I asked where Mrs. Weidel was. I said that my mother had always liked her mother, and missed her when she went away. But Ruth seemed not to hear. Her gaze had drifted. I said, "Why did you all move away?" Ruth did not reply, though I could hear her breathing hard. "Why did you abandon your house? It could have been fixed. It's still there. Your mom's hollyhocks are still there. You should come out and see it sometime. You could visit me." Ruth shrugged, and laughed. She gave me a sidelong glance, almost flirtatiously. It was startling to see how good-looking she could be, how sullen-sexy; to know how men would stare at her who would never so much as glance at a girl like me. Ruth said slowly, as if she'd come to a final, adamant conclusion to a problem that had long vexed her, "They all just went away."

Another time, after lunch with Ruth. I left a plastic change purse with a few coins in it on the ledge in one of the girls' lavatories, where Ruth was washing her hands. I don't recall whether I left it on purpose or not. But when I returned, after waiting for Ruth to leave the lavatory, the change purse was gone.

Once or twice, I invited Ruth Weidel to come home with me on the school bus some afternoon, to Millersport, to have supper with my family and stay the night. I must not have truly believed she might accept, for my mother would have been horrified and would have forced me to rescind the invitation. Ruth had hesitated, as if she wanted to say yes, wanted very badly to say yes, but finally she said, "No. I guess I better not."

Reflections and Responses

1. How does Joyce Carol Oates introduce the issue of class into the essay? How does her background differ from Ruth Weidel's? How would you describe her attitude toward the Weidel family? Why is she drawn to them? What does she find attractive about them?

2. How can you account for the abrupt introduction in the ninth paragraph of houses as the subject for famous American painters? Why do you think the author suddenly interjected this information? What does it contribute to the essay as a whole?

3. Where does the essay's title come from? Why do you think Joyce Carol Oates used this expression as the title? What does it suggest about the overall experience of the essay?

JOE QUEENAN

Matriculation Fixation

"In real life," writes Joe Queenan, "some children get the finest educations but still become first-class screwups." Sick and tired of listening to parents talk about what schools their college-bound children will or should attend, Queenan does what few other parents ever do—he decides to address the issue in an essay intended to point out the utter silliness of the quest for the "right" college, which he labels "Matriculation Fixation," to identify it as the psychological disorder he believes it is. His irritation with parents who obsess over their offspring's successes or failures mainly stems from the conversations about the topic, which he finds "banal, self-aggrandizing, self-flagellatory, or punitive." He then, with his usual sharp humor, proceeds to classify the various types of annoying conversations.

Joe Queenan is the author of seven books, including If You're Talking to Me, Your Career Must Be in Trouble *and* Balsamic Dreams: A Short But Self-Important History of the Baby Boomers. *A columnist for* GQ, *he has written essays and humor and researched articles for numerous magazines. He lives in Tarrytown, New York. Originally appearing in* The New York Times Education Life, *"Matriculation Fixation" was selected by Stephen Jay Gould for* The Best American Essays 2002.

Two years ago, I was languishing in the waiting room of a Philadelphia hospital when a complete stranger unexpectedly began telling me about his daughter's college plans. As my seventy-nine-year-old mother was recovering from major surgery that afternoon, I could not give him my complete and undivided attention. But as the briefing session wore on, I did manage to garner most of the relevant details.

The girl, bright but not brilliant, had been accepted to a first-tier university without financial aid but had also been accepted to a local, second-echelon university where she was promised a free ride. Money being tight, with other college-bound children in the family queue, the man had persuaded his daughter to accept the second university's offer. Now he was worried that she would one day rue this decision. Because she would be graduating from a less prestigious institution, fewer contacts would be made and fewer doors would be opened. Her degree would put her within striking distance of the yellow brick road, but not physically on the road itself. Did this make her father the spawn of Satan?

As a man of the world accustomed to being told the most intimate details about complete strangers' marriages, careers, and hobbies, I had long ago acquired the requisite skills to mediate this crisis. I told the man that many of my high school chums had graduated from the second-tier university in question and had gone on to live rich, full lives.

I told him that I myself had graduated from a second-echelon Philadelphia university not unlike the one his daughter was entering, and had managed to carve out a nice little niche for myself. I told him that my college days had been among the happiest of my life, that the sun never set without my thanking God for the illumination and inspiration provided by my talented, dedicated professors. Pressed for biographical data, I explained that I was a freelance writer, ticked off a list of my credentials, and said I was pretty happy with the way my career had turned out.

The man had never heard of me, had never read anything I'd written. Though he tried to feign interest in my pathetic curriculum vitae, I could see that he was devastated. By following an academic path similar to mine, his daughter, who was also planning a career in journalism, was going to end up as big a failure as I.

I never did find out why he was visiting the hospital.

I mention this incident because it illustrates the neurotic gabbiness that afflicts parents when it comes time to send their children to college. I know whereof I speak. Next fall, my daughter goes to college. Three years later my son will follow suit. I will be sorry to see them go; over the years they have proved to be remarkably amusing. But every dark cloud has a silver lining. Once my children have left the house, I will never again have to participate in a mind-numbing discussion about where my children or my friends' children or my neighbors' children are going to college, and why. On this subject, I am completely tapped out. This lack of interest does not stem from pure selfishness or un-alloyed contempt for other people's offspring. Rather, I feel this way because I find almost all conversations about the college selec-tion process to be banal, self-aggrandizing, self-flagellatory, or punitive. I'd rather talk about cribbage.

The most infuriating conversation is the one where the parent clearly seeks a decisive, career-validating moment of emotional closure. Such individuals believe that securing admission to a top-flight university provides a child with an irrevocable passport to success, guaranteeing a life of uninterrupted economic mirth. Par-ents such as these upwardly mobile chuckleheads exude an almost Prussian belligerence when announcing their children's destina-tions, congratulating themselves on a job well done, while issuing a sotto voce taunt to parents of the less gifted. For them, the hard part of child rearing is now over. Junior went to the right prep school, made the right friends, signed up for the right activities, and is now headed for the right school. Now we can get the heck out of here and move to Tuscany.

But in reality, life doesn't end at age seventeen. Or twenty-one. In real life, some children get the finest educations but still be-come first-class screwups. My own profession is filled with people who went to the right school but ended up in the wrong career. (They should have been flacks; the phone ringing in the next room is not and never will be the Pulitzer committee.) Some of those boys and girls most likely to succeed are going to end up on welfare or skid row. At which point they'll need parental input. Or cash. A parent's responsibility doesn't end once the kids leave. A parent's responsibility never ends. That's why Nature gives you the job.

A second, far more numerous class of obsessives consists of people who suddenly realize that their Brand X children aren't going to make the cut. Seventeen years of unread textbooks, unvis-ited museums, and untaken AP courses are now finally taking their toll, and those grandiose delivery-room dreams of Amherst, Bard, and Duke are suddenly going up in smoke. Bashfully, shame-facedly, miserably, these parents now mumble the names of the glamourless institutions their progeny are skulking off to. Invariably, they are colleges you never heard of in towns no one wants to visit in states whose capitals only repeat winners on *Jeopardy!* can name. The market has spoken, the glum parental expressions seem to say. My child is an idiot.

But once again, reality has a way of upsetting the worst-laid plans of mice and Mensa. Some kids are late bloomers. Some kids are better off in a less competitive environment. Lots of people achieve huge success in this society without a degree from a prestigious university. Just because your child has failed to clear the first, or even the twentieth, hurdle doesn't mean you should disown him. Matisse didn't get rolling until he was in his forties. Bill Gates, David Geffen, Michael Dell, Graydon Carter, and Madonna are all college dropouts. Ronald Reagan attended tiny Eureka College, while Warren Buffet went to Football U in Lincoln, Nebraska. Despite what you may have read in F. Scott Fitzgerald (who dropped out of Princeton in 1917), life doesn't have just one act. There is often act two. And act five. Not to mention the sequels.

Matriculation fixation reaches its dottiest form during the obligatory campus visit. Here it is never entirely clear what parents are looking for, particularly in high-profile institutions whose renown has in some way preceded them. During a recent visit to MIT, I watched the first thirty seconds of an admissions office video poking fun at the university's reputation as a nerd factory. While my wife and daughter watched the rest of the video, which assured applicants that MIT nerds were hard to find, I took a stroll around the campus. I saw a lot of nerds. And I do not mean this as a criticism.

Later that morning, a guide showed a bunch of us around campus. At one juncture, she pointed out a restaurant where students could grab a fast, inexpensive meal. "How much?" asked one highstrung mother. "About eight bucks," she was told. The woman shuddered, noting that forking over eight dollars for dinner every night could get pretty darned expensive.

"It's going to cost you forty grand to send your kid to school here," I interjected. "Don't start worrying about dinner prices."

Since that visit this fall, this incident has become an invaluable part of my repertory. Now, whenever I am dragooned into the 30,000th interminable conversation about the college selection process, I indicate that sedulous monitoring of on-campus restaurant prices should be a vital component of the winnowing procedure, particularly vis-à-vis panini. People who hear me say things like this can't decide whether I am insensitive or ornery or flat-out dumb. Well, let's just put it this way: I was never MIT material.

Reflections and Responses

1. Why do you think Queenan opens his short essay with the account of a conversation he has in a hospital waiting room? How does that set the stage and tone for what follows? Consider other ways Queenan might have gotten into his topic: for example, could he have used his final conversation as an opening?

2. Although the essay is essentially humorous, what serious matters does Queenan confront? What is he saying about elitism and education? Why don't we hear from college-bound students themselves? Do you think his attack on Americans' obsession over elite institutions would have been more persuasive if he had written a serious essay examining the subject fully? Why or why not?

3. Note that after his attack on parental obsessions over elite colleges, he winds up taking his daughter to one of the nation's most elite, Massachusetts Institute of Technology (MIT). Do you think this contradicts his points about other parents' obsessions? Is he too being "self-aggrandizing" by identifying MIT (note that he didn't specifically identify the college he attended)? Or is the MIT experience an extension of his humorous or "ornery" streak? How do you respond to his concluding paragraph?

GAY TALESE

Ali in Havana

When one of America's leading journalists was assigned to profile one of the world's biggest celebrities on a humanitarian-aid visit to one of the world's most controversial political figures, the result was bound to be a fascinating piece of writing and disclosure. In "Ali in Havana," Gay Talese accompanies the great fighter Muhammad Ali as he travels with his wife and entourage, along with many other visitors, to a reception at Havana's Palace of the Revolution to meet aging communist leader Fidel Castro. What ensues is both comic and poignant, as the magical Ali, stricken with Parkinson's disease, leaves Castro — who has been struggling to keep the small talk flowing — with a very odd parting token. A connoisseur of the unnoticed detail, Talese captures all of the humor, tension, and awkwardness of this nearly surrealistic scene.

Gay Talese is one of the founders of the New Journalism, a literary movement that irrevocably altered both the art of reporting and the art of the essay. He is the best-selling author of books about the New York Times (The Kingdom and the Power), *the inside story of a Mafia family* (Honor Thy Father), *the changing moral values of America* (Thy Neighbor's Wife), *and a historical memoir* (Unto the Sons). *Other nonfiction books include* The Bridge, New York: A Serendipiter's Journey, *and* Fame and Obscurity. *Talese served as guest editor of* The Best American Essays 1987. *"Ali in Havana" originally appeared in* Esquire *and was selected by Ian Frazier for the 1997 volume.*

It is a warm, breezy, palm-flapping winter evening in Havana, and the leading restaurants are crowded with tourists from Europe, Asia, and South America being serenaded by guitarists relentlessly singing *"Guan-tan-a-mera . . . guajira . . . Guan-tan-a-mera";* and at the

Café Cantante there are clamorous salsa dancers, mambo kings, grunting, bare-chested male performers lifting tables with their teeth, and turbaned women swathed in hip-hugging skirts, blowing whistles while gyrating their glistening bodies into an erotic frenzy. In the café's audience as well as in the restaurants, hotels, and other public places throughout the island, cigarettes and cigars are smoked without restraint or restriction. Two prostitutes are smoking and talking privately on the corner of a dimly lit street bordering the manicured lawns of Havana's five-star Hotel Nacional. They are copper-colored women in their early twenties wearing faded miniskirts and halters, and as they chat, they are watching attentively while two men — one white, the other black — huddle over the raised trunk of a parked red Toyota, arguing about the prices of the boxes of black-market Havana cigars that are stacked within.

The white man is a square-jawed Hungarian in his mid-thirties, wearing a beige tropical suit and a wide yellow tie, and he is one of Havana's leading entrepreneurs in the thriving illegal business of selling top-quality hand-rolled Cuban cigars below the local and international market price. The black man behind the car is a well-built, baldish, gray-bearded individual in his mid-fifties from Los Angeles named Howard Bingham; and no matter what price the Hungarian quotes, Bingham shakes his head and says, "No, no — that's too much!"

"You're crazy!" cries the Hungarian in slightly accented English, taking one of the boxes from the trunk and waving it in Howard Bingham's face. "These are Cohiba Esplendidos! The best in the world! You will pay one thousand dollars for a box like this in the States."

"Not me," says Bingham, who wears a Hawaiian shirt with a camera strapped around his neck. He is a professional photographer, and he is staying at the Hotel Nacional with his friend Muhammad Ali. "I wouldn't give you more than fifty dollars."

"You really are crazy," says the Hungarian, slicing through the box's paper seal with his fingernail, opening the lid to reveal a gleaming row of labeled Esplendidos.

"Fifty dollars," says Bingham.

"A hundred dollars," insists the Hungarian. "And hurry! The police could be driving around." The Hungarian straightens up and stares over the car toward the palm-lined lawn and stanchioned lights that glow in the distance along the road leading to the hotel's ornate portico, which is now jammed with people and vehicles; then he turns and flings a glance back toward the nearby public street, where he notices that the prostitutes are now blowing smoke in his direction. He frowns.

"Quick, quick," he says to Bingham, handing him the box. "One hundred dollars."

Howard Bingham does not smoke. He and Muhammad Ali and their traveling companions are leaving Havana tomorrow, after participating in a five-day American humanitarian-aid mission that brought a planeload of medical supplies to hospitals and clinics depleted by the United States' embargo, and Bingham would like to return home with some fine contraband cigars for his friends. But, on the other hand, one hundred is still too much.

"Fifty dollars," says Bingham determinedly, looking at his watch. He begins to walk away.

"O.K., O.K.," the Hungarian says petulantly. "Fifty."

Bingham reaches into his pocket for the money, and the Hungarian grabs it and gives him the Esplendidos before driving off in the Toyota. One of the prostitutes takes a few steps toward Bingham, but the photographer hurries on to the hotel. Fidel Castro is having a reception tonight for Muhammad Ali, and Bingham has only a half hour to change and be at the portico to catch the chartered bus that will take them to the government's headquarters. He will be bringing one of his photographs to the Cuban leader: an enlarged, framed portrait showing Muhammad Ali and Malcolm X walking together along a Harlem sidewalk in 1963. Malcolm X was thirty-seven at the time, two years away from an assassin's bullet; the twenty-one-year-old Ali was about to win the heavyweight title in a remarkable upset over Sonny Liston in Miami. Bingham's photograph is inscribed, TO PRESIDENT FIDEL CASTRO, FROM MUHAMMAD ALI. Under his signature, the former champion has sketched a little heart.

Although Muhammad Ali is now fifty-four and has been retired from boxing for more than fifteen years, he is still one of the most famous men in the world, being identifiable throughout five continents; and as he walks through the lobby of the Hotel Nacional toward the bus, wearing a gray sharkskin suit and a white cotton shirt buttoned at the neck without a tie, several guests approach him and request his autograph. It takes him about thirty seconds to write "Muhammad Ali," so shaky are his hands from the effects of Parkinson's syndrome; and though he walks without support, his movements are quite slow, and Howard Bingham and Ali's fourth wife, Yolanda, are following nearby.

Bingham met Ali thirty-five years ago in Los Angeles, shortly after the fighter had turned professional and before he discarded his "slave name" (Cassius Marcellus Clay) and joined the Black Muslims. Bingham subsequently became his closest male friend and has photographed every aspect of Ali's life: his rise and fall three times as the heavyweight champion; his three-year expulsion from boxing, beginning in 1967, for refusing to serve in the American military during the Vietnam War ("I ain't got no quarrel with them Vietcong"); his four marriages; his fatherhood of nine children (one adopted, two out of wedlock); his endless public appearances in all parts of the world — Germany, England, Egypt (sailing on the Nile with a son of Elijah Muhammad's), Sweden, Libya, Pakistan (hugging refugees from Afghanistan), Japan, Indonesia, Ghana (wearing a dashiki and posing with President Kwame Nkrumah), Zaire (beating George Foreman), Manila (beating Joe Frazier) . . . and now, on the final night of his 1996 visit to Cuba, he is en route to a social encounter with an aging contender he has long admired — one who has survived at the top for nearly forty years despite the ill will of nine American presidents, the CIA, the Mafia, and various militant Cuban Americans.

Bingham waits for Ali near the open door of the charter bus that is blocking the hotel's entrance; but Ali lingers within the crowd in the lobby, and Yolanda steps aside to let some people get closer to her husband.

She is a large and pretty woman of thirty-eight, with a radiant smile and a freckled, fair complexion that reflects her interracial ancestry. A scarf is loosely draped over her head and shoulders, her arms are covered by long sleeves, and her well-designed dress in vivid hues hangs below her knees. She converted to Islam from Catholicism when she married Ali, a man sixteen years her senior but one with whom she shared a familial bond dating back to her girlhood in their native Louisville, where her mother and Ali's mother were sisterly soul mates who traveled together to attend his fights. Yolanda had occasionally joined Ali's entourage, becoming acquainted with not only the boxing element but with Ali's female contemporaries who were his lovers, his wives, the mothers of his children; and she remained in touch with Ali throughout the 1970s, while she majored in psychology at Vanderbilt and later earned her master's degree in business at UCLA. Then — with the end of Ali's boxing career, his third marriage, and his vibrant health —Yolanda intimately entered his life as casually and naturally as she now stands waiting to reclaim her place at his side.

She knows that he is enjoying himself. There is a slight twinkle in his eyes, not much expression on his face, and no words forthcoming from this once most talkative of champions. But the mind behind his Parkinson's mask is functioning normally, and he is characteristically committed to what he is doing: he is spelling out his full name on whatever cards or scraps of paper his admirers are handing him. "Muhammad Ali." He does not settle for a time-saving "Ali" or his mere initials. He has never shortchanged his audience.

And in this audience tonight are people from Latin America, Canada, Africa, Russia, China, Germany, France. There are two hundred French travel agents staying at the hotel in conjunction with the Cuban government's campaign to increase its growing tourist trade (which last year saw about 745,000 visitors spending an estimated one billion dollars on the island). There is also on hand an Italian movie producer and his lady friend from Rome and a onetime Japanese wrestler, Antonio Inoki, who injured Ali's legs during a 1976 exhibition in Tokyo (but who warmly embraced him two nights ago in the hotel's lounge as they sat listening to Cuban pianist Chucho Valdes playing jazz on a Russian-made Moskva baby grand); and there is also in the crowd, standing taller than the rest, the forty-three-year-old, six-foot five-inch Cuban heavyweight hero Teófilo Stevenson, who was a three-time Olympic gold medalist, in 1972, 1976 and 1980, and who, on this island at least, is every bit as renowned as Ali or Castro.

Though part of Stevenson's reputation derives from his erstwhile power and skill in the ring (although he never fought Ali), it is also attributable to his not having succumbed to the offers of professional boxing promoters, stubbornly resisting the Yankee dollar — although Stevenson hardly seems deprived. He dwells among his countrymen like a towering Cuban peacock, occupying high positions within the government's athletic programs and gaining sufficient attention from the island's women to have garnered four wives so far, who are testimony to his eclectic taste.

His first wife was a dance instructor. His second was an industrial engineer. His third was a medical doctor. His fourth and present wife is a criminal attorney. Her name is Fraymari, and she is a girlishly petite olive-skinned woman of twenty-three who, standing next to her husband in the lobby, rises barely higher than the midsection of his embroidered guayabera — a tightly tailored, short-sleeved shirt that accentuates his tapered torso, his broad shoulders, and the length of his dark, muscular arms, which once prevented his opponents from doing any injustice to his winning Latin looks.

Stevenson always fought from an upright position, and he maintains that posture today. When people talk to him, his eyes look downward, but his head remains high. The firm jaw of his oval-shaped head seems to be locked at a right angle to his straight-spined back. He is a proud man who exhibits all of his height. But he does listen, especially when the words being directed up at him are coming from the perky little attorney who is his wife. Fraymari is now reminding him that it is getting late — everyone should be on the bus; Fidel may be waiting.

Stevenson lowers his eyes toward her and winks. He has gotten the message. He has been Ali's principal escort throughout this visit. He was also Ali's guest in the United States during the fall of 1995; and though he knows only a few words of English, and Ali no Spanish, they are brotherly in their body language.

Stevenson edges himself into the crowd and gently places his right arm around the shoulders of his fellow champion. And then, slowly but firmly, he guides Ali toward the bus.

The road to Fidel Castro's Palace of the Revolution leads through a memory lane of old American automobiles chugging along at about twenty-five miles an hour — springless, pre-embargo Ford coupes and Plymouth sedans, DeSotos and LaSalles, Nashes and Studebakers, and various vehicular collages created out of Cadillac grilles and Oldsmobile axles and Buick fenders patched with pieces of oil-drum metal and powered by engines interlinked with kitchen utensils and pre-Batista lawn mowers and other gadgets that have elevated the craft of tinkering in Cuba to the status of high art.

The relatively newer forms of transportation seen on the road are, of course, non-American products — Polish Fiats, Russian Ladas, German motor scooters, Chinese bicycles, and the glistening, newly imported, air-conditioned Japanese bus from which Muhammad Ali is now gazing through a closed window out toward the street. At times, he raises a hand in response to one of the waving pedestrians or cyclists or motorists who recognize the bus, which has been shown repeatedly on the local TV news conveying Ali and his companions to the medical centers and tourist sites that have been part of the busy itinerary.

On the bus, as always, Ali is sitting alone, spread out across the two front seats in the left aisle directly behind the Cuban driver. Yolanda sits a few feet ahead of him to the right; she is adjacent to the driver and within inches of the windshield. The seats behind her are occupied by Teófilo Stevenson, Fraymari, and the photographer Bingham. Seated behind Ali, and also occupying two seats, is an American screenwriter named Greg Howard, who weighs more than three hundred pounds. Although he has traveled with Ali for only a few months while researching a film on the fighter's life, Greg Howard has firmly established himself as an intimate sidekick, and as such is among the very few on this trip who have heard Ali's voice. Ali speaks so softly that it is impossible to hear him in a crowd, and as a result whatever public comments or sentiments he is expected to, or chooses to, express are verbalized by Yolanda, or Bingham, or Teófilo Stevenson, or even at times by this stout young screenwriter.

"Ali is in his Zen period," Greg Howard has said more than once, in reference to Ali's quiescence. Like Ali, he admires what he has seen so far in Cuba — "There's no racism here" — and as a black man he has long identified with many of Ali's frustrations and confrontations. His student thesis at Princeton analyzed the Newark race riots of 1967, and the Hollywood script he most recently completed focuses on the Negro baseball leagues of the pre–World War II years. He envisions his new work on Ali in the genre of *Gandhi*.

* * *

The two-dozen bus seats behind those tacitly reserved for Ali's inner circle are occupied by the secretary-general of the Cuban Red Cross and the American humanitarian personnel who have entrusted him with $500,000 worth of donated medical supplies; and there are also the two Cuban interpreters and a dozen members of the American media, including the CBS-TV commentator Ed Bradley and his producers and camera crew from *60 Minutes*.

Ed Bradley is a gracious but reserved individualist who has appeared on television for a decade with his left earlobe pierced by a small circular ring — which, after some unfavorable comment initially expressed by his colleagues Mike Wallace and Andy Rooney, prompted Bradley's explanation: "It's *my* ear." Bradley also indulges in his identity as a cigar smoker; and as he sits in the midsection of the bus next to his Haitian lady friend, he is taking full advantage of the Communist regime's laissez-faire attitude toward tobacco, puffing away on a Cohiba Robusto, for which he paid full price at the Nacional's tobacco shop — and which now exudes a costly cloud of fragrance that appeals to his friend (who occasionally also smokes cigars) but is not appreciated by the two California women who are seated two rows back and are affiliated with a humanitarian-aid agency.

Indeed, the women have been commenting about the smoking habits of countless people they have encountered in Havana, being especially disappointed to discover earlier this very day that the pediatric hospital they visited (and to which they committed donations) is under the supervision of three tobacco-loving family physicians. When one of the American women, a blonde from Santa Barbara, reproached one of the cigarette-smoking doctors indirectly for setting such a poor example, she was told in effect that the island's health statistics regarding longevity, infant mortality, and general fitness compared favorably with those in the United States and were probably better than those of Americans residing in the capital city of Washington. On the other hand, the doctor made it clear that he did not believe that smoking was good for one's health — after all, Fidel himself had given it up; but unfortunately, the doctor added, in a classic understatement, "Some people have not followed him."

Nothing the doctor said appeased the woman from Santa Barbara. She did not, however, wish to appear confrontational at the hospital's news conference, which was covered by the press; nor during her many bus rides with Ed Bradley did she ever request that he discard his cigar. "Mr. Bradley intimidates me," she confided to her California coworker. But he was of course living within the law on this island that the doctor had called "the cradle of the best tobacco in the world." In Cuba, the most available American periodical on the newsstands is *Cigar Aficionado*.

The bus passes through the Plaza de la Revolución and comes to a halt at a security checkpoint near the large glass doors that open onto the marble-floored foyer of a 1950s modern building that is the center of communism's only stronghold in the Western Hemisphere.

As the bus door swings open, Greg Howard moves forward in his seat and grabs the 235-pound Muhammad Ali by the arms and shoulders and helps him to his feet; and after Ali has made his way down to the metal step, he turns and stretches back into the bus to take hold of the extended hands and forearms of the 300-pound screenwriter and pulls him to a standing position. This routine, repeated at each and every bus stop throughout the week, is never accompanied by either man's acknowledging that he had received any assistance, although Ali is aware that some passengers find the pas de deux quite amusing, and he is not reluctant to use his friend to further comic effect. After the bus had made an earlier stop in front of the sixteenth-century Morro Castle — where Ali had followed Teófilo Stevenson up a 117-step spiral staircase for a rooftop view of Havana Harbor — he spotted the solitary figure of Greg Howard standing below in the courtyard. Knowing that there was no way the narrow staircase could accommodate Howard's wide body, Ali suddenly began to wave his arms, summoning Howard to come up and join him.

Castro's security guards, who know in advance the names of all the bus passengers, guide Ali and the others through the glass doors and then into a pair of waiting elevators for a brief ride that is followed by a short walk through a corridor and finally into a large white-walled reception room, where it is announced that Fidel Castro will soon join them. The room has high ceilings and potted palms in every corner and is sparsely furnished with modern tan leather furniture. Next to a sofa is a table with two telephones, one gray and the other red. Overlooking the sofa is an oil painting of the Viñales valley, which lies west of Havana; and among the primitive art displayed on a circular table in front of the sofa is a grotesque tribal figure similar to the one Ali had examined earlier in the week at a trinket stand while touring with the group in Havana's Old Square. Ali had then whispered into the ear of Howard Bingham, and Bingham had repeated aloud what Ali had said: "Joe Frazier."

Ali now stands in the middle of the room, next to Bingham, who carries under his arm the framed photograph he plans to give Castro. Teófilo Stevenson and Fraymari stand facing them. The diminutive and delicate-boned Fraymari has painted her lips scarlet and has pulled back her hair in a matronly manner, hoping no doubt to appear more mature than her twenty-three years suggest, but standing next to the three much older and heavier and taller men transforms her image closer to that of an anorexic teenager. Ali's wife and Greg Howard are wandering about within the group that is exchanging comments in muted tones, either in English or Spanish, sometimes assisted by the interpreters. Ali's hands are shaking uncontrollably at his sides; but since his companions have witnessed this all week, the only people who are now paying attention are the security guards posted near the door.

Also waiting near the door for Castro is the four-man CBS camera team, and chatting with them and his two producers is Ed Bradley, without his cigar. There are no ashtrays in this room! This is a most uncommon sight in Cuba. Its implications might be political. Perhaps the sensibilities of the blond woman from Santa Barbara were taken into account by the doctors at the hospital and communicated to Castro's underlings, who are now making a conciliatory gesture toward their American benefactress.

Since the security guards have not invited the guests to be seated, everybody remains standing — for ten minutes, for twenty minutes, and then for a full half hour. Teófilo Stevenson shifts his weight from foot to foot and gazes over the heads of the crowd toward the upper level of the portal through which Castro is expected to enter — if he shows up. Stevenson knows from experience that Castro's schedule is unpredictable. There is always a crisis of some sort in Cuba, and it has long been rumored on the island that Castro constantly changes the location of where he sleeps. The identity of his bed partners is, of course, a state secret. Two nights ago, Stevenson and Ali and the rest were kept waiting until midnight for an expected meeting with Castro at the Hotel Biocaribe (to which Bingham had brought his gift photograph). But Castro never appeared. And no explanation was offered.

Now in this reception room, it is already 9 P.M. Ali continues to shake. No one has had dinner. The small talk is getting smaller: A few people would like to smoke. The regime is not assuaging anyone in this crowd with a bartender. It is a cocktail party without cocktails. There are not even canapés or soft drinks. Everyone is becoming increasingly restless — and then suddenly there is a collective sigh. The very familiar man with the beard strides into the room, dressed for guerrilla combat; and in a cheerful, high-pitched voice that soars beyond his whiskers, he announces, "Buenas noches!"

In an even higher tone, he repeats, "Buenas noches," this time with a few waves to the group while hastening toward the guest of honor; and then, with his arms extended, the seventy-year-old Fidel Castro immediately obscures the lower half of Ali's expressionless face with a gentle embrace and his flowing gray beard.

"I am glad to see you," Castro says to Ali, via the interpreter who followed him into the room, a comely, fair-skinned woman with a refined English accent. "I am very, very glad to see you," Castro continues, backing up to look into Ali's eyes while holding on to his trembling arms, "and I am thankful for your visit." Castro then releases his grip and awaits a possible reply. Ali says nothing. His expression remains characteristically fixed and benign, and his eyes do not blink despite the flashbulbs of several surrounding photographers. As the silence persists, Castro turns toward his old friend Teófilo Stevenson, feigning a jab. The Cuban boxing champion lowers his eyes and, with widened lips and cheeks, registers a smile. Castro then notices the tiny brunette standing beside Stevenson.

"Stevenson, who is this young woman?" Castro asks aloud in a tone of obvious approval. But before Stevenson can reply, Fraymari steps forward with a hint of lawyerly indignation: "You mean you don't remember me?"

Castro seems stunned. He smiles feebly, trying to conceal his confusion. He turns inquiringly toward his boxing hero, but Stevenson's eyes only roll upward. Stevenson knows that Castro has met Fraymari socially on earlier occasions, but unfortunately the Cuban leader has forgotten, and it is equally unfortunate that Fraymari is now behaving like a prosecutor.

"You held my son in your arms before he was one year old!" she reminds him while Castro continues to ponder. The crowd is attentive; the television cameras are rolling.

"At a volleyball game?" Castro asks tentatively.

"No, no," Stevenson interrupts, before Fraymari can say anything more, "that was my former wife. The doctor."

Castro slowly shakes his head in mock disapproval. Then he abruptly turns away from the couple, but not before reminding Stevenson, "You should get name tags."

Castro redirects his attention to Muhammad Ali. He studies Ali's face.

"Where is your wife?" he asks softly. Ali says nothing. There is more silence and turning of heads in the group until Howard Bingham spots Yolanda standing near the back and waves her to Castro's side.

Before she arrives, Bingham steps forward and presents Castro with the photograph of Ali and Malcolm X in Harlem in 1963. Castro holds it up level with his eyes and studies it silently for several seconds. When this picture was taken, Castro had been in control of Cuba for nearly four years. He was then thirty-seven. In 1959, he defeated the U.S.-backed dictator Fulgencio Batista, overcoming odds greater than Ali's subsequent victory over the supposedly unbeatable Sonny Liston. Batista had actually announced Castro's death back in 1956. Castro, then hiding in a secret outpost, thirty years old and beardless, was a disgruntled Jesuit-trained lawyer who was born into a landowning family and who craved Batista's job. At thirty-two, he had it. Batista was forced to flee to the Dominican Republic.

During this period, Muhammad Ali was only an amateur. His greatest achievement would come in 1960, when he received a gold medal in Rome as a member of the United States Olympic boxing team. But later in the sixties, he and Castro would share the world stage as figures moving against the American establishment — and now, in the twilight of their lives, on this winter's night in Havana, they meet for the first time: Ali silent and Castro isolated on his island.

"*Que bien!*" Castro says to Howard Bingham before showing the photograph to his interpreter. Then Castro is introduced by Bingham to Ali's wife. After they exchange greetings through the interpreter, he asks her, as if surprised, "You don't speak Spanish?"

"No," she says softly. She begins to caress her husband's left wrist, on which he wears a $250 silver Swiss Army watch she bought him. It is the only jewelry Ali wears.

"But I thought I saw you speaking Spanish on the TV news this week," Castro continues wonderingly before acknowledging that her voice had obviously been dubbed.

"Do you live in New York?"

"No, we live in Michigan."

"Cold," says Castro.

"Very cold," she repeats.

"In Michigan, don't you find many people that speak Spanish?"

"No, not many," she says. "Mostly in California, New York . . ." and, after a pause, "Florida."

Castro nods. It takes him a few seconds to think up another question. Small talk has never been the forte of this man who specializes in nonstop haranguing monologues that can last for hours; and yet here he is, in a room crowded with camera crews and news photographers — a talk-show host with a guest of honor who is speechless. But Fidel Castro plods on, asking Ali's wife if she has a favorite sport.

"I play a little tennis," Yolanda says, and then asks him, "Do you play tennis?"

"Ping-Pong," he replies, quickly adding that during his youth he had been active in the ring. "I spent hours boxing . . ." he begins to reminisce, but before he finishes his sentence, he sees the slowly rising right fist of Muhammad Ali moving toward his chin! Exuberant cheering and handclapping resound through the room, and Castro jumps sideways toward Stevenson, shouting, "*Asesorame!*" — "Help me!"

Stevenson's long arms land upon Ali's shoulders from behind, squeezing him gently; and then, after he releases him, the two ex-champions face each other and begin to act out in slow motion the postures of competing prizefighters — bobbing, weaving, swinging, ducking — all of it done without touching and all of it accompanied by three minutes of ongoing applause and the click-ing of cameras, and also some feelings of relief from Ali's friends because, in his own way, he has decided to join them. Ali still says nothing, his face still inscrutable, but he is less remote, less alone, and he does not pull away from Stevenson's embrace as the latter eagerly tells Castro about a boxing exhibition that he and Ali had staged earlier in the week at the Balado gym, in front of hundreds of fans and some of the island's up-and-coming contenders.

Stevenson did not actually explain that it had been merely an-other photo opportunity, one in which they sparred openhanded in the ring, wearing their street clothes and barely touching each other's bodies and faces; but then Stevenson had climbed out of the ring, leaving Ali to the more taxing test of withstanding two ab-breviated rounds against one and then another young bully of grade school age who clearly had not come to participate in a kid-die show. They had come to floor the champ. Their bellicose little bodies and hot-gloved hands and helmeted hell-bent heads were consumed with fury and ambition; and as they charged ahead, swinging wildly and swaggering to the roars of their teenage friends and relatives at ringside, one could imagine their future boastings to their grandchildren: On one fine day back in the winter of '96, I whacked Muhammad Ali! Except, in truth, on this particular day, Ali was still too fast for them. He backpedaled and shifted and swayed, stood on the toes of his black woven-leather pointed shoes, and showed that his body was made for motion — his Parkinson's problems were lost in his shuffle, in the thrusts of his butterfly sting that whistled two feet above the heads of his aspiring assailants, in the dazzling dips of his rope-a-dope that had con-founded George Foreman in Zaire, in his ever-memorable style, which in this Cuban gym moistened the eyes of his ever-observant photographer friend and provoked the overweight screenwriter to cry out in a voice that few in this noisy Spanish crowd could under-stand, "Ali's on a high! Ali's on a high!"

Teófilo Stevenson raises Ali's right arm above the head of Cas-tro, and the news photographers spend several minutes posing the three of them together in flashing light. Castro then sees Fray-mari watching alone at some distance. She is not smiling. Castro nods toward her. He summons a photographer to take a picture of Fraymari and himself. But she relaxes only after her husband comes over to join her in the conversation, which Castro immediately directs to the health and growth of their son, who is not yet two years old.

"Will he be as tall as his father?" Castro asks.

"I assume so," Fraymari says, glancing up toward her husband. She also has to look up when talking to Fidel Castro, for the Cuban leader is taller than six feet and his posture is nearly as erect as her husband's. Only the six-foot three-inch Muhammad Ali, who is standing with Bingham on the far side of her husband — and whose skin coloring, oval-shaped head, and burr-style haircut are very similar to her husband's — betrays his height with the slope-shouldered forward slouch he has developed since his illness.

"How much does your son weigh?" Castro continues.

"When he was one year old, he was already twenty-six pounds," Fraymari says. "This is three above normal. He was walking at nine months."

"She still breast-feeds him," Teófilo Stevenson says, seeming pleased.

"Oh, that's very nourishing," agrees Castro.

"Sometimes the kid becomes confused and thinks my chest is his mother's breast," Stevenson says, and he could have added that his son is also confused by Ali's sunglasses. The little boy engraved teeth marks all over the plastic frames while chewing on them during the days he accompanied his parents on Ali's bus tour.

As a CBS boom pole swoops down closer to catch the conversation, Castro reaches out to touch Stevenson's belly and asks, "How much do you weigh?"

"Two hundred thirty-eight pounds, more or less."

"That's thirty-eight more than me," Castro says, but he complains, "I eat very little. Very little. The diet advice I get is never accurate. I eat around fifteen hundred calories — less than thirty grams of protein, less than that."

Castro slaps a hand against his own midsection, which is relatively flat. If he does have a potbelly, it is concealed within his well-tailored uniform. Indeed, for a man of seventy, he seems in fine health. His facial skin is florid and unsagging, his dark eyes dart around the room with ever-alert intensity, and he has a full head of lustrous gray hair not thinning at the crown. The attention he pays to himself might be measured from his manicured finger-nails down to his square-toed boots, which are unscuffed and smoothly buffed without the burnish of a lackey's spit shine. But his beard seems to belong to another man and another time. It is excessively long and scraggly. Wispy white hairs mix with the faded black and dangle down the front of his uniform like an old shroud, weather-worn and drying out. It is the beard from the hills. Castro strokes it constantly, as if trying to revive the vitality of its fiber.

Castro now looks at Ali.

"How's your appetite?" he asks, forgetting that Ali is not speaking.

"Where's your wife?" he then asks aloud, and Howard Bingham calls out to her. Yolanda has once more drifted back into the group.

When she arrives, Castro hesitates before speaking to her. It is as if he is not absolutely sure who she is. He has met so many people since arriving, and with the group rotating constantly due to the jostling of the photographers, Castro cannot be certain whether the woman at his side is Muhammad Ali's wife or Ed Bradley's friend or some other woman he has met moments ago who has left him with an unlasting impression. Having already committed a faux pas regarding one of the wives of the two multimarried ex-champions standing nearby, Castro waits for some hint from his interpreter. None is offered. Fortunately, he does not have to worry in this country about the women's vote — or any vote, for that matter — but he does sigh in mild relief when Yolanda reintroduces herself as Ali's wife and does so by name.

"Ah, Yolanda," Castro repeats, "what a beautiful name. That's the name of a queen somewhere."

"In our household," she says.

"And how is your husband's appetite?"

"Good, but he likes sweets."

"We can send you some of our ice cream to Michigan," Castro says. Without waiting for her to comment, he asks, "Michigan is very cold?"

"Oh, yes," she replies, not indicating that they had already discussed Michigan's winter weather.

"How much snow?"

"We didn't get hit with the blizzard," Yolanda says, referring to a storm in January, "but it can get three, four feet —"

Teófilo Stevenson interrupts to say that he had been in Michigan during the previous October.

"Oh," Castro says, raising an eyebrow. He mentions that during the same month he had also been in the United States (attending the United Nations' fiftieth-anniversary tribute). He asks Stevenson the length of his American visit.

"I was there for nineteen days," says Stevenson.

"Nineteen days!" Castro repeats. "Longer than I was."

Castro complains that he was limited to five days and prohibited from traveling beyond New York.

"Well, *comandante,*" Stevenson responds offhandedly, in a slightly superior tone, "if you like, I will sometime show you my video."

Stevenson appears to be very comfortable in the presence of the Cuban leader, and perhaps the latter has habitually encouraged this; but at this moment, Castro may well be finding his boxing hero a bit condescending and worthy of a retaliatory jab. He knows how to deliver it.

"When you visited the United States," Castro asks pointedly, "did you bring your wife, the lawyer?"

Stevenson stiffens. He directs his eyes toward his wife. She turns away.

"No," Stevenson answers quietly. "I went alone."

Castro abruptly shifts his attention to the other side of the room, where the CBS camera crew is positioned, and he asks Ed Bradley, "What do you do?"

"We're making a documentary on Ali," Bradley explains, "and we followed him to Cuba to see what he was doing in Cuba and . . ."

Bradley's voice is suddenly overwhelmed by the sounds of laughter and handclapping. Bradley and Castro turn to discover that Muhammad Ali is now reclaiming everyone's attention. He is holding his shaky left fist in the air; but instead of assuming a boxer's pose, as he had done earlier, he is beginning to pull out from the top of his upraised fist, slowly and with dramatic delicacy, the tip of a red silk handkerchief that is pinched between his right index finger and thumb.

After he has pulled out the entire handkerchief, he dangles it in the air for a few seconds, waving it closer and closer to the

278 *Ali in Havana*

forehead of the wide-eyed Fidel Castro. Ali seems bewitched. He continues to stare stagnantly at Castro and the others, surrounded by applause that he gives no indication he hears. Then he proceeds to place the handkerchief back into the top of his cupped left hand — pecking with the pinched fingers of his right — and then quickly opens his palms toward his audience and reveals that the handkerchief has disappeared.

"Where is it?" cries Castro, who seems to be genuinely surprised and delighted. He approaches Ali and examines his hands, repeating, "Where is it? Where have you put it?"

Everyone who has traveled on Ali's bus during the week knows where he has hidden it. They have seen him perform the trick repeatedly in front of some of the patients and doctors at the hospitals and clinics as well as before countless tourists who have recognized him in his hotel lobby or during his strolls through the town square. They have also seen him follow up each performance with a demonstration that exposes his method. He keeps hidden in his fist a flesh-colored rubber thumb that contains the handkerchief that he will eventually pull out with the fingers of his other hand; and when he is reinserting the handkerchief, he is actually shoving the material back into the concealed rubber thumb, into which he then inserts his own right thumb. When he opens his hands, the uninformed among his onlookers are seeing his empty palms and missing the fact that the handkerchief is tucked within the rubber thumb that is covering his outstretched right thumb. Sharing with his audience the mystery of his magic always earns him additional applause.

After Ali has performed and explained the trick to Castro, he gives Castro the rubber thumb to examine — and, with more zest than he has shown all evening, Castro says, "Oh, let me try it, I want to try — it's the first time I have seen such a wonderful thing!" And after a few minutes of coaching from Howard Bingham, who long ago learned how to do it from Ali, the Cuban leader performs with sufficient dexterity and panache to satisfy his magical ambitions and to arouse another round of applause from the guests.

Meanwhile, more than ten minutes have passed since Ali began his comic routine. It is already after 9:30 P.M., and the commenta-

tor Ed Bradley, whose conversation with Castro had been inter-
rupted, is concerned that the Cuban leader might leave the room
without responding to the questions Bradley has prepared for his
show. Bradley edges close to Castro's interpreter, saying in a voice
that is sure to be heard, "Would you ask him if he followed . . . was
able to follow Ali when he was boxing professionally?"

The question is relayed and repeated until Castro, facing the
CBS cameras, replies, "Yes, I recall the days when they were discussing the possibilities of a match between the two of them" — he
nods toward Stevenson and Ali — "and I remember when he went
to Africa."

"In Zaire," Bradley clarifies, referring to Ali's victory in 1974
over George Foreman. And he follows up: "What kind of impact
did he have in this country, because he was a revolutionary as well
as . . . ?"

"It was great," Castro says. "He was very much admired as a
sportsman, as a boxer, as a person. There was always a high opinion of him. But I never guessed one day we would meet here, with
this kind gesture of bringing medicine, seeing our children, visiting our polyclinics. I am very glad, I am thrilled, to have the opportunity to meet him personally, to appreciate his kindness. I see
he is strong. I see he has a very kind face."

Castro is speaking as if Ali were not in the room, standing a few
feet away. Ali maintains his fixed façade even as Stevenson whis-
pers into his ear, asking in English, "Muhammad, Muhammad,
why you no speak?" Stevenson then turns to tell the journalist who
stands behind him, "Muhammad does speak. He speaks to me."
Stevenson says nothing more because Castro is now looking at him
while continuing to tell Bradley, "I am very glad that he and
Stevenson have met." After a pause, Castro adds, "And I am glad
that they never fought."

"He's not so sure," Bradley interjects, smiling in the direction of
Stevenson.

"I find in that friendship something beautiful," Castro insists
softly.

"There is a tie between the two of them," Bradley says.

"Yes," says Castro. "It is true." He again looks at Ali, then at
Stevenson, as if searching for something more profound to say.

"And how's the documentary?" he finally asks Bradley.

"It'll be on *60 Minutes.*"

"When?"

"Maybe one month," Bradley says, reminding Castro's interpreter, "This is the program on which the *comandante* has been interviewed by Dan Rather a number of times in the past, when Dan Rather was on *60 Minutes.*"

"And who's there now?" Castro wants to know.

"I am," Bradley answers.

"You," Castro repeats, with a quick glance at Bradley's earring. "So you are there — the boss now?"

Bradley responds as a media star without illusions: "I'm a worker."

Trays containing coffee, tea, and orange juice finally arrive, but only in amounts sufficient for Ali and Yolanda, Howard Bingham, Greg Howard, the Stevensons, and Castro — although Castro tells the waiters he wants nothing.

Castro motions for Ali and the others to join him across the room, around the circular table. The camera crews and the rest of the guests follow, standing as near to the principals as they can. But throughout the group there is a discernible restlessness. They have been standing for more than an hour and a half. It is now approaching 10 P.M. There has been no food. And for the vast majority, it is clear that there will also be nothing to drink. Even among the special guests, seated and sipping from chilled glasses or hot cups, there is a waning level of fascination with the evening. Indeed, Muhammad Ali's eyes are closed. He is sleeping.

Yolanda sits next to him on the sofa, pretending not to notice. Castro also ignores it, although he sits directly across the table, with the interpreter and the Stevensons.

"How large is Michigan?" Castro begins a new round of questioning with Yolanda, returning for the third time to a subject they had explored beyond the interest of anyone in the room except Castro himself.

"I don't know how big the state is as far as demographics," Yolanda says. "We live in a very small village [Barrien Springs] with about two thousand people."

"Are you going back to Michigan tomorrow?"

"Yes."

"What time?"

"Two-thirty."

"Via Miami?" Castro asks.

"Yes."

"From Miami, where do you fly?"

"We're flying to Michigan."

"How many hours' flight?"

"We have to change at Cincinnati — about two and a half hours."

"Flying time?" asks Castro.

Muhammad Ali opens his eyes, then closes them.

"Flying time," Yolanda repeats.

"From Miami to Michigan?" Castro continues.

"No," she again explains, but still with patience, "we have to go to Cincinnati. There are no direct flights."

"So you have to take two planes?" Castro asks.

"Yes," she says, adding for clarification, "Miami to Cincinnati — and then Cincinnati to South Bend, Indiana."

"From Cincinnati . . . ?"

"To South Bend," she says. "That's the closest airport."

"So," Fidel goes on, "it is on the outskirts of the city?"

"Yes."

"You have a farm?"

"No," Yolanda says, "just land. We let someone else do the growing."

She mentions that Teófilo Stevenson has traveled through this part of the Midwest. The mention of his name gains Stevenson's attention.

"I was in Chicago," Stevenson tells Castro.

"You were at their home?" Castro asks.

"No," Yolanda corrects Stevenson, "you were in Michigan."

"I was in the countryside," Stevenson says. Unable to resist, he adds, "I have a video of that visit. I'll show it to you sometime."

Castro seems not to hear him. He directs his attention back to Yolanda, asking her where she was born, where she was educated, when she became married, and how many years separate her age from that of her husband, Muhammad Ali.

After Yolanda acknowledges being sixteen years younger than Ali, Castro turns toward Fraymari and with affected sympathy says that she married a man who is twenty years her senior.

"*Comandante!*" Stevenson intercedes, "I am in shape. Sports keep you healthy. Sports add years to your life and life to your years!"

"Oh, what conflict she has," Castro goes on, ignoring Stevenson and catering to Fraymari — and to the CBS cameraman who steps forward for a closer view of Castro's face. "She is a lawyer, and she does not put this husband in jail." Castro is enjoying much more than Fraymari the attention this topic is now getting from the group. Castro had lost his audience and now has it back and seemingly wants to retain it, no matter at what cost to Stevenson's harmony with Fraymari. Yes, Castro continues, Fraymari had the misfortune to select a husband "who can never settle down. . . . Jail would be an appropriate place for him."

"*Comandante,*" Stevenson interrupts in a jocular manner that seems intended to placate both the lawyer who is his spouse and the lawyer who rules the country, "I might as well be locked up!" He implies that should he deviate from marital fidelity, his lawyer wife "will surely put me in a place where she is the only woman who can visit me!"

Everyone around the table and within the circling group laughs. Ali is now awake. The banter between Castro and Stevenson resumes until Yolanda, all but rising in her chair, tells Castro, "We have to pack."

"You're going to have dinner now?" he asks.

"Yes, sir," she says. Ali stands, along with Howard Bingham. Yolanda thanks Castro's interpreter directly, saying, "Be sure to tell him, 'You're always welcome in our home.'" The interpreter quotes Castro as again complaining that when he visits America, he is usually restricted to New York, but he adds, "Things change."

The group watches as Yolanda and Ali pass through, and Castro follows them into the hallway. The elevator arrives, and its door is held open by a security guard. Castro extends his final farewell with handshakes — and only then does he discover that he holds Ali's rubber thumb in his hand. Apologizing, he tries to hand it back to Ali, but Bingham politely protests. "No, no," Bingham says, "Ali wants you to have it."

Castro's interpreter at first fails to understand what Bingham is saying.

"He wants you to keep it," Bingham repeats.

Bingham enters the elevator with Ali and Yolanda. Before the door closes, Castro smiles, waves goodbye, and stares with curiosity at the rubber thumb. Then he puts it in his pocket.

Reflections and Responses

1. Read Gay Talese's comments "On Certain Magazine Interviews" and "Listening to People Think" (page 31). How do you think his journalistic procedures in this essay compare to his comments about the art of interviewing?

2. How would you describe Talese's role in the essay? Where does he seem visible? Where does he seem almost invisible? How does he fit himself as a participant or as an observer into different situations?

3. Consider how Talese sets up the drama at the palace reception. How does he build tension? How does he mix both the leading and minor roles? Why do you think he focuses so closely on the different conversations? What do you think he wants the conversations to convey in general about the overall event? Consider, too, the strange gift Ali leaves with Castro. Do you think the gift can have any larger significance? Do you think Talese finds it significant? What exactly is it and what might it represent?

JOHN UPDIKE

The Disposable Rocket

We have already seen several selections that consider the human body from a woman's perspective, most notably Marcia Aldrich's "Hair," Lucy Grealy's "Mirrorings," and Gretel Ehrlich's "Spring." In "The Disposable Rocket," John Updike, one of America's preeminent novelists, delivers his version of the male body. He states at the outset that it is quite different from the female body in that "it is a low-maintenance proposition." Men don't necessarily identify themselves with their bodies. In his characteristic metaphorical manner, Updike concludes, "A man and his body are like a boy and the buddy who has a driver's license and the use of his father's car for the evening; he goes along, gratefully, for the ride."

Updike was born in 1932 in Shillington, Pennsylvania. After graduation from Harvard in 1954 and a year at an English art school, he worked for The New Yorker's *"Talk of the Town" department for two years. Since 1957 he has lived in Massachusetts as a freelance writer. A novelist, poet, essayist, and reviewer, Updike is one of the nation's most distinguished authors. His fiction has won the Pulitzer Prize, the National Book Award, the American Book Award, and the National Book Critics Circle Award. He has published numerous books and collections; his most recent novels are* Toward the End of Time *(1997),* Gertrude and Claudius *(2000), and* Seek My Face *(2002). "The Disposable Rocket" originally appeared in* Michigan Quarterly Review *and was selected by Tracy Kidder for* The Best American Essays 1994.

Inhabiting a male body is much like having a bank account; as long as it's healthy, you don't think much about it. Compared to the female body, it is a low-maintenance proposition: a shower now and then, trim the fingernails every ten days, a haircut once a month. Oh yes, shaving — scraping or buzzing away at your face every morning. Byron, in *Don Juan*, thought the repeated nuisance of shaving balanced out the periodic agony, for females, of childbirth. Women are, his lines tell us,

> Condemn'd to child-bed, as men for their sins
> Have shaving too entail'd upon their chins, —
>
> A daily plague, which in the aggregate
> May average on the whole with parturition.

From the standpoint of reproduction, the male body is a delivery system, as the female is a mazy device for retention. Once the delivery is made, men feel a faint but distinct falling-off of interest. Yet against the enduring female heroics of birth and nurture should be set the male's superhuman frenzy to deliver his goods: he vaults walls, skips sleep, risks wallet, health, and his political future all to ram home his seed into the gut of the chosen woman. The sense of the chase lives in him as the key to life. His body is, like a delivery rocket that falls away in space, a disposable means. Men put their bodies at risk to experience the release from gravity.

When my tenancy of a male body was fairly new — of six or so years' duration — I used to jump and fall just for the joy of it. Falling — backwards, downstairs — became a specialty of mine, an attention-getting stunt I was practicing into my thirties, at suburban parties. Falling is, after all, a kind of flying, though of briefer duration than would be ideal. My impulse to hurl myself from high windows and the edges of cliffs belongs to my body, not my mind, which resists the siren call of the chasm with all its might; the interior struggle knocks the wind from my lungs and tightens my scrotum and gives any trip to Europe, with its Alps, castle parapets, and gargoyled cathedral lookouts, a flavor of nightmare. Falling, strangely, no longer figures in my dreams, as it often did when I was a boy and my subconscious was more honest with me. An airplane, that necessary evil, turns the earth into a map so quickly the brain turns aloof and calm; still, I marvel that there is no end of young men willing to become jet pilots.

Any accounting of male-female differences must include the male's superior recklessness, a drive not, I think, toward death, as the darker feminist cosmogonies would have it, but to test the limits, to see what the traffic will bear — a kind of mechanic's curiosity. The number of men who do lasting damage to their young bodies is striking; war and car accidents aside, secondary-school sports, with the approval of parents and the encouragement of brutish coaches, take a fearful toll of skulls and knees. We were made for combat, back in the post-simian, East African days, and the bumping, the whacking, the breathlessness, the pain-smothering adrenaline rush, form a cumbersome and unfashionable bliss, but bliss nevertheless. Take your body to the edge, and see if it flies.

The male sense of space must differ from that of the female, who has such interesting, active, and significant inner space. The space that interests men is outer. The fly ball high against the sky, the long pass spiraling overhead, the jet fighter like a scarcely visible pinpoint nozzle laying down its vapor trail at forty thousand feet, the gazelle haunch flickering just beyond arrow-reach, the uncountable stars sprinkled on their great black wheel, the horizon, the mountaintop, the quasar — these bring portents with them, and awaken a sense of relation with the invisible, with the empty. The ideal male body is taut with lines of potential force, a diagram extending outward; the ideal female body curves around centers of repose. Of course, no one is ideal, and the sexes are somewhat androgynous subdivisions of a species: Diana the huntress is a more trendy body-type nowadays than languid, overweight Venus, and polymorphous Dionysus poses for more underwear ads than Mars. Relatively, though, men's bodies, however elegant, are designed for covering territory, for moving on.

An erection, too, defies gravity, flirts with it precariously. It extends the diagram of outward direction into downright detachability — objective in the case of the sperm, subjective in the case of the testicles and penis. Men's bodies, at this juncture, feel only partly theirs; a demon of sorts has been attached to their lower torsos, whose performance is erratic and whose errands seem, at times, ridiculous. It is like having a (much) smaller brother toward whom you feel both fond and impatient; if he is you, it is you in curiously simplified and ignoble form. This sense, of the male body being two of them, is acknowledged in verbal love play and erotic writing, where the penis is playfully given its own name, an individuation not even the rarest rapture grants a vagina. Here, where maleness gathers to a quintessence of itself, there can be no insincerity, there can be no hiding; for sheer nakedness, there is nothing like a hopeful phallus; its aggressive shape is indivisible from its tender-skinned vulnerability. The act of intercourse, from the point of view of a consenting female, has an element of mothering, of enwrapment, of merciful concealment, even. The male body, for this interval, is tucked out of harm's way.

To inhabit a male body, then, is to feel somewhat detached from it. It is not an enemy, but not entirely a friend. Our essence seems to lie not in cells and muscles but in the traces our thoughts and actions inscribe on the air. The male body skims the surface of nature's deep, wherein the blood and pain and mysterious cravings of women perpetuate the species. Participating less in nature's processes than the female body, the male body gives the impression — false — of being exempt from time. Its powers of strength and reach descend in early adolescence, along with acne and sweaty feet, and depart, in imperceptible increments, after thirty or so. It surprises me to discover, when I remove my shoes and socks, the same paper-white hairless ankles that struck me as pathetic when I observed them on my father. I felt betrayed when, in some tumble of touch football twenty years ago, I heard my tibia snap; and when, between two reading engagements in Cleveland, my appendix tried to burst; and when, the other day, not for the first time, there arose to my nostrils out of my own body the musty attic smell my grandfather's body had.

A man's body does not betray its tenant as rapidly as a woman's. Never as fine and lovely, it has less distance to fall; what rugged beauty it has is wrinkle-proof. It keeps its capability of procreation indecently long. Unless intense athletic demands are made on it, the thing serves well enough to sixty, which is my age now. From here on, it's chancy. There are no breasts or ovaries to admit cancer to the male body, but the prostate, that awkwardly located little source of seminal fluid, shows the strain of sexual function with fits of hysterical cell replication, and all that beer and potato chips add up in the coronary arteries. A writer, whose physical equipment can be minimal, as long as it gets him to the desk, the lectern, and New York City once in a while, cannot but be grateful to his body, especially to his eyes, those tender and intricate sites where the brain extrudes from the skull, and to his hands, which hold the pen or tap the keyboard. His body has been, not himself exactly, but a close pal, pot-bellied and balding like most of his other pals now. A man and his body are like a boy and the buddy who has a driver's license and the use of his father's car for the evening; he goes along, gratefully, for the ride.

Reflections and Responses

1. Updike's essay is constructed around numerous points of comparison between the male and the female body. What are the essential differences? Do you agree with Updike about the different ways men and women perceive their bodies? Are there points about which you disagree?

2. To what does the essay's title refer? Why do you think Updike chose this particular metaphor? Why is the rocket "disposable"? In what ways is the essay's central metaphor of a rocket reinforced by other imagery Updike uses in the essay?

3. Do you think Updike believes the male body is superior to the female — or vice versa? Can you detect any hints of preference for either one, or do you think he takes a neutral position?

3

The Public Sphere: Advocacy, Argument, Controversy

WENDELL BERRY

In Distrust of Movements

Why do so many social and political movements, no matter how useful and well-intentioned, fail to produce the changes their members advocate? Noted essayist and environmental activist Wendell Berry carefully attempts to answer this rarely asked question in "In Distrust of Movements." Although his explanations apply to all movements, he is particularly concerned with the way the world's industrial economy violently abuses our land and natural resources in the name of corporate interests and incessant "development." Any movement that tries to fix the problem piecemeal is doomed to failure, Berry argues, because the problem's solution lies only in a radical transformation of the economy that has caused all the problems to begin with.

One of the nation's leading nature essayists, Wendell Berry is the author of numerous books, including The Long-Legged House *(1969),* The Hidden Wound *(1970),* The Unsettling of America: Culture and Agriculture *(1977),* Recollected Essays 1965–1980 *(1981),* Standing By Words *(1983),* Home Economics *(1987),* What Are People For? *(1990),* Standing on Earth *(1991),* Sex, Economy, Freedom, and Community *(1993), and* Another Turn of the Crank *(1995). A long essay,* Life Is a Miracle, *and a novel,* The Life Story of Jayber Crow, *both appeared in 2000. "In Distrust of Movements" was published in* Orion *and selected by Alan Lightman for* The Best American Essays 2000.

I have had with my friend Wes Jackson a number of useful conversations about the necessity of getting out of movements — even movements that have seemed necessary and dear to us — when they have lapsed into self-righteousness and self-betrayal, as movements seem almost invariably to do. People in movements too readily learn to deny to others the rights and privileges they demand for themselves. They too easily become unable to mean their own language, as when a "peace movement" becomes violent. They often become too specialized, as if finally they cannot help taking refuge in the pinhole vision of the institutional intellectuals. They almost always fail to be radical enough, dealing finally in effects rather than causes. Or they deal with single issues or single solutions, as if to assure themselves that they will not be radical enough.

And so I must declare my dissatisfaction with movements to promote soil conservation or clean water or clean air or wilderness preservation or sustainable agriculture or community health or the welfare of children. Worthy as these and other goals may be, they cannot be achieved alone. I am dissatisfied with such efforts because they are too specialized, they are not comprehensive enough, they are not radical enough, they virtually predict their own failure by implying that we can remedy or control effects while leaving causes in place. Ultimately, I think, they are insincere; they propose that the trouble is caused by *other* people; they would like to change policy but not behavior.

The worst danger may be that a movement will lose its language either to its own confusion about meaning and practice or to preemption by its enemies. I remember, for example, my naive confusion at learning that it was possible for advocates of organic agriculture to look upon the "organic method" as an end in itself. To me, organic farming was attractive both as a way of conserving nature and as a strategy of survival for small farmers. Imagine my surprise in discovering that there could be huge "organic" monocultures. And so I was not too surprised by the recent attempt of the United States Department of Agriculture to appropriate the "organic" label for food irradiation, genetic engineering, and other desecrations of the corporate food economy. Once we allow our language to mean anything that anybody wants it to mean, it becomes impossible to mean what we say. When "homemade" ceases to mean neither more nor less than "made at home," then it means anything, which is to say that it means nothing.

As you see, I have good reasons for declining to name the movement I think I am part of. I am reconciled to the likelihood that from time to time it will name itself and have slogans, but I am not going to use its slogans or call it by any of its names.

Let us suppose that we have a Nameless Movement for Better Land Use and that we know we must try to keep it active, responsive, and intelligent for a long time. What must we do?

What we must do above all, I think, is try to see the problem in its full size and difficulty. If we are concerned about land abuse, then we must see that this is an economic problem. Every economy is, by definition, a land-using economy. If we are using our land wrong, then something is wrong with our economy. This is difficult. It becomes more difficult when we recognize that in modern times, every one of us is a member of the economy of everybody else.

But if we are concerned about land abuse, we have begun a profound work of economic criticism. Study of the history of land use (and any local history will do) informs us that we have had for a long time an economy that thrives by undermining its own foundations. Industrialism, which is the name of our economy, and which is now virtually the only economy of the world, has been from its beginnings in a state of riot. It is based squarely upon the principle of violence toward everything on which it depends, and it has not mattered whether the form of industrialism was communist or capitalist or whatever; the violence toward nature, human communities, traditional agricultures, local economies has been constant. The bad news is coming in, literally, from all over the world. Can such an economy be fixed without being radically changed? I don't think it can.

The Captains of Industry have always counseled the rest of us "to be realistic." Let us, therefore, be realistic. Is it realistic to assume that the present economy would be just fine if only it would stop poisoning the air and water, or if only it would stop soil erosion, or if only it would stop degrading watersheds and forest ecosystems, or if only it would stop seducing children, or if only it would quit buying politicians, or if only it would give women and favored minorities an equitable share of the loot? Realism, I think, is a very limited program, but it informs us at least that we should not look for bird eggs in a cuckoo clock.

Or we can show the hopelessness of single-issue causes and single-issue movements by following a line of thought such as this: We need a continuous supply of uncontaminated water. Therefore, we need (among other things) soil- and water-conserving ways of agriculture and forestry that are not dependent on monoculture, toxic chemicals, or the indifference and violence that always accompany big-scale industrial enterprises on the land. Therefore, we need diversified, small-scale land economies that are dependent on people. Therefore, we need people with the knowledge, skills, motives, and attitudes required by diversified, small-scale land economies. And all this is clear and comfortable enough, until we recognize the question we have come to: *where are the people?*

Well, all of us who live in the suffering rural landscapes of the United States know that most people are available to those landscapes only recreationally. We see them bicycling or boating or hiking or camping or hunting or fishing or driving along and looking around. They do not, in Mary Austin's phrase, "summer and winter with the land." They are unacquainted with the land's human and natural economies. Though people have not progressed beyond the need to eat food and drink water and wear clothes and live in houses, most people have progressed beyond the domestic arts — the husbandry and wifery of the world — by which those needful things are produced and conserved. In fact, the comparative few who still practice that necessary husbandry and wifery often are inclined to apologize for doing so, having been carefully taught in our education system that those arts are degrading and unworthy of people's talents. Educated minds, in the modern era, are unlikely to know anything about food and drink, clothing and shelter. In merely taking these things for granted, the modern educated mind reveals itself also to be as superstitious a mind as ever has existed in the world. What could be more superstitious than the idea that money brings forth food?

I am not suggesting, of course, that everybody ought to be a farmer or a forester. Heaven forbid! I am suggesting that most people now are living on the far side of a broken connection, and that this is potentially catastrophic. Most people are now fed, clothed, and sheltered from sources toward which they feel no gratitude and exercise no responsibility. There is no significant urban constituency, no formidable consumer lobby, no noticeable political leadership, for good land use practices, for good farming and good forestry, for restoration of abused land, or for halting the destruction of land by so-called development.

We are involved now in a profound failure of imagination. Most of us cannot imagine the wheat beyond the bread, or the farmer beyond the wheat, or the farm beyond the farmer, or the history beyond the farm. Most people cannot imagine the forest and the forest economy that produced their houses and furniture and paper, or the landscapes, the streams, and the weather that fill their pitchers and bathtubs and swimming pools with water. Most people appear to assume that when they have paid their money for these things, they have entirely met their obligations.

Money does not bring forth food. Neither does the technology of the food system. Food comes from nature and from the work of people. If the supply of food is to be continuous for a long time, then people must work in harmony with nature. That means that people must find the right answers to a lot of hard practical questions. The same applies to forestry and the possibility of a continuous supply of timber.

One way we could describe the task ahead of us is by saying that we need to enlarge the consciousness and the conscience of the economy. Our economy needs to know — and care — what it is doing. This is revolutionary, of course, if you have a taste for revolution, but it is also a matter of common sense.

Undoubtedly some people will want to start a movement to bring this about. They probably will call it the Movement to Teach the Economy What It Is Doing — the MTEWIID. Despite my very considerable uneasiness, I will agree to this, but on three conditions.

My first condition is that this movement should begin by giving up all hope and belief in piecemeal, one-shot solutions. The present scientific quest for odorless hog manure should give us sufficient proof that the specialist is no longer with us. Even now, after centuries of reductionist propaganda, the world is still intricate and vast, as dark as it is light, a place of mystery, where we cannot do one thing without doing many things, or put two things together without putting many things together. Water quality, for example, cannot be improved without improving farming and forestry, but farming and forestry cannot be improved without improving the education of consumers — and so on.

The proper business of a human economy is to make one whole thing of ourselves and this world. To make ourselves into a practical wholeness with the land under our feet is maybe not altogether possible — how would *we* know? — but as a goal, it at least carries us beyond hubris, beyond the utterly groundless assumption that we can subdivide our present great failure into a thousand separate problems that can be fixed by a thousand task forces of academic and bureaucratic specialists. That program has been given more than a fair chance to prove itself, and we ought to know by now that it won't work.

My second condition is that the people in this movement (the MTEWIID) should take full responsibility for themselves as members of the economy. If we are going to teach the economy what it is doing, then we need to learn what we are doing. This is going to have to be a private movement as well as a public one. If it is unrealistic to expect wasteful industries to be conservers, then obviously we must lead in part the public life of complainers, petitioners, protesters, advocates, and supporters of stricter regulations and saner policies. But that is not enough. If it is unreasonable to expect a bad economy to try to become a good one, then *we* must go to work to build a good economy. It is appropriate that this duty should fall to us, for good economic behavior is more possible for us than it is for the great corporations with their miseducated managers and their greedy and oblivious stockholders. Because it is possible for us, we must try in every way we can to make good economic sense in our own lives, in our households, and in our communities. We must do more for ourselves and our neighbors. We must learn to spend our money with our friends and not with our enemies. But to do this, it is necessary to renew local economies and revive the domestic arts. In seeking to change our economic use of the world, we are seeking inescapably to change our lives. The outward harmony that we desire between our economy and the world depends finally upon an inward harmony between our own hearts and the originating spirit that is the life of all creatures, a spirit as near us as our flesh and yet forever beyond the measures of this obsessively measuring age. We can grow good wheat and make good bread only if we understand that we do not live by bread alone.

My third condition is that this movement should content itself to be poor. We need to find cheap solutions, solutions within the reach of everybody, and the availability of a lot of money prevents the discovery of cheap solutions. The solutions of modern medicine and modern agriculture are all staggeringly expensive, and this is caused in part, and maybe altogether, because of the availability of huge sums of money for medical and agricultural research.

Too much money, moreover, attracts administrators and experts as sugar attracts ants — look at what is happening in our universities. We should not envy rich movements that are organized and led by an alternative bureaucracy living on the problems it is supposed to solve. We want a movement that is a movement because it is advanced by all its members in their daily lives.

Now, having completed this very formidable list of the problems and difficulties, fears and fearful hopes that lie ahead of us, I am relieved to see that I have been preparing myself all along to end by saying something cheerful. What I have been talking about is the possibility of renewing human respect for this earth and all the good, useful, and beautiful things that come from it. I have made it clear, I hope, that I don't think this respect can be adequately enacted or conveyed by tipping our hats to nature or by representing natural loveliness in art or by prayers of thanksgiving or by preserving tracts of wilderness — although I recommend all those things. The respect I mean can be given only by using well the world's goods that are given to us. This good use, which renews respect — which is the only currency, so to speak, of respect — also renews our pleasure. The callings and disciplines that I have spoken of as the domestic arts are stationed all along the way from the farm to the prepared dinner, from the forest to the dinner table, from stewardship of the land to hospitality to friends and strangers. These arts are as demanding and gratifying, as instructive and as pleasing, as the so-called fine arts. To learn them is, I believe, the work that is our profoundest calling. Our reward is that they will enrich our lives and make us glad.

Reflections and Responses

1. What does Berry have against movements? What limitations does he find with them? In what ways does language enter into his distrust of movements? Why does he object to "single-issue" causes?

2. Berry's essay takes the form of an argument. With whom do you think he is arguing? Who are his opponents? What groups or individuals is he attempting to convince?

3. Are you surprised that, after clearly announcing his dissatisfaction with environmental movements, Berry spends the latter part of his essay designing such a movement? How do you explain his shift from distrusting movements to actually proposing one?

FRANK CONROY

Think About It

Though educators don't like to think so, education is often a mysterious process. How we come to understand something — both in and out of school — can be far less direct and systematic than methodically minded teachers might acknowledge. Illumination sometimes takes time: "The light bulb may appear over your head," Frank Conroy writes, "but it may be a while before it actually goes on." In this brief but deeply intriguing essay, Conroy explores several episodes from his younger years and shows how some puzzling things he couldn't quite understand at first finally revealed their meaning to him long afterward. But not every such illumination came with "a resolving kind of click." Conroy also recalls a series of enigmatic meetings with two of America's most famous legal minds and how they led to the strange satisfaction of an unresolved problem.

Conroy, director of the prestigious Iowa Writers' Workshop, is the author of Stop-Time *(1967) and* Midair *(1985). His stories and essays have appeared in* The New Yorker, Esquire, Harper's Magazine, GQ, *and many other publications. He has worked as a jazz pianist and has often written about American music. Music is the theme of his latest novel,* Body & Soul *(1993). "Think About It" originally appeared in* Harper's Magazine *(1988) and was selected by Geoffrey Wolff for* The Best American Essays 1989.

When I was sixteen I worked selling hot dogs at a stand in the Fourteenth Street subway station in New York City, one level above the trains and one below the street, where the crowds continually flowed back and forth. I worked with three Puerto Rican men who could not speak English. I had no Spanish, and although we understood each other well with regard to the tasks at hand, sensing and adjusting to each other's body movements in the extremely confined space in which we operated, I felt isolated with no one to talk to. On my break I came out from behind the counter and passed the time with two old black men who ran a shoeshine stand in a dark corner of the corridor. It was a poor location, half hidden by columns, and they didn't have much business. I would sit with my back against the wall while they stood or moved around their ancient elevated stand, talking to each other or to me, but always staring into the distance as they did so.

As the weeks went by I realized that they never looked at anything in their immediate vicinity — not at me or their stand or anybody who might come within ten or fifteen feet. They did not look at approaching customers once they were inside the perimeter. Save for the instant it took to discern the color of the shoes, they did not even look at what they were doing while they worked, but rubbed in polish, brushed, and buffed by feel while looking over their shoulders, into the distance, as if awaiting the arrival of an important person. Of course there wasn't all that much distance in the underground station, but their behavior was so focused and consistent they seemed somehow to transcend the physical. A powerful mood was created, and I came almost to believe that these men could see through walls, through girders, and around corners to whatever hyperspace it was where whoever it was they were waiting and watching for would finally emerge. Their scattered talk was hip, elliptical, and hinted at mysteries beyond my white boy's ken, but it was the staring off, the long, steady staring off, that had me hypnotized. I left for a better job, with handshakes from both of them, without understanding what I had seen.

Perhaps ten years later, after playing jazz with black musicians in various Harlem clubs, hanging out uptown with a few young artists and intellectuals, I began to learn from them something of the extraordinarily varied and complex riffs and rituals embraced by different people to help themselves get through life in the ghetto. Fantasy of all kinds — from playful to dangerous — was in the very air of Harlem. It was the spice of uptown life.

Only then did I understand the two shoeshine men. They were trapped in a demeaning situation in a dark corner in an underground corridor in a filthy subway system. Their continuous staring off was a kind of statement, a kind of dance. Our bodies are here, went the statement, but our souls are receiving nourishment from distant sources only we can see. They were powerful magic dancers, sorcerers almost, and thirty-five years later I can still feel the pressure of their spell.

The light bulb may appear over your head, is what I'm saying, but it may be a while before it actually goes on. Early in my attempts to learn jazz piano, I used to listen to recordings of a fine player named Red Garland, whose music I admired. I couldn't quite figure out what he was doing with his left hand, however; the chords eluded me. I went uptown to an obscure club where he was playing with his trio, caught him on his break, and simply asked him. "Sixths," he said cheerfully. And then he went away.

I didn't know what to make of it. The basic jazz chord is the seventh, which comes in various configurations, but it is what it is. I was a self-taught pianist, pretty shaky on theory and harmony, and when he said sixths I kept trying to fit the information into what I already knew, and it didn't fit. But it stuck in my mind — a tantalizing mystery.

A couple of years later, when I began playing with a bass player, I discovered more or less by accident that if the bass played the root and I played a sixth based on the fifth note of the scale, a very interesting chord involving both instruments emerged. Ordinarily, I suppose I would have skipped over the matter and not paid much attention, but I remembered Garland's remark and so I stopped and spent a week or two working out the voicings, and greatly strengthened my foundations as a player. I had remembered what I hadn't understood, you might say, until my life caught up with the information and the light bulb went on.

I remember another, more complicated example from my sophomore year at the small liberal-arts college outside Philadelphia. I seemed never to be able to get up in time for breakfast in the dining hall. I would get coffee and a doughnut in the Coop instead — a basement area with about a dozen small tables where students could get something to eat at odd hours. Several mornings in a row I noticed a strange man sitting by himself with a cup of coffee. He was in his sixties, perhaps, and sat straight in his chair with very little extraneous movement. I guessed he was some sort of distinguished visitor to the college who had decided to put in some time at a student hangout. But no one ever sat with him. One morning I approached his table and asked if I could join him.

"Certainly," he said. "Please do." He had perhaps the clearest eyes I had ever seen, like blue ice, and to be held in their steady gaze was not, at first, an entirely comfortable experience. His eyes gave nothing away about himself while at the same time creating in me the eerie impression that he was looking directly into my soul. He asked a few quick questions, as if to put me at my ease, and we fell into conversation. He was William O. Douglas from the Supreme Court, and when he saw how startled I was he said, "Call me Bill. Now tell me what you're studying and why you get up so late in the morning." Thus began a series of talks that stretched over many weeks. The fact that I was an ignorant sophomore with literary pretensions who knew nothing about the law didn't seem to bother him. We talked about everything from Shakespeare to the possibility of life on other planets. One day I mentioned that I was going to have dinner with Judge Learned Hand. I explained that Hand was my girlfriend's grandfather. Douglas nodded, but I could tell he was surprised at the coincidence of my knowing the chief judge of the most important court in the country save the Supreme Court itself. After fifty years on the bench Judge Hand had become a famous man, both in and out of legal circles — a living legend, to his own dismay. "Tell him hello and give him my best regards," Douglas said.

Learned Hand, in his eighties, was a short, barrel-chested man with a large, square head, huge, thick, bristling eyebrows, and soft brown eyes. He radiated energy and would sometimes bark out remarks or questions in the living room as if he were in court. His humor was sharp, but often leavened with a touch of self-mockery. When something caught his funny bone he would burst out with explosive laughter — the laughter of a man who enjoyed laughing. He had a large repertoire of dramatic expressions involving the use of his eyebrows — very useful, he told me conspiratorially, when looking down on things from behind the bench. (The court stenographer could not record the movement of his eyebrows.) When I told him I'd been talking to William O. Douglas, they first shot up in exaggerated surprise, and then lowered and moved forward in a glower.

"*Justice* William O. Douglas, young man," he admonished. "Justice

Douglas, if you please." About the Supreme Court in general, Hand insisted on a tone of profound respect. Little did I know that in private correspondence he had referred to the Court as "The Blessed Saints, Cherubim and Seraphim," "The Jolly Boys," "The Nine Tin Jesuses," "The Nine Blameless Ethiopians," and my particular favorite, "The Nine Blessed Chalices of the Sacred Effluvium."

Hand was badly stooped and had a lot of pain in his lower back. Martinis helped, but his strict Yankee wife approved of only one before dinner. It was my job to make the second and somehow slip it to him. If the pain was particularly acute he would get out of his chair and lie flat on the rug, still talking, and finish his point without missing a beat. He flattered me by asking for my impression of Justice Douglas, instructed me to convey his warmest regards, and then began talking about the Dennis case, which he described as a particularly tricky and difficult case involving the prosecution of eleven leaders of the Communist party. He had just started in on the First Amendment and free speech when we were called in to dinner.

William O. Douglas loved the outdoors with a passion, and we fell into the habit of having coffee in the Coop and then strolling under the trees down toward the duck pond. About the Dennis case, he said something to this effect: "Eleven Communists arrested by the government. Up to no good, said the government; dangerous people, violent overthrow, etc. First Amendment, said the defense, freedom of speech, etc." Douglas stopped walking. "Clear and present danger."

"What?" I asked. He often talked in a telegraphic manner, and one was expected to keep up with him. It was sometimes like listening to a man thinking out loud.

"Clear and present danger," he said. "That was the issue. Did they constitute a clear and present danger? I don't think so. I think everybody took the language pretty far in Dennis." He began walking, striding along quickly. Again, one was expected to keep up with him. "The FBI was all over them. Phones tapped, constant surveillance. How could it be clear and present danger with the FBI watching every move they made? That's a ginkgo," he said suddenly, pointing at a tree. "A beauty. You don't see those every day. Ask Hand about clear and present danger."

I was in fact reluctant to do so. Douglas's argument seemed to me to be crushing — the last word, really — and I didn't want to embarrass Judge Hand. But back in the living room, on the second martini, the old man asked about Douglas. I sort of scratched my nose and recapitulated the conversation by the ginkgo tree. "What?" Hand shouted. "Speak up, sir, for heaven's sake."

"He said the FBI was watching them all the time so there couldn't be a clear and present danger," I blurted out, blushing as I said it.

A terrible silence filled the room. Hand's eyebrows writhed on his face like two huge caterpillars. He leaned forward in the wing chair, his face settling, finally, into a grim expression. "I am astonished," he said softly, his eyes holding mine, "at Justice Douglas's newfound faith in the Federal Bureau of Investigation." His big, granite head moved even closer to mine, until I could smell the martini. "I had understood him to consider it a politically corrupt, incompetent organization, directed by a power-crazed lunatic." I realized I had been holding my breath throughout all of this, and as I relaxed, I saw the faintest trace of a smile cross Hand's face. Things are sometimes more complicated than they first appear, his smile seemed to say. The old man leaned back. "The proximity of the danger is something to think about. Ask him about that. See what he says."

I chewed the matter over as I returned to campus. Hand had pointed out some of Douglas's language about the FBI from other sources that seemed to bear out his point. I thought about the words "clear and present danger," and the fact that if you looked at them closely they might not be as simple as they had first appeared. What degree of danger? Did the word "present" allude to the proximity of the danger, or just the fact that the danger was there at all — that it wasn't an anticipated danger? Were there other hidden factors these great men were weighing of which I was unaware?

But Douglas was gone, back to Washington. (The writer in me is tempted to create a scene here — to invent one for dramatic purposes — but of course I can't do that.) My brief time as a messenger boy was over, and I felt a certain frustration, as if, with a few more exchanges, the matter of *Dennis* v. *United States* might have been resolved to my satisfaction. They'd left me high and dry.

But, of course, it is precisely because the matter did not resolve that has caused me to think about it, off and on, all these years. "The Constitution," Hand used to say to me flatly, "is a piece of paper. The Bill of Rights is a piece of paper." It was many years before I understood what he meant. Documents alone do not keep democracy alive, nor maintain the state of law. There is no particular safety in them. Living men and women, generation after generation, must continually remake democracy and the law, and that involves an ongoing state of tension between the past and the present which will never completely resolve.

Education doesn't end until life ends, because you never know when you're going to understand something you hadn't understood before. For me, the magic dance of the shoeshine men was the kind of experience in which understanding came with a kind of click, a resolving kind of click. The same with the experience at the piano. What happened with Justice Douglas and Judge Hand was different, and makes the point that understanding does not always mean resolution. Indeed, in our intellectual lives, our creative lives, it is perhaps those problems that will never resolve that rightly claim the lion's share of our energies. The physical body exists in a constant state of tension as it maintains homeostasis, and so too does the active mind embrace the tension of never being certain, never being absolutely sure, never being done, as it engages the world. That is our special fate, our inexpressibly valuable condition.

Reflections and Responses

1. How does Conroy finally come to understand why the two shoeshine men always seemed to be looking into the distance? What has Conroy learned that illuminates their behavior? Can you think of other explanations?

2. What connections can you see between Conroy's insight into the behavior of the shoeshine men and his later understanding of the elusive jazz chords? In what ways does the insight go beyond music?

3. Consider the conclusion of the episode involving William O. Douglas and Learned Hand. How does it end? Conroy says: "The writer in me is tempted to create a scene here — to invent one for dramatic purposes — but of course I can't do that." What do you think he means by the "writer in me"? Why is the refusal to "create a scene" significant to both Conroy's theme and his technique?

ALAN M. DERSHOWITZ

Shouting "Fire!"

Artists and performers are not the only ones who explore the boundaries of free expression. Lawyers and judges, too, frequently find themselves struggling to ascertain the limits of free speech. In the following essay, one of America's best-known trial lawyers, Alan M. Dershowitz, takes a close look at one of the most commonly used arguments against free speech, the idea that some speech should be suppressed because it is "just like" falsely shouting fire in a crowded theater. In his investigation into the source of this famous analogy, Dershowitz demonstrates how it has been widely misused and abused by proponents of censorship. Indeed, it was an "inapt analogy even in the context in which it was originally offered." As an expression to suppress expression, the "shouting fire" analogy, Dershowitz maintains, has been "invoked so often, by so many people, in such diverse contexts, that it has become part of our national folk language."

Alan M. Dershowitz is Felix Frankfurter professor of law at Harvard Law School. He is the author of many books, including The Best Defense *(1982),* Taking Liberties *(1988),* Chutzpah *(1991),* Contrary to Public Opinion *(1992),* The Abuse Excuse *(1994),* Reasonable Doubts *(1996), and* Sexual McCarthyism *(1998). His most recent books include* Supreme Injustice *(2001),* Letters to a Young Lawyer *(2001), and* Why Terrorism Works *(2002). In addition to his teaching and writing, Professor Dershowitz is an active criminal defense and civil liberties lawyer. "Shouting 'Fire!'" originally appeared in* The Atlantic *(1989) and was selected by Justin Kaplan for* The Best American Essays *1990.*

When the Reverend Jerry Falwell learned that the Supreme Court had reversed his $200,000 judgment against *Hustler* magazine for the emotional distress that he had suffered from an outrageous parody, his response was typical of those who seek to censor speech: "Just as no person may scream 'Fire!' in a crowded theater when there is no fire, and find cover under the First Amendment, likewise, no sleazy merchant like Larry Flynt should be able to use the First Amendment as an excuse for maliciously and dishonestly attacking public figures, as he has so often done."

Justice Oliver Wendell Holmes's classic example of unprotected speech — falsely shouting "Fire!" in a crowded theater — has been invoked so often, by so many people, in such diverse contexts, that it has become part of our national folk language. It has even appeared — most appropriately — in the theater: in Tom Stoppard's play *Rosencrantz and Guildenstern Are Dead* a character shouts at the audience, "Fire!" He then quickly explains: "It's all right — I'm demonstrating the misuse of free speech." Shouting "Fire!" in the theater may well be the only jurisprudential analogy that has assumed the status of a folk argument. A prominent historian recently characterized it as "the most brilliantly persuasive expression that ever came from Holmes' pen." But in spite of its hallowed position in both the jurisprudence of the First Amendment and the arsenal of political discourse, it is and was an inapt analogy, even in the context in which it was originally offered. It has lately become — despite, perhaps even because of, the frequency and promiscuousness of its invocation — little more than a caricature of logical argumentation.

The case that gave rise to the "Fire!"-in-a-crowded-theater analogy, *Schenck v. United States,* involved the prosecution of Charles Schenck, who was the general secretary of the Socialist party in Philadelphia, and Elizabeth Baer, who was its recording secretary. In 1917 a jury found Schenck and Baer guilty of attempting to cause insubordination among soldiers who had been drafted to fight in the First World War. They and other party members had circulated leaflets urging draftees not to "submit to intimidation" by fighting in a war being conducted on behalf of "Wall Street's chosen few."

Schenck admitted, and the Court found, that the intent of the pamphlets' "impassioned language" was to "influence" draftees to resist the draft. Interestingly, however, Justice Holmes noted that nothing in the pamphlet suggested that the draftees should use unlawful or violent means to oppose conscription: "In form at least [the pamphlet] confined itself to peaceful measures, such as a petition for the repeal of the act" and an exhortation to exercise "your right to assert your opposition to the draft." Many of its most impassioned words were quoted directly from the Constitution.

Justice Holmes acknowledged that "in many places and in ordinary times the defendants, in saying all that was said in the circular, would have been within their constitutional rights." "But," he added, "the character of every act depends upon the circumstances in which it is done." And to illustrate that truism he went on to say:

> The most stringent protection of free speech would not protect a man in falsely shouting fire in a theater, and causing a panic. It does not even protect a man from an injunction against uttering words that may have all the effect of force.

Justice Holmes then upheld the convictions in the context of a wartime draft, holding that the pamphlet created "a clear and present danger" of hindering the war effort while our soldiers were fighting for their lives and our liberty.

The example of shouting "Fire!" obviously bore little relationship to the facts of the Schenck case. The Schenck pamphlet contained a substantive political message. It urged its draftee readers to *think* about the message and then — if they so chose — to act on it in a lawful and nonviolent way. The man who shouts "Fire!" in a crowded theater is neither sending a political message nor inviting his listener to think about what he has said and decide what to do in a rational, calculated manner. On the contrary, the message is designed to force action *without* contemplation. The message "Fire!" is directed not to the mind and the conscience of the listener but, rather, to his adrenaline and his feet. It is a stimulus to immediate *action,* not thoughtful reflection. It is — as Justice Holmes recognized in his follow-up sentence — the functional equivalent of "uttering words that may have all the effect of force."

Indeed, in that respect the shout of "Fire!" is not even speech, in any meaningful sense of that term. It is a *clang* sound, the equivalent of setting off a nonverbal alarm. Had Justice Holmes been more honest about his example, he would have said that freedom of speech does not protect a kid who pulls a fire alarm in the absence of a fire. But that obviously would have been irrelevant to the case at hand. The proposition that pulling an alarm is not protected speech certainly leads to the conclusion that shouting the word "fire" is also not protected. But the core analogy is the nonverbal alarm, and the derivative example is the verbal shout. By cleverly substituting the derivative shout for the core alarm, Holmes made it possible to analogize one set of words to another — as he could not have done if he had begun with the self-evident proposition that setting off an alarm bell is not free speech.

The analogy is thus not only inapt but also insulting. Most Americans do not respond to political rhetoric with the same kind of automatic acceptance expected of schoolchildren responding to a fire drill. Not a single recipient of the Schenck pamphlet is known to have changed his mind after reading it. Indeed, one draftee, who appeared as a prosecution witness, was asked whether reading the pamphlet asserting that the draft law was unjust would make him "immediately decide that you must erase that law." Not surprisingly, he replied, "I do my own thinking." A theatergoer would probably not respond similarly if asked how he would react to a shout of "Fire!"

Another important reason why the analogy is inapt is that Holmes emphasizes the factual falsity of the shout "Fire!" The Schenck pamphlet, however, was not factually false. It contained political opinions and ideas about the causes of the war and about appropriate and lawful responses to the draft. As the Supreme Court recently reaffirmed (in *Falwell* v. *Hustler*), "The First Amendment recognizes no such thing as a 'false' idea." Nor does it recognize false opinions about the causes of or cures for war.

A closer analogy to the facts of the Schenck case might have been provided by a person's standing outside a theater, offering the patrons a leaflet advising them that in his opinion the theater was structurally unsafe, and urging them not to enter but to complain to the building inspectors. That analogy, however, would not have served Holmes's argument for punishing Schenck. Holmes needed an analogy that would appear relevant to Schenck's political speech but that would invite the conclusion that censorship was appropriate.

Unsurprisingly, a war-weary nation — in the throes of a know-nothing hysteria over immigrant anarchists and socialists — welcomed the comparison between what was regarded as a seditious political pamphlet and a malicious shout of "Fire!" Ironically, the

"Fire!" analogy is nearly all that survives from the Schenck case; the ruling itself is almost certainly not good law. Pamphlets of the kind that resulted in Schenck's imprisonment have been circulated with impunity during subsequent wars.

Over the past several years I have assembled a collection of instance — cases, speeches, arguments — in which proponents of censorship have maintained that the expression at issue is "just like" or "equivalent to" falsely shouting "Fire!" in a crowded theater and ought to be banned, "just as" shouting "Fire!" ought to be banned. The analogy is generally invoked, often with self-satisfaction, as an absolute argument-stopper. It does, after all, claim the high authority of the great Justice Oliver Wendell Holmes. I have rarely heard it invoked in a convincing, or even particularly relevant, way. But that, too, can claim lineage from the great Holmes.

Not unlike Falwell, with his silly comparison between shouting "Fire!" and publishing an offensive parody, courts and commentators have frequently invoked "Fire!" as an analogy to expression that is not an automatic stimulus to panic. A state supreme court held that "Holmes' aphorism . . . applies with equal force to pornography" — in particular to the exhibition of the movie *Carmen Baby* in a drive-in theater in close proximity to highways and homes. Another court analogized "picketing . . . in support of a secondary boycott" to shouting "Fire!" because in both instances "speech and conduct are brigaded." In the famous Skokie case one of the judges argued that allowing Nazis to march through a city where a large number of Holocaust survivors live "just might fall into the same category as one's 'right' to cry fire in a crowded theater."

Outside court the analogies become even more badly stretched. A spokesperson for the New Jersey Sports and Exposition Authority complained that newspaper reports to the effect that a large number of football players had contracted cancer after playing in the Meadowlands — a stadium atop a landfill — were the "journalistic equivalent of shouting fire in a crowded theater." An insect researcher acknowledged that his prediction that a certain amusement park might become roach-infested "may be tantamount to shouting fire in a crowded theater." The philosopher Sidney Hook, in a letter to the *New York Times* bemoaning a Supreme Court decision that required a plaintiff in a defamation action to prove that the offending statement was actually false, argued that the First Amendment does not give the press carte blanche to accuse innocent persons "anymore than the First Amendment protects the right of someone falsely to shout fire in a crowded theater."

Some close analogies to shouting "Fire!" or setting off an alarm are, of course, available: calling in a false bomb threat; dialing 911 and falsely describing an emergency; making a loud, gunlike sound in the presence of the President; setting off a voice-activated sprinkler system by falsely shouting "Fire!" In one case in which the "Fire!" analogy was directly to the point, a creative defendant tried to get around it. The case involved a man who calmly advised an airline clerk that he was "only here to hijack the plane." He was charged, in effect, with shouting "Fire!" in a crowded theater, and his rejected defense — as quoted by the court — was as follows: "If we built fire-proof theaters and let people know about this, then the shouting of 'Fire!' would not cause panic."

Here are some more-distant but still related examples: the recent incident of the police slaying in which some members of an onlooking crowd urged a mentally ill vagrant who had taken an officer's gun to shoot the officer; the screaming of racial epithets during a tense confrontation; shouting down a speaker and preventing him from continuing his speech.

Analogies are, by their nature, matters of degree. Some are closer to the core example than others. But any attempt to analogize political ideas in a pamphlet, ugly parody in a magazine, offensive movies in a theater, controversial newspaper articles, or any of the other expressions and actions catalogued above to the very different act of shouting "Fire!" in a crowded theater is either self-deceptive or self-serving.

The government does, of course, have some arguably legitimate bases for suppressing speech which bear no relationship to shouting "Fire!" It may ban the publication of nuclear-weapon codes, of information about troop movements, and of the identity of undercover agents. It may criminalize extortion threats and conspiratorial agreements. These expressions may lead directly to serious harm, but the mechanisms of causation are very different from that at work when an alarm is sounded. One may also argue — less persuasively, in my view — against protecting certain forms of public obscenity and defamatory statements. Here, too, the mechanisms of causation are very different. None of these exceptions to the First Amendment's exhortation that the government "shall make no law . . . abridging the freedom of speech, or of the press" is anything like falsely shouting "Fire!" in a crowded theater; they all must be justified on other grounds.

A comedian once told his audience, during the stand-up routine, about the time he was standing around a fire with a crowd of people and got in trouble for yelling "Theater, theater!" That, I think, is about as clever and productive a use as anyone has ever made of Holmes's flawed analogy.

Reflections and Responses

1. Consider Dershowitz's analysis of Justice Holmes's decision in the Schenck case. What does Dershowitz find wrong with Holmes's reasoning? In what ways is Holmes's analogy "flawed"?

2. To what kinds of expression does Dershowitz find Holmes's analogy applicable? Go through Dershowitz's examples of protected and unprotected speech. Why is the "falsely shouting fire" analogy appropriate in some instances and not in others?

3. Consider Dershowitz's anecdote in the last paragraph about the comedian who yells "Theater, theater!" What was the comedian expressing? Why does Dershowitz find this response to Holmes's analogy "clever and productive"?

DEBRA DICKERSON

Who Shot Johnny?

On July 27, 1995, Debra Dickerson's sixteen-year-old nephew was shot in the back for no apparent reason and paralyzed. Although relatives kept trying to find out why ("Being black, male and shot, he must, apparently, be gang- or drug-involved"), his story held up and there was no way for anyone to make sense of the shooting. In this brief, tough, and unforgettable essay, Dickerson introduces us to her hospitalized nephew and angrily confronts his unknown assailant, whom she feels she knows all too well: "We rarely wonder about or discuss the brother who shot him because we already know everything about him."

Debra Dickerson is a contributing editor of US News & World Report. *Her articles have appeared in* The New Republic, Slate, Good Housekeeping, The Washington Post Book World, Allure, The Christian Science Monitor Report, The Nation, Underwire, Boston Review, *and* Reconstruction. *She is a graduate of the Harvard Law School and is at work on a memoir about social and political conflict within the black community. "Who Shot Johnny?" originally appeared in* The New Republic *(1996) and was selected by Ian Frazier for* The Best American Essays 1997.

Given my level of political awareness, it was inevitable that I would come to view the everyday events of my life through the prism of politics and the national discourse. I read *The Washington Post, The New Republic, The New Yorker, Harper's, The Atlantic Monthly, The Nation, National Review, Black Enterprise,* and *Essence* and wrote a weekly column for the Harvard Law School *Record* during my three years just ended there. I do this because I know that those of us who are not well-fed white guys in suits must not yield the debate to them, however well-intentioned or well-informed they may be. Accordingly, I am unrepentant and vocal about having gained admittance to Harvard through affirmative action; I am a feminist, stoic about my marriage chances as a well-educated, thirty-six-year-old black woman who won't pretend to need help taking care of herself. My strength flags, though, in the face of the latest role assigned to my family in the national drama. On July 27, 1995, my sixteen-year-old nephew was shot and paralyzed.

Talking with friends in front of his house, Johnny saw a car he thought he recognized. He waved boisterously — his trademark — throwing both arms in the air in a full-bodied, hip-hop Y. When he got no response, he and his friends sauntered down the walk to join a group loitering in front of an apartment building. The car followed. The driver got out, brandished a revolver, and fired into the air. Everyone scattered. Then he took aim and shot my running nephew in the back.

Johnny never lost consciousness. He lay in the road, trying to understand what had happened to him, why he couldn't get up. Emotionlessly, he told the story again and again on demand, remaining apologetically firm against all demands to divulge the missing details that would make sense of the shooting but obviously cast him in a bad light. Being black, male, and shot, he must apparently be involved with gangs or drugs. Probably both. Witnesses corroborate his version of events.

Nearly six months have passed since that phone call in the night and my nightmarish headlong drive from Boston to Charlotte. After twenty hours behind the wheel, I arrived haggard enough to reduce my mother to fresh tears and to find my nephew reassuring well-wishers with an eerie sang-froid.

I take the day shift in his hospital room; his mother and grandmother, a clerk and cafeteria worker, respectively, alternate nights there on a cot. They don their uniforms the next day, gaunt after hours spent listening to Johnny moan in his sleep. How often must his subconscious replay those events and curse its host for saying hello without permission, for being carefree and young while a would-be murderer hefted the weight of his uselessness and failure like Jacob Marley's* chains? How often must he watch

---

*Jacob Marley: The doomed ghost in Charles Dickens's *A Christmas Carol.* — Ed.

himself lying stubbornly immobile on the pavement of his nightmares while the sound of running feet syncopate his attacker's
taunts?

I spend these days beating him at gin rummy and Scrabble,
holding a basin while he coughs up phlegm and crying in the corridor while he catheterizes himself. There are children here much
worse off than he. I should be grateful. The doctors can't, or won't,
say whether he'll walk again.

I am at once repulsed and fascinated by the bullet, which remains lodged in his spine (having done all the damage it can do,
the doctors say). The wound is undramatic — small, neat, and perfectly centered — an impossibly pink pit surrounded by an otherwise undisturbed expanse of mahogany. Johnny has asked me
several times to describe it but politely declines to look in the mirror I hold for him.

Here on the pediatric rehab ward, Johnny speaks little, never
cries, never complains, works diligently to become independent.
He does whatever he is told; if two hours remain until the next pain
pill, he waits quietly. Eyes bloodshot, hands gripping the bed rails.
During the week of his intravenous feeding, when he was tormented
by the primal need to masticate, he never asked for food. He just
listened while we counted down the days for him and planned his
favorite meals. Now required to dress himself unassisted, he does
so without demur, rolling himself back and forth valiantly on the
bed and shivering afterward, exhausted. He "ma'am"s and "sir"s
everyone politely. Before his "accident," a simple request to take
out the trash could provoke a firestorm of teenage attitude. We,
the women who have raised him, have changed as well; we've finally come to appreciate those boxer-baring, oversized pants we
used to hate — it would be much more difficult to fit properly
sized pants over his diaper.

He spends a lot of time tethered to rap music still loud enough
to break my concentration as I read my many magazines. I hear
him try to soundlessly mouth the obligatory "mothafuckers" over-
laying the funereal dirge of the music tracks. I do not normally tolerate disrespectful music in my or my mother's presence, but if it
distracts him now . . .

"Johnny," I ask later, "do you still like gangster rap?" During the
long pause I hear him think loudly, I'm paralyzed Auntie, not

stupid. "I mostly just listen to hip-hop," he says evasively into his *Sports Illustrated.*

Miserable though it is, time passes quickly here. We always seem to be jerking awake in our chairs just in time for the next pill, his every-other-night bowel program, the doctor's rounds. Harvard feels a galaxy away — the world revolves around Family Members Living with Spinal Cord Injury class, Johnny's urine output, and strategizing with my sister to find affordable, accessible housing. There is always another long-distance uncle in need of an update, another church member wanting to pray with us, or Johnny's little brother in need of some attention.

We Dickerson women are so constant a presence the ward nurses and cleaning staff call us by name and join us for cafeteria meals and cigarette breaks. At Johnny's birthday pizza party, they crack jokes and make fun of each other's husbands (there are no men here). I pass slices around and try not to think, Seventeen with a bullet.

Oddly, we feel little curiosity or specific anger toward the man who shot him. We have to remind ourselves to check in with the police. Even so, it feels pro forma, like sending in those $2 rebate forms that come with new pantyhose: you know your request will fall into a deep, dark hole somewhere, but still, it's your duty to try. We push for an arrest because we owe it to Johnny and to ourselves as citizens. We don't think about it otherwise — our low expectations are too ingrained. A Harvard aunt notwithstanding, for people like Johnny, Marvin Gaye was right that only three things are sure: taxes, death, and trouble. At least it wasn't the second.

We rarely wonder about or discuss the brother who shot him because we already know everything about him. When the call came, my first thought was the same one I'd had when I'd heard about Rosa Parks's beating: a brother did it. A non-job-having, middle-of-the-day malt-liquor-drinking, crotch-clutching, loud-talking brother with many neglected children born of many forgotten women. He lives in his mother's basement with furniture rented at an astronomical interest rate, the exact amount of which he does not know. He has a car phone, an $80 monthly cable bill, and every possible phone feature but no savings. He steals Social Security numbers from unsuspecting relatives and assumes their identities to acquire large TV sets for which he will never pay. On the slim chance that he is brought to justice, he will have a colorful criminal history and no coherent explanation to offer for his act. His family will raucously defend him and cry cover-up. Some liberal lawyer just like me will help him plea-bargain his way to yet another short stay in a prison pesthouse that will serve only to add another layer to the brother's sociopathology and formless, mindless nihilism. We know him. We've known and feared him all our lives.

As a teenager, he called, "Hey, baby, gimme somma that boodie!" at us from car windows. Indignant at our lack of response, he followed up with, "Fuck you, then, 'ho!" He called me a "white-boy-lovin' nigger bitch oreo" for being in the gifted program and loving it. At twenty-seven, he got my seventeen-year-old sister pregnant with Johnny and lost interest without ever informing her that he was married. He snatched my widowed mother's purse as she waited in predawn darkness for the bus to work and then broke into our house while she soldered on an assembly line. He chased all the small entrepreneurs from our neighborhood with his violent thievery and put bars on our windows. He kept us from sitting on our own front porch after dark and laid the foundation for our periodic bouts of self-hating anger and racial embarrassment. He made our neighborhood a ghetto. He is the poster fool behind the maddening community knowledge that there are still some black mothers who raise their daughters but merely love their sons. He and his cancerous carbon copies eclipse the vast majority of us who are not sociopaths and render us invisible. He is the Siamese twin who has died but cannot be separated from his living, vibrant sibling; which of us must attract more notice? We despise and disown this anomalous loser, but for many he *is* black America. We know him, we know that he is outside the fold, and we know that he will only get worse. What we didn't know is that, because of him, my little sister would one day be the latest hysterical black mother wailing over a fallen child on TV.

Alone, lying in the road bleeding and paralyzed but hideously conscious, Johnny had lain helpless as he watched his would-be murderer come to stand over him and offer this prophecy: "Betch'ou won't be doin' nomo' wavin', mothafucker."

Fuck you, asshole. He's fine from the waist up. You just can't do anything right, can you?

Reflections and Responses

---

1. Why do you think the author begins her essay by telling us about herself? What does her introductory paragraph establish? Does it predispose you in any way to the events she narrates?

2. Consider the essay's final line. What criticism is Dickerson making of Johnny's assailant? How effective do you find it?

3. How would you answer the question posed by the essay's title? Do we really know who shot Johnny? Whom do you hold responsible?

DAVID HALBERSTAM

Who We Are

Manhattan is such a large island that when the World Trade Center towers were attacked on September 11, 2001, the author of the following essay was walking his dogs in Central Park and knew nothing of what happened until he returned home and received a phone call from a friend telling him to turn on the television. "By then," David Halberstam notes, "the world had already changed, mine and virtually everyone else's." The essay "Who We Are" was written in immediate response to the attacks and appeared in the November issue of Vanity Fair. *It represents one of the first contributions to what might be called "The Literature of 9/11." For Halberstam, the attacks provide a somber occasion to consider the resiliency of America's political system and its people, as he charts the historical course that took us from an isolationist nation at the start of the twentieth century to the world's foremost superpower at its end.*

One of the nation's most distinguished authors, David Halberstam has written numerous books on politics and international affairs, civil rights, American culture and industry, sports, and the news media. Among his major books are The Making of a Quagmire *(1965),* Ho *(1971),* The Best and the Brightest *(1972),* The Powers That Be *(1979),* The Reckoning *(1986),* The Fifties *(1993),* The Children *(1998),* Playing for Keeps *(1999), a book about Michael Jordan, and most recently,* Firehouse *(2002). He won the Pulitzer Prize in 1964 for his pessimistic* New York Times *dispatches from Vietnam. "Who We Are" was selected by Stephen Jay Gould for* The Best American Essays 2002.

The night before the world changed completely I was driving back to New York late, after lecturing at Drew University in exurban New Jersey. The sky was relatively clear, and I did what I often do on such occasions — I looked up at the Twin Towers as a kind of beacon for my approach, the first sign that Manhattan was close and that I was almost home. The next morning, when I got up to walk the dogs, I was still in a somewhat churlish mood because the New York Giants, whose fortunes I took very seriously, had opened their season the night before by playing terribly. At the moment I was about to go out the door, eight A.M., that game still seemed exceptionally important to me.

After I got back, at a few minutes before nine, a telephone call came from my friend the writer John Gregory Dunne, who told me to turn on the television set — a plane had struck the World Trade Center and one of the towers was in flames. By then the world had already changed, mine and virtually everyone else's. Perhaps only once before in our history, with the attack on Pearl Harbor, has there been such a difference between yesterday and today, between then and now. Looking now at the newspaper headlines of Tuesday morning, September 11, 2001, I find them distant and removed from our reality — like museum pieces, relics from another time, aged memorabilia from another city, another country.

We are left with the rubble at Ground Zero, a term that was not much in our vocabulary a few weeks ago. The rubble is even worse than it appears to be on television. In some ways it is reminiscent of Berlin in April 1945, because the two World Trade Center buildings were so grand; in truth, they were self-contained little cities, and so the rubble is that of small cities. When the attack happened, we who live here were shocked — but in some ways not surprised — that that which we had always feared had finally happened. Slowly in the days afterward we began to come to terms with the complexity of our emotions, first with the sheer horror of the event itself, destructive and violent, and then with the more terrible knowledge of the magnitude of the long-range implications of it: that it is a threat *in continuum,* the abrupt start of a new chapter in our lives, a deadly struggle that is all too familiar in other parts of the world but absolutely new to us here.

Yet the threat was always there. And New York was always uniquely vulnerable to it — despite the cinematic versions, in which protection was offered by Schwarzenegger, Stallone, and Willis, who always got the bad guy in the last sequence of any movie that deigned to address terrorism. We dealt with terrorism in the past, it seems, by turning to Hollywood; we believed that we were protected by our fantasies. But when the unthinkable happened, there was no action hero to rescue us at the end.

Anyone who paid any attention to the way the world was going knew deep down before the attack that America was no longer immune; on the last page of a book that I was in the process of publishing in mid-September, there is a sentence about the missile shield, which has always struck me as a kind of high-tech Maginot Line. I wrote that the real threat to this country would come not from some rogue state vulnerable to our power, but from terrorists who could walk into any American city with a crude atomic bomb in a suitcase. That sentence was born not of any great prophetic sense on my part but, regrettably, of mere common sense.

Our very strength makes us a target, and the symbols of that strength — the tallest edifices of capitalism, and the center of our military command — are targets in particular. We have had a good deal of time — some twenty-five years, perhaps more — to understand two things. First, that the great threat to our country is not from another developed nation with a nuclear-strike force, against which our immense military power is so readily deployed, but from terrorists who do not offer an easy target, and who hate the United States for what it represents (a pervasive, in their eyes, corrupting, decadent culture) and for its alliances (not just with Israel but, equally important, with moderate Arab states). These terrorists were at war with us before we were at war with them. Second, that these groups are increasingly well financed, and that the level of their craft was bound to improve; they have allies, overt and covert, who are helping them bridge the vast gap between the primitive conditions that have given birth to their hatreds and the modern sophistication that enables them to pull off violent acts like this.

We have witnessed a turning point in American history, the beginning of what I think is going to be the most challenging of our geopolitical struggles — because the enemy is so difficult to do battle with, because he offers so poor a target for our high-technology weaponry, and because no small part of his strength is his patience, which he matches against our innate impatience, an inevitable byproduct of a dynamic society constantly in some sort of overdrive. If we are wise, strong, and patient, and if the fates smile upon us, we will be able to say years from now that the people who launched this attack succeeded beyond their own best interests, in that they finally got on our radar screen, thereby forcing us to focus our national attention on something so elemental as our survival as a free society. We have dealt with the issue only sporadically and haphazardly in the past, precisely because we were so free, so strong, and so eager to enjoy the benefits of our great freedom and affluence.

Rarely have our previous concerns and agendas, that which seemed so important and galvanizing — Connie Chung's semi-famous get of Congressman Gary Condit, the trials and tribulations of Lizzie Grubman, the ever-absorbing saga of movie-star romances and divorces — come to seem so inconsequential so fast. Even before the bombing of Pearl Harbor occurred, in December 1941, there had been all kinds of evidence that the rest of the civilized world was already deeply involved in a titanic struggle that would surely determine the future of civilization as we knew it.

I was seven at the time of Pearl Harbor, and I have very clear memories of that critical day. We lived in the Bronx, where my father, who had served in World War I, was a doctor. I can remember that we were in the family car, and we got the news from the radio, as almost everyone did that Sunday — in a stream of interruptions by announcers with stentorian, doomsday voices. My brother, who was two years older, and I had never heard of Pearl Harbor, and we had little idea of where Hawaii was, but hearing the radio, hearing the hushed serious tones with which our parents discussed the news, tones that we had never heard them use before, we knew in some instinctive way that our lives had changed fatefully. Which they had.

It was not just that the next morning when we got to school we performed air-raid drills, and then repeated them almost daily for two weeks. Within a few months my father went back into the service — he was forty-six at the time — and we gave up our apartment in the Bronx, moving first to my uncle's house in Winsted, Connecticut, and then to El Paso, and Austin, and Rochester, Minnesota, as my father was posted to different, domestic army bases before going overseas. But I remember that we, and I use the word "we" in the larger sense — not just my family but everyone around us — were not fearful. There seemed at the moment an odd steadiness and confidence — perhaps it was fatalism about what was going to happen next and the fact that it was not going to be easy. All we wanted to know was what we were supposed to do from that moment on.

Looking back at those days and reading books about that time, most Americans will be struck by that sense of immediate unity and lack of panic, how everyone seemed to understand and accept what his or her role was supposed to be. The challenge before us then, though very difficult at the time, seems easier than the one before us now, because it so readily fitted our strengths — even if we did not yet know it — and because we had no alternative to the singular focus of our energies. Hearing that the Japanese had bombed us at Pearl Harbor, Winston Churchill, vastly relieved, immediately understood the changed equation of the war, and wrote that the deed was done, that the Allies would win, that the colossus of America (he knew we were a colossus before we knew we were a colossus) would rise to the occasion. Japan, in his phrase, would be "ground to powder." He understood that our vast industrial resources — the arsenal of democracy — operated outside the reach of enemy planes and would become the determining factor in the war.

That enemy back in 1941 was more easily definable, the definition of the war more traditional, and our power more readily applicable against the Axis than against the elusive enemy we now face, working in the shadows, often at so great a distance and often, it turns out, right among us. Never has there been an enemy less visible to our intelligence operations and so invulnerable to any military strike.

This is a brand-new era, and war has come home to us as it never has before. At Pearl Harbor we were attacked, but it was a distant attack. By contrast, this is an attack against two of our best-known and most symbolic edifices; as such it has ended a unique historical span for us as a great, untouchable power, a span that I would place at eighty-seven years, to be exact. In that period the immense carnage of the modern era was always somewhere else. Because of that we were permitted many illusions. We became somewhat schizophrenic, isolationist — due to our geography, our size, our power, our wealth, and our self-sufficiency — but still the guardian and shield, in a shrewd kind of enlightened self-interest, of like-minded democratic regimes. Yet true internationalism has always been an uneasy role for America.

For our geography has always dominated our psyche; we are apart from Europe and we *like* being apart from Europe. Our modern history confirms our love/hate relationship with internationalism. Even as America was beginning to surge forward as a major industrial player, when the First World War began, we came in three years after the other major powers. With most of Europe already bled white and exhausted, we eventually played the decisive role. Then, still protected by our two oceans, we went back to our old ways and rejected President Wilson's attempt at internationalism. During World War II, we once again came in later than most of the other players — two years later if you mark the calendar from the war's beginnings in Europe, longer if you count Asian events.

That war ended with us emerging as a new superpower, one dramatically more internationalist than when we had entered. We were brought into close connection with the rest of the world by the generation of men who had actually fought and who had witnessed firsthand the calamity caused by the previous generation's isolationism. They understood the importance and synergy of the new weaponry unsheathed at the very end of the war, the atomic bomb and the German V-2 rockets. All this made isolationism no longer viable. Thus for the first time did we begin to deal with the knowledge that the immunities and protections that had been ours no longer existed.

Still, we remained very different from the rest of the world. Unlike almost any other nation that had been part of World War II, we felt better about ourselves when it was over than we had before it began. The devastation inflicted on others — some 20 million people dead in Russia, 6 million in Germany, 6 million in Poland — was on a different scale from our losses. We sacrificed, to be sure, some 400,000 men and women on both fronts, but our soil was essentially untouched. Europe was shattered; the British, exhausted emotionally, physically, and financially, could no longer sustain their role as the leader of the West.

Thus did we begin the ascent to superpower status. That the ascent has not been much desired, and is probably even unwanted, is critically important to understanding how America responds to crises in foreign policy, why it does so more slowly and more awkwardly, but, when finally aroused, does so with a certain finality. Our instinct is to be apart. We are a vast country, with all kinds of different regions and people; we do not unite lightly or quickly for any single purpose. It is, I think, in the long run, a source of strength and tolerance.

The period that followed World War II was a new and chilling one, a hot war followed by a cold one. In Eastern Europe lines were drawn, and we quickly found ourselves facing the challenge of the formidable new Soviet empire. The lessons of World War II were applied to the new demands of the Cold War. That which had always protected us in the past — our geographical isolation — no longer existed; the oceans had become ponds.

There were still powerful pockets of isolationism in this country, especially in the Midwest. It is easy to underestimate today the resistance to much of the policy containing communism in the late forties, and the number of Americans who wanted to never again become involved in Europe, who did not want to help support and strengthen our fragile European allies, and who in some cases believed that our old alliances were a source of vulnerability. (In the Midwest the fear that it was the old eastern establishment doing the work of the British was powerful. The least Secretary of State Dean Acheson — he of a certain generational Anglophilia, with his fancy old-boy manners and British tailoring — could do to help a politically embattled President Truman, Averell Harriman once said, was to shave off his British guard's mustache.) Resistance to Soviet imperialism could not be sold in too low-key and abstract a way, as Senator Arthur Vandenberg of Michigan, a last-minute convert to internationalism, understood. If Truman wanted his containment policy to go through the Congress, Vandenberg said, he could have it, but he would have to go and scare the hell out of the American people.

Still, through all the paranoia in both societies, and the terror of the Cold War, there was an equilibrium of power, a mutuality of terror. There were certain fears of a nuclear attack earlier in the struggle, but they gradually receded. Once again our scientific-industrial base was more than adequate — indeed, by the end of the Cold War we were, because of our vast technological superiority, systematically widening the gap on the Soviet Union, something of which Mikhail Gorbachev, with his extensive ties to the KGB, was all too aware.

Then the Soviet empire collapsed. The threat that had hung over this country for some forty years disappeared. The oceans, which had become ponds, were, in the minds of far too many people here, oceans once again. John F. Kennedy, taking as his topic the period before England rallied itself against the threat posed by Hitler, wrote a college thesis that was turned into a short book called *Why England Slept.* If someone were to write a book about America from the collapse of the Berlin Wall in 1989 to September 11, 2001, it might be called *Why America Napped.*

When social historians come to measure us in the future, they may look at the decade that just passed with unusual distaste, as a time of trivial pursuits and debate in the public sector and singular greed in the private one, where the heads of our biggest corporations were given unacceptably large rewards. A poem which W. H. Auden wrote at the time of the start of World War II seems particularly apropos at this moment. It is called "September 1, 1939." The first five lines go: "I sit in one of the dives / On Fifty-second Street / Uncertain and afraid / As the clever hopes expire / Of a low dishonest decade." With luck, and I say this very carefully, with luck, that era is past.

What is at stake here is something elemental to what we are as a people and a nation: the survival of the open and free society. Our very openness makes us unusually vulnerable to enemies. When we show up at hotels or airports, we do not have to lug with us all kinds of documentation to prove that we are who we say we are; that has been a curious kind of privilege, and it is going to be more difficult to preserve in the future. But our freedom in a larger sense is much more than that.

Those of us, I suspect, who have over the years worked in societies that are not free have treasured, more than most, freedom in America, not just the freedom to move about but the freedom to be who and what you want to be, to be different from those who went before you in your own family, to if necessary reinvent yourself and become the person of your own imagination. I believe as a matter of political faith not merely that freedom represents an easier, more pleasurable life in the simplest sense for the individual, but also that all our great strengths — industrial, scientific, military, and artistic — flow from it. The freer we are, the more we are able to use the talents of all our people. We waste less human potential than any other society that I know of.

What an irony that we, who have always depended on this scientific excellence and industrial might to protect us, are threatened not by a First World or even Second or Third World country, but by a terrorist guerrilla group, rootless in terms of nationhood and with a medieval vision for the future. Yet this group has managed to find exceptional financing and to adapt itself to a shrewd if minimalist application of borrowed or stolen modern technology. Even as we reel from this assault, our enemies are trying to buy the most modern weapons of mass destruction, and they have shown a remarkable ability to move money around the world to finance such operations.

This, then, is the ultimate challenge to us as a society, far more difficult and complicated than the one that followed Pearl Harbor; Pearl Harbor had the ability not merely to unify the country — as this attack has — but also to *sustain* that unity for as long as was required. The phrase we used in those days, lest we forget, was "for the duration." The September 11 assault is infinitely more insidious, and it strikes a nation that after a half century of relentless affluence is quite different — much more materialistic, with a significantly more abbreviated and fragmented attention span. The responses the attack inspired at different levels of our society are quite complicated and in some ways terribly revealing: contrast, if you will, the selfless behavior of those magnificent New York firefighters, rushing into the inferno of the Twin Towers to save strangers, with that of the stock-market players, architects of the greatest one-week drop in the stock market since the Depression. Both the firefighters and the Wall Street operators were, I suppose, merely doing their jobs.

The America of 1941 was poorer, and expectations were much, much lower, much closer to a certain kind of Calvinist root. There was a greater sense, I believe, on the part of ordinary citizens of what they *owed* back. That is very different from today. We have been quite differently conditioned than our parents and grandparents were in what to expect out of life. This is a much more self-absorbed society, one that demands ever quicker results; it is

accustomed to being secure — and *entertained*. When things go
wrong it is likely to be thought of as someone else's fault, and
therefore merely a mistake that ought to be rectified. And quickly.
What is especially difficult about this new challenge is that it challenges our attention span.

Of the many results of the end of the Cold War — the amazing
surge in the American economy, the rise of nationalism and tribalism in certain parts of the world — the most surprising and distressing was the trivialization of the American political agenda.
This was reflected in the media, most especially in the decline in
foreign reporting among the three main networks. Any serious
look at the larger world was presumed to be boring. Fifty-six years
after World War II ended I can still tell you the names of the great
CBS radio reporters of that era: Edward R. Murrow, Eric Sevareid,
Charles Collingwood, David Schoenbrun, Winston Burdett. Who
can name five foreign correspondents for the networks today?
Sadly, the people who make the biggest salaries, our new specialists in instant, artificial empathy, have, with some exceptions, by
and large produced the most frivolous work — the sum of which
has seemed to say that America was unthreatened, that there was
no challenge to us, and that we need not know anything about the
rest of the world. Not surprisingly, our national debates on important issues atrophied. During the last election, allegedly serious
political commentators would sit around telling us which of the
candidates seemed more likable, as if they were judging a campaign for high school class president.

We have been bingeing for a decade, all of us in different degrees. (I include in this myself, and this magazine as well.) For
many in the rest of the world, especially people who wish us well, it
has been inexplicable, a nation of so much power and responsibility paying so little attention to the world around it. It was as if the
old isolationist impulse had been restored and magnified.

We have gone from having a serious agenda, worthy of a
monopoly superpower, to an ever more trivial one of scandal and
celebrity. When we have wanted (or needed) in the last decade or
so to exercise our power in certain foreign policy crises, the dis-
connect between our complex international role and the lack of
public knowledge and interest — and our government's innate
caution about taking any risks — has mandated what is virtually a

zero-casualties approach, especially after the events in Somalia in 1993. Whatever else, that era ended on September 11.

I have always thought the concept, so fashionable in the last few years, of a "greatest generation" as exceptional historical foolishness. I say that with the most profound admiration for those who survived the Depression and fought in World War II. They bore an uncommonly heavy burden; my father — the man I revere more than anyone else, an immigrants' son who put himself through college and medical school and finished his medical training just in time for the Great Depression — was a member of it. But the idea that he belonged to a better generation than that of his father, who had helped bring our family here from the Old Country, would have surely appalled him. Generations aren't greater or lesser, weaker, noisier, or more silent. (Mine was supposedly the silent generation.) They are composed of human beings who respond to different circumstances and different challenges in different ways. Challenged in the right way and properly led, in a free society, they will almost invariably do the right thing. A world of easy security and easy affluence, with an elite, all-volunteer, professional army, will inevitably bring out lesser qualities. Responding together to a genuine threat to national security, especially in a time of economic reversals, will surely bring out other, better ones.

What is important about generations are the challenges before them, and how well those challenges are explained by their leaders. We talk now about the need for leadership as though it were George Bush's responsibility alone. But leadership during World War II came from all parts of the society. Today there must be within the private sector a parallel sense of obligation. If this country is to enter a new era — "a long twilight struggle," to use John Kennedy's extremely apt phrase — with a very difficult adversary, then it needs patient, thoughtful leadership in all walks of life. For we are being brought back into contact with a part of the world that is hard for us to understand and where it is extremely difficult to exercise power. We will not do well by simply lashing out at a supple, elusive adversary in a way that makes us feel better but does little to change his modus operandi.

One of the advantages of being older and having some degree of historical knowledge is the faith in the free society that eventually

comes with it. The terrible thing about the Communists, the poet
Allen Ginsberg once told me years ago, when we were in Eastern
Europe and he had had a difficult little struggle with the Czech
and Polish authorities, is that all the clichés about them were true.
I would add to that a corollary: that one of the good things about
our democracy is that many of the clichés about it are also true —
you just have to stick around long enough to bear witness. In my
lifetime I have seen the resilience of American democracy time
and again — in those months after World War II, when we moved
so quickly from being a sleeping isolationist nation to becoming
an awesome new international power. And post-*Sputnik*, when we
showed our capacity to go all out in space, with the pledge of John
Kennedy in 1961 to put a man on the moon, which resulted, only
eight years later, in our doing exactly that. Over the years, I have
come to admire in our society the loyalty and energies and resolve
of free men and women freely summoned.

What I have also learned is that opponents of a free society —
whether it was the Nazis and the leaders of imperial Japan, or the
Soviets during the Cold War, or even more recently Slobodan
Milosevic, who kept telling America's diplomats that he could out-
bluff us because he could accept death and we could not — tend
to underestimate our strengths and even see them as weaknesses.
The most recent example of that kind of thinking comes from
Osama bin Laden, who was quoted in a 1996 interview as saying that his battle with America was easier than the one with the
Russians, who were more courageous and above all more patient.
Men such as bin Laden believe that what I consider to be our
strengths — the slowness of our political responses, the complexity and diversity of our social fabric — reflect a certain kind of
decadence.

Getting America to change directions and attitudes from one
era to another sometimes must seem like trying to change the direction of an aircraft carrier by trailing your hand behind it in the
water. But our strengths, when summoned and focused, when the
body politic is aroused and connects to the top of the political process, are never to be underestimated.

In some ways this inevitably comes back to the personal. I am a
New Yorker. What was bombed was the city in which I live. It is an
assault upon so many things that I cherish: the way I live — that is,

the love of the constant possibilities in a free society — and the place where I live as well. Among those killed were eleven firefighters at Engine Company 40, Ladder Company 35, whose station house is only two blocks from our apartment, men who have protected me and my family for years.

Being a New Yorker is as much a condition as it is a description of where I reside. Not that many of us are born here: one becomes a New Yorker in most instances by choice. I happen to have been born in one of the boroughs, but I did not grow up here, and I came back quite warily in my thirties, twenty-five years after World War II had driven us from the city. Then I was not at all sure whether I wanted to stay. But I did, tentatively at first and then, in time, lovingly. I came to love New York's grittiness and excitement, even coming to accept its edgier, harsher, often angrier side; Rudy Giuliani in that sense is the perfect New York mayor, reflecting all of our best and, on occasion, a good many of our lesser qualities. I came to understand that that very edginess was a critical part of the New York condition, and sometimes I have surely made my own contributions to it. I understand that being a true New Yorker is not necessarily a warm and fuzzy role. True New Yorkers celebrate the flaws of their city as much as they do its virtues.

I have lived here almost thirty-five years now. My wife and I were married here, our daughter was born here and grew up here. I always start my day by walking our dogs through Central Park, and I thrill every morning to the vista in front of me as I look south, over the bucolic Sheep Meadow, then down to the skyscrapers that begin on Central Park South. There are constant changes and gradations of light, according to the time of day and year. For me, it still remains, for all its flaws, an alabaster city, always gleaming. Living here now seems more important than ever before. There are many things worth cherishing in life, and I have found all of them here — above all, the human pulse of the city itself, which has always seemed to me so regenerative, perhaps now more than ever.

Reflections and Responses

1. Although Halberstam places the events of 9/11 in a large historical framework, he also frequently introduces his personal

history into the essay. How has he blended his own and his nation's histories into one? How does this mixture of public and personal affect the way we read the essay?

2. Of what significance is Pearl Harbor to American history and Halberstam's personal history? How does Halberstam compare and contrast these two attacks? In what ways does he see them as similar? What important differences does he also find?

3. Does Halberstam, in your opinion, try to find an underlying reason for the terrorist attacks of 9/11? If so, what reasons does he suggest? If not, why do you think he suggests no reasons? Finally, how would you summarize Halberstam's response to 9/11 in a sentence or two?

VICKI HEARNE

What's Wrong with
Animal Rights

*When people argue for the rights of animals, what exactly do they mean by
"rights"? Does their definition of animal rights take into account the "certain unalienable rights" that Thomas Jefferson wrote into the Declaration
of Independence — the right to "life, liberty and the pursuit of happiness"?
In the following essay, Vicki Hearne skillfully combines personal and professional experience with philosophical reflections on happiness as she
builds a case against the reductive view of animals that typifies the animal-rights movement. In Hearne's opinion, the problem with animal-rights advocates is not that they take their position too far; "it's that they've got it all
wrong."*

*A professional dog trainer and Yale University professor, Hearne has
published three volumes of poetry,* Nervous Horses *(1980),* In the Absence of Horses *(1983), and* Parts of Light *(1994); three books of
essays,* Adam's Task: Calling Animals by Name *(1986),* Bandit: Dossier of a Dangerous Dog *(1991), and* Animal Happiness *(1994); and
a novel,* The White German Shepherd *(1988). "What's Wrong with
Animal Rights" originally appeared in* Harper's Magazine *in 1991
and was selected by Susan Sontag for* The Best American Essays 1992.
Vicki Hearne died of lung cancer in August 2001.

Not all happy animals are alike. A Doberman going over a hurdle
after a small wooden dumbbell is sleek, all arcs of harmonious
power. A basset hound cheerfully performing the same exercise exhibits harmonies of a more lugubrious nature. There are chimpanzees who love precision the way musicians or fanatical housekeepers
or accomplished hypochondriacs do; others for whom happiness

is a matter of invention and variation — chimp vaudevillians. There is a rhinoceros whose happiness, as near as I can make out, is in needing to be trained every morning, all over again, or else he "forgets" his circus routine, and in this you find a clue to the slow, deep, quiet chuckle of his happiness and to the glory of the beast. Happiness for Secretariat is in his ebullient bound, that joyful length of stride. For the draft horse or the weight-pull dog, happiness is of a different shape, more awesome and less obviously intelligent. When the pulling horse is at its most intense, the animal goes into himself, allocating all of the educated power that organizes his desire to dwell in fierce and delicate intimacy with that power, leans into the harness, and MAKES THAT SUCKER MOVE.

If we are speaking of human beings and use the phrase "animal happiness," we tend to mean something like "creature comforts." The emblems of this are the golden retriever rolling in the grass, the horse with his nose deep in the oats, the kitty by the fire. Creature comforts are important to animals — "Grub first, then ethics" is a motto that would describe many a wise Labrador retriever, and I have a pit bull named Annie whose continual quest for the perfect pillow inspires her to awesome feats. But there is something more to animals, a capacity for satisfactions that come from work in the fullest sense — what is known in philosophy and in this country's Declaration of Independence as "happiness." This is a sense of personal achievement, like the satisfaction felt by a good wood-carver or a dancer or a poet or an accomplished dressage horse. It is a happiness that, like the artist's, must come from something within the animal, something trainers call "talent." Hence, it cannot be imposed on the animal. But it is also something that does not come *ex nihilo*.* If it had not been a fairly ordinary thing, in one part of the world, to teach young children to play the pianoforte, it is doubtful that Mozart's music would exist.

Happiness is often misunderstood as a synonym for pleasure or as an antonym for suffering. But Aristotle associated happiness with ethics — codes of behavior that urge us toward the sensation of getting it right, a kind of work that yields the "click" of satisfaction upon solving a problem or surmounting an obstacle. In his *Ethics*, Aristotle wrote, "If happiness is activity in accordance with

*__ex nihilo:__ Latin, "out of nothing." — Ed.

excellence, it is reasonable that it should be in accordance with the highest excellence." Thomas Jefferson identified the capacity for happiness as one of the three fundamental rights on which all others are based: "life, liberty, and the pursuit of happiness."

I bring up this idea of happiness as a form of work because I am an animal trainer, and work is the foundation of the happiness a trainer and an animal discover together. I bring up these words also because they cannot be found in the lexicon of the animal-rights movement. This absence accounts for the uneasiness toward the movement of most people, who sense that rights advocates have a point but take it too far when they liberate snails or charge that goldfish at the county fair are suffering. But the problem with the animal-rights advocates is not that they take it too far; it's that they've got it all wrong.

Animal rights are built upon a misconceived premise that rights were created to prevent us from unnecessary suffering. You can't find an animal-rights book, video, pamphlet, or rock concert in which someone doesn't mention the Great Sentence, written by Jeremy Bentham* in 1789. Arguing in favor of such rights, Bentham wrote: "The question is not, Can they *reason?* nor, can they *talk?* but, can they suffer?"

The logic of the animal-rights movement places suffering at the iconographic center of a skewed value system. The thinking of its proponents — given eerie expression in a virtually sadoporno-graphic sculpture of a tortured monkey that won a prize for its compassionate vision — has collapsed into a perverse conundrum. Today the loudest voices calling for — demanding — the destruction of animals are the humane organizations. This is an inevitable consequence of the apotheosis of the drive to relieve suffering: death is the ultimate release. To compensate for their contradictions, the humane movement has demonized, in this century and the last, those who made animal happiness their business: veterinarians, trainers, and the like. We think of Louis Pasteur as the man whose work saved you and me and your dog and cat from rabies, but antivivisectionists of the time claimed that rabies increased in areas where there were Pasteur Institutes.

---

*Jeremy Bentham: British philosopher and social reformer (1748–1832) whose *Introduction to the Principles of Morals and Legislation* appeared in 1789. — Ed.

An anti-rabies public relations campaign mounted in England in the 1880s by the Royal Society for the Prevention of Cruelty to Animals and other organizations led to orders being issued to club any dog found not wearing a muzzle. England still has her cruel and unnecessary law that requires an animal to spend six months in quarantine before being allowed loose in the country. Most of the recent propaganda about pit bulls — the crazy claim that they "take hold with their front teeth while they chew away with their rear teeth" (which would imply, incorrectly, that they have double jaws)— can be traced to literature published by the Humane Society of the United States during the fall of 1987 and earlier. If your neighbors want your dog or horse impounded and destroyed because he is a nuisance — say the dog barks, or the horse attracts flies — it will be the local Humane Society to whom your neighbors turn for action.

In a way, everyone has the opportunity to know that the history of the humane movement is largely a history of miseries, arrests, prosecutions, and death. The Humane Society is the pound, the place with the decompression chamber or the lethal injections. You occasionally find worried letters about this in Ann Landers's column.

Animal-rights publications are illustrated largely with photographs of two kinds of animals — "Helpless Fluff" and "Agonized Fluff," the two conditions in which some people seem to prefer their animals, because any other version of an animal is too complicated for propaganda. In the introduction to his book *Animal Liberation,* Peter Singer says somewhat smugly that he and his wife have no animals and, in fact, don't much care for them. This is offered as evidence of his objectivity and ethical probity. But it strikes me as an odd, perhaps obscene underpinning for an ethical project that encourages university and high school students to cherish their ignorance of, say, great bird dogs as proof of their devotion to animals.

I would like to leave these philosophers behind, for they are inept connoisseurs of suffering who might revere my Airedale for his capacity to scream when subjected to a blowtorch but not for his wit and courage, not for his natural good manners that are a gentle rebuke to ours. I want to celebrate the moment not long ago when, at his first dog show, my Airedale, Drummer, learned that there can be a public place where his work is respected. I want to celebrate his meticulousness, his happiness upon realizing at the dog show that no one would swoop down upon him and swamp him with the goo-goo excesses known as the "teddy-bear complex" but that people actually got out of his way, gave him room to work. I want to say, "There can be a six-and-a-half-month-old puppy who can care about accuracy, who can be fastidious, and whose fastidiousness will be a foundation for courage later." I want to say, "Leave my puppy alone!"

I want to leave the philosophers behind, but I cannot, in part because the philosophical problems that plague academicians of the animal-rights movement are illuminating. They wonder, do animals have rights or do they have interests? Or, if these rightists lead particularly unexamined lives, they dismiss that question as obvious (yes, of course animals have rights, prima facie) and proceed to enumerate them, James Madison style. This leads to the issuance of bills of rights — the right to an environment, the right not to be used in medical experiments — and other forms of trivialization.

The calculus of suffering can be turned against the philosophers of festering flesh, even in the case of food animals, or exotic animals who perform in movies and circuses. It is true that it hurts to be slaughtered by man, but it doesn't hurt nearly as much as some of the cunningly cruel arrangements meted out by "Mother Nature." In Africa, 75 percent of the lions cubbed do not survive to the age of two. For those who make it to two, the average age at death is ten years. Asali, the movie and TV lioness, was still working at age twenty-one. There are fates worse than death, but twenty-one years of a close working relationship with Hubert Wells, Asali's trainer, is not one of them. Dorset sheep and polled Herefords would not exist at all were they not in a symbiotic relationship with human beings.

A human being living in the "wild" — somewhere, say, without the benefits of medicine and advanced social organization — would probably have a life expectancy of from thirty to thirty-five years. A human being living in "captivity" — in, say, a middle-class neighborhood of what the Centers for Disease Control call a Metropolitan Statistical Area — has a life expectancy of seventy or more years. For orangutans in the wild in Borneo and Malaysia, the life expectancy is thirty-five years; in captivity, fifty years. The wild is not a suffering-free zone or all that frolicsome a location.

The questions asked by animal-rights activists are flawed, because they are built on the concept that the origin of rights is in the avoidance of suffering rather than in the pursuit of happiness. The question that needs to be asked — and that will put us in closer proximity to the truth — is not, do they have rights? or, what are those rights? but rather, what is a right?

Rights originate in committed relationships and can be found, both intact and violated, wherever one finds such relationships — in social compacts, within families, between animals, and between people and nonhuman animals. This is as true when the nonhuman animals in question are lions or parakeets as when they are dogs. It is my Airedale whose excellencies have my attention at the moment, so it is with reference to him that I will consider the question, what is a right?

When I imagine situations in which it naturally arises that A defends or honors or respects B's rights, I imagine situations in which the relationship between A and B can be indicated with a possessive pronoun. I might say, "Leave her alone, she's my daughter" or "That's what she wants, and she is my daughter. I think I am bound to honor her wants." Similarly, "Leave her alone, she's my mother." I am more tender of the happiness of my mother, my father, my child, than I am of other people's family members; more tender of my friends' happinesses than your friends' happinesses, unless you and I have a mutual friend.

Possession of a being by another has come into more and more disrepute, so that the common understanding of one person possessing another is slavery. But the important detail about the kind of possessive pronoun that I have in mind is reciprocity: if I have a friend, she has a friend. If I have a daughter, she has a mother. The possessive does not bind one of us while freeing the other; it cannot do that. Moreover, should the mother reject the daughter, the word that applies is "disown." The form of disowning that most often appears in the news is domestic violence. Parents abuse children; husbands batter wives.

Some cases of reciprocal possessives have built-in limitations, such as "my patient/my doctor" or "my student/my teacher" or "my agent/my client." Other possessive relations are extremely limited but still remarkably binding: "my neighbor" and "my country" and "my president."

The responsibilities and the ties signaled by reciprocal possession typically are hard to dissolve. It can be as difficult to give up an enemy as to give up a friend, and often the one becomes the other, as though the logic of the possessive pronoun outlasts the forms it chanced to take at a given moment, as though we were stuck with one another. In these bindings, nearly inextricable, are found the origin of our rights. They imply a possessiveness but also recognize an acknowledgment by each side of the other's existence.

The idea of democracy is dependent on the citizens' having knowledge of the government; that is, realizing that the government exists and knowing how to claim rights against it. I know this much because I get mail from the government and see its "representatives" running about in uniforms. Whether I actually have any rights in relationship to the government is less clear, but the idea that I do is symbolized by the right to vote. I obey the government, and, in theory, it obeys me, by counting my ballot, reading the *Miranda* warning to me, agreeing to be bound by the Constitution. My friend obeys me as I obey her; the government "obeys" me to some extent, and, to a different extent, I obey it.

What kind of thing can my Airedale, Drummer, have knowledge of? He can know that I exist and through that knowledge can claim his happinesses, with varying degrees of success, both with me and against me. Drummer can also know about larger human or dog communities than the one that consists only of him and me. There is my household — the other dogs, the cats, my husband. I have had enough dogs on campuses to know that he can learn that Yale exists as a neighborhood or village. My older dog, Annie, not only knows that Yale exists but can tell Yalies from townies, as I learned while teaching there during labor troubles.

Dogs can have elaborate conceptions of human social structures, and even of something like their rights and responsibilities within them, but these conceptions are never elaborate enough to construct a rights relationship between a dog and the state, or a dog and the Humane Society. Both of these are concepts that depend on writing and memoranda, officers in uniform, plaques and seals of authority. All of these are literary constructs, and all of them are beyond a dog's ken, which is why the mail carrier who doesn't also happen to be a dog's friend is forever an intruder — this is why dogs bark at mailmen.

It is clear enough that natural rights relations can arise between people and animals. Drummer, for example, can insist, "Hey, let's go outside and do something!" if I have been at my computer several days on end. He can both refuse to accept various of my suggestions and tell me when he fears for his life — such as the time when the huge, white flapping flag appeared out of nowhere, as it seemed to him, on the town green one evening when we were working. I can (and do) say to him either, "Oh, you don't have to worry about that" or, "Uh oh, you're right, Drum, that guy looks dangerous." Just as the government and I— two different species of organism — have developed improvised ways of communicating, such as the vote, so Drummer and I have worked out a number of ways to make our expressions known. Largely through obedience, I have taught him a fair amount about how to get responses from me. Obedience is reciprocal; you cannot get responses from a dog to whom you do not respond accurately. I have enfranchised him in a relationship to me by educating him, creating the conditions by which he can achieve a certain happiness specific to a dog, maybe even specific to an Airedale, inasmuch as this same relationship has allowed me to plumb the happiness of being a trainer and writing this article.

Instructions in this happiness are given terms that are alien to a culture in which liver treats, fluffy windup toys, and miniature sweaters are confused with respect and work. Jack Knox, a sheepdog trainer originally from Scotland, will shake his crook at a novice handler who makes a promiscuous move to praise a dog, and will call out in his Scottish accent, "Eh! Eh! Get back, get BACK! Ye'll no be abusin' the dogs like that in my clinic." America is a nation of abused animals, Knox says, because we are always swooping at them with praise, "no gi'ing them their freedom." I am reminded of Rainer Maria Rilke's* account in which the Prodigal Son leaves — has to leave — because everyone loves him, even the dogs love him, and he has no path to the delicate and fierce

*__Rainer Maria Rilke:__ Austrian lyric poet (1875–1926). — Ed.

truth of himself. Unconditional praise and love, in Rilke's story, disenfranchise us, distract us from what truly excites our interest.

In the minds of some trainers and handlers, praise is dishonesty. Paradoxically, it is a kind of contempt for animals that masquerades as a reverence for helplessness and suffering. The idea of freedom means that you do not, at least not while Jack Knox is nearby, helpfully guide your dog through the motions of, say, herding over and over — what one trainer calls "explainy-wainy." This is rote learning. It works tolerably well on some handlers, because people have vast unconscious minds and can store complex preprogrammed behaviors. Dogs, on the other hand, have almost no unconscious minds, so they can learn only by thinking. Many children are like this until educated out of it.

If I tell my Airedale to sit and stay on the town green, and someone comes up and burbles, "What a pretty thing you are," he may break his stay to go for a caress. I pull him back and correct him for breaking. Now he holds his stay because I have blocked his way to movement but not because I have punished him. (A correction blocks one path as it opens another for desire to work; punishment blocks desire and opens nothing.) He holds his stay now, and — because the stay opens this possibility of work, new to a heedless young dog — he watches. If the person goes on talking, and isn't going to gush with praise, I may heel Drummer out of his stay and give him an "Okay" to make friends. Sometimes something about the person makes Drummer feel that reserve is in order. He responds to an insincere approach by sitting still, going down into himself, and thinking, "This person has no business pawing me. I'll sit very still, and he will go away." If the person doesn't take the hint from Drummer, I'll give the pup a little backup by saying, "Please don't pet him, he's working," even though he was not under any command.

The pup reads this, and there is a flicker of a working trust now stirring in the dog. Is the pup grateful? When the stranger leaves, does he lick my hand, full of submissive blandishments? This one doesn't. This one says nothing at all, and I say nothing much to him. This is a working trust we are developing, not a mutual congratulation society. My backup is praise enough for him; the use he makes of my support is praise enough for me.

Listening to a dog is often praise enough. Suppose it is just after

dark and we are outside. Suddenly there is a shout from the house.
The pup and I both look toward the shout and then toward each
other: "What do you think?" I don't so much as cock my head, because Drummer is growing up, and I want to know what he thinks.
He takes a few steps toward the house, and I follow. He listens
again and comprehends that it's just Holly, who at fourteen is
much given to alarming cries and shouts. He shrugs at me and
goes about his business. I say nothing. To praise him for this performance would make about as much sense as praising a human
being for the same thing. Thus:

> A. What's that?
> B. I don't know. [Listens] Oh, it's just Holly.
> A. What a goooooood human being!
> B. Huh?

This is one small moment in a series of like moments that will
culminate in an Airedale who on a Friday will have the discrimination and confidence required to take down a man who is attacking
me with a knife and on Saturday clown and play with the children
at the annual Orange Empire Dog Club Christmas party.

People who claim to speak for animal rights are increasingly devoted to the idea that the very keeping of a dog or a horse or a ger-
bil or a lion is in and of itself an offense. The more loudly they
speak, the less likely they are to be in a rights relation to any given
animal, because they are spending so much time in airplanes or
transmitting fax announcements of the latest Sylvester Stallone
anti-fur rally. In a 1988 *Harper's* forum, for example, Ingrid New-
kirk, the national director of People for the Ethical Treatment of
Animals, urged that domestic pets be spayed and neutered and ultimately phased out. She prefers, it appears, wolves — and wolves
someplace else — to Airedales and, by a logic whose interior structure is both emotionally and intellectually forever closed to Drummer, claims thereby to be speaking for "animal rights."

She is wrong. I am the only one who can own up to my Airedale's inalienable rights. Whether or not I do it perfectly at any
given moment is no more refutation of this point than whether I
am perfectly my husband's mate at any given moment refutes the

fact of marriage. Only people who know Drummer, and whom he can know, are capable of this relationship. PETA and the Humane Society and the ASPCA and the Congress and NOW—as institutions—do have the power to affect my ability to grant rights to Drummer but are otherwise incapable of creating conditions or laws or rights that would increase his happiness. Only Drummer's owner has the power to obey him — to obey who he is and what he is capable of—deeply enough to grant him his rights and open up the possibility of happiness.

Reflections and Responses

1. How does Hearne define happiness? What is its relation to work? Why, in her opinion, are the interrelated concepts of happiness and work not "in the lexicon of the animal-rights movement"?

2. Why does Hearne bring up the life-expectancy statistics of animals living "in the wild"? In what way do these statistics reinforce her argument? How might an animal-rights advocate respond to her use and interpretation of these statistics?

3. The Declaration of Independence reads: "We hold these truths to be self-evident, that all men are created equal, that they are endowed by their Creator with certain unalienable rights, that among these are life, liberty and the pursuit of happiness." Do you think Hearne legitimately or illegitimately extends Jefferson's words to apply to nonhumans? Explain your position.

JAMAICA KINCAID

On Seeing England
for the First Time

One of the most sinister sides of imperialism is the way it promotes the ruling nation's culture and rejects the colony's. The effect of this on an impressionable young person is vividly described in Jamaica Kincaid's sensitive and angry autobiographical essay about growing up in Antigua with the dark shadow of England continually looming over her. England and a reverence for things English invaded every aspect of her daily life and education. Yet it was not until adulthood that she finally journeyed to England and really saw it for the first time. "The space between the idea of something and its reality," Kincaid writes, "is always wide and deep and dark." The real England she finally sees is far different from the other England, whose maps and history she was made to memorize as a schoolgirl in Antigua.

Kincaid is the author of At the Bottom of the River *(1983),* Annie John *(1985),* A Small Place *(1988),* Lucy *(1990),* The Autobiography of My Mother *(1996),* My Brother *(1997), and* Mr. Potter *(2002). A staff writer for* The New Yorker, *her stories and essays have also appeared in* Rolling Stone, Paris Review, *and other literary periodicals. She was born in Antigua and currently lives in Vermont. "On Seeing England for the First Time" originally appeared in* Transition *(1991) and was selected by Susan Sontag for* The Best American Essays 1992.

When I saw England for the first time, I was a child in school sitting at a desk. The England I was looking at was laid out on a map gently, beautifully, delicately, a very special jewel; it lay on a bed of sky blue — the background of the map — its yellow form mysterious, because though it looked like a leg of mutton, it could not really look like anything so familiar as a leg of mutton because it was England — with shadings of pink and green, unlike any shadings of pink and green I had seen before, squiggly veins of red running in every direction. England was a special jewel all right, and only special people got to wear it. The people who got to wear England were English people. They wore it well and they wore it everywhere: in jungles, in deserts, on plains, on top of the highest mountains, on all the oceans, on all the seas, in places where they were not welcome, in places they should not have been. When my teacher had pinned this map up on the blackboard, she said, "This is England" — and she said it with authority, seriousness, and adoration, and we all sat up. It was as if she had said, "This is Jerusalem, the place you will go to when you die but only if you have been good." We understood then — we were meant to understand then — that England was to be our source of myth and the source from which we got our sense of reality, our sense of what was meaningful, our sense of what was meaningless — and much about our own lives and much about the very idea of us headed that last list.

At the time I was a child sitting at my desk seeing England for the first time, I was already very familiar with the greatness of it. Each morning before I left for school, I ate a breakfast of half a grapefruit, an egg, bread and butter and a slice of cheese, and a cup of cocoa; or half a grapefruit, a bowl of oat porridge, bread and butter and a slice of cheese, and a cup of cocoa. The can of cocoa was often left on the table in front of me. It had written on it the name of the company, the year the company was established, and the words "Made in England." Those words, "Made in England," were written on the box the oats came in too. They would also have been written on the box the shoes I was wearing came in; a bolt of gray linen cloth lying on the shelf of a store from which my mother had bought three yards to make the uniform that I was wearing had written along its edge those three words. The shoes I wore were made in England; so were my socks and cotton undergarments and the satin ribbons I wore tied at the end of two plaits of my hair. My father, who might have sat next to me at breakfast, was a carpenter and cabinet maker. The shoes he wore to work would have been made in England, as were his khaki shirt and trousers, his underpants and undershirt, his socks and brown felt hat. Felt was not the proper material from which a hat that was expected to provide shade from the hot sun should be made, but my father must have seen and admired a picture of an Englishman wearing such a hat in England, and this picture that he saw must have been so compelling that it caused him to wear the wrong hat for a hot climate most of his long life. And this hat — a brown felt hat — became so central to his character that it was the first thing he put on in the morning as he stepped out of bed and the last thing he took off before he stepped back into bed at night. As we sat at breakfast a car might go by. The car, a Hillman or a Zephyr, was made in England. The very idea of the meal itself, breakfast, and its substantial quality and quantity was an idea from England; we somehow knew that in England they began the day with this meal called breakfast and a proper breakfast was a big breakfast. No one I knew liked eating so much food so early in the day; it made us feel sleepy, tired. But this breakfast business was Made in England like almost everything else that surrounded us, the exceptions being the sea, the sky, and the air we breathed.

At the time I saw this map — seeing England for the first time — I did not say to myself, "Ah, so that's what it looks like," because there was no longing in me to put a shape to those three words that ran through every part of my life, no matter how small; for me to have had such a longing would have meant that I lived in a certain atmosphere, an atmosphere in which those three words were felt as a burden. But I did not live in such an atmosphere. My father's brown felt hat would develop a hole in its crown, the lining would separate from the hat itself, and six weeks before he thought that he could not be seen wearing it — he was a very vain man — he would order another hat from England. And my mother taught me to eat my food in the English way: the knife in the right hand, the fork in the left, my elbows held still close to my side, the food carefully balanced on my fork and then brought up to my mouth. When I had finally mastered it, I overheard her saying to a friend, "Did you see how nicely she can eat?" But I knew then that I enjoyed my food more when I ate it with my bare hands, and I continued to do so when she wasn't looking. And when my teacher showed us the map, she asked us to study it carefully, because no test we would ever take would be complete without this statement: "Draw a map of England."

I did not know then that the statement "Draw a map of England" was something far worse than a declaration of war, for in fact a flat-out declaration of war would have put me on alert, and again in fact, there was no need for war — I had long ago been conquered. I did not know then that this statement was part of a process that would result in my erasure, not my physical erasure, but my erasure all the same. I did not know then that this statement was meant to make me feel in awe and small whenever I heard the word "England": awe at its existence, small because I was not from it. I did not know very much of anything then — certainly not what a blessing it was that I was unable to draw a map of England correctly.

After that there were many times of seeing England for the first time. I saw England in history. I knew the names of all the kings of England. I knew the names of their children, their wives, their disappointments, their triumphs, the names of people who betrayed them, I knew the dates on which they were born and the dates they died. I knew their conquests and was made to feel glad if I figured in them; I knew their defeats. I knew the details of the year 1066 (the Battle of Hastings, the end of the reign of the Anglo-Saxon kings) before I knew the details of the year 1832 (the year slavery was abolished). It wasn't as bad as I make it sound now; it was worse. I did like so much hearing again and again how Alfred the Great, traveling in disguise, had been left to watch cakes, and because he wasn't used to this the cakes got burned, and Alfred burned his hands pulling them out of the fire, and the woman who had left him to watch the cakes screamed at him. I loved King Alfred. My grandfather was named after him; his son, my uncle, was named after King Alfred; my brother is named after King Alfred. And so there are three people in my family named after a man they have never met, a man who died over ten centuries ago. The first view I got of England then was not unlike the first view received by the person who named my grandfather.

This view, though — the naming of the kings, their deeds, their disappointments — was the vivid view, the forceful view. There were other views, subtler ones, softer, almost not there — but these were the ones that made the most lasting impression on me, these

were the ones that made me really feel like nothing. "When morning touched the sky" was one phrase, for no morning touched the
sky where I lived. The mornings where I lived came on abruptly,
with a shock of heat and loud noises. "Evening approaches" was
another, but the evenings where I lived did not approach; in fact, I
had no evening — I had night and I had day and they came and
went in a mechanical way: on, off; on, off. And then there were
gentle mountains and low blue skies and moors over which people
took walks for nothing but pleasure, when where I lived a walk was
an act of labor, a burden, something only death or the automobile
could relieve. And there were things that a small turn of a head
could convey — entire worlds, whole lives would depend on this
thing, a certain turn of a head. Everyday life could be quite tiring,
more tiring than anything I was told not to do. I was told not to
gossip, but they did that all the time. And they ate so much food,
violating another of those rules they taught me: do not indulge in
gluttony. And the foods they ate actually: if only sometime I could
eat cold cuts after theater, cold cuts of lamb and mint sauce, and
Yorkshire pudding and scones, and clotted cream, and sausages
that came from upcountry (imagine, "up-country"). And having
troubling thoughts at twilight, a good time to have troubling
thoughts, apparently; and servants who stole and left in the middle
of a crisis, who were born with a limp or some other kind of defor-
mity, not nourished properly in their mother's womb (that last
part I figured out for myself; the point was, oh to have an untrust-
worthy servant); and wonderful cobbled streets onto which solid
front doors opened; and people whose eyes were blue and who had
fair skins and who smelled only of lavender, or sometimes sweet
pea or primrose. And those flowers with those names: delphini-
ums, foxgloves, tulips, daffodils, floribunda, peonies; in bloom, a
striking display, being cut and placed in large glass bowls, crystal,
decorating rooms so large twenty families the size of mine could fit
in comfortably but used only for passing through. And the weather
was so remarkable because the rain fell gently always, only occasionally in deep gusts, and it colored the air various shades of gray,
each an appealing shade for a dress to be worn when a portrait was
being painted; and when it rained at twilight, wonderful things
happened: people bumped into each other unexpectedly and that
would lead to all sorts of turns of events — a plot, the mere weather

caused plots. I saw that people rushed: they rushed to catch trains, they rushed toward each other and away from each other; they rushed and rushed and rushed. That word: rushed! I did not know what it was to do that. It was too hot to do that, and so I came to envy people who would rush, even though it had no meaning to me to do such a thing. But there they are again. They loved their children; their children were sent to their own rooms as a punishment, rooms larger than my entire house. They were special, everything about them said so, even their clothes; their clothes rustled, swished, soothed. The world was theirs, not mine; everything told me so.

If now as I speak of all this I give the impression of someone on the outside looking in, nose pressed up against a glass window, that is wrong. My nose was pressed up against a glass window all right, but there was an iron vise at the back of my neck forcing my head to stay in place. To avert my gaze was to fall back into something from which I had been rescued, a hole filled with nothing, and that was the word for everything about me, nothing. The reality of my life was conquests, subjugation, humiliation, enforced amnesia. I was forced to forget. Just for instance, this: I lived in a part of St. John's, Antigua, called Ovals. Ovals was made up of five streets, each of them named after a famous English seaman — to be quite frank, an officially sanctioned criminal: Rodney Street (after George Rodney), Nelson Street (after Horatio Nelson), Drake Street (after Francis Drake), Hood Street, and Hawkins Street (after John Hawkins). But John Hawkins was knighted after a trip he made to Africa, opening up a new trade, the slave trade. He was then entitled to wear as his crest a Negro bound with a cord. Every single person living on Hawkins Street was descended from a slave. John Hawkins's ship, the one in which he transported the people he had bought and kidnapped, was called *The Jesus*. He later became the treasurer of the Royal Navy and rear admiral.

Again, the reality of my life, the life I led at the time I was being shown these views of England for the first time, for the second time, for the one-hundred-millionth time, was this: the sun shone with what sometimes seemed to be a deliberate cruelty; we must have done something to deserve that. My dresses did not rustle in the evening air as I strolled to the theater (I had no evening, I had no theater; my dresses were made of a cheap cotton, the weave of

which would give way after not too many washings). I got up in the
morning, I did my chores (fetched water from the public pipe for
my mother, swept the yard), I washed myself, I went to a woman to
have my hair combed freshly every day (because before we were
allowed into our classroom our teachers would inspect us, and
children who had not bathed that day, or had dirt under their
fingernails, or whose hair had not been combed anew that day,
might not be allowed to attend class). I ate that breakfast. I walked
to school. At school we gathered in an auditorium and sang a
hymn, "All Things Bright and Beautiful," and looking down on us
as we sang were portraits of the Queen of England and her husband; they wore jewels and medals and they smiled. I was a
Brownie. At each meeting we would form a little group around a
flagpole, and after raising the Union Jack, we would say, "I
promise to do my best, to do my duty to God and the Queen, to
help other people every day and obey the scouts' law."

Who were these people and why had I never seen them, I mean
really seen them, in the place where they lived? I had never been
to England. No one I knew had ever been to England, or I should
say, no one I knew had ever been and returned to tell me about it.
All the people I knew who had gone to England had stayed there.
Sometimes they left behind them their small children, never to see
them again. England! I had seen England's representatives. I had
seen the governor general at the public grounds at a ceremony celebrating the Queen's birthday. I had seen an old princess and I
had seen a young princess. They had both been extremely not
beautiful, but who of us would have told them that? I had never
seen England, really seen it, I had only met a representative, seen
a picture, read books, memorized its history. I had never set foot,
my own foot, in it.

The space between the idea of something and its reality is always
wide and deep and dark. The longer they are kept apart — idea of
thing, reality of thing — the wider the width, the deeper the
depth, the thicker and darker the darkness. This space starts out
empty, there is nothing in it, but it rapidly becomes filled up with
obsession or desire or hatred or love — sometimes all of these
things, sometimes some of these things, sometimes only one of
these things. The existence of the world as I came to know it was a

result of this: idea of thing over here, reality of thing way, way over there. There was Christopher Columbus, an unlikable man, an unpleasant man, a liar (and so, of course, a thief) surrounded by maps and schemes and plans, and there was the reality on the other side of that width, that depth, that darkness. He became obsessed, he became filled with desire, the hatred came later, love was never a part of it. Eventually, his idea met the longed-for reality. That the idea of something and its reality are often two completely different things is something no one ever remembers; and so when they meet and find that they are not compatible, the weaker of the two, idea or reality, dies. That idea Christopher Columbus had was more powerful than the reality he met, and so the reality he met died.

And so finally, when I was a grown-up woman, the mother of two children, the wife of someone, a person who resides in a powerful country that takes up more than its fair share of a continent, the owner of a house with many rooms in it and of two automobiles, with the desire and will (which I very much act upon) to take from the world more than I give back to it, more than I deserve, more than I need, finally then, I saw England, the real England, not a picture, not a painting, not through a story in a book, but England, for the first time. In me, the space between the idea of it and its reality had become filled with hatred, and so when at last I saw it I wanted to take it into my hands and tear it into little pieces and then crumble it up as if it were clay, child's clay. That was impossible, and so I could only indulge in not-favorable opinions.

There were monuments everywhere; they commemorated victories, battles fought between them and the people who lived across the sea from them, all vile people, fought over which of them would have dominion over the people who looked like me. The monuments were useless to them now, people sat on them and ate their lunch. They were like markers on an old useless trail, like a piece of old string tied to a finger to jog the memory, like old decoration in an old house, dirty, useless, in the way. Their skins were so pale, it made them look so fragile, so weak, so ugly. What if I had the power to simply banish them from their land, send boat after boatload of them on a voyage that in fact had no destination, force them to live in a place where the sun's presence was a constant? This would rid them of their pale complexion and make

them look more like me, make them look more like the people I
love and treasure and hold dear, and more like the people who occupy the near and far reaches of my imagination, my history, my
geography, and reduce them and everything they have ever known
to figurines as evidence that I was in divine favor, what if all this
was in my power? Could I resist it? No one ever has.

And they were rude, they were rude to each other. They didn't
like each other very much. They didn't like each other in the way
they didn't like me, and it occurred to me that their dislike for me
was one of the few things they agreed on.

I was on a train in England with a friend, an English woman.
Before we were in England she liked me very much. In England
she didn't like me at all. She didn't like the claim I said I had on
England, she didn't like the views I had of England. I didn't like
England, she didn't like England, but she didn't like me not liking
it too. She said, "I want to show you my England, I want to show
you the England that I know and love." I had told her many times
before that I knew England and I didn't want to love it anyway. She
no longer lived in England; it was her own country, but it had not
been kind to her, so she left. On the train, the conductor was rude
to her; she asked something, and he responded in a rude way. She
became ashamed. She was ashamed at the way he treated her;
she was ashamed at the way he behaved. "This is the new England,"
she said. But I liked the conductor being rude; his behavior
seemed quite appropriate. Earlier this had happened: we had
gone to a store to buy a shirt for my husband; it was meant to be a
special present, a special shirt to wear on special occasions. This
was a store where the Prince of Wales has his shirts made, but the
shirts sold in this store are beautiful all the same. I found a shirt I
thought my husband would like and I wanted to buy him a tie to go
with it. When I couldn't decide which one to choose, the salesman
showed me a new set. He was very pleased with these, he said, because they bore the crest of the Prince of Wales, and the Prince of
Wales had never allowed his crest to decorate an article of clothing
before. There was something in the way he said it; his tone was
slavish, reverential, awed. It made me feel angry; I wanted to hit
him. I didn't do that. I said, my husband and I hate princes, my
husband would never wear anything that had a prince's anything
on it. My friend stiffened. The salesman stiffened. They both drew

themselves in, away from me. My friend told me that the prince was a symbol of her Englishness, and I could see that I had caused offense. I looked at her. She was an English person, the sort of English person I used to know at home, the sort who was nobody in England but somebody when they came to live among the people like me. There were many people I could have seen England with; that I was seeing it with this particular person, a person who reminded me of the people who showed me England long ago as I sat in church or at my desk, made me feel silent and afraid, for I wondered if, all these years of our friendship, I had had a friend or had been in the thrall of a racial memory.

I went to Bath — we, my friend and I, did this, but though we were together, I was no longer with her. The landscape was almost as familiar as my own hand, but I had never been in this place before, so how could that be again? And the streets of Bath were familiar, too, but I had never walked on them before. It was all those years of reading, starting with Roman Britain. Why did I have to know about Roman Britain? It was of no real use to me, a person living on a hot, drought-ridden island, and it is of no use to me now, and yet my head is filled with this nonsense, Roman Britain. In Bath, I drank tea in a room I had read about in a novel written in the eighteenth century. In this very same room, young women wearing those dresses that rustled and so on danced and flirted and sometimes disgraced themselves with young men, soldiers, sailors, who were on their way to Bristol or someplace like that, so many places like that where so many adventures, the outcome of which was not good for me, began. Bristol, England. A sentence that began "That night the ship sailed from Bristol, England" would end not so good for me. And then I was driving through the countryside in an English motorcar, on narrow winding roads, and they were so familiar, though I had never been on them before; and through little villages the names of which I somehow knew so well though I had never been there before. And the countryside did have all those hedges and hedges, fields hedged in. I was marveling at all the toil of it, the planting of the hedges to begin with and then the care of it, all that clipping, year after year of clipping, and I wondered at the lives of the people who would have to do this, because wherever I see and feel the hands that hold up the world, I see and feel myself and all the people who look like me.

And I said, "Those hedges" and my friend said that someone, a woman named Mrs. Rothchild, worried that the hedges weren't being taken care of properly; the farmers couldn't afford or find the help to keep up the hedges, and often they replaced them with wire fencing. I might have said to that, well if Mrs. Rothchild doesn't like the wire fencing, why doesn't she take care of the hedges herself, but I didn't. And then in those fields that were now hemmed in by wire fencing that a privileged woman didn't like was planted a vile yellow flowering bush that produced an oil, and my friend said that Mrs. Rothchild didn't like this either; it ruined the English countryside, it ruined the traditional look of the English countryside.

It was not at that moment that I wished every sentence, everything I knew, that began with England would end with "and then it all died; we don't know how, it just all died." At that moment, I was thinking, who are these people who forced me to think of them all the time, who forced me to think that the world I knew was incomplete, or without substance, or did not measure up because it was not England; that I was incomplete, or without substance, and did not measure up because I was not English. Who were these people? The person sitting next to me couldn't give me a clue; no one person could. In any case, if I had said to her, I find England ugly, I hate England; the weather is like a jail sentence, the English are a very ugly people, the food in England is like a jail sentence, the hair of English people is so straight, so dead looking, the English have an unbearable smell so different from the smell of people I know, real people of course, she would have said that I was a person full of prejudice. Apart from the fact that it is I — that is, the people who look like me — who made her aware of the unpleasantness of such a thing, the idea of such a thing, prejudice, she would have been only partly right, sort of right: I may be capable of prejudice, but my prejudices have no weight to them, my prejudices have no force behind them, my prejudices remain opinions, my prejudices remain my personal opinion. And a great feeling of rage and disappointment came over me as I looked at England, my head full of personal opinions that could not have public, my public, approval. The people I come from are powerless to do evil on grand scale.

The moment I wished every sentence, everything I knew, that began with England would end with "and then it all died, we don't know how, it just all died" was when I saw the white cliffs of Dover. I had sung hymns and recited poems that were about a longing to see the white cliffs of Dover again. At the time I sang the hymns and recited the poems, I could really long to see them again because I had never seen them at all, nor had anyone around me at the time. But there we were, groups of people longing for something we had never seen. And so there they were, the white cliffs, but they were not that pearly majestic thing I used to sing about, that thing that created such a feeling in these people that when they died in the place where I lived they had themselves buried facing a direction that would allow them to see the white cliffs of Dover when they were resurrected, as surely they would be. The white cliffs of Dover, when finally I saw them, were cliffs, but they were not white; you would only call them that if the word "white" meant something special to you; they were dirty and they were steep; they were so steep, the correct height from which all my views of England, starting with the map before me in my classroom and ending with the trip I had just taken, should jump and die and disappear forever.

Reflections and Responses

1. Note that Kincaid opens her essay with various images of England. What do these images have in common? How do they reflect colonialism? How do they reflect literature? Why do you think Kincaid begins by placing the images in the context of a classroom?

2. Consider Kincaid's account of her father's hat. In what ways does the "brown felt hat" represent England? How does Kincaid view the hat?

3. When Kincaid finally visits England, what aspects of the country does she dislike the most? What does she mean when she says toward the end of her essay that "I may be capable of prejudice, but my prejudices have no weight to them"? Do you find her opinions prejudiced? In your opinion has she or has she not "prejudged" England?

ASHRAF RUSHDY

Exquisite Corpse

When Emmett Till — a fourteen year old from Chicago visiting relatives in
Mississippi — was viciously murdered and then tossed into the Talla-
hatchie River in 1955, his mother insisted on an open-coffin funeral that
allowed photographs of her son's horribly mutilated corpse to be published
across the nation. It was a momentous political gesture; it shocked the
country and the photographs had an enormous impact on the course of the
Civil Rights movement. But why didn't the public see photographs of James
Byrd who in 1998 was brutally dragged from a pickup truck in Texas
until his body was dismembered? Would such photos, however sickening,
have had a positive effect by making us vividly see what racial hatred is ca-
pable of? In "Exquisite Corpse," African American scholar Ashraf Rushdy
compares these two racial incidents, separated by nearly a half-century,
and examines the moral authority of photography. "So why do we need to
see the corpse?" he asks. His essay provides a compelling answer.

Ashraf Rushdy is Professor of African American Studies and English
Literature at Wesleyan University. He is the author of one book on John
Milton, The Empty Garden *(1992), and two books on contemporary*
African American cultural and literary history, Neo-Slave Narratives
(1999) and Remembering Generations *(2001). Written while he was*
a Fellow at the National Humanities Center, "Exquisite Corpse" first ap-
peared in Transition *and was selected by Kathleen Norris for* The Best
American Essays 2001.

In an earlier time, a lynch mob would display the body of its victim
with impunity, often gathering around it for a group photograph.
These images, and the bodies they represented, were the icons of
white supremacy. Circulated in newspapers, the pictures displayed

the power of the white mob and the powerlessness of the black community. After the highly publicized lynching of Claude Neal in 1934, photographers took hundreds of shots of his mutilated body and sold them for fifty cents each. The photograph of Neal's hanging body eventually became a postcard. One group of white people, gathered around a burned black body, was communicating to another group in another county: they had done their part, asserted their place in the world. The image was certain to incite other communities to follow their example: this was the golden age of lynching.

The body of the victim assumed a magical quality for the lynch mob: the corpse was an object to be tortured, mutilated, collected, displayed. To snuff out life was rarely enough: more ritual was required. In 1937, when a Georgia mob was unable to lynch Willie Reid because the police had already killed him, they broke into the funeral home where he lay, carried his body to a baseball diamond, and burned it. Even a mob that had already hanged, maimed, and burned a man might still feel compelled to exhume his body in order to inflict further indignities; so it was with the corpse of George Armwood, in 1933.

As the historian Jacquelyn Dowd Hall has noted, the spectacle of lynching dramatized a social hierarchy where whites and blacks, women and men, knew their place. Blacks were terrorized, white women were vulnerable, and white men were on top, invulnerable and free. Still, whites projected immense sexual power onto blacks; the terror of lynching reflected their own anxieties.

Indeed lynching also seems to be the expression of a peculiar necrophilia, manifest in the desire to possess the bodies of victims, in the passion with which dead bodies were handled and displayed — as if they were talismans of life itself. The East Texas lynch mob that killed David Gregory in 1933 pulled out his heart and cut off his penis before tossing his body onto a pyre: those were the most potent emblems of vitality. Such actions bespeak nothing so much as a perverse fondness for the dead body.

While lynch mobs subjected the corpses of their victims to the most spectacular abuse, victims' families were more concerned with matters of the spirit. Most often they buried their loved ones in silence: for these families, the corpse was less important than the soul.

The same can be said of those families who refused to bury lynch victims. In 1889, after a mob broke into a Barnwell, South Carolina, jail and lynched eight African American men, the local black community displayed its solidarity at the funeral. More than five hundred people lined the street, and several women implored the Lord to "burn Barnwell to the ground." The community refused to bury six of the men, claiming that the whites who killed them should bear that responsibility. In Virginia, Joseph McCoy's aunt refused to bury the body of her nephew, who was lynched in 1897. "As the people killed him, they will have to bury him," she explained. The body, whether buried or left to the elements, had become a symbol of the injustice and barbarism of the white community, the failure of the nation's founding principles: let the dead bury their dead.

When Emmett Till was lynched in 1955, Mamie Till Bradley refused to hide her son's corpse. His mutilated and decomposed body was found in the Tallahatchie River three days after he died. Despite the sheriff's opposition, she insisted that her son be returned to Chicago. Bradley opened the casket as soon as it arrived at Illinois Central Terminal and promptly announced that she wanted an open-casket funeral so everyone could "see what they did to my boy." On the first day the casket was open for viewing, ten thousand people saw it; on the day of the funeral, at least two thousand mourners stood outside the packed church where the services were held. The body of Emmett Till — "his head . . . swollen and bashed in, his mouth twisted and broken" — became a new kind of icon. Emmett Till showed the world exactly what white supremacy looked like.

According to one report, Till's funeral created an "emotional explosion": "thousands of cursing, shrieking, fainting Negroes" responded to the "corpse . . . displayed 'as is.'" The Southern media denounced Bradley's decision as "macabre exhibitionism" and cheap political "exploitation." But African Americans who attended the funeral or saw pictures of Till's body were transformed. One reader congratulated the *Amsterdam News* for "putting the picture of the murdered Till boy on the front page"; a writer for the *Pittsburgh Courier* predicted that Mrs. Bradley's decision might "easily become an opening gun in a war on Dixie which can rever-

berate around the world." A photo-essay in *Jet* proved electrify-
ing: Representative Charles Diggs remarked that the "picture in
Jet magazine showing Emmett Till's mutilation . . . stimulated . . .
anger on the part of blacks all over the country." A black sociolo-
gist later wrote that "the *Jet* magazine photograph of Emmett Till's
grotesque body left an indelible impression on young Southern
blacks"; they went on to become "the vanguard of the Southern
student movement."

The influence of the *Jet* photographs has been well documented. As a girl, civil rights activist Joyce Ladner kept clippings
in a scrapbook. She responded to the picture of Till's bloated body
in the magazine "with horror that transformed itself into a promise
to alter the political and racial terrain where such a crime could
happen." Cleveland Sellers, an activist and field director in the Student Nonviolent Coordinating Committee, remembers how pictures of the corpse in black newspapers and magazines — showing
"terrible gashes and tears in the flesh . . . [giving] the appearance
of a ragged, rotting sponge" — created a stir about civil rights when
he was a youth in South Carolina. A thirteen-year-old boy named
Cassius Clay stood on a street corner in Louisville, transfixed by
pictures of Emmett Till in black newspapers and magazines: in
one picture, smiling and happy; in the other, a gruesome mockery
of a face. Muhammad Ali says he admired Mrs. Bradley, who had
"done a bold thing" in forcing the world to look at her son. Fifteen
years later, Ali met Brother Judge Aaron, a man who had survived
a Klan lynching attempt in the 1960s. (They had carved the letters
KKK into his chest and castrated him to send a "message" to
"smart-alecky . . . niggers like Martin Luther King and Reverend
Shuttleworth.") Ali responded by dedicating all his future fights to
"the unprotected people, to the victims."

By the time of Emmett Till's murder, lynching had begun to decline, and pictures of lynching victims were becoming scarce.
What had once been viewed with pride now seemed like barbarity:
the victim's body became less an icon of white supremacy than a
denunciation of it. As popular opinion turned against lynching,
the sight of lynched bodies became an embarrassment for white
communities squirming under the glare of national and international scrutiny. In fact, these corpses became potent weapons in

the political struggle to enact a law against lynching — a struggle that continues today.

The 1959 murder of Mack Charles Parker was representative of this new climate. The lynch mob wore masks to hide the identity of its members; they gave up on their original plan to castrate their victim and hang the body from a bridge: instead, they weighted the body and dumped it into the river. When Parker's body was recovered ten days later, town officials worked furiously to keep it from being entered as evidence before the Senate during deliberations on antilynching legislation. Police officers and state troopers guarded the body in a funeral home, and after *Chicago Defender* reporter Tony Rhoden managed to sneak in and take a picture of the badly mutilated body, there was a frantic search for him and his camera. Two hours after the coroner's inquest, before Parker's mother had even heard that his body had been recovered, he was buried in a hasty ceremony.

It is not clear what happened to Rhoden's photograph of Parker's body. If it was not published, it might have been because of the censorship that has restrained mainstream photojournalism in times of extremity. *Life* magazine had to wait eight months while government censors debated whether it could publish a picture of a dead American soldier on Buna Beach, New Guinea, in 1943. While pictures of dead bodies were widely published during the Vietnam War, a *Detroit Free Press* photographer had to beg military censors to approve a photograph of an American soldier crying over a body bag during the Persian Gulf War. And even in the absence of official censorship, Americans' delicate sensibilities have prevented the widespread dissemination of gruesome pictures. A *New York Times* reader wrote an angry letter to complain about a photograph of a Kosovo massacre victim in October 1998. His brief comment — "This is not something I wish to see alongside my breakfast" — aptly characterizes a reading public that does not expect graphic violence in the responsible media.

In June 1998 an African American named James Byrd was murdered in Jasper, Texas, by a white ex-con named John William King and two accomplices. It was determined that Byrd's body had been dragged from a pickup truck and that the body had been dismembered along the route: the head, neck, and right arm were severed from the torso. During King's trial in February 1999, the prosecution presented photographs that documented Byrd's suffering: his knees, heels, buttocks, and elbows were ground to the bone; eight of his left ribs and nine of his right were broken; his ankles were cut to the bone by the chains that attached him to the truck. A pathologist testified that Byrd's "penis and testicles [were] shredded from his body," and we learned, with horror, that "Mr. Byrd was alive up to the point where he hit the culvert and his head separated from his body." For months, the story of James Byrd's brutal slaying transfixed the nation.

No picture of James Byrd's corpse has ever been published. Indeed, when the *New York Times* interviewed several editors for a story on newspaper photography, none had seen the prosecution's photographs. In a strange twist of fate, however, King's own body served as evidence in the state's case against him: it seems he had a passion for racist tattoos. Prosecutors showed thirty-three slides and photographs of the images inscribed on King's body: a cross with a black man hanging from it, a swastika, the insignia of Hitler's SS, a woodpecker peeking out from a Ku Klux Klan hood, the Virgin Mary holding a horned baby Jesus, images of Church of Satan founder Anton La Vey, goat heads, Valentine hearts turned upside down, playing cards showing eights and aces (the dead man's poker hand), a dragon emblazoned with the words *Beto I* (the Texas prison where King was incarcerated from 1995 to 1997), the slogan *Aryan Pride,* and several allusions to "peckerwoods" — rednecks — in prison. (It had been reported earlier that King had a tattoo of Tinkerbell on his penis; the DA declined to mention this.) It was King's body, not Byrd's, that became an advertisement for white supremacy, and judging by the John William King tribute pages that have sprung up on the Internet, the advertisement has been successful.

It is not likely that anyone other than the lawyers, the jury, and the courtroom spectators will ever see the photographs that the court accepted as evidence. In the only well-known image of Byrd, he is wearing a Colorado Rockies baseball cap, looking directly into the camera. The most graphic picture appeared on the cover of the *Boston Globe* on June 12, 1998: it showed the dried blood that stained the Jasper street where Byrd's torso had been dragged.

The Byrd family was singularly gracious in promoting reconciliation and defusing racial hatred in the aftermath of the murder, and it may have been out of respect for their feelings that photographs of James Byrd's body were not published. Indeed, for about six weeks after the murder, the major story in Jasper was the tension between the Byrd family's desire for privacy and activists' eagerness for publicity. Even as reporters set up a media circus around the funeral, they wrote compassionately of the pain that politicians and political advocacy groups created for the Byrds. When the Klan gathered for a rally to distance themselves from John William King and his cohorts, and the Dallas-based New Black Panthers gathered to respond to the Klan, the Byrd family tried to remain above the fray. As the *Houston Chronicle* reported, "Byrd's family was uncomfortable with the idea of turning him into a national symbol, and would have preferred to have had a quieter service without the political rallying cries."

Despite these pleas, this case demanded national attention. In newspaper stories that pit a grieving family wishing for peace and quiet against a flock of politically motivated vultures intent on creating a self-serving spectacle, the true complexity of the Jasper saga is lost. It is despicable, of course, to use Byrd's funeral to promote racism, as the Klan did; and it is wrongheaded to use the event to promote armed self-defense, as the New Black Panthers did. But there are other considerations — considerations that are at least as compelling as a family's grief. Those who attempted to situate the murder in its historical context, while respecting the family's wishes for a degree of privacy, should be praised.

At James Byrd's funeral, Jesse Jackson said that "Brother Byrd's innocent blood alone could very well be the blood that changes the course of our country, because no one has captured the nation's attention like this tragedy." Jackson asked the town of Jasper to erect a monument in Byrd's memory, "as a tangible protest against hate crimes." I applaud Jackson's sense of urgency, but his proposal is in the wrong tenor. Indeed, I would suggest that Jackson went wrong precisely when he departed from his insight: spilled blood is a valuable representation of the search for justice. In his resolve to create a monument, he shifted his focus from blood to image, from body to stone.

The connections between the Till and Byrd lynchings are striking. Part of the evidence against King was an *Esquire* article on the Till lynching that he had kept in his apartment: this suggested that his actions were premeditated. Mamie Till Bradley spoke about the

Jasper murder on a New York radio talk show; two weeks later, she held the hand of James Byrd's father at a Harlem memorial service. There were some coincidences, too: after the trial of Till's lynchers, newspapers reported that Till's father had been hanged in 1944, after he was convicted of rape and murder while stationed in Italy with the army; after the trial in the Jasper case, it was revealed that John William King's uncle had been acquitted of killing a gay man in 1939. More than half a century of hate crimes has ensnared these families — the Tills, the Byrds, the Kings — in America's quiet history of guilt and grief.

But there are disparities. In 1955, the American public learned about Emmett Till's life and they saw his death: the contrast between a vibrant youth and a violent end helped ignite the outcry that followed. In 1998, even as contemporary readers learned about James Byrd's life, they were denied the pictures that might have inspired a greater and more productive outrage. On February 24, 1999, the same day the *New York Times* reported the jury's verdict in the Jasper trial, it ran two other stories about hate crimes: in Virginia, a jury convicted a white teenager of burning a cross on the lawn of an interracial couple; and in Louisiana, a white man was sentenced to twenty years in prison for trying to set fire to two cars and their African American occupants. Hatred is far more pervasive than we would like to admit, and representations of it are critical to the education of the majority of white Americans who believe that racism was a phenomenon that ended sometime in the sixties.

Of course, publishing pictures of James Byrd's corpse might fan the flames of white supremacy. There were reports of copycat crimes within a week of Byrd's murder: in Louisiana, where three white men taunted a black man with racial epithets while trying to drag him alongside their car; and in Illinois, where three white boys assaulted a black teenager in almost exactly the same way. Three months later, New York City police officers and firefighters parodied Byrd's murder by imitating it in a Labor Day parade float. And while the trial was under way, a Washington, D.C., radio announcer — the "Greaseman" — responded to a clip from a song by soul singer Lauryn Hill by commenting, "No wonder people drag them behind trucks." (He was fired the next day.) In a climate where people still respond to lynching with jokes and mimicry, pictures of James Byrd's body might have fed this evil appetite.

So why do we need to see the corpse? It is possible that pictures of graphic violence still have the power to make an impression. At least one member of the jury found the pictures of Byrd's body almost unbearable; she had to force herself to turn each page. Indeed, one Jasper resident suggested that the lynchers should be sentenced to life in a cell "with pictures of James Byrd's body parts pasted all over the walls" — expressing the hope that even the murderers would find such images sickening. This kind of shock therapy might work for the public at large. It would have been difficult for policemen and firemen in New York, or a DJ in Washington, to joke about the murder of James Byrd if their jokes summoned images of the horrific crimes they were taking so lightly.

These photographs could also turn the tide of history once again. African American men have long been portrayed as comic buffoons or dangerous criminals, and a large segment of this nation remains incapable of imagining black suffering. A study concerning the effects of race on the death penalty found that there is "neither strong nor consistent" evidence of discrimination against black defendants in death penalty trials. But the study also concluded that the race of the victim matters greatly in juries' decisions to sentence a murderer to death. Convicted murderers who kill a white victim are more than four times as likely to be condemned to death as those who kill a black victim. Only 8 whites have been executed for murdering black Americans since the death penalty was reinstated in 1977, but 123 blacks have been put to death for murdering whites. Predominantly white juries seem unable to sympathize with black crime victims. It is possible that this crime, fixed in memory, could transform the nation's moral imagination.

To have wounded the Byrd family any more would have been intolerable; and pictures of their relative's body would have wounded them. To have created conditions that satisfied the blood lust of white supremacists would have been criminal; and photographs of the remains of James Byrd would have given them glee. To lower the already low level of public discourse would be shameful; and publishing more photographs of violence is not likely to elevate it. But our primary concern must be to prevent another family from feeling as the Byrd family now feels; we cannot determine how best to combat hatred by focusing on the response of the most incorri-

gible purveyors of hatred. The past teaches us that images of terror — used responsibly — can foster a climate in which terror is no
longer tolerated. I suggest that we aspire to the courageous example of Mamie Till Bradley, not the cautious compromises of newspaper editors who fear to offend their readerships. A citizenry
alert to the horror of hate crimes would be compensation enough.

Reflections and Responses

1. Why is Emmett Till's murder important to the argument Rushdy
constructs? Do you think the two incidents are similar enough to
make his case or do you think important distinctions can be made?

2. Why do you think Rushdy avoids simply contrasting only the Till
and Byrd murders? Why does he introduce many other examples of
lynchings and murders? What historical point is he making?

3. Note that Rushdy's argument does not merely dismiss those
who opposed publishing the Byrd photographs. What are their arguments? Why might Byrd's family not want to publicize the photos? Why would newspapers oppose? What other reasons does
Rushdy offer in favor of those who oppose making the photos
available? Do you agree with Rushdy or do you think Byrd's photos
would have served no useful purpose?

PETER SINGER

The Singer Solution
to World Poverty

Philosophy can sometimes be quite practical: the following essay, which argues for our moral responsibility to behave altruistically, even contains two toll-free telephone numbers the reader can use to make a two-hundred-dollar contribution. Peter Singer, the famous and controversial ethical philosopher, sincerely hopes that his argument will convince you to contribute. He reinforces his argument with several intriguing hypothetical situations that put readers in the driver's seat of a moral dilemma. How will you respond? Would you agree not to buy another hooded Gap sweatshirt or that new Eminem CD that you don't really need and instead give the money to UNICEF?

Peter Singer was born in Melbourne, Australia, and studied philosophy there and at the University of Oxford. One of the leading thinkers of the animal-rights movement, his influential books on ethical issues include Animal Liberation *(1975),* Practical Ethics *(1979), and* Rethinking Life and Death *(1995). His recent publications are* Writings on an Ethical Life *and* A Darwinian Left: Politics, Evolution, and Cooperation, *both of which appeared in 2000. He is currently DeCamp Professor of Bioethics in the Center for Human Values, Princeton University. "The Singer Solution to World Poverty" originally appeared in* The New York Times Magazine *and was selected by Alan Lightman for* The Best American Essays, *2000.*

In the Brazilian film *Central Station,* Dora is a retired schoolteacher who makes ends meet by sitting at the station writing letters for illiterate people. Suddenly she has an opportunity to pocket a thousand dollars. All she has to do is persuade a homeless nine-year-old boy to follow her to an address she has been given. (She is told he will be adopted by wealthy foreigners.) She delivers the boy, gets the money, spends some of it on a television set, and settles down to enjoy her new acquisition. Her neighbor spoils the fun, however, by telling her that the boy was too old to be adopted — he will be killed and his organs sold for transplantation. Perhaps Dora knew this all along, but after her neighbor's plain speaking, she spends a troubled night. In the morning Dora resolves to take the boy back.

Suppose Dora had told her neighbor that it is a tough world, other people have nice new TVs too, and if selling the kid is the only way she can get one, well, he was only a street kid. She would then have become, in the eyes of the audience, a monster. She redeems herself only by being prepared to bear considerable risks to save the boy.

At the end of the movie, in cinemas in the affluent nations of the world, people who would have been quick to condemn Dora if she had not rescued the boy go home to places far more comfortable than her apartment. In fact, the average family in the United States spends almost one third of his income on things that are no more necessary to them than Dora's new TV was to her. Going out to nice restaurants, buying new clothes because the old ones are no longer stylish, vacationing at beach resorts — so much of our income is spent on things not essential to the preservation of our lives and health. Donated to one of a number of charitable agencies, that money could mean the difference between life and death for children in need.

All of which raises a question: in the end, what is the ethical distinction between a Brazilian who sells a homeless child to organ peddlers and an American who already has a TV and upgrades to a better one, knowing that the money could be donated to an organization that would use it to save the lives of kids in need?

Of course, there are several differences between the two situations that could support different moral judgments about them. For one thing, to be able to consign a child to death when he is standing right in front of you takes a chilling kind of heartlessness; it is much easier to ignore an appeal for money to help children you will never meet. Yet for a utilitarian philosopher like myself — that is, one who judges whether acts are right or wrong by their consequences — if the upshot of the American's failure to donate the money is that one more kid dies on the streets of a Brazilian city, then it is in some sense just as bad as selling the kid to the organ peddlers. But one doesn't need to embrace my utilitarian ethic to see that at the very least, there is a troubling incongruity in being so quick to condemn Dora for taking the child to the organ peddlers while at the same time not regarding the American consumer's behavior as raising a serious moral issue.

In his 1996 book, *Living High and Letting Die,* the New York University philosopher Peter Unger presented an ingenious series of imaginary examples designed to probe our intuitions about whether it is wrong to live well without giving substantial amounts of money to help people who are hungry, malnourished, or dying from easily treatable illnesses like diarrhea. Here's my paraphrase of one of these examples:

Bob is close to retirement. He has invested most of his savings in a very rare and valuable old car, a Bugatti, which he has not been able to insure. The Bugatti is his pride and joy. In addition to the pleasure he gets from driving and caring for his car, Bob knows that its rising market value means that he will always be able to sell it and live comfortably after retirement. One day when Bob is out for a drive, he parks the Bugatti near the end of a railway siding and goes for a walk up the track. As he does so, he sees that a runaway train, with no one aboard, is running down the railway track. Looking farther down the track, he sees the small figure of a child very likely to be killed by the runaway train. He can't stop the train and the child is too far away to warn of the danger, but he can throw a switch that will divert the train down the siding where his Bugatti is parked. Then nobody will be killed — but the train will destroy his Bugatti. Thinking of his joy in owning the car and the financial security it represents, Bob decides not to throw the switch. The child is killed. For many years to come, Bob enjoys owning his Bugatti and the financial security it represents.

Bob's conduct, most of us will immediately respond, was gravely wrong. Unger agrees. But then he reminds us that we too have opportunities to save the lives of children. We can give to organizations like UNICEF or Oxfam America. How much would we have to give one of these organizations to have a high probability of saving the life of a child threatened by easily preventable diseases? (I do not believe that children are more worth saving than adults, but since no one can argue that children have brought their poverty on themselves, focusing on them simplifies the issues.) Unger called up some experts and used the information they provided to offer some plausible estimates that include the cost of raising money, administrative expenses, and the cost of delivering aid where it is most needed. By his calculation, $200 in donations would help a sickly two-year-old transform into a healthy six-year-old — offering safe passage through childhood's most dangerous years. To show how practical philosophical argument can be, Unger even tells his readers that they can easily donate funds by using their credit card and calling one of these toll-free numbers: (800) 367-5437 for UNICEF; (800) 693-2687 for Oxfam America.

Now you too have the information you need to save a child's life. How should you judge yourself if you don't do it? Think again about Bob and his Bugatti. Unlike Dora, Bob did not have to look into the eyes of the child he was sacrificing for his own material comfort. The child was a complete stranger to him and too far away to relate to in an intimate, personal way. Unlike Dora too, he did not mislead the child or initiate the chain of events imperiling him. In all these respects, Bob's situation resembles that of people able but unwilling to donate to overseas aid and differs from Dora's situation.

If you still think that it was very wrong of Bob not to throw the switch that would have diverted the train and saved the child's life, then it is hard to see how you could deny that it is also very wrong not to send money to one of the organizations listed above. Unless, that is, there is some morally important difference between the two situations that I have overlooked.

Is it the practical uncertainties about whether aid will really reach the people who need it? Nobody who knows the world of overseas aid can doubt that such uncertainties exist. But Unger's figure of $200 to save a child's life was reached after he had made conservative assumptions about the proportion of the money donated that will actually reach its target.

One genuine difference between Bob and those who can afford to donate to overseas aid organizations but don't is that only Bob can save the child on the tracks, whereas there are hundreds of millions of people who can give $200 to overseas aid organizations. The problem is that most of them aren't doing it. Does this mean that it is all right for you not to do it?

Suppose that there were more owners of priceless vintage cars — Carol, Dave, Emma, Fred, and so on, down to Ziggy — all in exactly the same situation as Bob, with their own siding and their own switch, all sacrificing the child in order to preserve their own cherished car. Would that make it all right for Bob to do the same? To answer this question affirmatively is to endorse follow-the-crowd ethics — the kind of ethics that led many Germans to look away when the Nazi atrocities were being committed. We do not excuse them because others were behaving no better.

We seem to lack a sound basis for drawing a clear moral line between Bob's situation and that of any reader of this article with $200 to spare who does not donate it to an overseas aid agency. These readers seem to be acting at least as badly as Bob was acting when he chose to let the runaway train hurtle toward the unsuspecting child. In the light of this conclusion, I trust that many readers will reach for the phone and donate that $200. Perhaps you should do it before reading further.

Now that you have distinguished yourself morally from people who put their vintage cars ahead of a child's life, how about treating yourself and your partner to dinner at your favorite restaurant? But wait. The money you will spend at the restaurant could also help save the lives of children overseas! True, you weren't planning to blow $200 tonight, but if you were to give up dining out just for one month, you would easily save that amount. And what is one month's dining out compared to a child's life? There's the rub. Since there are a lot of desperately needy children in the world, there will always be another child whose life you could save for another $200. Are you therefore obliged to keep giving until you have nothing left? At what point can you stop?

Hypothetical examples can easily become farcical. Consider Bob. How far past losing the Bugatti should he go? Imagine that Bob had got his foot stuck in the track of the siding, and if he diverted the train, then before it rammed the car it would also amputate his big toe. Should he still throw the switch? What if it would amputate his foot? His entire leg?

As absurd as the Bugatti scenario gets when pushed to extremes, the point it raises is a serious one: only when the sacrifices become very significant indeed would most people be prepared to say that Bob does nothing wrong when he decides not to throw the switch. Of course, most people could be wrong; we can't decide moral issues by taking opinion polls. But consider for yourself the level of sacrifice that you would demand of Bob, and then think about how much money you would have to give away in order to make a sacrifice that is roughly equal to that. It's almost certainly much, much more than $200. For most middle-class Americans, it could easily be more like $200,000.

Isn't it counterproductive to ask people to do so much? Don't we run the risk that many will shrug their shoulders and say that morality, so conceived, is fine for saints but not for them? I accept that we are unlikely to see, in the near or even medium-term future, a world in which it is normal for wealthy Americans to give the bulk of their wealth to strangers. When it comes to praising or blaming people for what they do, we tend to use a standard that is relative to some conception of normal behavior. Comfortably off Americans who give, say, 10 percent of their income to overseas aid organizations are so far ahead of most of their equally comfortable fellow citizens that I wouldn't go out of my way to chastise them for not doing more. Nevertheless, they should be doing much more, and they are in no position to criticize Bob for failing to make the much greater sacrifice of his Bugatti.

At this point various objections may crop up. Someone may say, "If every citizen living in the affluent nations contributed his or her share, I wouldn't have to make such a drastic sacrifice, because long before such levels were reached the resources would have been there to save the lives of all those children dying from lack of food or medical care. So why should I give more than my fair share?" Another, related objection is that the government ought to increase its overseas aid allocations, since that would spread the burden more equitably across all taxpayers.

Yet the question of how much we ought to give is a matter to be decided in the real world — and that, sadly, is a world in which we know that most people do not, and in the immediate future will not, give substantial amounts to overseas aid agencies. We

know too that at least in the next year, the United States government is not going to meet even the very modest United Nations–
recommended target of 0.7 percent of gross national product; at the
moment it lags far below that, at 0.09 percent, not even half of
Japan's 0.22 percent or a tenth of Denmark's 0.97 percent. Thus, we
know that the money we can give beyond that theoretical "fair share"
is still going to save lives that would otherwise be lost. While the idea
that no one need do more than his or her fair share is a powerful
one, should it prevail if we know that others are not doing their fair
share and that children will die preventable deaths unless we do
more than our fair share? That would be taking fairness too far.

Thus, this ground for limiting how much we ought to give also
fails. In the world as it is now, I can see no escape from the conclusion that each one of us with wealth surplus to his or her essential
needs should be giving most of it to help people suffering from
poverty so dire as to be life-threatening. That's right: I'm saying
that you shouldn't buy that new car, take that cruise, redecorate
the house, or get that pricy new suit. After all, a thousand-dollar
suit could save five children's lives.

So how does my philosophy break down in dollars and cents? An
American household with an income of $50,000 spends around
$30,000 annually on necessities, according to the Conference
Board, a nonprofit economic research organization. Therefore,
for a household bringing in $50,000 a year, donations to help the
world's poor should be as close as possible to $20,000. The $30,000
required for necessities holds for higher incomes as well. So a
household making $100,000 could cut a yearly check for $70,000.
Again, the formula is simple: whatever money you're spending on
luxuries, not necessities, should be given away.

Now, evolutionary psychologists tell us that human nature just
isn't sufficiently altruistic to make it plausible that many people
will sacrifice so much for strangers. On the facts of human nature,
they might be right, but they would be wrong to draw a moral conclusion from those facts. If it is the case that we ought to do things
that, predictably, most of us won't do, then let's face that fact head-on.
Then, if we value the life of a child more than going to fancy
restaurants, the next time we dine out we will know that we could
have done something better with our money. If that makes living a
morally decent life extremely arduous, well, then that is the way
things are. If we don't do it, then we should at least know that we

are failing to live a morally decent life — not because it is good to wallow in guilt but because knowing where we should be going is the first step toward heading in that direction.

When Bob first grasped the dilemma that faced him as he stood by that railway switch, he must have thought how extraordinarily unlucky he was to be placed in a situation in which he must choose between the life of an innocent child and the sacrifice of most of his savings. But he was not unlucky at all. We are all in that situation.

Reflections and Responses

1. Do you find Singer's hypothetical examples convincing? If you place yourself in the situations he describes, do you reach the same conclusions he does? Can you refute his hypothetical situations?

2. At one point, Singer identifies himself as a "utilitarian philosopher," that is, "one who judges whether acts are right or wrong by their consequences." Do you find any limitations with this manner of evaluating right and wrong? Can you rewrite Singer's hypothetical examples in such a way that the "right" decision would perhaps lead to a bad consequence? Suppose, for example, that Bob pulled the switch and saved the boy's life, but another child hiding in the runaway train was killed in the collision with Bob's fancy automobile. Would that child's death be a direct consequence of Bob's apparently generous act? Would criminal charges be filed against Bob? Consider other variations.

3. Note that throughout the essay Singer argues for just one cause — child poverty. Why do you think he chose this and not a different sort of cause? What if he had selected AIDS research or Amnesty International as likely ways to help human suffering? Would these be just as effective? Why or why not? And if you did give your money to relieve child poverty, would you be making a conscious decision NOT to assist the causes of AIDS or cancer research or the Red Cross, or any other legitimate charitable organization?

SHELBY STEELE

On Being Black
and Middle Class

One of the most controversial selections to have appeared in The Best
American Essay *series, Shelby Steele's 1988 essay disturbed readers who
saw it not as a black writer's candid account of his divided identity but
rather as an assimilationist endorsement of white America. In refusing to
define himself solely along racial lines, Steele appeared to be turning his
back on his own people. His essay, however, calls into question this very
dilemma: Steele wonders why black middle-class Americans are somehow expected to celebrate the black underclass as the "purest" representation of
African American identity. While maintaining that he has more in common with middle-class Americans than with underclass blacks, Steele con-
fesses that he often finds himself contriving to be black, aligning himself
with a "victim-focused black identity." He concludes his essay with a distinction he believes African Americans must make if they are to enjoy the opportunities open to them: they must learn, he says, to distinguish between
"actual victimization" and "identification with the victim's status." In his
resistance to that kind of "identification," Steele establishes his own "identity" as a writer and individual.*

*Shelby Steele is a research fellow at the Hoover Institution, Stanford
University. His collection of essays,* The Content of Our Character,
won the National Book Critics Circle Award *for general nonfiction in
1991. His essays have appeared in a wide variety of periodicals, including*
Harper's, The American Scholar, Commentary, The New Republic, Confrontation, Black World, *and* The New York Times Magazine. *His most recent book is* A Dream Deferred: The Second Betrayal
of Black Freedom in America *(1998). "On Being Black and Middle*

Class" originally appeared in Commentary *(1988) and was selected by* Geoffrey Wolff *for* The Best American Essays 1989.

Not long ago, a friend of mine, black like myself, said to me that the term "black middle class" was actually a contradiction in terms. Race, he insisted, blurred class distinctions among blacks. If you were black, you were just black and that was that. When I argued, he let his eyes roll at my naiveté. Then he went on. For us, as black professionals, it was an exercise in self-flattery, a pathetic pretension, to give meaning to such a distinction. Worse, the very idea of class threatened the unity that was vital to the black community as a whole. After all, since when had white America taken note of anything but color when it came to blacks? He then reminded me of an old Malcolm X line that had been popular in the sixties. Question: What is a black man with a Ph.D.? Answer: A nigger.

For many years I had been on my friend's side of this argument. Much of my conscious thinking on the old conundrum of race and class was shaped during my high school and college years in the race-charged sixties, when the fact of my race took on an almost religious significance. Progressively, from the mid-sixties on, more and more aspects of my life found their explanation, their justification, and their motivation in race. My youthful concerns about career, romance, money, values, and even styles of dress became a subject to consultation with various oracular sources of racial wisdom. And these ranged from a figure as ennobling as Martin Luther King, Jr., to the underworld elegance of dress I found in jazz clubs on the South Side of Chicago. Everywhere there were signals, and in those days I considered myself so blessed with clarity and direction that I pitied my white classmates who found more embarrassment than guidance in the fact of *their* race. In 1968, inflated by my new power, I took a mischievous delight in calling them culturally disadvantaged.

But now, hearing my friend's comment was like hearing a priest from a church I'd grown disenchanted with. I understood him, but my faith was weak. What had sustained me in the sixties sounded monotonous and off the mark in the eighties. For me, race had lost much of its juju, its singular capacity to conjure meaning. And today, when I honestly look at my life and the lives of many other middle-class blacks I know, I can see that race never fully explained our situation in American society. Black though I may be, it is impossible for me to sit in my single-family house with two cars in the driveway and a swing set in the back yard and *not* see the role class has played in my life. And how can my friend, similarly raised and similiarly situated, not see it?

Yet despite my certainty I felt a sharp tug of guilt as I tried to explain myself over my friend's skepticism. He is a man of many comedic facial expressions and, as I spoke, his brow lifted in extreme moral alarm as if I were uttering the unspeakable. His clear implication was that I was being elitist and possibly (dare he suggest?) anti-black — crimes for which there might well be no redemption. He pretended to fear for me. I chuckled along with him, but inwardly I did wonder at myself. Though I never doubted the validity of what I was saying, I felt guilty saying it. Why?

After he left (to retrieve his daughter from a dance lesson) I realized that the trap I felt myself in had a tiresome familiarity and, in a sort of slow-motion epiphany, I began to see its outline. It was like the suddenly sharp vision one has at the end of a burdensome marriage when all the long-repressed incompatibilities come undeniably to light.

What became clear to me is that people like myself, my friend, and middle-class blacks generally are caught in a very specific double bind that keeps two equally powerful elements of our identity at odds with each other. The middle-class values by which we were raised — the work ethic, the importance of education, the value of property ownership, of respectability, of "getting ahead," of stable family life, of initiative, of self-reliance, etc. — are, in themselves, raceless and even assimilationist. They urge us toward participation in the American mainstream, toward integration, toward a strong identification with the society — and toward the entire constellation of qualities that are implied in the word "individualism." These values are almost rules for how to prosper in a democratic, free-enterprise society that admires and rewards individual effort. They tell us to work hard for ourselves and our families and to seek our opportunities whenever they appear, inside or outside the confines of whatever ethnic group we may belong to.

But the particular pattern of racial identification that emerged in the sixties and that still prevails today urges middle-class blacks (and all blacks) in the opposite direction. This pattern asks us to see

ourselves as an embattled minority, and it urges an adversarial
stance toward the mainstream, an emphasis on ethnic consciousness
over individualism. It is organized around an implied separatism.
The opposing thrust of these two parts of our identity results in
the double bind of middle-class blacks. There is no forward movement on either plane that does not constitute backward movement
on the other. This was the familiar trap I felt myself in while talking with my friend. As I spoke about class, his eyes reminded me
that I was betraying race. Clearly, the two indispensable parts of
my identity were a threat to each other.

Of course when you think about it, class and race are both similar in some ways and also naturally opposed. They are two forms of
collective identity with boundaries that intersect. But whether they
clash or peacefully coexist has much to do with how they are defined. Being both black and middle class becomes a double bind
when class and race are defined in sharply antagonistic terms, so
that one must be repressed to appease the other.

But what is the "substance" of these two identities, and how does
each establish itself in an individual's overall identity? It seems to
me that when we identify with any collective we are basically identifying with images that tell us what it means to be a member of
that collective. Identity is not the same thing as the fact of membership in a collective; it is, rather, a form of self-definition, facili-
tated by images of what we wish our membership in the collective
to mean. In this sense, the images we identify with may reflect the
aspirations of the collective more than they reflect reality, and
their content can vary with shifts in those aspirations.

But the process of identification is usually dialectical. It is just as
necessary to say what we are *not* as it is to say what we are — so that
finally identification comes about by embracing a polarity of positive and negative images. To identify as middle class, for example, I
must have both positive and negative images of what being middle
class entails; then I will know what I should and should not be
doing in order to be middle class. The same goes for racial identity.

In the racially turbulent sixties the polarity of images that came
to define racial identification was very antagonistic to the polarity
that defined middle-class identification. One might say that the
positive images of one lined up with the negative images of the
other, so that to identify with both required either a contortionist's

flexibility or a dangerous splitting of the self. The double bind of the black middle class was in place. . . .

The black middle class has always defined its class identity by means of positive images gleaned from middle- and upper-class white society, and by means of negative images of lower-class blacks. This habit goes back to the institution of slavery itself, when "house" slaves both mimicked the whites they served and held themselves above the "field" slaves. But in the sixties the old bourgeois impulse to dissociate from the lower classes (the "we-they" distinction) backfired when racial identity suddenly called for the celebration of this same black lower class. One of the qualities of a double bind is that one feels it more than sees it, and I distinctly remember the tension and strange sense of dishonesty I felt in those days as I moved back and forth like a bigamist between the demands of class and race.

Though my father was born poor, he achieved middle-class standing through much hard work and sacrifice (one of his favorite words) and by identifying fully with solid middle-class values — mainly hard work, family life, property ownership, and education for his children (all four of whom have advanced degrees). In his mind these were not so much values as laws of nature. People who embodied them made up the positive images in his class polarity. The negative images came largely from the blacks he had left behind because they were "going nowhere."

No one in my family remembers how it happened, but as time went on, the negative images congealed into an imaginary character named Sam, who, from the extensive service we put him to, quickly grew to mythic proportions. In our family lore he was sometimes a trickster, sometimes a boob, but always possessed of a catalogue of sly faults that gave up graphic images of everything we should not be. On sacrifice: "Sam never thinks about tomorrow. He wants it now or he doesn't care about it." On work: "Sam doesn't favor it too much." On children: "Sam likes to have them but not to raise them." On money: "Sam drinks it up and pisses it out." On fidelity: "Sam has to have two or three women." On clothes: "Sam features loud clothes. He likes to see and be seen." And so on. Sam's persona amounted to a negative instruction manual in class identity.

I don't think that any of us believed Sam's faults were accurate representations of lower-class black life. He was an instrument of self-definition, not of sociological accuracy. It never occurred to us that he looked very much like the white racist stereotype of blacks, or that he might have been a manifestation of our own racial self-hatred. He simply gave us a counterpoint against which to express our aspirations. If self-hatred was a factor, it was not, for us, a matter of hating lower-class blacks but of hating what we did not want to be.

Still, hate or love aside, it is fundamentally true that my middle-class identity involved a dissociation from images of lower-class black life and a corresponding identification with values and patterns of responsibility that are common to the middle class everywhere. These values sent me a clear message: be both an individual and a responsible citizen; understand that the quality of your life will approximately reflect the quality of effort you put into it; know that individual responsibility is the basis of freedom and that the limitations imposed by fate (whether fair or unfair) are no excuse for passivity.

Whether I live up to these values or not, I know that my acceptance of them is the result of lifelong conditioning. I know also that I share this conditioning with middle-class people of all races and that I can no more easily be free of it than I can be free of my race. Whether all this got started because the black middle class modeled itself on the white middle class is no longer relevant. For the middle-class black, conditioned by these values from birth, the sense of meaning they provide is as immutable as the color of his skin.

I started the sixties in high school feeling that my class-conditioning was the surest way to overcome racial barriers. My racial identity was pretty much taken for granted. After all, it was obvious to the world that I was black. Yet I ended the sixties in graduate school a little embarrassed by my class background and with an almost desperate need to be "black." The tables had turned. I knew very clearly (though I struggled to repress it) that my aspirations and my sense of how to operate in the world came from my class background, yet "being black" required certain attitudes and stances that made me feel secretly a little duplicitous. The inner compatibility of class and race I had known in 1960 was gone.

For blacks, the decade between 1960 and 1969 saw racial identification undergo the same sort of transformation that national identity undergoes in times of war. It became more self-conscious, more narrowly focused, more prescribed, less tolerant of opposition. It spawned an implicit party line, which tended to disallow competing forms of identity. Race-as-identity was lifted from the relative slumber it knew in the fifties and pressed into service in a social and political war against oppression. It was redefined along sharp adversarial lines and directed toward the goal of mobilizing the great mass of black Americans in this warlike effort. It was imbued with a strong moral authority, useful for denouncing those who opposed it and for celebrating those who honored it as a positive achievement rather than as a mere birthright.

The form of racial identification that quickly evolved to meet this challenge presented blacks as a racial monolith, a singular people with a common experience of oppression. Differences within the race, no matter how ineradicable, had to be minimized. Class distinctions were one of the first such differences to be sacrificed, since they not only threatened racial unity but also seemed to stand in contradiction to the principle of equality which was the announced goal of the movement for racial progress. The discomfort I felt in 1969, the vague but relentless sense of duplicity, was the result of a historical necessity that put my race and class at odds, that was asking me to cast aside the distinction of my class and identify with a monolithic view of my race.

If the form of this racial identity was the monolith, its substance was victimization. The civil rights movement and the more radical splinter groups of the late sixties were all dedicated to ending racial victimization, and the form of black identity that emerged to facilitate this goal made blackness and victimization virtually synonymous. Since it was our victimization more than any other variable that identified and unified us, moreover, it followed logically that the purest black was the poor black. It was images of him that clustered around the positive pole of the race polarity; all other blacks were, in effect, required to identify with him in order to confirm their own blackness.

Certainly there were more dimensions to the black experience than victimization, but no other had the same capacity to fire the indignation needed for war. So, again out of historical necessity, victimization became the overriding focus of racial identity. But this only deepened the double bind for middle-class blacks like me.

When it came to class we were accustomed to defining ourselves against lower-class blacks and identifying with at least the values of middle-class whites; when it came to race we were now being asked to identify with images of lower-class blacks and to see whites, middle class or otherwise, as victimizers. Negative lining up with positive, we were called upon to reject what we had previously embraced and to embrace what we had previously rejected. To put it still more personally, the Sam figure I had been raised to define myself against had now become the "real" black I was expected to identify with.

The fact that the poor black's new status was only passively earned by the condition of his victimization, not by assertive, positive action, made little difference. Status was status apart from the means by which it was achieved, and along with it came a certain power — the power to define the terms of access to that status, to say who was black and who was not. If a lower-class black said you were not really "black" — a sellout, an Uncle Tom — the judgment was all the more devastating because it carried the authority of his status. And this judgment soon enough came to be accepted by many whites as well.

In graduate school I was once told by a white professor, "Well, but . . . you're not really black. I mean, you're not disadvantaged." In his mind my lack of victim status disqualified me from the race itself. More recently I was complimented by a black student for speaking reasonably correct English, "proper" English as he put it. "But I don't know if I really want to talk like that," he went on. "Why not?" I asked. "Because then I wouldn't be black no more," he replied without a pause.

To overcome his marginal status, the middle-class black had to identify with a degree of victimization that was beyond his actual experience. In college (and well beyond) we used to play a game called "nap matching." It was a game of one-upmanship, in which we sat around outdoing each other with stories of racial victimization, symbolically measured by the naps of our hair. Most of us were middle class and so had few personal stories to relate, but if we could not match naps with our own biographies, we would move on to those legendary tales of victimization that came to us from the public domain.

The single story that sat atop the pinnacle of racial victimization for us was that of Emmett Till, the Northern black teenager who, on a visit to the South in 1955, was killed and grotesquely mutilated for supposedly looking at or whistling at (we were never sure which, though we argued the point endlessly) a white woman. Oh, how we probed his story, finding in his youth and Northern upbringing the quintessential embodiment of black innocence, brought down by a white evil so portentous and apocalyptic, so gnarled and hideous, that it left us with a feeling not far from awe. By telling his story and others like it, we came to *feel* the immutability of our victimization, its utter indigenousness, as a thing on this earth like dirt or sand or water.*

Of course, these sessions were a ritual of group identification, a means by which we, as middle-class blacks, could be at one with our race. But why were we, who had only a moderate experience of victimization (and that offset by opportunities our parents never had), so intent on assimilating or appropriating an identity that in so many ways contradicted our own? Because, I think, the sense of innocence that is always entailed in feeling victimized filled us with a corresponding feeling of entitlement, or even license, that helped us endure our vulnerability on a largely white college campus.

In my junior year in college I rode to a debate tournament with three white students and our faculty coach, an elderly English professor. The experience of being the lone black in a group of whites was so familiar to me that I thought nothing of it as our trip began. But then halfway through the trip the professor casually turned to me and, in an isn't-the-world-funny sort of tone, said that he had just refused to rent an apartment in a house he owned to a "very nice" black couple because their color would "offend" the white couple who lived downstairs. His eyebrows lifted helplessly over his hawkish nose, suggesting that he too, like me, was a victim of America's racial farce. His look assumed a kind of comradeship: he and I were above this grimy business of race, though for expediency we had occasionally to concede the world its madness.

My vulnerability in this situation came not so much from the professor's blindness to his own racism as from his assumption

---

*For more on the subject of Emmett Till, see Ashraf Rushdy's "Exquisite Corpse" on page 356. — Ed.

that I would participate in it, that I would conspire with him against my own race so that he might remain comfortably blind. Why did he think I would be amenable to this? I can only guess that he assumed my middle-class identity was so complete and all-encompassing that I would see his action as nothing more than a trifling concession to the folkways of our land, that I would in fact applaud his decision not to disturb propriety. Blind to both his own racism and to me — one blindness serving the other — he could not recognize that he was asking me to betray my race in the name of my class.

His blindness made me feel vulnerable because it threatened to expose my own repressed ambivalence. His comment pressured me to choose between my class identification, which had contributed to my being a college student and a member of the debating team, and my desperate desire to be "black." I could have one but not both; I was double-bound.

Because double binds are repressed there is always an element of terror in them: the terror of bringing to the conscious mind the buried duplicity, self-deception, and pretense involved in serving two masters. This terror is the stuff of vulnerability, and since vulnerability is one of the least tolerable of all human feelings, we usually transform it into an emotion that seems to restore the control of which it has robbed us; most often, that emotion is anger. And so, before the professor had even finished his little story, I had become a furnace of rage. The year was 1967, and I had been primed by endless hours of nap-matching to feel, at least consciously, completely at one with the victim-focused black identity. This identity gave me the license, and the impunity, to unleash upon this professor one of those volcanic eruptions of racial indignation familiar to us from the novels of Richard Wright. Like Cross Damon in *Outsider,* who kills in perfectly righteous anger, I tried to annihilate the man. I punished him not according to the measure of his crime but according to the measure of my vulnerability, a measure set by the cumulative tension of years of repressed terror. Soon I saw that terror in *his* face, as he stared hollow-eyed at the road ahead. My white friends in the back seat, knowing no conflict between their own class and race, were astonished that someone they had taken to be so much like themselves could harbor a rage that for all the world looked murderous.

Though my rage was triggered by the professor's comment, it was deepened and sustained by a complex of need, conflict, and repression in myself of which I had been wholly unaware. Out of my racial vulnerability I had developed the strong need of an identity with which to defend myself. The only such identity available was that of me as victim, him as victimizer. Once in the grip of this paradigm, I began to do far more damage to myself than he had done.

Seeing myself as a victim meant that I clung all the harder to my racial identity, which, in turn, meant that I suppressed my class identity. This cut me off from all the resources my class values might have offered me. In those values, for instance, I might have found the means to a more dispassionate response, the response less of a victim attacked by a victimizer than of an individual offended by a foolish old man. As an individual I might have reported this professor to the college dean. Or I might have calmly tried to reveal his blindness to him, and possibly won a convert. (The flagrancy of his remark suggested a hidden guilt and even self-recognition on which I might have capitalized. Doesn't confession usually signal a willingness to face oneself?) Or I might have simply chuckled and then let my silence serve as an answer to his provocation. Would not my composure, in any form it might take, deflect into his own heart the arrow he'd shot at me?

Instead, my anger, itself the hair-trigger expression of a long-repressed double bind, not only cut me off from the best of my own resources, it also distorted the nature of my true racial problem. The righteousness of this anger and the easy catharsis it brought buoyed the delusion of my victimization and left me as blind as the professor himself.

As a middle-class black I have often felt myself *contriving* to be "black." And I have noticed this same contrivance in others — a certain stretching away from the natural flow of one's life to align oneself with a victim-focused black identity. Our particular needs are out of sync with the form of identity available to meet those needs. Middle-class blacks need to identify racially; it is better to think of ourselves as black and victimized than not black at all; so we contrive (more unconsciously than consciously) to fit ourselves into an identity that denies our class and fails to address the true source of our vulnerability.

For me this once meant spending inordinate amounts of time at black faculty meetings, though these meetings had little to do with my real racial anxieties or my professional life. I was new to the university, one of two blacks in an English department of over seventy, and I felt a little isolated and vulnerable, though I did not admit it to myself. But at these meetings we discussed the problems of black faculty and students within a framework of victimization. The real vulnerability we felt was covered over by all the adversarial drama the victim/victimized polarity inspired, and hence went unseen and unassuaged. And this, I think, explains our rather chronic ineffectiveness as a group. Since victimization was not our primary problem — the university had long ago opened its doors to us — we had to contrive to make it so, and there is not much energy in contrivance. What I got at these meetings was ultimately an object lesson in how fruitless struggle can be when it is not grounded in actual need.

At our black faculty meetings, the old equation of blackness with victimization was ever present — to be black was to be a victim; therefore, not to be a victim was not to be black. As we contrived to meet the terms of this formula there was an inevitable distortion of both ourselves and the larger university. Through the prism of victimization the university seemed more impenetrable than it actually was, and we more limited in our powers. We fell prey to the victim's myopia, making the university an institution from which we could seek redress but which we could never fully join. And this mind-set often led us to look more for compensations for our supposed victimization than for opportunities we could pursue as individuals.

The discomfort and vulnerability felt by middle-class blacks in the sixties, it could be argued, was a worthwhile price to pay considering the progress achieved during that time of racial confrontation. But what may have been tolerable then is intolerable now. Though changes in American society have made it an anachronism, the monolithic form of racial identification that came out of the sixties is still very much with us. It may be more loosely held, and its power to punish heretics has probably diminished, but it continues to catch middle-class blacks in a double bind, thus impeding not only their own advancement but even, I would contend, that of blacks as a group.

The victim-focused black identity encourages the individual to feel that his advancement depends almost entirely on that of the group. Thus he loses sight not only of his own possibilities but of the inextricable connection between individual effort and individual advancement. This is a profound encumbrance today, when there is more opportunity for blacks than ever before, for it reimposes limitations that can have the same oppressive effect as those the society has only recently begun to remove.

It was the emphasis on mass action in the sixties that made the victim-focused black identity a necessity. But in the eighties and beyond, when racial advancement will come only through a multitude of individual advancements, this form of identity inadvertently adds itself to the forces that hold us back. Hard work, education, individual initiative, stable family life, property ownership — these have always been the means by which ethnic groups have moved ahead in America. Regardless of past or present victimization, these "laws" of advancement apply absolutely to black Americans also. There is no getting around this. What we need is a form of racial identity that energizes the individual by putting him in touch with both his possibilities and his responsibilities.

It has always annoyed me to hear from the mouths of certain arbiters of blackness that middle-class blacks should "reach back" and pull up those blacks less fortunate than they — as though middle-class status were an unearned and essentially passive condition in which one needed a large measure of noblesse oblige to occupy one's time. My own image is of reaching back from a moving train to lift on board those who have no tickets. A noble enough sentiment — but might it not be wiser to show them the entire structure of principles, efforts, and sacrifice that puts one in a position to buy a ticket any time one likes? This, I think, is something members of the black middle class can realistically offer to other blacks. Their example is not only a testament to possibility but also a lesson in method. But they cannot lead by example until they are released from a black identity that regards that example as suspect, that sees them as "marginally" black, indeed that holds *them* back by catching them in a double bind.

To move beyond the victim-focused black identity we must learn to make a difficult but crucial distinction: between actual victimization, which we must resist with every resource, and identification with the victim's status. Until we do this we will continue to wrestle more with ourselves than with the new opportunities which so many paid so dearly to win.

Reflections and Responses

1. Consider the two people Steele introduces us to in his essay — a black friend (pages 375–376) and a white college professor (pages 382–384). What does each person represent? Of what importance are they to Steele's own self-identity? How does he establish his differences toward each one? Why are these differences important to Steele's own identity?

2. What do you think of Steele's contention that poorer and less-educated African Americans are generally considered more "black" than those from the middle class? What evidence does Steele offer to support this idea? On what grounds is black "authenticity" or "purity" based? Do you think the media — especially film, music, and television — reinforce certain images of "blackness"?

3. Note that toward the conclusion of his essay Steele uses the word "we." What is the significance of this shift? What identification is he establishing and with whom?

JOY WILLIAMS

The Killing Game

In today's world, survival is a theme that includes all of nature, not merely human life. When the following angry attack on hunting originally appeared in a popular men's magazine, the editors were deluged with equally angry letters from hundreds of subscribers. As you read the essay, you'll see at once why it enraged hunters and hunting advocates. Williams did not choose to write a calm, composed, and gently persuasive critique of hunting but went all out in a savage and often sarcastic attack on American hunters, a group she considers "overequipped . . . insatiable, malevolent, and vain."

Williams is the author of several novels and two collections of stories, Taking Care *(1982) and* Escapes *(1989), as well as a 1987 history and guide to the Florida Keys. Her nonfiction includes articles on sharks, James Dean, the environment, and the electric chair. In 1993 she received the Strauss Living Award from the American Academy of Arts and Letters. "The Killing Game" originally appeared in* Esquire *(1990) and was selected by Joyce Carol Oates for* The Best American Essays 1991.

Death and suffering are a big part of hunting. A big part. Not that you'd ever know it by hearing hunters talk. They tend to downplay the killing part. To kill is to put to death, extinguish, nullify, cancel, destroy. But from the hunter's point of view, it's just a tiny part of the experience. *The kill is the least important part of the hunt,* they often say, or, *Killing involves only a split second of the innumerable hours we spend surrounded by and observing nature . . .* For the animal, of course, the killing part is of considerable more importance. José Ortega y Gasset, in *Meditations on Hunting,* wrote, *Death is a sign of reality in hunting. One does not hunt in order to kill; on the contrary, one kills in order to have hunted.* This is the sort of intellectual blather that the "thinking" hunter holds dear. The conservation editor of *Field & Stream*, George Reiger, recently paraphrased this sentiment by saying, *We kill to hunt, and not the other way around*, thereby making it truly fatuous. A hunter in West Virginia, one Mr. Bill Neal, blazed through this philosophical fog by explaining why he blows the toes off tree raccoons so that they will fall down and be torn apart by his dogs. *That's the best part of it. It's not any fun just shooting them.*

Instead of monitoring animals — many animals in managed areas are tagged, tattooed, and wear radio transmitters — wildlife managers should start hanging telemetry gear around hunters' necks to study their attitudes and listen to their conversations. It would be grisly listening, but it would tune out for good the *suffering as sacrament* and *spiritual experience* blather that some hunting apologists employ. *The unease with which the good hunter inflicts death is an unease not merely with his conscience but with affirming his animality in the midst of his struggles toward humanity and clarity,* Holmes Rolston III drones on in his book *Environmental Ethics*.

There is a formula to this in literature — someone the protagonist loves has just died, so he goes out and kills an animal. This makes him feel better. But it's kind of a sad feeling-better. He gets to relate to Death and Nature in this way. Somewhat. But not really. Death is still a mystery. Well, it's hard to explain. It's sort of a semireligious thing . . . Killing and affirming, affirming and killing, it's just the cross the "good" hunter must bear. The bad hunter just has to deal with postkill letdown.

Many are the hunter's specious arguments. Less semireligious but a long-standing favorite with them is the vegetarian approach: you eat meat, don't you? If you say no, they feel they've got you — you're just a vegetarian attempting to impose your weird views on others. If you say yes, they accuse you of being hypocritical, of allowing your genial A&P butcher to stand between you and reality. The fact is, the chief attraction of hunting is the pursuit and murder of animals — the meat-eating aspect of it is trivial. If the hunter chooses to be *ethical* about it, he might cook his kill, but the meat of most animals is discarded. Dead bear can even be dangerous! A bear's heavy hide must be skinned at once to prevent meat spoilage. With effort, a hunter can make okay chili, *something to keep in mind*, a sports rag says, *if you take two skinny spring bears.*

As for subsistence hunting, please . . . Granted that there might be one "good" hunter out there who conducts the kill as spiritual exercise and two others who are atavistic enough to want to supplement their Chicken McNuggets with venison, most hunters hunt for the hell of it.

For hunters, hunting is fun. Recreation is play. Hunting is recreation. Hunters kill for play, for entertainment. They kill for the thrill of it, to make an animal "theirs." (The Gandhian doctrine of nonpossession has never been a big hit with hunters.) The animal becomes the property of the hunter by its death. Alive, the beast belongs only to itself. This is unacceptable to the hunter. *He's yours . . . He's mine . . . I decided to . . . I decided not to . . . I debated shooting it, then I decided to let it live . . .* Hunters like beautiful creatures. A "beautiful" deer, elk, bear, cougar, bighorn sheep. A "beautiful" goose or mallard. Of course, they don't stay "beautiful" for long, particularly the birds. Many birds become rags in the air, shredded, blown to bits. *Keep shooting till they drop!* Hunters get a thrill out of seeing a plummeting bird, out of seeing it crumple and fall. *The big pheasant folded in classic fashion.* They get a kick out of "collecting" new species. *Why not add a unique harlequin duck to your collection?* Swan hunting is satisfying. *I let loose a three-inch Magnum. The large bird only flinched with my first shot and began to gain altitude. I frantically ejected the round, chambered another, and dropped the swan with my second shot. After retrieving the bird I was amazed by its size. The swan's six-foot wingspan, huge body, and long neck made it an impressive trophy.* Hunters like big animals, trophy animals. A "trophy" usually means that the hunter doesn't deign to eat it. Maybe he skins it or mounts it. Maybe he takes a picture. *We took pictures, we took pictures.* Maybe he just looks at it for a while. The disposition of the "experience" is up to the hunter. He's entitled to do whatever he wishes with the damn thing. It's dead.

Hunters like categories they can tailor to their needs. There are the "good" animals — deer, elk, bear, moose — which are allowed to exist for the hunter's pleasure. Then there are the "bad" animals, the vermin, varmints, and "nuisance" animals, the rabbits and raccoons and coyotes and beavers and badgers, which are disencouraged to exist. The hunter can have fun killing them, but the pleasure is diminished because the animals aren't "magnificent."

Then there are the predators. These can be killed any time, because, hunters argue, they're predators, for godsakes.

Many people in South Dakota want to exterminate the red fox

because it preys upon some of the ducks and pheasant they want
to hunt and kill each year. They found that after they killed the
wolves and coyotes, they had more foxes than they wanted. The ring-
necked pheasant is South Dakota's state bird. No matter that it was
imported from Asia specifically to be "harvested" for sport, it's
South Dakota's state bird and they're proud of it. A group called
Pheasants Unlimited gave some tips on how to hunt foxes. *Place a
small amount of larvicide* [a grain fumigant] *on a rag and chuck it
down the hole . . . The first pup generally comes out in fifteen minutes . . . Use
a .22 to dispatch him . . . Remove each pup shot from the hole. Following
gassing, set traps for the old fox who will return later in the evening . . .*
Poisoning, shooting, trapping — they make up a sort of sportsman's triathlon.

In the hunting magazines, hunters freely admit the pleasure of
killing to one another. *Undeniable pleasure radiated from her smile.
The excitement of shooting the bear had Barb talking a mile a minute.* But
in public, most hunters are becoming a little wary about raving on
as to how much fun it is to kill things. Hunters have a tendency to
call large animals by cute names — "bruins" and "muleys," "berry-
fed blackies" and "handsome cusses" and "big guys," thereby implying a balanced jolly game of mutual satisfaction between the
hunter and the hunted — *Bam, bam, bam, I get to shoot you and you get
to be dead.* More often, though, when dealing with the nonhunting
public, a drier, businesslike tone is employed. Animals become a
"resource" that must be "utilized." Hunting becomes "a legitimate
use of the resource." Animals become a product like wool or lumber or a crop like fruit or corn that must be "collected" or "taken"
or "harvested." Hunters love to use the word *legitimate.* (Oddly, Tol-
stoy referred to hunting as "evil legitimized.") *A legitimate use, a legitimate form of recreation, a legitimate escape, a legitimate pursuit.* It's a
word they trust will slam the door on discourse. Hunters are increasingly relying upon their spokesmen and supporters, state and
federal game managers and wildlife officials, to employ the drone
of a solemn bureaucratic language and toss around a lot of questionable statistics to assure the nonhunting public (93 percent!)
that there's nothing to worry about. The pogrom is under control.
The mass murder and manipulation of wild animals is just another
business. Hunters are a tiny minority, and it's crucial to them that
the millions of people who don't hunt not be awakened from their

long sleep and become antihunting. Nonhunters are okay. Dweeby, probably, but okay. A hunter *can respect the rights* of a nonhunter. It's the "antis" he despises, those *misguided, emotional, not-in-possession-of-the-facts, uninformed zealots who don't understand nature . . . Those dime-store ecologists cloaked in ignorance and spurred by emotion . . . Those doggy-woggy types, who under the guise of being environmentalists and conservationists are working to deprive him of his precious right to kill.* (Sometimes it's just a *right*; sometimes it's a *God-given* right.) Antis can be scorned, but nonhunters must be pacified, and this is where the number crunching of wildlife biologists and the scripts of *professional resource managers* come in. Leave it to the professionals. They know what numbers are the good numbers. Utah determined that there were six hundred sandhill cranes in the state, so permits were issued to shoot one hundred of them. Don't want to have too many sandhill cranes. California wildlife officials reported "sufficient numbers" of mountain lions to "justify" renewed hunting, even though it doesn't take a rocket scientist to know the animal is extremely rare. (It's always a dark day for hunters when an animal is adjudged *rare*. How can its numbers be "controlled" through hunting if it scarcely exists?) A recent citizens' referendum prohibits the hunting of the mountain lion in perpetuity — not that the lions aren't killed anyway, in California and all over the West, hundreds of them annually by the government as part of the scandalous Animal Damage Control Program. Oh, to be the lucky hunter who gets to be an official government hunter and can legitimately kill animals his buddies aren't supposed to! Montana officials, led by K. L. Cool, that state's wildlife director, have definite ideas on the number of buffalo they feel can be tolerated. Zero is the number. Yellowstone National Park is the only place in America where bison exist, having been annihilated everywhere else. In the winter of 1988, nearly six hundred buffalo wandered out of the north boundary of the park and into Montana, where they were immediately shot at point-blank range by lottery-winning hunters. It was easy. And it was obvious from a video taken on one of the blow-away-the-bison days that the hunters had a heck of a good time. The buffalo, Cool says, threaten ranchers' livelihoods by doing damage to property — by which he means, I guess, that they eat the grass. Montana wants zero buffalos; it also wants zero wolves.

Large predators — including grizzlies, cougars, and wolves — are often the most "beautiful," the smartest and wildest animals of all. The gray wolf is both a supreme predator and an endangered species, and since the Supreme Court recently affirmed that ranchers have no constitutional right to kill endangered predators — apparently some God-given rights are not constitutional ones — this makes the wolf a more or less lucky dog. But not for long. A small population of gray wolves has recently established itself in northwestern Montana, primarily in Glacier National Park, and there is a plan, long a dream of conservationists, to "reintroduce" the wolf to Yellowstone. But to please ranchers and hunters, part of the plan would involve immediately removing the wolf from the endangered-species list. Beyond the park's boundaries, he could be hunted as a "game animal" or exterminated as a "pest." (Hunters kill to hunt, remember, except when they're hunting to kill.) The area of Yellowstone where the wolf would be restored is the same mountain and high-plateau country that is abandoned in winter by most animals, including the aforementioned luckless bison. Part of the plan, too, is compensation to ranchers if any of their far-ranging livestock is killed by a wolf. It's a real industry out there, apparently, killing and controlling and getting compensated for losing something under the Big Sky.

Wolves gotta eat — a fact that disturbs hunters. Jack Atcheson, an outfitter in Butte, said, *Some wolves are fine if there is control. But there never will be control. The wolf-control plan provided by the Fish and Wildlife Service speaks only of protecting domestic livestock. There is no plan to protect wildlife . . . There are no surplus deer or elk in Montana . . . Their numbers are carefully managed. With uncontrolled wolf populations, a lot of people will have to give up hunting just to feed wolves. Will you give up your elk permit for a wolf?*

It won't be long before hunters start demanding compensation for animals they aren't able to shoot.

Hunters believe that wild animals exist only to satisfy their wish to kill them. And it's so easy to kill them! The weaponry available is staggering, and the equipment and gear limitless. *The demand for big boomers has never been greater than right now, Outdoor Life* crows, *and the makers of rifles and cartridges are responding to the craze with a variety of light artillery that is virtually unprecedented in the history of sporting arms* . . . Hunters use grossly overpowered shotguns and rifles and compound bows. They rely on four-wheel-drive vehicles and three-wheel ATVs and airplanes . . . *He was interesting, the only moving, living creature on that limitless white expanse. I slipped a cartridge into the barrel of my rifle and threw the safety off* . . . They use snowmobiles to run down elk, and dogs to run down and tree cougars. It's easy to shoot an animal out of a tree. It's virtually impossible to miss a moose, a conspicuous and placid animal of steady habits . . . *I took a deep breath and pulled the trigger. The bull dropped. I looked at my watch: 8:22. The big guy was early. Mike started whooping and hollering and I joined him. I never realized how big a moose was until this one was on the ground. We took pictures* . . . Hunters shoot animals when they're resting . . . *Mike selected a deer, settled down to a steady rest, and fired. The buck was his when he squeezed the trigger. John decided to take the other buck, which had jumped up to its feet. The deer hadn't seen us and was confused by the shot echoing about in the valley. John took careful aim, fired, and took the buck. The hunt was over* . . . And they shoot them when they're eating . . . *The bruin ambled up the stream, checking gravel bars and backwaters for fish. Finally he plopped down on the bank to eat. Quickly, I tiptoed into range* . . . They use decoys and calls . . . *The six-point gave me a cold-eyed glare from ninety steps away. I hit him with a 130-grain Sierra boat-tail handload. The bull went down hard. Our hunt was over* . . . They use sex lures . . . *The big buck raised its nose to the air, curled back its lips, and tested the scent of the doe's urine. I held my breath, fought back the shivers, and jerked off a shot. The 180-grain spire-point bullet caught the buck high on the back behind the shoulder and put it down. It didn't get up* . . . They use walkie-talkies, binoculars, scopes . . . *With my 308 Browning BLR, I steadied the 9X cross hairs on the front of the bear's massive shoulders and squeezed. The bear cartwheeled backward for fifty yards* . . . *The second Federal Premium 165-grain bullet found its mark. Another shot anchored the bear for good* . . . They bait deer with corn. They spread popcorn on golf courses for Canada geese and they douse meat baits with fry grease and honey for bears . . . *Make the baiting site redolent of inner-city doughnut shops.* They use blinds and tree stands and mobile stands. They go out in groups, in gangs, and employ "pushes" and "drives." So many methods are effective. So few rules apply. It's fun! . . . *We kept on repelling the swarms of birds as they came in looking for shelter from that big ocean wind, emptying our shell belts* . . .

A species can, in the vernacular, be *pressured by hunting* (which means that killing them has decimated them), but that just increases the fun, the *challenge*. There is practically no criticism of conduct within the ranks . . . *It's mostly a matter of opinion and how hunters have been brought up to hunt* . . . Although a recent editorial in *Ducks Unlimited* magazine did venture to primly suggest that one should *not fall victim to greed-induced stress through piggish competition with others*.

But hunters are piggy. They just can't seem to help it. They're overequipped . . . insatiable, malevolent, and vain. They maim and mutilate and despoil. And for the most part, they're inept. Grossly inept.

Camouflaged toilet paper is a must for the modern hunter, along with his Bronco and his beer. Too many hunters taking a dump in the woods with their roll of Charmin beside them were mistaken for white-tailed deer and shot. Hunters get excited. They'll shoot anything — the pallid ass of another sportsman or even themselves. A Long Island man died last year when his shotgun went off as he clubbed a wounded deer with the butt. Hunters get mad. They get restless and want to fire! They want to use those assault rifles and see foamy blood on the ferns. Wounded animals can travel for miles in fear and pain before they collapse. Countless gut-shot deer — *if you hear a sudden, squashy thump, the animal has probably been hit in the abdomen* — are "lost" each year. "Poorly placed shots" are frequent, and injured animals are seldom tracked, because most hunters never learned how to track. The majority of hunters will shoot at anything with four legs during deer season and anything with wings during duck season. Hunters try to nail running animals and distant birds. They become so overeager, so *aroused,* that they misidentify and misjudge, spraying their "game" with shots but failing to bring it down.

The fact is, hunters' lack of skill is a big, big problem. And nowhere is the problem worse than in the new glamour recreation, bow hunting. These guys are elitists. They doll themselves up in camouflage, paint their faces black, and climb up into tree stands from which they attempt the penetration of deer, elk, and turkeys with modern, multiblade, broadhead arrows shot from sophisticated, easy-to-draw compound bows. This "primitive" way of hunting appeals to many, and even the nonhunter may feel that it's a "fairer" method, requiring more strength and skill, but bow hunting is the cruelest, most wanton form of wildlife disposal of all. Studies conducted by state fish and wildlife departments repeatedly show that bow hunters wound and fail to retrieve as many animals as they kill. An animal that flees, wounded by an arrow, will most assuredly die of the wound, but it will be days before he does. Even with a "good" hit, the time elapsed between the strike and death is exceedingly long. *The rule of thumb has long been that we should wait thirty to forty-five minutes on heart and lung hits, an hour or more on a suspected liver hit, eight to twelve hours on paunch hits, and that we should follow immediately on hindquarter and other muscle-only hits, to keep the wound open and bleeding,* is the advice in the magazine *Fins and Feathers.* What the hunter does as he hangs around waiting for his animal to finish with its terrified running and dying hasn't been studied — maybe he puts on more makeup, maybe he has a highball.

Wildlife agencies promote and encourage bow hunting by permitting earlier and longer seasons, even though they are well aware that, in their words, *crippling is a by-product of the sport,* making archers pretty sloppy for elitists. The broadhead arrow is a very inefficient killing tool. Bow hunters are trying to deal with this problem with the suggestion that they use poison pods. These poisoned arrows are illegal in all states except Mississippi *(Ah'm gonna get ma deer even if ah just nick the little bastard),* but they're widely used anyway. You wouldn't want that deer to suffer, would you?

The mystique of the efficacy and decency of the bow hunter is as much an illusion as the perception that a waterfowler is a refined and thoughtful fellow, a *romantic aesthete,* as Vance Bourjaily put it, equipped with his faithful Labs and a love for solitude and wild places. More sentimental drivel has been written about bird shooting than any other type of hunting. It's a soul-wrenching pursuit, apparently, the execution of birds in flight. Ducks Unlimited — an organization that has managed to put a spin on the word *conservation* for years — works hard to project the idea that duck hunters are blue bloods and that duck stamps with their pretty pictures are responsible for saving all the saved puddles in North America. *Sportsman's conservation* is a contradiction in terms (We protect things now so that we can kill them later) and is broadly interpreted (Don't kill them all, just kill most of them). A hunter is a conservationist in the same way a farmer or a rancher is: he's not. Like the rancher who kills everything that's not stock on his (and the public's) land, and the farmer who scorns wildlife because "they don't pay their freight," the hunter uses nature by destroying its parts, mastering it by simplifying it through death.

George ("We kill to hunt and not the other way around") Reiger, the conservationist-hunter's spokesman (he's the best they've got, apparently), said that the "dedicated" waterfowler will shoot other game "of course," but *we do so much in the same spirit of the lyrics, that when we're not near the girl we love, we love the girl we're near.* (Duck hunters practice tough love.) The fact is, far from being a "romantic aesthete," the waterfowler is the most avaricious of all hunters . . . *That's when Scott suggested the friendly wager on who would take the most birds* . . . and the most resistant to minimum ecological decency. Millions of birds that managed to elude shotgun blasts were dying each year from ingesting the lead shot that rained down in the wetlands. Year after year, birds perished from feeding on spent lead, but hunters were "reluctant" to switch to steel. They worried that it would impair their shooting, and ammunition manufacturers said a changeover would be "expensive." State and federal officials had to weigh the poisoning against these considerations. It took forever, this weighing, but now steel-shot loads are required almost everywhere, having been judged "more than adequate" to bring down the birds. This is not to say, of course, that most duck hunters use steel shot almost everywhere. They're traditionalists and don't care for all the new, pesky rules. Oh, for the golden age of waterfowling, when a man could measure a good day's shooting by the pickup load. But those days are gone. Fall is a melancholy time, all right.

Spectacular abuses occur wherever geese congregate, Shooting Sportsman notes quietly, something that the more cultivated Ducks Unlimited would hesitate to admit. Waterfowl populations are plummeting and waterfowl hunters are out of control. "Supervised" hunts are hardly distinguished from unsupervised ones. A biologist with the Department of the Interior who observed a hunt at Sand Lake in South Dakota said, *Hunters repeatedly shot over the line at incoming flights where there was no possible chance of retrieving. Time and time again I was shocked at the behavior of hunters. I heard them laugh at the plight of dazed cripples that stumbled about. I saw them striking the heads of retrieved cripples against fence posts.* In the South, wood ducks return to their roosts after sunset when shooting hours are closed. Hunters find this an excellent time to shoot them. Dennis Anderson, an outdoors writer, said, *Roost shooters just fire at the birds as fast as they can, trying to drop as many as they can. Then they grab what birds they can find. The birds they can't find in the dark, they leave behind.*

Carnage and waste are the rules in bird hunting, even during legal seasons and open hours. Thousands of wounded ducks and geese are not retrieved, left to rot in the marshes and fields . . . *When I asked Wanda where hers had fallen, she wasn't sure.* Cripples, and there are many cripples made in this pastime, are still able to run and hide, eluding the hunter even if he's willing to spend time searching for them, which he usually isn't . . . *It's one thing to run down a cripple in a picked bean field or a pasture, and quite another to watch a wing-tipped bird drop into a huge block of switch grass.* Oh nasty, nasty switch grass. A downed bird becomes invisible on the ground and is practically unfindable without a good dog, and few "water-fowlers" have them these days. They're hard to train — usually a professional has to do it — and most hunters can't be bothered. Birds are easy to tumble . . . *Canada geese—blues and snows—can all take a good amount of shot. Brant are easily called and decoyed and come down easily. Ruffed grouse are hard to hit but easy to kill. Sharptails are harder to kill but easier to hit* . . . It's just a nuisance to recover them. But it's fun, fun, fun swatting them down . . . *There's distinct pleasure in watching a flock work to a good friend's gun.*

Teal, the smallest of common ducks, are really easy to kill. Hunters in the South used to *practice* on teal in September, prior to the "serious" waterfowl season. But the birds were so diminutive and the limit so low (four a day) that many hunters felt it hardly worth going out and getting bit by mosquitoes to kill them. Enough did, however, brave the bugs and manage to "harvest" 165,000 of the little migrating birds in Louisiana in 1987 alone. *Shooting is usually best on opening day. By the second day you can sometimes detect a decline in local teal numbers. Areas may deteriorate to virtually no action by the third day* . . . The area *deteriorates.* When a flock is wiped out, the skies are empty. *No action.*

Teal declined more sharply than any duck species except mallard

last year; this baffles hunters. Hunters and their procurers—
wildlife agencies—will *never* admit that hunting is responsible for
the decimation of a species. John Turner, head of the federal Fish
and Wildlife Service, delivers the familiar and litanic line. Hunting
is not the problem. *Pollution* is the problem. *Pesticides, urbanization,
deforestation, hazardous waste,* and *wetlands destruction* are the problem. And drought! There's been a big drought! Antis should devote their energies to solving these problems if they care about
wildlife, and leave the hunters alone. While the Fish and Wildlife
Service is busily conducting experiments in cause and effect, like
releasing mallard ducklings on a wetland sprayed with the insecti-
cide ethyl parathion (they died—it was known they would, but
you can never have enough studies that show guns aren't a duck's
only problem), hunters are killing some 200 million birds and animals each year. But these deaths are incidental to the problem,
according to Turner. A factor, perhaps, but a *minor* one. Ducks
Unlimited says the problem isn't hunting, it's *low recruitment* on the
part of the birds. To the hunter, *birth* in the animal kingdom is *recruitment.* They wouldn't want to use an emotional, sentimental
word like *birth.* The black duck, a very "popular" duck in the
Northeast, so "popular," in fact, that game agencies felt that
hunters couldn't be asked to refrain from shooting it, is scarce
and getting scarcer. Nevertheless, it's still being hunted. *A number
of studies are currently under way in an attempt to discover why black
ducks are disappearing, Sports Afield* reports. Black ducks are disappearing because they've been shot out, their elimination being a
dreadful example of game management, and managers who are
loath to "displease" hunters. The skies— *flyways* —of America
have been divided into four administrative regions, and the states,
advised by a federal government coordinator, have to agree on
policies.

There's always a lot of squabbling that goes on in flyway meetings— lots of complaints about short-stopping, for example. Short-
stopping is the deliberate holding of birds in a state, often by
feeding them in wildlife refuges, so that their southern migration
is slowed or stopped. Hunters in the North get to kill more than
hunters in the South. This isn't fair. Hunters demand equity in opportunities to kill.

Wildlife managers hate closing the season on anything. Closing the season on a species would indicate a certain amount of *mis*management and misjudgment at the very least — a certain reliance on overly optimistic winter counts, a certain overappeasement of hunters who would be "upset" if they couldn't kill their favorite thing. And worse, closing a season would be considered victory for the antis. Bird-hunting "rules" are very complicated, but they all encourage killing. There are shortened seasons and split seasons and special seasons for "underutilized" birds. (Teal were very recently considered "underutilized.") The limit on coots is fifteen a day — shooting them, it's easy! They don't fly high — giving the hunter something to do while he waits in the blind. Some species are "protected," but bear in mind that hunters begin blasting away one half hour before sunrise and that most hunters can't identify a bird in the air even in broad daylight. Some of them can't identify birds in hand either, and even if they can (#%*! *I got me a canvasback, that duck's frigging protected . . .*), they are likely to bury unpopular or "trash" ducks so that they can continue to hunt the ones they "love."

Game "professionals," in thrall to hunters' "needs," will not stop managing bird populations until they've doled out the final duck (*I didn't get my limit but I bagged the last one, by golly . . .*). The Fish and Wildlife Service services legal hunters as busily as any madam, but it is powerless in tempering the lusts of the illegal ones. Illegal kill is a monumental problem in the not-so-wonderful world of waterfowl. Excesses have always pervaded the "sport," and bird shooters have historically been the slobs and profligates of hunting. *Doing away with hunting would do away with a vital cultural and historical aspect of American life,* John Turner claims. So, do away with it. Do away with those who have already done away with so much. Do away with them before the birds they have pursued so relentlessly and for so long drop into extinction, sink, in the poet Wallace Stevens's words, "downward to darkness on extended wings."

"Quality" hunting is as rare as the Florida panther. What you've got is a bunch of guys driving over the plains, up the mountains, and through the woods with their stupid tag that cost them a couple of bucks and immense coolers full of beer and body parts. There's a price tag on the right to destroy living creatures for play, but it's not much. *A big-game hunting license is the greatest deal going since the Homestead Act,* Ted Kerasote writes in *Sports Afield. In many*

states residents can hunt big game for more than a month for about $20.
It's cheaper than taking the little woman out to lunch. It's cheap all
right, and it's because killing animals is considered *recreation* and is
underwritten by state and federal funds. In Florida, state moneys
are routinely spent on "youth hunts," in which kids are guided to
shoot deer from stands in wildlife-management areas. The organ-
izers of these events say that these staged hunts *help youth to understand man's role in the ecosystem.* (Drop a doe and take your place in
the ecological community, son . . .)

Hunters claim (they don't actually believe it but they've learned
to say it) that they're doing nonhunters a favor, for if they didn't
use wild animals, wild animals would be useless. They believe that
they're just *helping Mother Nature control populations (you wouldn't
want those deer to die of starvation, would you?).* They claim that their
tiny fees provide *all* Americans with wild lands and animals. (People who don't hunt get to enjoy animals all year round while
hunters get to enjoy them only during hunting season . . .) Ducks
Unlimited feels that it, in particular, is a selfless provider and environmental champion. Although members spend most of their
money lobbying for hunters and raising ducks in pens to release
later over shooting fields, they do save some wetlands, mostly by
persuading farmers not to fill them in. *See that little pothole there the
ducks like? Well, I'm gonna plant more soybeans there if you don't pay me
not to . . .* Hunters claim many nonsensical things, but the most
nonsensical of all is that they *pay their own way.* They do not pay
their own way. They *do* pay into a perverse wildlife-management
system that manipulates "stocks" and "herds" and "flocks" for
hunters' killing pleasure, but these fees in no way cover the
cost of highly questionable ecological practices. For some spare
change . . . *the greatest deal going* . . . hunters can hunt on public
land — national parks, state forests — preserves for hunters! —
which the nonhunting and antihunting public pay for. (Access to
private lands is becoming increasingly difficult for them, as experience has taught people that hunters are obnoxious.) Hunters kill
on millions of acres of land all over America that are maintained
with general taxpayer revenue, but the most shocking, really twisted
subsidization takes place on national wildlife refuges. Nowhere is
the arrogance and the insidiousness of this small, aggressive minority more clearly demonstrated. Nowhere is the murder of animals,

the manipulation of language, and the distortion of public intent more flagrant. The public perceives national wildlife refuges as safe havens, as sanctuaries for animals. And why wouldn't they? The word *refuge* of course *means* shelter from danger and distress. But the dweeby nonhunting public — they tend to be so literal. The word has been reinterpreted by management over time and now hunters are invited into more than half of the country's more than 440 wildlife "sanctuaries" each year to bang them up and kill more than half a million animals. This is called *wildlife-oriented recreation.* Hunters think of this as being no less than their due, claiming that refuge lands were purchased with duck stamps *(. . . our duck stamps paid for it . . . our duck stamps paid for it . . .).* Hunters equate those stupid stamps with the mystic, multiplying power of the Lord's loaves and fishes, but of 90 million acres in the Wildlife Refuge System, only 3 million were bought with hunting-stamp revenue. Most wildlife "restoration" programs in the states are translated into clearing land to increase deer habitats (so that too many deer will require hunting . . . you wouldn't want them to die of starvation, would you?) and trapping animals for restocking and study (so hunters can shoot more of them). Fish and game agencies hustle hunting — instead of conserving wildlife, they're killing it. It's time for them to get in the business of protecting and preserving wildlife and creating balanced ecological systems instead of pimping for hunters who want their deer/duck/pheasant/turkey — animals stocked to be shot.

Hunters' self-serving arguments and lies are becoming more preposterous as nonhunters awake from their long, albeit troubled, sleep. Sport hunting is immoral; it should be made illegal. Hunters are persecutors of nature who should be prosecuted. They wield a disruptive power out of all proportion to their numbers, and pandering to their interests — the special interests of a group that just wants to kill things — is mad. It's preposterous that every year less than 7 percent of the population turns the skies into shooting galleries and the woods and fields into abattoirs. It's time to stop actively supporting and passively allowing hunting, and time to stigmatize it. It's time to stop being conned and cowed by hunters, time to stop pampering and coddling them, time to get them off the government's duck-and-deer dole, time to stop thinking of wild animals as "resources" and "game," and start think-

ing of them as sentient beings that deserve our wonder and respect, time to stop allowing hunting to be creditable by calling it
"sport" and "recreation." Hunters make wildlife *dead, dead, dead.*
It's time to wake up to this indisputable fact. As for the hunters, it's
long past check-out time.

Reflections and Responses

1. In her sixth paragraph, Williams introduces the following quotes:
*"He's yours . . . He's mine . . . I decided to . . . I decided not to . . . I de-
bated shooting it, then I decided to let it live . . ."* Who is supposedly
saying these things? What point is Williams making about hunters?

2. Williams criticizes not only the morality of hunting but the "manipulation of language" by "hunting apologists." To what extent
does she focus her argument on language? What aspects of the
pro-hunting language does she most dislike? What euphemisms
does she satirize? Do you think she criticizes this language fairly?
Explain.

3. Go through the essay systematically and list the pro-hunting arguments Williams introduces. How many can you identify? How do
you think she handles them? For example, do you agree with her
refutation of the position that people who eat meat are hypocritical in their criticism of hunters?

GARRY WILLS

The Dramaturgy of Death

*The continued reliance on the death penalty in many states has long re-
mained one of our nation's most divisive issues. The debate becomes especially heated whenever a capital crime becomes a major news story, such as
in the case of Timothy McVeigh's 1993 Oklahoma City bombing or the fall
2002 serial sniper killings in the Washington, D.C., area. When such tragic
events receive around-the-clock attention, the media will certainly rehearse
all the customary arguments for or against the death penalty. In "The Dramaturgy of Death," noted author Garry Wills—borrowing from the German
philosopher Friedrich Nietzsche (1844–1900)—systemically reviews all the
reasons that societies throughout the ages have advanced in favor of some
type of capital punishment. Although he finds them flawed, he nevertheless
observes that they had a common justification in their drama (thus the "dramaturgy" of his title) altogether missing in today's use of the death penalty.*

*Garry Wills, who teaches history at Northwestern University, has pub-
lished more than thirty books on a wide variety of subjects that include
history, biography, criticism, politics, and religion. His most recent publications include* Papal Sin: Structures of Deceit *(2000);* Venice: Lion
City *(2001);* James Madison *(2002);* Mr. Jefferson's University *(2002);
and* Why I Am a Catholic *(2002). He has received the Pulitzer Prize, the
National Book Critics Circle Award (twice), and the Presidential Medal of
the National Endowment for the Humanities. "The Dramaturgy of Death"
originally appeared in* The New York Review of Books *and was selected
by Stephen Jay Gould for* The Best American Essays 2002.

1. Capital Punishment: The Rationales

A slight perusal of the laws by which the measures of vindictive and
coercive justice are established will discover so many disproportions

between crimes and punishments, such capricious distinctions of guilt,
and such confusion of remissness and severity as can scarcely be believed
to have been produced by public wisdom, sincerely and calmly studious
of public happiness.

—Samuel Johnson, *Rambler* 114

Nietzsche denied that capital punishment ever arose from a single
or consistent theory of its intent or effect. It erupted from a tangle
of overlapping yet conflicting urges, which would be fitted out with
later rationalizations. The only common denominator he found in
the original urges was some form of grievance (he used the French
term *ressentiment*). One can expand his own list of such urges:

Killing as exclusion. This occurs when society does not want to
admit any responsibility for persons considered outsiders. Abandonment of wounded or captured people one does not want to
feed or support is an example, or exposure of unwanted children,
or exiling the defenseless (as the blind and old Oedipus was extruded from Thebes), or "outlawing"—leaving people without
protection to any predators on them. Outlawing was an English
practice continued in our colonies. In fact, Thomas Jefferson,
when he revised the laws of Virginia for the new republic, left certain categories of offenders "out of the protection of the laws"—
freed slaves who either enter the state or refuse to leave it, a white
woman bearing a black child who does not leave the state within a
year. These could be killed or mistreated in any way without remedy at law. The ancient Greeks denied offenders recourse to law by
the penalty of *atimia* (loss of rights). There were lesser degrees of
this, but the full degree of "atimia . . . and condemnation to death
are interchangeable." Nietzsche calls this "Punishment as the expulsion of a degenerate element . . . as a means of preserving the
purity of a race or maintaining a social type."

Killing as cleansing. Outlawing abandons people to possible or
probable death but does not directly bring it about. Other forms
of extrusion require society's purification by *destruction* of a pol-
luted person. Unless society or its agents effect this purification,
the pollution continues to taint them. Lesser pollutions can be
robbed of their effect by simply driving away the affected person.
But deeper taints are removed only by accompanying the expulsion with something like stoning the polluter to death or throwing
him off a cliff. Plato said that the murderer of anyone in his own

immediate family was to be killed by judicial officers and magistrate, then "thrown down naked on a designated crossroads outside the city; whereupon every official present must throw his own stone at the head of the corpse, to cleanse the whole city, and finally must take him beyond the land's outer boundaries and cast him out, all rites of burial denied" (*Laws* 873b–c).

Killing as execration. Sometimes the community must thrust away contamination by ritual curses *(arai)*, joining the punitive cry of the Furies, who are also called Arai (Aeschylus, *Eumenides* 417). When Prometheus is punished by exposure as the penalty of theft, Brute Force (Bia) tells the technician clamping him to the rock (Hephaistos) that he should curse as well as immobilize him (Aeschylus, *Prometheus* 38, 67–68). Southern lynch mobs stayed to curse with fury their hanged victim from a similar impulse.

Killing to maintain social order. Superiors dramatize their dominance by showing that it is easy for those higher in the social scale to kill those lower, but harder for the lower to kill the higher. Plato's legal code devised a penalty for a slave who kills a free man — public scourging to death before the free man's tomb and family — that had no symmetrical penalty for a free man who kills a slave (*Laws* 872b–c). In Jefferson's legal code, slaves could not testify against whites, but whites could testify against slaves. In parts of this country still, a black killing a white is far more likely to receive a death sentence than a white killing a black. Nietzsche calls this "Punishment as a means of inspiring fear of those who determine and execute the punishment."

Killing to delegitimize a former social order. Revolutionary tribunals execute officials of an overthrown regime. Even without a coup, critics of Athenian democracy claimed that mass juries were too ready to condemn their leaders. When the Turkish general Lala Mustafa Pasha captured Cyprus from the Venetians in 1570, the podestà who had held out against him, Marcantonio Bragadin, was mutilated (nose and ears cut off), dragged around the city walls, dangled from a ship's mast, tied naked to a post, skinned alive, beheaded, and "quartered" (his four limbs cut off). Then his skin, stuffed with straw, was tied to a cow and led through the streets of the Famagusta, before being returned as a victory prize to Constantinople. Venetian rule was pulverized in its representative. Nietzsche calls this "Punishment as a festival, namely as the rape and mockery of a finally defeated enemy."

Killing as posthumous delegitimation. Some inquisitors tried dead men and symbolically executed them. The leaders of the Gowrie Plot that tried to supplant King James VI of Scotland in 1600 were tried posthumously and their corpses were hanged, drawn (eviscerated), and quartered. In 897, Stephen VI had the corpse of his predecessor, Pope Formosus, exhumed, propped up in his papal garb, tried and condemned for usurpation, stripped of his vestments, his head (that had borne the tiara) cut off, along with the three fingers of his right hand used in benediction, and head, fingers, and body thrown in the Tiber — all to declare Formosus's consecration of bishops and ordination of priests invalid.

Killing as total degradation. The previous three forms of execution punished an offender as a member of a class (lower or higher); but other humiliating deaths are contrived to deprive a person of humanity as such. Public torture before death was one means for this — scourging that makes the offender scream and writhe, losing dignity along with his composure. The Greek punishment for theft was *apotympanismos,* the beating of a naked man clamped down in a crouched position before he was left to die of exposure (it is the punishment given to Prometheus in his play, though he cannot die). The death for traitors in Elizabethan England was an elaborate piece of theater. First the offender was dragged backward on a hurdle to the place of execution — signifying, said the attorney general Sir Edward Coke, that the man was "not worthy any more to tread upon the face of the earth whereof he was made; also for that he hath been retrograde to nature, therefore is he drawn backward at a horse-tail." Then the man (it was a male punishment) was stripped, hanged, cut down living, castrated, disemboweled, his heart and viscera thrown in boiling water, decapitated, quartered, and his head exposed on Tower Bridge. When Jesuit priests were hanged, drawn, and quartered, their head, members, torso, and clothes were hidden away to prevent the taking of relics.

Killing and posthumous degradation. Refusal of burial led the ancient Greeks to let bodies be exposed for ravaging by dogs and kites (Creon's treatment of Polyneices in Sophocles' *Antigone*). Romans let crucified bodies hang to be pecked at and decompose. Florentines in the Renaissance dangled the corpses of criminals from the high windows of the Bargello till they rotted, and commissioned artists like Andrea del Sarto to depict them there, prolonging the shame after they were gone. Joan of Arc was killed by a slow fire that consumed her clothes and skin, then the flames were raked away, to expose her body as a woman's and to show that no demon had spirited her away. Then intense fire was mounted to burn her down to ashes for scattering in the Seine, to prevent any collection of relics.

Killing by ordeal. In this punishment, the innocent were supposed to be protected if subjected to ordeal by combat, ordeal by fire (walking through it, as Saint Francis is supposed to have done in Egypt), or ordeal by water. The latter was especially reserved for suspected witches, who would sink only if innocent. A less lethal form of this punishment survived in the "ducking stool" for immersing witches. Jefferson's revised code says this: "All attempts to delude the people, or to abuse their understanding by exercise of the pretended [claimed] arts of witchcraft, conjuration, enchantment, or sorcery or by pretended prophecies, shall be punished by ducking and whipping at the discretion of a jury, not exceeding 15 stripes."

Threatened killing as inducement to remorse. Refusal to undergo trial by ordeal could be taken as a confession, leading to a lesser penalty than death. Recanting could have the same effect. Joan of Arc, when first brought out to the stake with its kindling, renounced her voices as "idolatry" (devil worship), and was given life imprisonment. Only when she abjured her recantation was she actually put to the stake. Scaffold repentance could reduce the sentence to less than death — or, at the least, make officials perform a "merciful" (a swifter, not a lingering) execution — e.g., letting a man die in the noose before being cut down for disemboweling. Nietzsche calls this punishment for the "improvement" of the criminal.

Killing as repayment. The *lex talionis,* as it exacts "an eye for an eye," must exact a life for a life. We say, "You're going to *pay* for this." Jefferson followed the logic of his state's *lex talionis:*

> Whosoever shall be guilty of Rape, Polygamy, or Sodomy with man or woman shall be punished, if a man, by castration, if a woman, by cutting thro' the cartilage of her nose a hole of one half inch diameter at the least . . . Whosoever on purpose and of malice forethought shall maim another, or shall disfigure him, by cutting out or disabling the tongue, slitting or cutting off a nose, lip or ear, branding, or otherwise, shall be maimed or disfigured in like sort: or if that cannot be for want of the

same part, then as nearly as may be in some other part of at least equal value and estimation in the opinion of a jury, and moreover shall forfeit one half of his lands and goods to the sufferer.

Taking a life for a life on this principle is called by Nietzsche "Punishment as recompense to the injured party for the harm done."

Killing as repayment-plus. In Athenian law, repayment was of equal value if the crime was unintentional, but of double if it was intentional. On that principle, death has not been reserved only for taking a life, but can be considered an added penalty for crimes like major theft, rape, treasonous speech, and the like.

Killing as victim therapy. The Attic orator Antiphon has the father of a son killed by accident plead that the unintentional killer must be punished; the death leaves the father aggrieved (*epithymion* — much like Nietzsche's *ressentiment*). The grievance, of course, would be even greater if the killing were intentional. Soothing this sense of grievance is now called "giving closure" to the ordeal of victims.

Killing as a form of pedagogy. We say that punishing a man will "teach him a lesson." More important, it may teach others the consequence of crime, deterring anyone who contemplates a similar offense. Kant said that the person should be treated as his own end, not as a means for others' advantage. But the person executed is, by this theory, turned into a teaching instrument for the benefit of others.

2. Public Execution

> Experience of past times gives us little reason to hope that any reformation will be effected by a periodical havoc of our fellow beings.
>
> — Samuel Johnson, *Rambler* 114

The fourteen types of capital punishment listed above do not exhaust all the possible urges expressed in our havocking of others. And as Nietzsche said, they are not neat little separate rationales. They conflict with each other at an intellectual level, but they reinforce each other at the emotional level. They are more powerful for certain people in certain combinations. But they have one thing in common: *they all demand, in logic, maximum display and publicity.*

The outlaw's status must be proclaimed for people to act on it. The other effects sought — whether cleansing, order enforcement, delegitimation, humiliation, repayment, therapy, deterrence — can only be achieved if an audience sees what is being done to satisfy, intimidate, soothe, or instruct it.

In fact, various means to dramatize the process, to make its meaning clear, to show the right way to "read" it, were invented. Those going to the scaffold often had their crimes blazoned on their backs. Joan of Arc wore a fool's cap with her four crimes printed on it. A crucified man had his crime posted on the cross. Lesser criminals were branded to sustain the memory of their crime. Ingenious means of execution were invented to express society's horror, anger, power, and the like. Any punishment that fits the crime should be *seen* to fit the crime. Indeed, the only urges that people now commonly admit to — the last four in the above list (repayment of two kinds, "closure," and deterrence) — are closely linked with publicity. The repayment is to us, to society as well as to the victims, the therapy is for the victims' contemplation, and an act meant to deter should vividly catch the attention of those who might benefit from it. How can they "learn their lesson" if it is not spelled out for them?

Our unconfessed difficulty is that we have given up whatever logic there was to the death penalty, since we have become unable to embrace most of the practices of the past. We no longer believe in a divine miasma to be purged, or divine guidance to be revealed in survival by ordeal. We have given up the desecration of corpses, killing as a reinforcement of class distinctions, torture, maiming, evisceration, and all the multiple methods used to reduce the criminal to a *corpus vile*. Even Jefferson wavered on the *lex talionis* when it came to blinding an offender (he could go as far as a nose for a nose, but not as far as an eye for an eye). Our Constitution forbids cruel and unusual punishment, and we take that to mean that there will be no gratuitous humiliation of the convict — we do not even put people in the stocks anymore, much less invite the public to see a condemned man being strapped onto a gurney. We want painless executions, so we have recurred to one of the few humane-looking methods of the Greeks — lethal injection (hemlock), though among the many deterrents to becoming a philosopher, Socrates' quiet (and self-chosen) death in his seventies has never ranked very high.

So far from stigmatizing or humiliating the inmate of death row, we now provide him with a long and costly process meant to ascertain guilt, with free legal aid if he cannot afford his own, with counseling and family visits, with reading of his choice and TV, a last meal to his specifications, a last request, religious attendance, guaranteed burial, a swift and nearly painless death. We shut up his last hours from the general public, and act as if this secret rite will deter by some magic of mere occurrence. We treat the killing as a dirty little secret, as if we are ashamed of it. Well, we should be ashamed. Having given up on most of the previous justifications for the death penalty, we cling to a mere vestige of the practice, relying most urgently on one of the least defensible defenses of it.

3. Deterrence

> The gibbet, indeed, certainly disables those who die upon it from infesting the community; but their death seems not to contribute more to the reformation of their associates than any other method of separation.
>
> —Samuel Johnson, *Rambler* 114

The bad faith of the process shows in the insistence on using the deterrence argument when it has been discredited by all the most reputable studies. This is an old story. In the eighteenth century, Samuel Johnson, who liked to defend any tradition he could, discovered no deterrent effect following on traditional executions, though they were far more numerous and far more public than they are now (factors, some people think, that add to deterrent effect). In the middle of the twentieth century, Arthur Koestler could refer to a strong scholarly record on the matter:

> This belief in the irreplaceable deterrent value of the death-penalty has been proved to be a superstition by the long and patient inquiries of the Parliamentary Select Committee of 1930 and the Royal Commission on Capital Punishment of 1948; yet it pops up again and again. Like all superstitions, it has the nature of a Jack-in-the-box; however often you hit it over the head with facts and statistics, it will solemnly pop up again, because the hidden spring inside it is the unconscious and irrational power of traditional beliefs.

Present and former presidents of the most prestigious criminolog-
ical societies, polled in 1995, overwhelmingly said they did not
think the death penalty significantly reduces the homicide rate
(94 percent), and they knew of no empirical evidence that would
support such a claim (94.1 percent). They held (79.2 percent)
that execution causes no reduction in crime — a finding confirmed by the fact that states with the death penalty have higher
murder rates than those without (the region with the highest number of homicides, the South, accounts for over 80 percent of the
nation's executions). Furthermore, countries in Europe that have
given up the death penalty have far lower murder rates than does
the United States (since those countries *do* have gun control laws).
Disbelief in the deterring power of execution is also expressed,
though not so overwhelmingly, by police chiefs and sheriffs — not
a far-left part of the community — surveyed by Peter D. Hart Research Associates in 1995. They did not think (67 percent) that
executions significantly reduce homicides. In fact, New York's former police chief Patrick V. Murphy responded that "the flimsy notion that the death penalty is an effective law enforcement tool is
being exposed as mere political puffery."

Expert criminologists said (100 percent, joined in this by 85 percent of the police chiefs) that politicians support the death penalty
for symbolic reasons, to show they are tough on crime, though that
distracts them (86.6 percent of the criminologists, 56 percent of
the police chiefs) from addressing better methods of reducing the
homicide rate. The police listed five things that would be more effective in fighting crime, including longer sentences, more police,
and gun control. It takes little observation of actual politicians to
confirm that politicians support the death penalty for electoral reasons. Now-Senator Dianne Feinstein, who had opposed capital punishment as a very active member of the California parole board,
embraced it in 1990 when she ran for governor. When I asked her
during that campaign what had made her change her position, she
said that she had become convinced that executions do deter other
criminals. I said that most studies I had seen denied this, but she
told me she had read new and better research, though she could
not name it for me. "I'll send it to you," she promised — but she
never did. The only empirical evidence that mattered to her was

her knowledge of the way Rose Bird had been resoundingly defeated for reelection as the chief justice of the Supreme Court of California because she opposed capital punishment. When Andrew Young ran for governor of Georgia in 1990, he too abandoned his earlier opposition to the death penalty (though his daughter remained an activist opponent of it, because of its disproportionate rate among blacks — the NAACP Legal Defense Fund discovered that a black's chance of being executed in Georgia was eleven times that of a white). I asked Young if he too had been convinced that executions deter. He said that he had not, but that as mayor of Atlanta he had listened to police tell him that it discouraged them to catch criminals and see them escape execution — "I did it for their morale." (He did it, though, only when he was leaving the mayor's office and addressing a much whiter constituency in his race for governor.)

Other politicians obviously look to the polls, not to policy studies, when taking their stand on executions. Campaigning to become the senator from New York, Hillary Clinton knew how much support the state's former governor Mario Cuomo had lost because of his resolute stand against executions. William Weld, while he was still governor of Massachusetts, said that he relied not on studies but on "my gut": "My gut is that . . . capital punishment is deterrent." The deft use of the death penalty issue by Bob Graham as governor of Florida and in his 1986 race for the Senate is studied in a book that Timothy McVeigh is known to have read in prison. In 1984, Graham dismissed scholarly studies on the death penalty by saying, "This is an issue that is inherently beyond what empirical research can validate," making him another gut-truster like Weld. But if we cannot know the deterrent effect, we are certainly killing one man for a hypothetical effect on others that is uncertain.

Actually, the deterrent theory of capital punishment, always weak, is especially flimsy now, when a rash of cases — some involving DNA evidence — has proved that some innocent men are on death row. The evidence of incompetent defenses, faked evidence, and negligent procedures has led to announced or informal moratoria on executions. In Oklahoma alone, where Timothy McVeigh's crime was committed, the evidence in approximately three thousand cases is now tainted by the defective lab work of one technician,

Joyce Gilchrist. The execution of the innocent is not a new issue, but widespread public awareness of it is. The British study by the Select Committee on Capital Punishment, cited by Arthur Koestler, found cases of mistaken executions, including "many" reported by the governor of Sing Sing in America.

Some try to separate the problem of killing the *right* person from the question of whether we should execute *any* person at all. But since the principal prop of the death penalty is deterrence theory, that prop is knocked out when uncertainty of guilt enters the national consciousness. Even if we were to grant that executions deter, they may not deter people who think it is a random matter whether the right person is caught. If they might get off while guilty, or be killed while innocent, that fact is not a very stable basis for forswearing a particular homicide. And executing the mentally defective or marginally juvenile, like the disproportionate killing of blacks, cannot much intimidate a would-be murderer who is mentally sound, of mature age, or white.

These considerations join longer-term flaws in the deterrence argument. Juries are readiest to convict people for crimes of passion, sexually charged rape-murders, child-abuse murders, or serial killings. To see these offenders caught will not necessarily affect the person most likely to have the coolness and calculation that deterrence requires. And obviously they do not affect other people in the grip of obsessions, mental instability, or drug- or alcohol-induced frenzy. Plato was against executing those guilty of a crime of passion (*Laws* 867c–d), but our juries reflect more the anger of society than the didactic strategies of deterrence. In doing this, the juries fail to make the calculations that we are told future murderers will make. The whole theory is senseless.

4. *"Closure"*

> [People come] in thousands to the legal massacre and look with carelessness, perhaps with triumph, on the utmost exacerbations of human misery.
>
> —Samuel Johnson, *Rambler* 114

"Closure" has become a buzzword, not only for discussing the death penalty but for addressing any kind of social discontent.

When the unmarried mother of Jesse Jackson's child sued Reverend Jackson, it was not about anything so crass as money, it was to find "closure" for herself and her child. Who can deprive a grieving person of solace? This is the argument Antiphon's prosecutor made when he demanded emotional relief for the loss of his child to an accident. Attorney General John Ashcroft endorsed the argument by arranging for the families of Timothy McVeigh's victims to see him die. This conflicts with the logic of deterrence, since the families are not viewing the event to deter them from becoming mass murderers. If the real point of executions is to act *in terrorem* for other criminals, the Oklahoma families are the least appropriate audience.

Ashcroft's response to the hot pressures of the McVeigh case is just that of Dianne Feinstein or Andrew Young to less emotionally charged instances of capital punishment, where no mass murder is involved. McVeigh, the cold killer revealed in *American Terrorist*, by Lou Michel and Dan Herbeck, triggers all the upsurges of emotion Nietzsche described. We feel that the very existence of a McVeigh is an affront to society, a pollutant of our life, a thing we cannot be clean of without execration. But the politician does not want to be seen ministering to atavistic reactions in their raw state. So he invokes deterrence where it does not apply, or says that humane consideration of the victims' sympathies trumps all other considerations. Seeing the murderer die, we are told, will just help the families to "close a chapter of their lives."

But is this really likely? The aim of emotional healing is to bring inflamed emotions of loss and *ressentiment* back into a manageable relationship with other parts of one's life. Does that happen when, for many years in most cases (six years so far in McVeigh's case), a victim's survivors focus on seeing that someone pays for his or her loss? This tends to reenact the outrage in a person's mind, rather than to transcend it. It prolongs the trauma, delaying and impeding the healing process. When I asked Sister Helen Prejean, the author of *Dead Man Walking*, what she has observed, she said that families are asked by prosecutors to attend the trial of a relative's murderer, but to show no emotion lest they cause a mistrial. "They learn new details of the crime, and with each new turn of the trial and its aftermath the media call them to get a reaction." This is less like healing than like tearing scabs open again and again. Some relatives who want to escape this process are accused by their own of not loving the victim, says Sister Helen: "I have seen families torn apart over the death penalty."

What's more, the sterile, anodyne, and bureaucratic procedures of a modern execution can baffle the desire for revenge encouraged before its performance. Sister Helen recalls a man who said he wished to see more suffering, and who comes with pro-death demonstrators to all later executions. This is hardly one who has found "closure." The eeriness of the closure language was revealed when McVeigh himself, through his lawyer, Rob Nigh, expressed sympathy for the relatives' "disappointment" after his execution was delayed. He is more the manipulator of these grieving people than an offering to them.

Emotional counselors work toward reconciliation with the facts, as religious leaders recommend forgiveness. Many church bodies oppose the death penalty, drawing on rich traditions in the various faiths. Saint Augustine resisted the killing of murderers, even of two men who had murdered one of his own priests, arguing that the fate of souls is in God's hands (Letters 133, 134). It is true that Thomas Aquinas likened the killing of murderers to the amputation of a limb for the good of the whole body, but his fellow Dominican Niceto Blázquez points out how defective this argument is: Thomas was drawing an analogy with the excommunication of sinners from the Church, the body of Christ — but that is a move meant to promote reunion, to rescue a person from the death of his soul, not to impose a death on the body.

Conservative Catholics, who are aghast at fellow believers' willingness to ignore the pope on matters like contraception, blithely ignore in their turn papal pleas to renounce the death penalty (addressed most recently to the McVeigh case). And I have not seen Bible-quoting fundamentalists refer to the one place in the Gospels where Jesus deals with capital punishment. At John 8:3–11, he interrupts a legal execution (for adultery) and tells the officers of the state that their own sinfulness deprives them of jurisdiction. Jesus himself gives up any jurisdiction for this kind of killing: "Neither do I condemn you." George W. Bush said during the campaign debates of last year that Jesus is his favorite philosopher — though he did not hesitate to endorse the execution of 152 human beings in Texas, where half of the public defenders of accused murderers were sanctioned by the Texas bar for legal mis-behavior or incompetence. Mr. Bush clearly needs some deeper consultation with the philosopher of his choice.

Reflections and Responses

1. Wills divides his essay into four parts. How are these parts related to each other? How, for example, does Part 3 grow out of Part 2? How does the sequence of parts establish the course of his argument about the death penalty and lead to his position?

2. What is the cumulative effect of Part 1? Why do you think Wills went so deeply into a history of execution to make his argument about present-day executions? Do you think he intends to show how much crueler and less humane past societies were as compared to ours today? Explain your response.

3. Why does Wills focus so much on deterrence as today's main justification of the death penalty? Do you think most people believe that capital punishment does have a deterrent effect? Or do you think there are other justifications for the death penalty that Wills ignores? Is "closure" a separate justification given by death penalty advocates or is it a part of the deterrence argument? How does Wills relate the two?

Alternative
Arrangements

Rhetorical Modes

Any distinguished essay will demonstrate a wide variety of rhetorical techniques. The essays in this volume are no exception. The following classification is designed for those who want to isolate a rhetorical strategy for observation and analysis. The five essays listed under each category were chosen because they distinctly and conveniently show a particular rhetorical mode in action.

NARRATING EVENTS

Anwar F. Accawi, *The Telephone*
Rudolph Chelminski, *Turning Point*
Yusef Komunyakaa, *The Blue Machinery of Summer*
Danielle Ofri, *Merced*
Jamaica Kincaid, *On Seeing England for the First Time*

DESCRIBING PEOPLE, PLACES, AND THINGS

Annie Dillard, *The Stunt Pilot*
Barry Lopez, *The Stone Horse*
Judith Ortiz Cofer, *Silent Dancing*
Henry Louis Gates, Jr., *In the Kitchen*
Gay Talese, *Ali in Havana*

DESCRIBING A PROCESS

Scott Russell Sanders, *The Inheritance of Tools*
Ann Hodgman, *No Wonder They Call Me a Bitch*
Annie Dillard, *The Stunt Pilot*
Frank Conroy, *Think About It*
Lucy Grealy, *Mirrorings*

DEFINING ONE'S TERMS

Shelby Steele, *On Being Black and Middle Class*
Alan M. Dershowitz, *Shouting "Fire!"*
Vicki Hearne, *What's Wrong with Animal Rights*
Wendell Berry, *In Distrust of Movements*
Ian Frazier, *A Lovely Sort of Lower Purpose*

CLASSIFYING IDEAS

Marcia Aldrich, *Hair*
Joe Queenan, *Matriculation Fixation*
Amy Tan, *Mother Tongue*
Edward Hoagland, *Heaven and Nature*
Garry Wills, *The Dramaturgy of Death*

PROVIDING EXAMPLES

Peter Singer, *The Singer Solution to World Poverty*
Alan M. Dershowitz, *Shouting "Fire!"*
Rebecca McClanahan, *Book Marks*
Marcia Aldrich, *Hair*
John McPhee, *Silk Parachute*

MAKING COMPARISONS

Ann Hodgman, *No Wonder They Call Me a Bitch*
Edward Hoagland, *Heaven and Nature*
Amy Tan, *Mother Tongue*
John Updike, *The Disposable Rocket*
Anne Fadiman, *Mail*

FORMING ANALOGIES

Alan M. Dershowitz, *Shouting "Fire!"*
Ashraf Rushdy, *Exquisite Corpse*
Annie Dillard, *The Stunt Pilot*
Gretel Ehrlich, *Spring*
Yusef Komunyakaa, *The Blue Machinery of Summer*

ANALYZING CAUSES

Danielle Ofri, *Merced*
Joyce Carol Oates, *They All Just Went Away*
David Halberstam, *Who We Are*
Edward Hoagland, *Heaven and Nature*
Debra Dickerson, *Who Shot Johnny?*

CONSTRUCTING ARGUMENTS

Garry Wills, *The Dramaturgy of Death*
Alan M. Dershowitz, *Shouting "Fire!"*
Peter Singer, *The Singer Solution to World Poverty*
Joy Williams, *The Killing Game*
Vicki Hearne, *What's Wrong with Animal Rights*

Some Literary and Journalistic Techniques

As noted in the Introduction, the contemporary essay can be considered in terms of both literature and journalism. Some of the essays in this volume offer excellent models of the essay as a literary form, while others illustrate the art and craft of reportage. The following arrangement focuses on some of the most important features of both kinds of writing.

CLOSE OBSERVATION AND DETAIL

Ian Frazier, *A Lovely Sort of Lower Purpose*
Scott Russell Sanders, *The Inheritance of Tools*
Barry Lopez, *The Stone Horse*
Gretel Ehrlich, *Spring*
Danielle Ofri, *Merced*

METAPHOR AND SYMBOL

Annie Dillard, *The Stunt Pilot*
John McPhee, *Silk Parachute*
John Updike, *The Disposable Rocket*
Scott Russell Sanders, *The Inheritance of Tools*
Yusef Komunyakaa, *The Blue Machinery of Summer*

IRONY AND SATIRE

Jamaica Kincaid, *On Seeing England for the First Time*
Vicki Hearne, *What's Wrong with Animal Rights*

Joy Williams, *The Killing Game*
Ann Hodgman, *No Wonder They Call Me a Bitch*
Joe Queenan, *Matriculation Fixation*

MOSAIC STRUCTURES

Lucy Grealy, *Mirrorings*
Rebecca McClanahan, *Book Marks*
Judith Ortiz Cofer, *Silent Dancing*
Gretel Ehrlich, *Spring*
Joyce Carol Oates, *They All Just Went Away*

INTERVIEW AND QUOTATION

Gay Talese, *Ali in Havana*
Frank Conroy, *Think About It*
Shelby Steele, *On Being Black and Middle Class*
Annie Dillard, *The Stunt Pilot*
Joy Williams, *The Killing Game*

RESEARCH AND INFORMATION

Garry Wills, *The Dramaturgy of Death*
Anne Fadiman, *Mail*
Ashraf Rushdy, *Exquisite Corpse*
Rudolph Chelminski, *Turning Point*
Alan M. Dershowitz, *Shouting "Fire!"*

Contemporary Issues

The essays in this volume are organized around three dominant types of writing. However, selections across the chapters share topical and thematic relationships as well. The following arrangement provides possibilities for linking these essays by their topics of contemporary interest.

THE MULTICULTURAL EXPERIENCE

Anwar F. Accawi, *The Telephone*
Jamaica Kincaid, *On Seeing England for the First Time*
Amy Tan, *Mother Tongue*
Edwidge Danticat, *Westbury Court*
Judith Ortiz Cofer, *Silent Dancing*
Henry Louis Gates, Jr., *In the Kitchen*
Yusef Komunyakaa, *The Blue Machinery of Summer*
Ashraf Rushdy, *Exquisite Corpse*
Shelby Steele, *On Being Black and Middle Class*

GENDER AND SEXUAL IDENTITY

Joyce Carol Oates, *They All Just Went Away*
Marcia Aldrich, *Hair*
John Updike, *The Disposable Rocket*
Edward Hoagland, *Heaven and Nature*
Rebecca McClanahan, *Book Marks*
Danielle Ofri, *Merced*

CLASS VALUES

Shelby Steele, *On Being Black and Middle Class*
Joyce Carol Oates, *They All Just Went Away*
Scott Russell Sanders, *The Inheritance of Tools*
Peter Singer, *The Singer Solution to World Poverty*
Yusef Komunyakaa, *The Blue Machinery of Summer*
Danielle Ofri, *Merced*

MEDIA AND CULTURAL ANALYSIS

Joy Williams, *The Killing Game*
Anne Fadiman, *Mail*
David Halberstam, *Who We Are*
Ann Hodgman, *No Wonder They Call Me a Bitch*
Ashraf Rushdy, *Exquisite Corpse*
Gay Talese, *Ali in Havana*
Edwidge Danticat, *Westbury Court*

NATURE AND THE ENVIRONMENT

Gretel Ehrlich, *Spring*
Ian Frazier, *A Lovely Sort of Lower Purpose*
Barry Lopez, *The Stone Horse*
Wendell Berry, *In Distrust of Movements*
Joy Williams, *The Killing Game*

SPEECH AND SILENCE

Amy Tan, *Mother Tongue*
Rebecca McClanahan, *Book Marks*
Jamaica Kincaid, *On Seeing England for the First Time*
Judith Ortiz Cofer, *Silent Dancing*
Debra Dickerson, *Who Shot Johnny?*
Alan M. Dershowitz, *Shouting "Fire!"*
Yusef Komunyakaa, *The Blue Machinery of Summer*
Danielle Ofri, *Merced*

RIGHTS AND REFORM

Index of Authors